CISTERCIAN FATHERS SERIES: NUMBER THIRTY-EIGHT

BALDWIN OF FORD

SPIRITUAL TRACTATES

CISTERCIAN FATHERS SERIES: NUMBER THIRTY-EIGHT

Baldwin of Ford

# Spiritual Tractates

Volumes One and Two

*Translated and annotated
with an introduction by*
David N. Bell

Cistercian Publications
cistercianpublications.org

LITURGICAL PRESS
Collegeville, Minnesota
litpress.org

A Cistercian Publications title published by Liturgical Press

**Cistercian Publications**
Editorial Offices
161 Grosvenor Street
Athens, Ohio 45701
www.cistercianpublications.org

Baldwin of Ford, monk of Ford Abbey 1169/70–1175, abbot of Ford, 1175–1180, bishop of Worcester, 1180–1184, archbishop of Canterbury 1184–1190.

This translation is based on the Latin text contained in Robert Thomas (ed.), *Baudouin de Ford, Traites; Pain de Cîteaux* 35–40 (Chimay, Belgium 1973–75), and compared with the text contained in J.-P. Migne, *Patrologiae cursus completus: series latina*, 204.

© 1986 Cistercian Publications. © 2008 by Order of Saint Benedict, Collegeville, Minnesota. All rights reserved. No part of this book may be used or reproduced in any manner whatsoever, except brief quotations in reviews, without written permission of Liturgical Press, Saint John's Abbey, PO Box 7500, Collegeville, MN 56321-7500.

**Library of Congress Cataloging-in-Publication Data**

Baldwin, Archbishop of Canterbury, ca. 1120–1190.
    Baldwin of Ford, spiritual tractates.

    (Cistercian Fathers series; no. 38, 41)
    "This translation is based on the Latin text contained in Robert Thomas (ed.), Baudouin de Ford, Traités; Pain de cîteaux 35–40 (Chimay, Belgium) 1973–75"—T.p. verso.
    Bibliography: p. 37
    Includes indexes.
    1. Catholic Church—Sermons.    2. Sermons, Latin.
I. Bell, David N., 1943– .    II. Baldwin, Archbishop of Canterbury, ca 1120–1190.    Traités.    III. Title.
IV. Series.
BX1756.B334B35    1986    252'.02    85-22363

ISBN 978-0-87907-447-0

TO
MAURICE MULLETT

Of right and wrong he taught
Truths as refin'd as ever Athens heard;
And (strange to tell!) he practis'd what he preach'd.

> John Armstrong,
> *The Art of Preserving Health*

VOLUME ONE

# TABLE OF CONTENTS

| | |
|---|---|
| Introduction | 9 |
|   Notes to the Introduction | 31 |
| Bibliography | 37 |
| Abbreviations | 40 |

Baldwin of Ford: Spiritual Tractates
Tractate I: *On the Most Holy Sacrament of the Eucharist* — 43
Tractate II: *On the Corrupt Way of Life of the Clergy and People* — 68
Tractate III: *On the Love of God* — 77
Tractate IV: *On the Twofold Resurrection Which is Obtained by Perseverance in Obedience* — 102
Tractate V: *On the Rest Which Christ Has Sought and Prepared for Himself and for Us* — 130
Tractate VI: *On the Power of the Word of God* — 152
Tractate VII: *On the Angelic Salutation* — 191
Tractate VIII: *On the Wound of Love Which the Bride Inflicts Upon the Bridegroom* — 214

# INTRODUCTION

### BALDWIN'S LIFE

BALDWIN OF EXETER, Baldwin of Ford, Baldwin of Worcester, and Baldwin of Canterbury: the distinguished ecclesiastical career of this complicated cleric reflects the different worlds in which, with varying degrees of success and acclamation, he lived and moved and had his being. He was a teacher, canonist, monk, abbot, papal legate, bishop, archbishop, and a candidate for the College of Cardinals. He was deeply learned, unquestionably ascetic, godly and gullible, and, according to Gerald of Wales, a better monk than abbot, a better abbot than bishop, a better bishop than archbishop.[1] His considerable writings as abbot of Ford reveal a man with a thorough, accurate, and perspicacious grasp of the nature and purpose of the spiritual life; his unfortunate activities as primate of England show us a bishop whose judgement neither of situations nor of persons could safely be trusted. All human beings are by nature complex, but Baldwin, perhaps, was more complex than most.

We know little of his early years. Gervase of Canterbury tells us that he was born at Exeter of humble stock,[2] but this comment on his parents' station may well reflect less the truth than the attitude of the Canterbury monks who (as we shall see) had good reason to dislike Baldwin and may well have calumniated him. As Christopher Holdsworth has pointed out, there is clear evidence from another source that Baldwin's mother could read Latin – a rare phenomenon among women of the time – and if this were so, it would indicate an aristocratic and educated background for Baldwin rather than a lowly one.[3]

Gervase, however, goes on to say that Baldwin was learned in both sacred and secular subjects,[4] and it is probable that his studies were begun, if not completed, at the cathedral school of Exeter. If, as seems eminently likely, the learned and influential Robert Pullen taught theology there before moving to Oxford in 1133, it is possible that Baldwin studied under him.[5] It is also possible, but by no means certain, that in the course of time he himself rose to become master of the school.[6] He did not, however, stay in England, for a letter of John of Salisbury reveals that Baldwin was in Italy in 1150 when he was presented to Pope Eugenius III at Ferentino.[7] The most likely reason for his being in Italy was to pursue his legal studies at one or other of the Italian universities, and it is possible (though this is pure speculation) that he studied at Bologna in the 1140's under the future Alexander III. The latter, as we shall see, knew him well, had a high opinion of his legal expertise, and in later years often appointed him papal judge-delegate. Already by 1150 he was known for his learning, for he was appointed as tutor to Gratian, a nephew of Innocent II. How long this relationship continued and how long Baldwin stayed in Europe we do not know, but he was certainly back at Exeter by 1159/60, for he is included in a list of clerks to the bishop of Exeter, Robert Warelwast, who died in 1160[8]. Robert's successor, Bartholomew, a friend of Baldwin and an eminent canonist in his own right, was also sufficiently impressed with him to appoint him archdeacon of Totnes shortly after his consecration in 1161[9].

Now the next year, 1162, was a year of great importance in the ecclesiastical history of England, for of far greater significance than Baldwin's elevation to the archdeaconry of Totnes was Thomas Becket's elevation to the archbishopric of Canterbury; and over the next eight years the great conflict of king and archbishop was gradually to embroil the whole of Europe and lead the archbishop to a martyr's death on the stones of Canterbury Cathedral. Baldwin's sympathies were unquestionably with Becket,[10] and there can surely be no doubt that the virulence of the controversy played a significant part in his decision to resign from his position of archdeacon and enter the monastic life in 1169 or 1170.[11] Baldwin's austere and ascetic tendencies (which were, in any case, not altogether suited to archidiaconal office) led him to choose the cistercian abbey of Ford, a daughter-house of Waverley, the first cistercian abbey to be established in England. In

1136, an abbot and twelve monks had moved from Waverley to Brightley in Devon, where they founded a house on land given to them by Richard fitzBaldwin de Brionis. This site, however, proved unsuitable, and the monks had left and were on their way back to Waverley when they met Richard's sister and heiress, Adelicia, who offered them the site at Ford. This they accepted, and the abbey at Ford (then in an enclave of Devon, but now included in the boundaries of Dorset) was founded in 1141, some thirty years before Baldwin arrived there.[12]

It was during his decade in the abbey that Baldwin produced nearly all of his extant spiritual writing: all but three of the *Tractates* translated in these present volumes, the lengthy *De sacramento altaris*,[13] the *De commendatione fidei*,[14] and the two sermons (*De sancta cruce* and *De obedienta*) which are being prepared for publication by Br. Bernard-J. Samain of the Abbaye d'Orval, and which we shall discuss in more detail a little later.[15] These works reveal a man thoroughly and happily at home in cistercian spirituality, an acute theologian well aware of contemporary currents and events, and one of the last true representatives of the rich patristic–monastic tradition which was so soon to give way to the often arid scholasticism of the thirteenth century. By 1175 Baldwin had risen to become abbot of Ford (his claustral prior, we might note, was John, whose important sermons on the Song of Songs have already been translated in this present series[16]), and three years later we find one of the cardinals of Alexander III recommending him for the red hat, and informing the pope that his learning, integrity, and religion were known throughout the whole cistercian order.[17] It seems, in fact, that Baldwin's relationship with the papacy for the entire period from 1170 to the early 1180s was fairly close. Apart from his abbatial duties and his spiritual writing, he was much involved with the development of decretal legislation in England and, as Charles Duggan has pointed out, of the four figures who played a major role in this matter (Baldwin, his friend and colleague Bartholomew of Exeter, Roger of Worcester, and Richard of Canterbury) Baldwin's was "the clearest and most decisive personality".[18] As we mentioned a little earlier, he was often commissioned as papal judge-delegate by Alexander, and both as abbot of Ford and bishop of Worcester (the see to which he was appointed in 1180) he was deeply concerned with the definition and codification of papal jurisdictional authority in England.[19]

His four years as bishop of Worcester were not especially eventful. He seems to have gone about his pastoral duties with care and diligence, and the only occurrence of any note which comes from these years is the dramatic story of how he saved one Gilbert of Plumpton from the gallows. This Gilbert, it seems, was unjustly accused of rape and condemned to be hanged, and despite the opposition of a large crowd, he had been taken to the gallows and actually hoisted aloft before the bishop of Worcester appeared on the scene. His Lordship, threatening the executioners with excommunication, demanded that they cease their business, both because it was a Sunday and because it was the feast of St Mary Magdalen. Accordingly, the rope was loosened and the knight lowered to the ground. His enemies could well wait until the next day and re-hang him on Monday. Overnight, however, the king intervened. He was aware of the injustice of the proceedings and therefore commanded that Gilbert should remain alive, but imprisoned, until he should decide what was to be done with him. And although his imprisonment was fairly lengthy (it lasted until the king's death some five years later), it was to Bishop Baldwin that Gilbert owed his salvation.[20] These remarkable events occurred towards the end of Baldwin's sojourn in Worcester, and they bring to end the happier part of his life, for in 1184 he was consecrated archbishop of Canterbury, and the story of his remaining years is, on the whole, gloomy and depressing.

'What can I say of Baldwin?', asks Gervase of Canterbury. 'My intention and my promise was to say favourable things about kings and archbishops, and to tell my readers in some way of the good things done in the church of Canterbury. But when I look at what Baldwin did, I am forced against my will to speak not of the good, but of the many evils'.[21] Herbert of Bosham, too, saw Baldwin's archiepiscopate in a dismal light,[22] and Gerald of Wales accuses him of being too lax, too lenient, and too easily led. Admittedly, Gerald says it more delicately than that, but that is what he means.[23]

## Introduction

His election to the primacy was itself contested. The monks of Christ Church, a disputatious body who had long claimed the sole right to elect the primate, objected to Baldwin as they always objected to the bishops' choice, and put forward three candidates of their own: Odo, the abbot of Battle, an able, charming, and saintly man; Peter de Leia, the Cluniac bishop of St David's; and Theobald, abbot of Cluny. The king was forced to intervene, and with some difficulty persuaded the contumacious monks to accept the bishop of Worcester. Baldwin himself had said that he would accept the primacy only if the prior and the monks agreed,[24] and after the compromise had been effected, he accordingly took office and expressed his hope, his first and highest desire, that he and the monks would be 'one in the Lord'.[25] His hope was not to be fulfilled. Indeed, it is doubtful if ever it could have been. Baldwin was a Cistercian and a canonist: learned, ascetic, and cosmopolitan. Christ Church was a powerful, luxurious, and jealous community, intent on preserving its own privileges, its own powers, and its own way of life – a way of life which by this time was monastic in name alone. 'The independence of the convent', says Hunt, 'was grievous to Baldwin as archbishop, and its luxury disgusted him as a Cistercian,'[26] and from the very beginning his relationship with the monks was doomed.

Clashes took place almost immediately. Certain offerings and revenues which were traditionally the perquisites of the monastery were seized by Baldwin, and the monks were deprived of the control of certain properties.[27] But these problems were as nothing compared to the furor that erupted as a result of the archbishop's plans to establish at Hackington (about half a mile from Canterbury) a collegiate church for secular priests, complete with prebendal stalls for the king and all the bishops.[28] The monks of Christ Church were (predictably) horrified. Apart from the fact that the college was to be endowed partly from Christ Church property, they saw in it a direct threat to their own prestige, and the beginning of a gradual take-over by which they would be deprived of their right to elect the primate. In this, we might add, they were probably correct, for the bishops, as also the king, had long been dissatisfied with the prevailing practice, and there is no doubt that they would have relished a reduction in the electoral powers of the Christ Church convent. Be that as it may, the monks resisted the plans of the archbishop and appealed to Rome, and the affair became more and more violent and its ramifications more and more wide-spread. A succession of inconsequential pontiffs – Urban III, Gregory VIII, Clement III – supported the monks, while Henry II supported Baldwin; and at one stage the situation became so bad that for more than eighteen months during 1188 and 1189 the monks were actually imprisoned within the conventual buildings, and for most of this period no liturgy was celebrated in the cathedral. It is not surprising that rumours were spread abroad that the archbishop was either mad or dead.[29]

After Henry's death in 1189, Baldwin attempted to effect a reconciliation, but when he failed to do so, turned instead to threats and violence, and tried to force the convent into submission. As part of his plan he appointed as prior Roger Norreys, an ungodly move which is surely comprehensible only in terms of out-and-out *realpolitik*.[30] Norreys had been treasurer of Christ Church, but there was nothing monastic about either his character or his conduct. He was intelligent, crafty, self-seeking, calculating, and tyrannical, and although we have no knowledge of his appreciation of music, he certainly liked wine and women. He may well have been a splendid raconteur and an entertaining dinner-guest, but he was utterly unsuitable for any ecclesiastical or monastic office. The monks were reduced to desperation, and had no option but to throw themselves on the mercy of the new king, Richard I. The king, after some preliminary negotiations, visited Canterbury in November 1189 and managed to effect a compromise which vindicated Baldwin and which, if not wholly satisfactory to the convent, at least rid them of their two greatest worries: Hackington and Norreys. On the one hand, it was acknowledged that the archbishop had the power to build himself a church wherever he pleased; on the other, the archbishop agreed to demolish the buildings at Hackington and construct his college elsewhere. On the one hand, it was acknowledged that the archbishop had the right to institute his own prior; on the other, the archbishop agreed to relieve Roger Norreys of his office.[31] The monks, as we have said, were far from happy about this final settlement, but had no choice but to accept it. The archbishop, for his part, kept his side of the bargain: he sent Norreys to Evesham, where he continued in his immorality, tyranny, and mismanagement unabated, and announced his intention of transferring his collegiate foundation from Hackington to Lambeth. Little was done in the matter, however, for Baldwin left England on crusade in March of the next year, and died in the Holy Land eight months later.

It seems that the crusade was something fairly close to his heart, for he had taken the cross at Geddington in 1188, and later that year preached the crusade in Wales, a country which he had visited a year earlier as papal legate. In so doing, he killed two birds with one stone, for not only did he attract large numbers of Welshmen to the cross, but as a 'token of investiture' (*investiturae signum*), he combined with his preaching the celebration of mass in all the cathedral churches of Wales.[32] His pilgrimage, in other words, was also a means of asserting his metropolitan authority in Wales and of demonstrating to the Welsh bishops that the see of Canterbury was truly supreme. The fact that certain of the Welsh bishops remained unpersuaded is not part of this story. In the course of this pilgrimage the archbishop also showed that his austerity and asceticism concealed a dry sense of humour, for while he and his party were on their way to Bangor they had occasion to pass through a steep and rocky valley, and by the time they had negotiated it, they were all panting and out of breath. It was at this juncture that the archbishop called for someone to whistle a tune. He himself could do it, he said, but no-one seems to have taken up his challenge. And all this, says Gerald of Wales (who was with him at the time), was 'a pleasantry highly laudable in a person of his approved gravity'.[33]

Shortly after the archbishop's return to England, Henry II died, and Baldwin, as was his duty, presided over the coronation of his successor. It is here that we come across another episode which reveals a different and darker aspect of the archbishop's character: that intolerance, anger, and less than Christian charity which also appears in some of the letters of the Hackington controversy. The coronation of

Richard I was a solemn and splendid affair, but only male Christians were permitted to attend. Women and Jews were banned from the proceedings 'because of the magic arts which they are wont to practise at royal coronations'.[34] Despite this ban, on the day of the coronation, a Jewish deputation bearing rich gifts presented itself at Westminster Hall, and a few of the Jews, most unwisely, slipped inside to see what was going on. They were immediately and violently driven out, and the event precipitated a riot. Several Jews were beaten and some were killed, and one, Benedict of York, escaped with his life only by being baptised in the nearby church of the Innocents by William, a priest who happened to come from his own city. The next day Benedict was ordered to appear before the king, and there renounced his recent baptism by identifying himself to the monarch not as William (the name with which he had been baptised) but as Benedict of York, "one of your Jews". The king then turned to Baldwin and asked him what should be done with the man, and Baldwin, 'less prudently than was fitting, and in a spirit of anger', said: 'If he will not be God's man, let him be the devil's!' His advice was followed, and Benedict remained a Jew, and died at Northampton shortly afterwards. Even then his troubles were not over, for the Jews refused him burial because he was a Christian and the Christians refused him burial because he was a Jew, and I have no idea what became of his body. Roger of Hoveden admits freely that Baldwin was wrong in this. He says that Baldwin should have answered: 'We demand a christian trial for him, since he became a Christian and now contradicts it', but as we have seen, this is not what the archbishop said, and there can be no doubt that this regrettable episode casts a further shadow upon Baldwin's reputation.[35]

After the coronation of Richard, Baldwin had little more than a year to live. In November 1189 the Hackington affair was resolved, and in December of that year Richard left for the crusade. In March 1190 Baldwin, together with Hubert Walter, bishop of Salisbury, 'who were the only English bishops to fulfil their vows, followed the king to Sicily, and arrived before him in the land of Judah'.[36] Baldwin's role in the crusade was an active one, both ecclesiastically and militarily:

## Introduction

on the one hand he deputised for the Patriarch, Heraclius, who was ill, and on the other he provided a company of two hundred knights (*milites*) and three hundred followers (*satellites*) to fight under the banner of St Thomas of Canterbury. He himself was one of those in charge of the christian camp, and it was he who blessed the army and gave it absolution as it set forth to fight the infidel.[37] By this time, however, he was an old man, and the conditions and climate of Palestine were less than kind to old men. The unchristian conduct of the crusading army further afflicted him, and having contracted a fever, he died during the siege of Acre on the 19th or 20th November, 1190.[38] This is how a contemporary chronicler describes the events:

> When the archbishop of Canterbury saw what he had earlier heard—that the army was wholly dissolute, and given to drinking, whoring, and gambling—his spirit, which was unable to endure such excesses, was afflicted with a weariness for life. And because a disease which is general is difficult to cure, on a day when the worst reports of this sort were coming more frequently to his ears, and knowing that though man has the care of things, God is over all, he sighed and burst out in these words: 'Lord God, now there is need to reprove and correct with holy grace, that if it please your mercy, I should be taken away from the turmoil of this present life; I have tarried long enough in this army!' It was as if the Lord had heard him, for not fifteen days had passed since these words than he began to feel somewhat cold and stiff, and giving way to a burning fever, he happily fell asleep in the Lord a few days later.[39]

The archbishop was buried where he died, and his will, leaving all his wealth for the relief of the Holy Land, was executed by his friend and fellow-bishop, Hubert of Salisbury.[40] His vestments—a tunicle, dalmatic, and chasuble, all rich with gold, and two mantles—were left at Canterbury.[41] News of his death reached England the following March (Gervase does not tell us of the glee with which this must have been greeted by the Christ Church convent), and in 1193 Baldwin's executor and co-crusader, Hubert Walter, was elected his successor as the next archbishop of Canterbury.

### BALDWIN'S TRACTATES

The Tractates account for just about half of Baldwin's published work, and the process by which they have arrived at their present form is somewhat complicated. There is no doubt that they were originally delivered at various times as sermons, but then, on two separate occasions, they were edited and in some instances amalgamated to form more literary productions. Most of the titles and sub-titles which appear throughout the Tractates would presumably have been added as part of this process. Now John Pits, writing in 1619, lists among the works of Baldwin a volume of thirty-three sermons but makes no mention of the Tractates, and Bertrand Tissier repeats this information in his *Bibliotheca Patrum Cisterciensium* published some forty years later.[42] No surviving manuscript, however, contains thirty-three sermons, and we may therefore ask what became of them and what was their relationship to the treatises which are here our concern. There seems little doubt that Pits' original manuscript has vanished, but in 1911-12, P. Guébin presented a persuasive case that part of it — perhaps two-thirds or even three-quarters — is to be found copied in a manuscript of the late twelfth or early thirteenth century which may originally have come from Bec and which is now in the collection of the Bibliothèque Nationale.[43] We may refer to this as Manuscript A, and a casual glance at its contents reveals immediately that the 'sermons' are in fact the 'tractates', even though they are not referred to as such and even though they appear in a quite different order from that in which they occur in this present translation.

What authority, then, do we have for this present arrangement? The answer is to be found in a second manuscript — Manuscript B — which originally formed part of the excellent library at Clairvaux and is now to be found at Troyes.[44] Manuscript B, I suspect, is a little later in date than Manuscript A, and it differs from the latter both in its content and in its arrangement. As far as content is concerned, it contains both more and less than Manuscript A. Two sermons which appear in the latter—an exegesis of 1 Samuel 15: 22, 'Obedience is better than sacrifices' (*De obedientia*), and an encomium on the Holy Cross (*De sancta cruce*)[45]—are not to be found in Manuscript B; but four sermons which do appear in B (Tractates IX/IV, X/II, XIII, and XIV) are absent from A. On the other hand, it seems likely that Manuscript A was never completed, and if Guébin was correct, it might well have gone on to include not only these sermons, but also certain others which are now irretrievably lost. The arrangement of the Tractates in Manuscript B is also quite different and reveals much more substantial editing than appears in Manuscript A. A certain amount of adjustment had already been made in the latter. Tractate XV, for example, almost certainly originated as a series of three separate sermons, each of about the same length, but in both Manuscripts A and B it is presented as one single treatise.[46] Yet although Manuscript A is at least one stage removed from the original sermons, Manuscript B is still further distant and represents the second major stage in editing. In Manuscript A, Tractates I/I, I/II, IX/I, IX/II, IX/III, and X/I still appear as separate sermons, whereas in Manuscript B they have been amalgamated to form Tractates I, IX, and X. Furthermore, we have already mentioned that two treatises included in Manuscript A make no appearance at all in Manuscript B, and of those which do appear only in the latter, I strongly suspect that two (IX/IV and X/II), which have either a very abrupt beginning or a very abrupt ending, are far from complete. The reasons for these amalgamations, omissions, and additions are still not wholly clear to me.

Why, then, should we decide to use this second and more severely edited manuscript as the basis for our translation? The answer is simple: it was this manuscript which was used by Tissier for his edition of the Tractates published in the *Bibliotheca Patrum Cisterciensium*, and it was this edition, in turn, which was reproduced in 1855 in the Migne Patrology. Like much in Migne, therefore, it is this arrangement of the Tractates which has become standard. Moreover, it was this same manuscript which was used by Fr Robert Thomas as the basis for his edition of the Latin text of the Tractates[47] – an edition, which while not strictly critical, is nevertheless much more accurate than that of the redoubtable Migne – and it was from this edition of Fr Thomas that the English version of the Tractates here presented was translated. We must also remember that Manuscript B is a good and accurate manuscript, and that the major differences between itself and Manuscript A relate not to the text, but to the arrangement of the materials therein contained.

In conclusion, therefore, what we have here are not Baldwin's sermons as they were originally delivered, but an incomplete thirteenth-century edited version of these sermons. How incomplete is difficult to say, but if we include the two sermons / tractates which appear only in Manuscript A, and treat Tractates I, IX, and X as eight separate treatises, we arrive at a total of twenty-three sermons. If we prefer to think of Tractate XV as comprising not one but three sermons, then the total comes to twenty-five. In other words, out of the volume of thirty-three sermons reported by Pits, it is quite possible that up to ten have been lost, and there seems now little chance of recovering them. They may very well still be extant – the number of anonymous twelfth-century sermons still in manuscript is legion – but the question of identification is entirely another matter.

The great majority of the treatises – all but three, in fact (Tractates I, II, and XII) – clearly derive from a monastic milieu. The other three date from Baldwin's later years as either bishop of Worcester or archbishop of Canterbury (I think probably the latter). Taken together they cover a very wide range of subjects and represent our main source for the elucidation of Baldwin's spiritual teaching. We find discussions of the meaning and symbolism of the eucharist, the purpose and importance of the incarnation, the nature of the Trinity, the place of Mary and her role in the process of redemption, the relationship of church and state, the responsibilities of the priestly life and ecclesiastical office, the nature of the soul and the process of its reformation, faith and reason, doubt and certainty, sin and contrition, abstinence and renunciation, humility and discipline, asceticism and mortification, the meaning of martyrdom, concupiscence and its control, the nature of true poverty, the theology of community and the common life, the idea and ideal of the monastic profession, and, of course, a great deal of material on those matters which lie at the very heart of the Cistercian way: charity and obedience, and the love of God and our neighbour. But throughout all this material, the author, as John Morson has pointed out, 'is constantly preoccupied with the stages towards union with God, from a rudimentary self-knowledge to that wisdom or charity which is a forerunner of the face-to-face vision'.[48] Baldwin, in other words, was truly a *spirituel* and did have a spiritual teaching—a teaching which was grounded in the ideas and ideals of Cîteaux, but which nevertheless bore the characteristic marks of his own ascetic and austere temperament.[49] The pivotal points of his thought are no different from those of the other great Cistercians; indeed, no different from those of twelfth-century monasticism as a whole. We have retained God's image, our potential for deification, but have lost his likeness; sin and self-will separate us from God. How, then, shall we restore this likeness and actualize our potential? There are two aspects to the answer, one which looks inwards and the other outwards. On the one hand we need the discipline, obedience, abstinence, and renunciation by which self-will and self-love are controlled, and on the other we need the love of God and of our neighbour. The two aspects are not, of course, separate: we cannot truly love God and yet reject his will; and his will, enshrined in his commandments, leaves us in no doubt as to what we should do.

> The charity of God and obedience are bound each to each with an unbreakable bond and in no way separated from each other. The Lord shows us that there cannot be charity without obedience when he says: 'If anyone loves me, he will keep my word' (Jn 14: 23): that is to say, he will observe my commandments, and in observing them, he will obey me. And he also shows us that there cannot be obedience without charity when he says: 'Whoever does not love me does not keep my words' (Jn 14: 24). If, then,

he who loves obeys, and he who does not love does not obey, it follows that just as there cannot be charity without obedience, neither can there be obedience without charity.[50]

Everything, therefore, centres on the love of God: to love God is to love your neighbour; to love God is to deny yourself; to love God is to keep his commandments; to love God is to imitate Christ; to love God is to die; and to die is to gain eternal life. The *via monastica* is neither more nor less than the *imitatio Christi*. This is Baldwin's teaching, just as it was the teaching of Bernard, Aelred, William of St Thierry, or any other of the cistercian writers; yet the fact that these abbots were one and all representatives of a great tradition did not prevent them from adding to this tradition their own elaborations and enrichments. William of St Thierry, for instance, offers us an awe-inspiring trinitarian mysticism, and Aelred of Rievaulx presents us with a vitally important theology of friendship. And Baldwin, whilst not the equal of these great figures, is no simple retailer of second-hand cistercian spirituality. In his fifteenth Tractate, for example, we find a theological analysis of the origins and nature of the common life which, as I have attempted to demonstrate elsewhere, presents us with a real and positive contribution to our understanding of this important subject,[51] and although his third Tractate is so deeply and so obviously indebted to Bernard, what he says he says in his own way and with his own emphases. His thought and his writings inevitably reflect his temperament, and it is for this reason that I have referred elsewhere to his spirituality as an ascetic spirituality.[52] This is not to deny the central importance of charity—for Baldwin, as we have seen, asceticism is a necessary concomitant of charity—but simply to indicate that when two different artists paint the same subject, their paintings will not be identical. We do not find in Baldwin the warm humanity of an Aelred of Rievaulx or the startling charisma of a Bernard. Why should we? Baldwin is Baldwin, and unlike some of the other abbots of his order, his life and personality may be difficult to understand, but they are far from shadowy. Together with his many faults he is very much his own man, and those who wish to know him and his teaching better will find in the Tractates a rich and profitable store of information. We may see in them a little library of medieval monastic thought, and they well repay intelligent browsing.

### BALDWIN'S SOURCES

No-one ever denied that Baldwin was learned. He was well and widely read, and as I have indicated elsewhere, thoroughly abreast of the theological developments and controversies of his times.[53] His learning, however, was that of a canonist, not that of a speculative theologian. Law and precedents were of first importance to him, and he had no time for the rational investigation of areas into which reason had no business to go. 'We ought not to enquire into what God has not wished to reveal',[54] he says, and what God has wished to reveal is to be found in the Scripture and in the writings of the 'orthodox Fathers'.[55] His faith is 'founded unshakeably on the words of God himself',[56] and if faith and reason conflict (as they often do), then the latter must give way to the former. 'The eye of human reason is often offended by the pious devotion of faith, but when it offends, it is cast out. It is better for you to enter life having one eye of sound faith, than to be cast into hell-fire with two eyes, one of faith and one of human reason'.[57] Faith is rooted in divine authority, and its beginning and its foundation is Truth itself.[58] For Baldwin, the defences of the faith reduce to the authority of Holy Scripture,[59] and the purpose of reason is two-fold: to make a rational decision between good and evil, and to understand as clearly as possible the meaning and significance of what God has revealed.[60] The Scriptures are central to his thought, his faith, and his style. His fundamental attitude, Leclercq has said, is a profound respect for the sacred text, and nothing alien should be mingled with it. He uses Scripture to interpret Scripture, and he sees the writings of the Fathers only as commentaries on this divine revelation.[61]

Baldwin's knowledge of the Bible, like that of most of his contemporaries, was encyclopedic. There are very few books which are not quoted at least once in his writing, though as we might expect, some appear much more frequently than others. In the Tractates, the *De sacramento altaris*, and the *De commendatione fidei*, there are more than three thousand direct quotations from Scripture, and a huge multitude of echoes, allusions, and reminiscences. The only biblical books from which I have been unable to find a quotation are Ruth, 1 Chronicles, 1 Esdras, Judith, Obadiah, Nahum, Haggai, Philemon, 2 and 3 John, and Jude, and it will not have escaped the reader that most of these books are notable for their brevity. Nor could I guarantee that some echo of their text is not to be found hidden away in Baldwin's work. As I mentioned, however, some parts of Scripture are cited much more frequently than others, and this is particularly true of the Psalms. They comprise more than fifty percent of the total number of Old Testament quotations and more than a quarter of the whole, and there is no doubt that these high proportions are a simple reflection of the place they occupied in the liturgy. They were engrained in the thought and speech of any monk or priest of Baldwin's day, and with a little manipulation could be used to illustrate virtually anything. And if we include with Psalms the four Gospels, we find that we have accounted for more than half the total number of biblical quotations in all Baldwin's spiritual writings.

In many cases, these quotations are not in accordance with the Vulgate text. Out of eighty-three direct quotations in Tractate IV, for example, one-third have been in some way amended, and these emendations, together with the many which appear elsewhere, may be classified into four main groups: (1) those in which there are minor additions (such as *enim* in [3] below) or omissions (such as in Hosea 2:19, *Et sponsabo te in justitia*, which omits *mihi* after *te*[62]); (2) those in which we find inversion or transposition of words or phrases (e.g. Song of Songs 1: 3, *Trahe me post te: in odorem unguentorum tuorum curremus*, for *Trahe me, post te curremus in odorem unguentorum tuorum*[63]); (3) those in which we have a conflation of two or more verses (e.g. *In custodiendis illis retributio multa. Justitiae enim Domini rectae, laetificantes corda*, which is a conflation of verses 12 and 9 of Psalm 18 [19] together with an additional *enim*[64]); and (4) those in which words have been changed. This last group may be further divided into two: (4.a) minor changes, such as *enim* for *autem*, *sive* . . . *sive* for *et* . . . *et*, a singular instead of a plural, or a different tense; and (4.b) major changes, in which the version given is completely different from that of the Vulgate. Two examples will suffice: in the Vulgate, Isaiah 66: 10 reads *Laetamini cum Jerusalem, et exsultate in ea, omnes qui diligitis eam*, but in Tractate IV, Baldwin renders this as *Laetare, Jerusalem, et diem factum agite omnes, qui diligitis eam*.[65] Again, the Vulgate version of Isaiah 7:9 reads *Si non credideritis, non permanebitis*, but in Tractate VI (and elsewhere), Baldwin gives this as *Nisi credideritis, non intelligetis*.[66]

What are the reasons for these changes, major and minor? Most of the minor variants can be explained simply by lapses of memory or a trifling adjustment so as to fit the context better, but the major variations are more interesting, and there are two main explanations which account for them. The first is that the passage concerned may have been drawn from the liturgy rather than directly from the bible, for there are a considerable number of cases in which the scriptural text as it appears in the liturgy represents a different tradition from that which appears in the Vulgate. The reasons for this are not our concern here, but the variant form of Isaiah 66: 10 quoted above is to be accounted for in this way. The second explanation is that the variant text represents not the Vulgate, but the Old Latin, and since we may rest assured that Baldwin did not have access to Old Latin manuscripts, the sources for these variants are undoubtedly the Church Fathers. This in itself is useful, for if we can trace the probable source from which the Old Latin version is taken, it gives us a profitable glimpse into our author's patristic authorities. The reading of Isaiah 7: 9 which we cited above is just such an Old Latin variant, and Baldwin may well have found it in Augustine's *De Trinitate* (see Tr. VI-4). Other possible sources for such Old Latin variants are Jerome (especially Jerome!), Ambrose, Gregory the Great, and even the *Rule of St Benedict* (see Trs. I-12, II-18, VI-4, VI-18, VI-42, VIII-5, VIII-9, IX/II-4, and IX/III-9).

It is not often that Baldwin names his patristic authorities. In the whole of the Tractates, for example, only Augustine is mentioned, and he only three times (see Trs. I-34, IV-29, and VII-9). But in his other works we find him referring by name to Ambrose, Gregory the Great, Hilary, Jerome, Origen, and pseudo-Dionysius, as well as the bishop of Hippo.[67] None of these names comes to us as any great surprise, save perhaps that of pseudo-Dionysius. Baldwin's quotation, 'The being of all is the Divinity which is beyond being',[68] appears to derive from John Scot Eriugena's translation of the *Celestial Hierarchy*[69], and we know that at least three works of pseudo-Dionysius – the *Celestial Hierarchy*, the *Ecclesiastical Hierarchy*, and the *Mystical Theology* – were all to be found in the library at Ford.[70] It is typical of Baldwin's approach, however, that his explanation of this phrase and the context in which it appears are alike augustinian, and there is no trace in Baldwin of that fascination with dionysian thought which we find in the work of his fellow Cistercians, Isaac of Stella or Garnier of Rochefort.

Augustine, without question, was Baldwin's master. Apart from naming him more often than any other writer, Baldwin penned a multitude of passages which either are founded on Augustine's thought, or in which we hear an echo of his teaching.[71] It is true that his approach to Augustine was not uncritical,[72] but there is no doubt that he held him in the highest veneration, and the fact that his name appears only three times in the Tractates is no reflection of his overwhelming importance. In any case, as we stated above, Baldwin rarely names his sources, and the determination of those he does not name is not always easy. The main reason for this is that Baldwin was not a plagiarist. He read the "orthodox Fathers", pondered and meditated upon them, and gradually assimilated them into his own thought and his own theology, but when he wrote, he wrote as Baldwin of Ford, and not as Augustine or Jerome. Sometimes we catch a glimpse of one or other of the Fathers – Benedict, for example (see Trs. VI–42, VI–43, XII–10, XV–25, XVI–15), or a couple of quotations from Gregory the Great (see Trs. X/1–16 and XV–28), or an echo of Hilary (see Tr. X/1–3), or the influence of Leo the Great (see Tr. XIII–2), or a snatch of Maximus of Turin or Venantius Fortunatus[73] – but more often we find ourselves in a spiritual and theological atmosphere which certainly has its roots in the patristic tradition, but in which individual voices can only rarely be distinguished.

Of his contemporaries, Baldwin names none at all, neither in the Tractates nor elsewhere, and it is difficult to get a clear picture of the extent to which he was acquainted with their works. Some of them certainly influenced him. Bernard, for instance, clearly had a profound effect on his conception of charity, and there is no difficulty in seeing his impact on the archbishop's third Tractate.[74] Similarly, I do not think there is any doubt that in his teaching on the common life and the nature of community, he was indebted to Aelred of Rievaulx, and I have attempted to demonstrate this indebtedness elsewhere.[75] His Mariology seems to echo Anselm of Canterbury, for I strongly suspect that the curious terms used in the seventh Tractate to describe the Mother of God—*superspeciosa, supergratiosa, supergloriosa*—derive from one of the *Orationes* of Baldwin's archiepiscopal predecessor (see Tr. VII-16). John of Fécamp may also have influenced him, for J. C. Didier has drawn our attention to a number of expressions which certainly seem inspired by passages in John's work.[76]

The influence of the Victorines is more difficult to determine. They were certainly represented in the library at Ford,[77] but I cannot recall any direct and incontrovertible evidence for Victorine influence. There is an expression in Tractate VIII which could possibly have come from Richard of St Victor (see Tr. VIII-15), but since it was a well-known saying at the time and could have come from any number of other places, it can hardly be considered as any real proof. It is true that I suspect that in one or two passages we may see the shadow of Hugh of St Victor, but the similarities are too general to permit any categorical statement. The situation with regard to the Cistercian William of St Thierry is in some ways similar. In a number of places, Robert Thomas has directed our attention to passages in William's work which seem to parallel Baldwin's ideas (see Trs. III-4, IX/1-9, IX/1-23, IX/2-11, and XIII-10), and it would be both interesting and important if we could demonstrate that William was indeed one of his sources. His *De contemplando Deo* and *De natura et dignitate amoris* were both available at Ford,[78] but the parallels adduced by Fr Thomas are too general and too indefinite to warrant any definite conclusion.

Among the pagan writers, we find in the Tractates quotations from Cicero, Ovid, Virgil, and Lucan, though none of them is cited by name.[79] Nor should we be surprised to find them, for the embellishing of one's works with classical quotations was a standard practice of the period. In its dispute with Baldwin, for example, the convent of Christ Church quoted Ovid, Lucan, Juvenal, and Horace in its letters of appeal and declarations of woe.[80] No attention was paid to the context from which the quotation was drawn (many, in any case, would have been taken from *florilegia*), and no difficulty was experienced in adorning writing which might be very spiritual (such as Baldwin's sixteenth Tractate) with Ovidian passages taken from a very secular work. What is notable—or perhaps what is typical—of Baldwin is not that he should quote these pagan poets, but that he should quote them so infrequently. He makes no public display of his undoubted learning, and has no interest in impressing his readers with his comprehensive knowledge of the classics. For Baldwin, it is the faith, rooted in the bed-rock of God's revelation, which is important, and there is no doubt that he would have agreed wholly with Tertullian that Athens and Jerusalem have very little in common:

> What has Athens to do with Jerusalem? What has the Academy to do with the Church? What have heretics to do with Christians? Our instruction is from the Porch of Solomon, and it was he himself who taught that the Lord should be sought in simplicity of heart (Ws 1:1). Away with those who would produce a Stoic and Platonic and dialectic Christianity! We have no need for curiosity after Christ Jesus, nor for investigations after the Gospel. We believe; and we want nothing beyond what we believe![81]

It is this spirit which is reincarnated in the teaching of the abbot of Ford.

Such, then, are some of Baldwin's sources, but what of Baldwin himself as a source? To what extent were his own spiritual writings used and read by his contemporaries? Copies of his works seem to have been fairly widely distributed—there were manuscripts at Alcobaça, Bec, Byland, Canterbury, Clairvaux, Durham (though this is not certain), Fountains Abbey, Glastonbury, Gloucester, Holme

Introduction 29

St Benets, Jervaulx, La Trappe, Longpont, Louvain, Margam, Oxford (Balliol College and Lincoln College), Ramsey, Reading, Revesby, Rievaulx, Saint-Sépulcre at Cambrai, Saint-Victor of Paris, Waltham, and possibly Windsor[82] – but how much these manuscripts were actually utilised is a different matter. Peter of Blois was certainly acquainted with Baldwin's treatise on the common life (Tractate xv),[83] and in the thirteenth and fourteenth centuries, substantial extracts from the archbishop's works were included in lengthy *catenae biblicae* which formed part of the library at Clairvaux.[84] Extensive extracts are also included in an early thirteenth-century *catena* of twelfth-century writers which enjoyed considerable popularity and which was printed a number of times in the sixteenth century.[85] Apart from these, however, I know of no other cases which demonstrate unequivocally the influence of our author. The appearance of certain passages from the very end of the *De sacramento altaris* in two commentaries on St Paul discovered by Arthur Landgraf in 1928 and 1935 are no evidence of this influence.[86] As Landgraf himself suggested, they come from an appendix to the *De sacramento altaris* which was not from Baldwin's pen, but which was subjoined to his treatise at a later date by a later editor. Although it appears as part of the work in Tissier and the Migne Patrology, it is rightly omitted in the text edited by John Morson and published in 1963.[87]

On the other hand, there is some evidence that interest in Baldwin's work survived at least into the 1500's. Two manuscripts were copied in the fifteenth century,[88] and in 1521, one of the first books ever printed at Cambridge contained the first two Tractates, that on the eucharist and that on the corrupt way of life of the clergy and people.[89] After this, however, the archbishop sinks into oblivion, and appears only twice in the course of the next three and a half centuries: once in the pages of Tissier's *Bibliotheca Patrum Cisterciensium* published in 1622, and once when this edition was reprinted in the Migne Patrology of 1855. But the times change and we change with them, and as is clear from such series as this present one, there has recently been a notable revival of interest in the spiritual writings of the twelfth century. New editions and new translations of Baldwin have appeared,[90] and he is only one among many obscure men who, in recent years, have been raised from their tombs in the later volumes of the Migne Patrology to a new and better life. The place which Baldwin should occupy in this goodly fellowship remains to be seen, but it is the hope of the translator that this English version of his Tractates will make the writings of this complex man a little more accessible, and assist those more qualified or more christian than I to make an accurate assessment of his worth.

## NOTES

*Abbreviations*

B. of F./B. de F. Baldwin of Ford / Baudouin de Ford.
CF   Cistercian Fathers Series, published by CP.
CP   Cistercian Publications, Kalamazoo, Michigan.
CS   Cistercian Studies Series, published by CP.
PC   *Pain de Cîteaux*, now published by La Documentation Cistercienne, Rochefort.
PL   *Patrologiae Cursus Completus, Series Latina*, ed. J. P. Migne, Paris.
RS   Rolls Series, published by H.M.S.O., London.
SCh  *Sources chrétiennes*, published by Les Éditions du Cerf, Paris.
Tr.  Tractate.

1. See Giraldus Cambrensis, *Itinerarium Kambriae* II, XIV (ed. J. Dimock; RS 21/6 [1868] 149) and *Vita Sancti Remigii* XXIX (Ed. J. Dimock; RS 21/7 [1877] 71).
2. See Gervase of Canterbury, *Historical Works* (ed. W. Stubbs; RS 73 [1879-80]) 2: 400: 'In Exonia ex infimo genere natus, litteris saecularibus et sacris eruditus est, et in omni honestate conversatus est'.
3. See C. J. Holdsworth, *Another Stage . . . A Different World: Ideas and People Around Exeter in the Twelfth-Century* (Exeter, 1979) 12.
4. See n. 2 above.
5. See R. L. Poole, 'The Early Lives of Robert Pullen and Nicholas Breakspear', in A. G. Little and F. M. Powicke, edd., *Essays in Medieval History Presented to T. F. Tout* (1925; rpt. New York, 1967) 62–63; K. Edwards, *The English Secular Cathedrals in the Middle Ages* (Manchester, 1967$^2$) 186–187.
6. Gerald of Wales calls him *scholarum magister egregius* (*Speculum Ecclesiae* II, xxv, ed. J. S. Brewer; RS 21/4 [1873] 81), but we cannot always believe Gerald. In R. Hakluyt's *The Principal Navigations, Voiages and Discoveries of the English Nation* (London, 1589) 1: 14, we are also told that Baldwin *scholarum rector primum erat*, but Hakluyt's source is probably Gerald.
7. See Poole, 69 citing John of Salisbury, *Letter* 292.
8. See Poole, 63.
9. For Bartholomew and his relationship with Baldwin, see A. Morey, *Bartholomew of Exeter: Bishop and Canonist* (Cambridge, 1937), especially 105–109. The precise date of Baldwin's appointment is uncertain: Morey suggests 1161 (see Morey, 105), but it may have been early in 1162.
10. See B. Smalley, *The Becket Conflict and the Schools: A Study of Intellectuals in Politics* (Totowa, N.J., 1973) 217–220. Smalley cites certain letters of John of Salisbury which make it clear that the latter regarded Baldwin as a strong supporter of Becket (see 217 n. 5).

11. The date has been established by Morey, 121.
12. For a brief account of the history of the abbey and a comprehensive bibliography, see M. A. Dimier's article 'Ford ou Forde' in the *Dictionnaire d'histoire et de géographie ecclésiastiques* (Paris, 1971) 17: 1020–1022.
13. PL 204: 641–774 reproduces the edition of Bertrand Tissier published in 1662 in the fifth volume of his *Bibliotheca Patrum Cisterciensium*. A critical edition of the text by John Morson was published in 1963: *Baudouin de Ford, Le sacrement de l'autel*, ed. J. Morson / tr. E. de Solms (SCh 93–94; Paris, 1963). In the dedicatory letter, Baldwin refers to himself as *frater B.*, *Fordensis monasterii servus* (PL 204: 641A; SCh 93: 70), so the work was produced sometime between 1170 and 1180. Leclercq's dating—between 1161 and 1180—is incorrect (see his introduction to Morson's critical edition, SCh 93: 9–10).
14. PL 204: 571–640 again reproduces Tissier's edition, but the present writer has a critical edition in preparation. The work was written probably between 1171 and 1178 (the arguments are presented in D. N. Bell, 'The Preface to the *De Commendatione Fidei* of Baldwin of Ford', forthcoming in *Cîteaux*.
15. These sermons were the subject of P. Guébin's brief but important article, 'Deux sermons inédits de Baldwin, archevêque de Canterbury 1184–1190', in *Journal of Theological Studies* O.S. 13 (1911–12) 571–574. Guébin provides summaries of the sermons, but no editions of the text.
16. See John of Ford, tr. W. M. Becket, *Sermons on the Final Verses of the Song of Songs* (CF 29, 39, 43–47; [1977–1984]). Seven volumes. For John's appointment as prior, see Hilary Costello's introduction to volume 1 of the translation (CF 29), 4.
17. See Morey, 106, n. 4 for the Latin text of the letter. See also P. Glorieux, 'Candidats pour la pourpre en 1178' in *Mélanges de science religieuse* 11 (1954) 17–19.
18. C. Duggan, *Twelfth-Century Decretal Collections and Their Importance in English History* (London, 1963) 119.
19. See generally *ibid.* 110–115, 149–151. For an excellent discussion of what a papal judge-delegate was and the sort of things he had to do, see Morey, chapter IV.
20. This is the story as recounted in the *Chronica* of Roger of Hoveden (see *Chronica Magistri Rogeri de Hovedene*, ed. W. Stubbs; RS 51/2 [1869] 286). There is an English translation in *The Annals of Roger de Hoveden*, tr. H. T. Riley (London, 1853) 2: 32–33.
21. Gervase, 2: 400.
22. See Smalley, 216, who cites as evidence Herbert's *Liber Melorum* III (PL 190: 1403A–1404A) and the dedicatory letter of his *Vita Sancti Thomae* (PL 190: 1073A–1074A).
23. See his comments in his *Itinerarium Kambriae* II, XIV (RS 21/6: 149) and *Vita Sancti Remigii* xxix (RS 21/7: 71). For other assessments of Baldwin's character, see my 'The Ascetic Spirituality of B. of F.' in *Cîteaux* 31 (1980) 227–228.
24. See Gervase 1: 324: 'As you know', said Baldwin, 'my brothers the bishops of England elected me against my will; but I say now what I said then: that I will not and I ought not undertake the government of the church of Canterbury, except through the prior and the convent'.
25. See *ibid.* 2: 401: 'Hoc est primum, fratres, et summum in desideriis meis, ut unum simus in Domino . . . .'.

Notes to Introduction    33

26. See W. Hunt's article 'Baldwin' in the *Dictionary of National Biography* 1: 952. Gerald of Wales bears eloquent witness to the luxury, laxity, and gluttony of Christ Church, and even if his account is somewhat exaggerated, it is clear that the Canterbury monks were guilty of very serious lapses from the monastic ideal (see Giraldus, *De Rebus a se Gestis* II, v [ed. J. S. Brewer; RS 21/1 (1861) 51–52] and *Speculum Ecclesiae* II, III–VI [RS 21/4: 38–46]. There are plenty of similar accounts in the contemporary literature).

27. See D. Knowles, *The Monastic Order in England* (Cambridge, 1950) 318–319, who cites the relevant authorities.

28. For a detailed history of the Hackington controversy, see W. Stubbs' introduction to his edition of *Chronicles and Memorials of the Reign of Richard I: II, Epistolae Cantuarienses* (RS 38/2 [1865]). A day by day calendar of the events will be found therein, CXXI–CLXVII. For a briefer account and a consideration of the motives of the various parties, see Knowles, 317–322.

29. See Gervase, 1: 423. The date is April 1188.

30. Cf. Stubbs, *Epistolae Cantuarienses* LXXV: 'It is hardly conceivable that Baldwin ever intended to maintain Roger Norreys in the position of prior. . . . The archbishop probably thought that such an appointment would compel the monks to submit, and that done, the obnoxious prior might be provided for elsewhere'. Further on the career and character of Roger Norreys, see Knowles, 331–343.

31. For a description of these dramatic events, which took place in the gloom and fog of a late November afternoon, see Gervase, 1: 475–481.

32. See Giraldus, *Itinerarium Kambriae* II, 1 (RS 21/6: 104–105).

33. See *ibid.* II, VI (RS 21/6: 124–125), quoted in the translation of Sir Richard Colt Hoare (see T. Wright (ed.), *The Historical Works of Giraldus Cambrensis* [London, 1894/442).

34. Roger of Wendover, *Flores Historiarum* (ed. H. G. Hewlett; RS 84/1 [1886]) 166. See C. Roth, *A History of the Jews in England* (Oxford, 1964³) 19, n. 1.

35. My account of the incident follows Roger of Hoveden, 3: 12–13 (see Riley's English translation, 2: 119–120). For other accounts in contemporary sources, see Roth, 20, n. 1. Roth also provides a more detailed description of this unfortunate episode.

36. Richard of Devizes, ed. J. T. Appleby, *The Chronicle of Richard of Devizes of the Time of King Richard the First* (London, 1963) 15.

37. See the *Itinerarium Regis Ricardi* lxi (ed. W. Stubbs; RS 38/1 [1864] 115–116).

38. For a brief discussion of the date of Baldwin's death, see my 'B. of F. and Twelfth-Century Theology' in E. R. Elder, ed., *Noble Piety and Reformed Monasticism: Studies in Medieval Cistercian History VII* (CS 65 [1981]) 144 n. 13.

39. *Itinerarium Regis Ricardi* LXV (RS 38/1: 123–124).

40. See Roger of Wendover, 1: 189.

41. See Gervase, 2: 406.

42. See J. Pits, *Relationum Historicarum de Rebus Anglicis* (Paris, 1619) 259–260, and B. Tissier, *Bibliotheca Patrum Cisterciensium* (Bonnefontaine, 1662) 5: 1 (Tissier's list is reproduced in PL 204: 401–404). The same list also appears in C. de Visch, *Bibliotheca Scriptorum Sacri Ordinis Cisterciensis* (Douai, 1649) 27–28.

43. For Guébin's article, see n. 15 above. The manuscript in question is Bibl. Nat. lat. 2601. My discussion of these manuscripts, their dates, and their relationships has

been deliberately simplified in this introduction, and for a more detailed account the reader must be referred to my 'The *Corpus* of the Works of B. of F.' in *Cîteaux* 35 (1984) 221.

44. This is Troyes 876. There are other manuscripts which also arrange the Tractates in this order, but for details the reader must once again be referred to my 'The *Corpus* of the Works of B. of F.'.

45. See n. 15 above.

46. See Tr. xv-1. Cf. also Beryl Smalley's views on the structure of the second Tractate (see Tr. II–12).

47. R. Thomas (ed./tr.), *B. de F., Traités*, PC 35–40 (Chimay, 1973–75), six volumes. This supercedes the Tissier/Migne text in PL 204: 403–572, but since the latter version is probably more readily accessible, I have indicated *in loc.* all the major areas in which revision or correction of the Migne text is necessary.

48. J. Morson, 'B. of F.: A Contemplative', in *Coll. O. C. R.* 27 (1965) 160.

49. For a more complete account of Baldwin's spirituality and of its relationship to that of his contemporaries, see my "Ascetic Spirituality of B. of F." *passim*.

50. See Tr. III PL 204: 426A–B (PC 35: 152; CF 29:92).

51. See my "Heaven on Earth: Celestial and Cenobitic Unity in the Thought of B. of F." in E. R. Elder, ed., *Heaven on Earth. Studies in Medieval Cistercian History IX* CS 68 (1983) 1–21.

52. See my article cited in n. 23 above.

53. See my 'B. of F. and Twelfth-Century Theology', *passim*.

54. *De commendatione fidei* PL 204: 607A.

55. See Baldwin's unequivocal statement in *De sacramento altaris* PL 204: 653B–C (SCh 93: 116) translated in Tr. vi–5 below. For his use of the term 'orthodox Fathers', see my 'B. of F. and Twelfth-Century Theology', 147, n. 67.

56. See *De sacramento altaris* PL 204: 679B (SCh 93: 208) and elsewhere.

57. Tr. I PL 204: 407D (PC 35: 46; CF 38:50).

58. See *ibid.* 408A–B (PC 35: 48; CF 38:51).

59. See *De commendatione fidei* PL 204: 621A translated in my 'B. of F. and Twelfth-Century Theology' 140 n. 60.

60. See generally *ibid.* 139–141, especially 140 n. 56.

61. See Leclercq's introduction to Morson's edition of the *De sacramento altaris*, Sch 93: 25–26.

62. Tr. IV PL 204: 439B (PC 36: 68; CF 38:121).

63. *Ibid.* 439C (PC 36: 70; CF 38:122).

64. *Ibid.* 435A (PC 36: 46; CF 38:113).

65. *Ibid.* 432D (PC 36: 34; CF 38:108).

66. Tr. vi PL 204: 452C (PC 37: 26; CF 38:154). These variants are not always to be found in the Migne Patrology; in some cases (in many cases in the *De sacramento altaris*), Baldwin's version has been tacitly corrected to conform to the *textus receptus*.

67. For a list of all these citations, see my 'B. of F. and Twelfth-Century Theology', 147–148 nn. 69–75. According to Gervase of Canterbury, 1: 476, the archbishop also appealed specifically to the *Rule of St Benedict* in his dispute with the monks of Christ Church. It would have been odd had he not done so.

68. See *De sacramento altaris*; PL 204:720B; SCh 94:374: 'Esse omnium est super esse divinitas'.

69. See PL 122:1046C.

70. Our evidence for this comes from the *Registrum Librorum Anglie*, 'a location list of selected books available in the cathedrals and monasteries of England and southern Scotland, compiled by Franciscans probably at Oxford in the second half of the 13th century' (R. H. and M. A. Rouse, 'The *Registrum Anglie*: the Franciscan 'union catalogue' of British libraries', in A. C. de la Mare and B. C. Barker-Benfield, *Manuscripts at Oxford: An Exhibition in Memory of R. W. Hunt* [Oxford 1980] 55). Professor Rouse is at present engaged in preparing an edition of the *Registrum*, and I am most grateful to him for his kindness in providing me with a list of the books from Ford.

71. See M. Pellegrino, 'Reminiscenze bibliche, liturgiche e agostiniane nel *De sacramento altaris* di Baldovino di Ford', in *Revenue des études augustiniennes* 10 (1964) 39-44, and the indexes of names both in Morson's edition of the *De sacramento altaris* and in this present translation, s.v. Augustin / Augustine.

72. Cf. *De sacramento altaris* PL 204: 732C-D; SCh 94: 424-426, in which Baldwin disagrees with Augustine on the matter of the exegesis of Ex 12: 5.

73. For the identification of Maximus, we are indebted to Henri de Lubac (see his *Exégèse médiévale, les quatre sens de l'Écriture* [Paris, 1959-64] 1: 343); for Venantius Fortunatus, see *De sacramento altaris* 671C (SCh 93: 180) where we find the phrase *hoc opus nostrae salutis* from the hymn *Pange, lingua, gloriosi proelium certaminis*. Baldwin would have been familiar with this hymn through the Easter liturgy. In my earlier note on Baldwin's sources (see my 'B. of F. and Twelfth-Century Theology' 141) I also suggested that we might see traces of the influence of Cassiodorus (see SCh 93: 130, n. 3), Isidore of Seville (see Tr. II-3), and Bede in Baldwin's writings. On further reading and reflection, I think that the evidence is too weak to permit the certain identification of these writers. The *Registrum* records their works at Ford and Baldwin would surely have known them, but I have not yet proved it to my own satisfaction.

74. See Tr. III-6, 15, 16. See further the index of names in this present translation, s.v. Bernard of Clairvaux, and in Morson's edition of the *De sacramento altaris*, s.v. Bernard, Saint. The *Registrum* (MS Oxford, Bodleian Library, Tanner 165, ff. 115-116) records eleven works at Ford by or attributed to Bernard. Of these, eight are genuine and three pseudonymous.

75. See my 'Heaven on Earth' *passim*. I suggested there that the most important direct sources for Baldwin's theology of the *vita communis* were Augustine, Aelred, Bernard, and Benedict.

76. See J. C. Didier, 'Le *De sacramento altaris* de B. de F.', in *Cahiers de civilisation médiévale* 8 (1965) 59-60 n. 4. The passages cited by Didier are to be found in John's prayer *Summe sacerdos*, and any priest who celebrated Mass would have been familiar with it. It is still to be found in the Missal, though attributed there to Ambrose of Milan. On the other hand, the works of John of Fécamp were very widely read, and it is quite possible that Baldwin knew more of his writing than just this single prayer.

77. The *Registrum* (ff. 119$^v$-120$^v$) records eight works at Ford by or attributed to Hugh of St Victor (five of these are genuinely his), and eleven works by Richard of St Victor, all of which appear to be genuine.

78. See the *Registrum*, f. 115ᵛ, where we find, attributed to Bernard of Clairvaux, a *De amore Dei*. This is a standard designation in medieval catalogues (and also in many manuscripts) for the *De contemplando Deo* and *De natura et dignitate amoris* of William of St Thierry.

79. For Cicero, see Tr. VI–7; for Ovid, Virgil, and Lucan, see Trs. VIII–10, IX/II–30, 32, XIV–2, XV–42, XVI–8, and my 'B. of F. and Twelfth-Century Theology' 148, nn. 82–84.

80. See Stubbs, *Epistolae Cantuarienses* 60, 69, 96, 151, 193 (Ovid); 32 (Lucan); 68 (Juvenal); 116, 157, 309 (Horace).

81. Tertullian, *De Praescriptione Haereticorum* VII PL 2: 20B–21A. We may compare Baldwin, *De Commendatione Fidei* PL 204: 591A, in which our author makes it clear that he has no time for Plato and worldly wisdom ('B. of F. and Twelfth-Century Theology' 142).

82. See my 'The *Corpus* of the Works of B. of F.' for the identification and locations of these manuscripts. I will not be in the least surprised if this list needs to be extended as a result of further researches.

83. See A. Landgraf, 'The Commentary on St Paul of the Codex Paris Arsenal, lat. 534 and Baldwin of Canterbury', in *Catholic Biblical Quarterly* 10 (1948) 61–62. In my earlier study ('B. of F. and Twelfth-Century Theology' 141), for reasons which now escape me, I suggested that Peter was one of Baldwin's sources rather than *vice-versa*. That suggestion was incorrect.

84. See Leclercq's introduction to Morson's edition of the *De sacramento altaris*, SCh 93: 46 n. 1, referring to Leclercq's 'Les écrits de Geoffroy d'Auxerre' in *Revue Bénédictine* 62 (1952) 289 (= J. Leclercq, *Recueil d'études sur saint Bernard et ses écrits* [Rome, 1962] 1: 42–43). The manuscripts in question are Troyes 1423 and 1696.

85. See T. M. Käppeli, "Eine aus frühscholastischen Werken exzerpierte Bibelkatene", in *Divus Thomas* Ser. 3 Vol. 9 (1931) 309–319.

86. For the commentary discovered in 1928, see A. Landgraf, 'Familienbildung bei Paulinenkommentaren des 12. Jahrhunderts' in *Biblica* 13 (1932) 169–193, and the same author's 'Untersuchungen zu den Paulinenkommentaren des 12. Jahrhunderts', in RTAM 8 (1936) 254; for the commentary discovered in 1935, see his article cited in n. 83 above, 55–62. Leclercq incorrectly accepts these passages as evidence of Baldwin's influence (see SCh 93: 46 n. 1).

87. See the discussion in SCh 93: 23 n. 1 (Leclercq) and 59–60 (Morson). Landgraf's doubts are expressed in his 'The Commentary on St Paul . . .' 59.

88. Cambridge, *Corpus Christi* 331 and the fine manuscript in Brussels, Bibl. Royale 5277, dated 1453. Both contain the *De sacramento altaris*. Further discussion of these manuscripts will be found in my 'The *Corpus* of the Works of B. of F.'.

89. *Reverendissimi in Christo patris, ac domini, dñi Balduini, Cantuariensis archiepiscopi, de venerabili, ac divinissimo altaris sacramento, sermo devotissimus, sacraeque scripturae floribus undiquaque respersus* (Cambridge, 1521). The volume was printed by John Siberch.

90. For the Tractates, see n. 47 above; for the *De sacramento altaris*, see n. 13 above, and B. of F., *Sacramento del Altar*, ed. Monasterio Ntra. Sra. de los Angeles (Azul, Argentina, 1978).

## BIBLIOGRAPHY

A. *Editions and Translations of Baldwin's Works*
  1. Collected Works (*Tractatus Diversi, De Commendatione Fidei, De Sacramento Altaris*)
     B. Tissier, *Bibliotheca Patrum Cisterciensium* (Bonnefontaine, 1662), volume 5.
     J. P. Migne (ed.), *Patrologiae Cursus Completus, Series Latina* (Paris, 1855), volume 204.
  2. *Tractatus Diversi*
     *Reverendissimi in Christo patris, ac domini, dñi Balduini, Cantuariensis archiepiscopi, de venerabili, ac divinissimo altaris sacramento, sermo devotissimus, sacraeque scripturae floribus undiquaque respersus* (Cambridge, 1521). Latin text of Trs. I and II.
     Baudouin de Ford, *Traités*, ed. / tr. R. Thomas (PC 35–40; Chimay, 1973–1975), six volumes. Latin text and French translation of Trs. I to XVI.
     C. Waddell, 'The Treatise *On the Common Life* by Baldwin, Archbishop of Canterbury and Quondam Abbot of Ford', in *Liturgy O.C.S.O.* II (1977) 19–65. English translation (together with a useful introduction) of Tr. XV.
  3. *De sacramento altaris*
     Baudouin de Ford, *Le sacrement de l'autel*, ed. J. Morson / tr. E. de Solms, introduction by J. Leclercq (SCh 93–94; Paris, 1963), two volumes with continuous pagination. Latin text and French translation.
     Baldwin of Ford, *Sacramento del Altar*, ed. Monasterio Ntra. Sra. de los Angeles (Padres Cistercienses; Azul, Argentina, 1978). Spanish translation. There is a review-article of this work by R. Summers in *Cistercian Studies* 15 (1980) 295–300.
  4. *Letters*
     W. Stubbs (ed.), *Chronicles and Memorials of the Reign of Richard I. Volume II: Epistolae Cantuarienses–The Letters of the Prior and Convent of Christ Church, Canterbury from A.D. 1187 to A.D. 1199.* (RS 38/2; London, 1865). Latin text of nine letters (Nos. 8, 22, 32, 84, 111, 140, 191, 338, 345).
     PL 202: 1533. Latin text of one letter.

B. *Dictionary Articles*
   By J. M. Canivez, in *Dictionnaire d'histoire et de géographie ecclésiastiques* 6: 1415–1416.
   By J. M. Canivez, in *Dictionnaire de spiritualité* 1: 1285–1286.
   By C. Duggan, in *New Catholic Encyclopedia* 2: 28.
   By W. Hunt, in *Dictionary of National Biography* 1: 952–954.
   By J. Morson, in *Dictionnaire des auteurs cisterciens* 90–91.

C. Early Works to 1900
For references to the works of Cave, Ceillier, de Visch, Fabricius, Henriques, Manrique, and Oudin, see the article by Canivez in the *Dictionnaire d'histoire et de géographie ecclésiastiques* cited in Section B above.

D. Works Devoted Entirely to Baldwin

Bell, D. N. 'The Ascetic Spirituality of Baldwin of Ford', in *Cîteaux* 31 (1980) 227-250

———. 'Baldwin of Ford and Twelfth-Century Theology', in E. R. Elder, ed., *Noble Piety and Reformed Monasticism*. Studies in Medieval Cistercian History VII, CS 65 (Kalamazoo, 1981) 136-148.

———. 'Heaven on Earth: Celestial and Cenobitic Unity in the Thought of Baldwin of Ford', in E. R. Elder, ed., *Heaven on Earth. Studies in Medieval Cistercian History IX*, CS 68 (Kalamazoo, 1983) 1-21.

———. 'The *Corpus* of the Works of Baldwin of Ford', in *Cîteaux* 35 (1984) 215-234.

———. 'Baldwin of Ford and the Sacrament of the Altar', forthcoming in Studies in Medieval Cistercian History XI.

———. 'The Preface to the *De Commendatione Fidei* of Baldwin of Ford', forthcoming in *Cîteaux*.

J. C. Didier, 'Le *De Sacramento Altaris* de Baudouin de Ford', in *Cahiers de civilisation médiévale* 8 (1965) 59-66.

———. 'Baudouin de Ford et la dévotion au Sacré Coeur de Jésus', in *Cîteaux* 26 (1975) 222-225.

P. Guébin, 'Deux sermons inédits de Baldwin, archevêque de Canterbury 1184-1190', in *Journal of Theological Studies* O.S. 13 (1911-12) 571-574.

C. Hallet, 'La communion des personnes d'après une oeuvre de Baudouin de Ford', in *Revue d'ascétique et de mystique* 42 (1966) 405-422.

———. 'Notes sur le vocabulaire du *De Vita Coenobitica* de Baudouin de Ford', in *Analecta Cisterciensia* 22 (1966) 272-278.

A. Landgraf, 'The Commentary on St Paul of the Codex Paris Arsenal, lat. 534 and Baldwin of Canterbury', in *Catholic Biblical Quarterly* 10 (1948) 55-62.

J. Morson, 'Baldwin of Ford: A Contemplative', in *Collectanea O.C.R.* 27 (1965) 160-164.

M. Pellegrino, 'Reminiscenze bibliche, liturgiche e agostiniane nel *De Sacramento Altaris* di Baldovino di Ford', in *Revue des études augustiniennes* 10 (1964) 39-44.

E. Works With Important Sections Devoted to Baldwin
Extremely valuable material may be found in the following two doctoral dissertations, neither of which has been published:

C. J. Holdsworth, *Learning and Literature of English Cistercians 1167-1214, with Special Reference to John of Ford* (Cambridge University, typescript, 1960).

B. E. A. Jones, *The Acta of Archbishops Richard and Baldwin: 1174-1190* (London University, typescript, 1964).

Lesser amounts of material may be found in the following works:

C. Duggan, *Twelfth-Century Decretal Collections and Their Importance in English History* (London, 1963) 110-115.

R. Foreville, *L'Église et la royauté en Angleterre sous Henri II Plantagenet* (Paris, 1943) 533-554.

C. J. Holdsworth, 'John of Ford and English Cistercian Writing, 1167-1214', in *Transactions of the Royal Historical Society*, Series V 11 (1961) 117-136.
D. Knowles, *The Monastic Order in England: A History of Its Development from the Times of St Dunstan to the Fourth Lateran Council, 943-1216* (Cambridge, 1950) 316-322.
A. Morey, *Bartholomew of Exeter: Bishop and Canonist. A Study in the Twelfth Century* (Cambridge, 1937) 105-109, 120-121.
B. Smalley, *The Becket Conflict and the Schools: A Study of Intellectuals in Politics* (Totowa, N.J., 1973) 216-220.

## ABBREVIATIONS

| | |
|---|---|
| B. | Baldwin |
| CF | De commendatione fidei |
| DLF | A. Blaise, *Dictionnaire Latin-Français des Auteurs Chrétiens* (Turnhout, 1954). |
| hom. | homoioteleuton |
| lit. | literally |
| M.T. | Massoretic Text |
| n. | note |
| O.L. | Old Latin |
| RB | *Regula S. Benedicti* |
| RSV | Revised Standard Version |
| SA | De sacramento altaris |
| SBO | *Sancti Bernardi Opera*, edd. J. Leclercq–H. M. Rochais–C. H. Talbot (Rome, 1957–) |
| SC | Sources chrétiennes (Paris: Cerf) |
| Tr. | Tractate |

Psalms have been cited according to Septuagint-Vulgate enumeration; Hebrew enumeration appears in brackets

### CITATION OF BALDWIN'S WORKS

*Tractates*: cited by volume and page number of Fr Robert Thomas's edition of the text: R. Thomas (ed./trans.), *Baudouin de Ford, Traités, Pain de Cîteaux* 35–40 (Chimay, 1973–75).

*De sacramento altaris*: cited by column number of PL 204 and (in parenthesis) by page number of Fr John Morson's edition of the text: J. Morson (ed.)/E. de Solms (trans.), *Baudouin de Ford, Le sacrement de l'autel*, SCh 93–94 [continuous pagination] (Paris, 1963).

*De commendatione fidei*: cited by column number of PL 204.

BALDWIN OF FORD
*SPIRITUAL TRACTATES*

# TRACTATE I
# ON THE MOST HOLY SACRAMENT
# OF THE EUCHARIST[1]

ON ACCOUNT OF ITS WORTH and reverence, the sacrament of the body and blood of the Lord is worthy to be handled worthily by those who are worthy, to be prepared worthily, to be received worthily, and to be distributed worthily. Great and inestimable is the worth of this sacrament, and who is there able [to conceive] it? Its greatness surpasses the limits of our understanding and exceeds the bounds of our capacity. Great indeed is the price of the world,[2] a price without price, a priceless price, which cannot be assessed or appraised. 'Great is the sacrament of godliness, says the Apostle, which was manifested in the flesh, was justified in the spirit, appeared to angels, was preached to the Gentiles, believed in the world and taken up in glory.'\*     1 Tm 3:16

This sacrament is the sacrifice of truth. Nothing in it is false, nothing in it is feigned, nothing counterfeit, nothing faked by magical manipulations. There is only true sincerity and sincere truth: truth in that which is evident; truth in that which is hidden. That which is evident is the true and visible form of bread.[3] Before the consecration, we have here the true substance of bread, but in the consecration, it is transubstantiated[4] and changed by virtue of the power of the words into the true flesh of Christ. After the consecration, the whole of Christ, who made darkness his hiding-place,* is hidden under the visible form. To him the prophet said, 'Truly you are the hidden God, the king of Israel, the Saviour.'

Christ was hidden from the beginning in the bosom of the Father; afterwards, he was hidden in the form of a servant which he assumed; and now he is hidden in the sacrament which he instituted. Faith finds him hidden in the bosom of the Father; no less does faith find him hidden in man; and it is faith which finds him hidden in the sacrament. The great power of faith possesses the great grace of intimacy with God. Wherever it finds him, it can approach him, and with a certain familiar and audacious intimacy, it rushes into his sanctuary and his bed-chamber. It gives no thought to being hindered by the guardians of the entrance or the door-keepers or the chamberlains: it enters carefree and unites itself confidently but reverently to the mysteries of God's intentions.

And is it surprising that God entrusts his intentions to the faith of his faithful? Do kings and princes of the people not impart the mystery of their intentions to their faithful [subjects]? God is faithful and without any iniquity,* and his faithful friends, who preserve their faith for him and serve him in faith, are [also] without iniquity. All his works are done in faith,* and without faith it is impossible to please him.⁵

God tests his faithful and his elect so as to find them worthy of him. He tests their faith, and he tests their hope, and he tests their love. But at the moment we are discussing faith, which is tested by God in many ways and is put to the proof most of all in this sacrament.

With an eternal intention, God determined to save the world by the death of his only-begotten Son and to send into the World its Saviour and its salvation; nor [did he intend to send] any other salvation apart from the Saviour himself.

That which he determined he also promised, and he revealed his intention to his faithful. [With this] the faith of the saints rested content; they believed it, and they awaited the fulfilment of his promise. But God delayed his Christ. Why he delayed him is known to him alone and is his secret, but in the meantime he was exercising the faith of the just. To test their faith, God wished to overshadow that which he had promised in a number of ways and to prefigure it with various symbolic objects and sacrifices. All the old rites of legal sacrifice, instituted by the law and approved by the prophets, were done as a reminder of the promise and as a mystical symbol of its future fulfilment. Thus, through the continual round of sacrifices it would be impossible to forget the object of this wonderful promise, whose future [realization] would be yet more wonderful and to which the law and the prophets bear witness.

In these signs of things yet to come, faith was being continually exercised in the service and honor of God, so that the fervor of its devotion would not grow cool from languishing in idleness and the hope of its expectation would not be lost as a result of forgetfulness. And if any of the faithful asked himself what these things meant for him, his reverence and devotion always regarded as certain that which remained hidden in the conviction of faith.

This was the way of things until the shadows withdrew and their place was taken by truth. He who was to come is come; the holy one of Israel is come! He was made man, was seen upon earth, and conversed with men.* He made known to the world the ways of life,* and when he had accomplished the divine plan⁶ for which he came, he ascended into heaven where now he is, seated on the right hand of God. [But] before he ascended into heaven, he comforted his disciples and the other faithful who would follow them that they might not lose hope or despair of his help when his bodily presence had been taken from their eyes: 'Behold', he said, 'I am with you, even to the end of the world.'*

Our Jesus, therefore, is with us. Why should I not call him 'ours' since he was given⁷ to us? 'For unto us the Son is given.⁸ He who says, 'As for me, I will rejoice in the Lord, and I will exult in God my Jesus,'⁹ claims for himself a certain right to this Jesus. This Jesus of ours, with whom God has given us all things,* cannot bear to be absent from us. He loves us so much that he who is the Wisdom of the Father says, 'My delight is to be with the sons of men.'* He was with us in the flesh before he died for us; he was with us in [his] death, insofar as his bodily presence was not yet lifted from the earth; [he was with us] after death, when he appeared to his disciples and gave them many proofs [of his resurrection];* and he is with us even now, even to the end of the world,* until [the day that] we shall be with him, for we shall be always with the Lord.* See how greatly Jesus loves us!¹⁰

Neither death nor life can separate him from us in the charity with which he loves us. For that reason, neither death nor life should separate us from his charity.* Whom should we love if not [Jesus]? Or rather whom should we love in the way that he [is loved]? For apart from all else, if we are not ungrateful and mean, it should be enough that he loves us. To someone who loves is owed above all an exchange of love. He who loves wants to be loved, and this is indeed right and proper. But if someone wants to be loved and does not want to love, it would be very strange if he judged himself and acquitted himself of being unjust. It is a true judgement that he who does not love the one that loves him is himself unworthy to be loved, and truly, he who does not love Jesus puts himself in great danger, worthy of the Apostle's execration and curse: 'If anyone does not love our Lord Jesus Christ, let him be anathema, Maranatha!'* [But] contrary to this is the same [Apostle's] prayer: 'Grace be with all them that love our Lord Jesus Christ in incorruption.'¹¹*

1 Co 16:22

Eph 6:24

Jesus loved us first indeed, and lest we not love him, he is with us even to the end of the world. 'The Lord of hosts is with us, the God of Jacob, our protector.'* From the time that the God of Jacob, the wrestler who supplanted [his brother], was made our protector and assumed our flesh, the Lord of Hosts is with us. He himself says of the just, 'I am with him in tribulation',* and to him the just man says, 'Though I should walk in the midst of the shadow of death, I will fear no evils, for you are with me'.* Emmanuel is with us against those who oppress us and who rejoice at the evils which befall us. He is with us in our moment of need, aiding and protecting us, favoring us with every [possible] help and consolation.

Ps 45:8[46:7]

Ps 90[91]:15

Ps 22[23]:4

This is also the way it was with the just men of days gone by, but now, through the mystery of the Incarnation, [he is] with us by his fellowship in our common nature. But even this extremity of love, when he is with us in such a way, is not enough for Jesus. He clasps us with a tighter embrace and unites [himself to us] in a wonderful way through the sacrament of communion, so that he might be in us and we in him, as he says, 'Anyone who eats my flesh and drinks my blood remains in me, and I in him'.* But the Christ who remains in us also lives in us, as the Apostle says, 'It is no longer I who live, but Christ who lives in me'.* If Christ lives in us, the Spirit of God also dwells in us,* and according to the same apostle, 'Anyone who does not have the spirit of Christ does not belong to him. But if Christ is in us, the body indeed is dead because of sin, but the spirit is alive because of righteousness. And if the Spirit of him that raised Jesus Christ from the dead dwells in you, he that raised Jesus Christ from the dead will give life to your mortal bodies also through his Spirit dwelling in you.'* And the Lord himself says, 'Anyone who eats my flesh and drinks my blood has eternal life.'*

In this sacrament, therefore, our life is hidden with Christ in God.* Here is hidden eternal life, and that true salvation which was promised to those of old and given to us, [salvation] which will be revealed to us when God comes to be glorified in his saints and to be made wonderful in all who have believed.* The Lord has done great things for us,* for what he promised to those of old he has already in large part shown to us. In this sacrament he has shown us the truth of that intention [he had from] of old, of which the Prophet says: 'Lord, let your intention of old be true'.¹² This is the truth of God's promises, the truth of the signs, the truth of the sacrifices, the truth of the shadows and prefigurements. In short, it is the Truth himself, Christ, who says, 'I am the Truth',* the truth which Pilate failed to recognize when he said, 'What is truth?', and went outside.* Let him remain outside who has gone outside, and if he who is faithless departs, let him depart!\* But as for us, lest we remain outside and be counted among the faithless, let us enter into the sanctuary of God; let us be led by faith and enter into the powers of the Lord.\* In the faith of this sacrament let us consider the powers of God,¹³ for whom nothing is impossible,\* whose word is all-powerful and always true, and who can always do what he wills when he wills.¹⁴

As a testimony to this faith, it is enough for us that Christ, who is the power of God and the wisdom of God,\* said to his disciples, 'Take this, this is my body'.\* If our human wisdom murmurs [against this] in our heart, let the pious devotion¹⁵ of faith restrain its murmurs. Let us show honor to the words of God in the humility of faith; let us offer all [our] reverence to so venerable a sacrament and so excellent a grace with cleanness of hands\* and purity of life.

When the time came for him to pass from this world to the Father, Jesus, in his great kindness and generosity,¹⁶ left us this pledge of his love, and in his desire to test the faith and charity of his own, he made this sacrament a sort of arena in which those he chose to test might be exercised. First and foremost, it is divine faith and human reason which struggle together. This they do that one might gouge out the other's eye, and there is no end to the combat until one of them is blinded. Human reason has its eye, and so does faith, but the eye of reason is dim and often cannot see things which are visible and placed near to it. The eye of faith, however, is keen and with it are clearly seen the invisible things of God.\*

Faced with the power of this sacrament, the mind is dulled, the eye of reason darkened, and every

*Margin references:*
1 Co 7:15
Ps 70[71]:16
Lk 1:37
1 Co 1:24
Mt 26:26
2K 22:25, Jb 22:30
Rm 1:20

sense of the body blunted. Our hands, which are so inquisitive and so diligent in touching things, put forth all their skill, but all they can find are normal characteristics of ordinary bread. When we taste it and examine it carefully with our eyes, its flavor, color, appearance,[17] form, and other qualities [again] suggest to our thoughts that it is bread and not flesh. When our reason is consulted, it replies that these fleshly thoughts have persuaded it and the bodily senses have convinced it. The eye of human reason cannot comprehend the invisible things of God unless it be anointed with the eye-salve of grace and enlightened with the true light, of which it is written, 'The commandment of the Lord is full of light, enlightening the eyes.'* If your eye offends you', says the Lord, 'pluck it out and cast it from you',* and it is not inappropriate to regard this as [referring to] the eye of human reason. It is often offended by the pious devotion of faith, but when it offends it is cast out. It is better for you to enter life having one eye of sound faith than to be cast into hell-fire with two eyes—one of faith and the other of human reason.* And whoever is led by human wisdom, accepting only those parts of faith which appear to be in accord with human reasonings, is just like a man with two eyes.

Our faith, however, has a greater testimony than that [which comes] from human reason. It is based on divine authority, which is the supreme reason, incomparably surpassing every human reason. What human reason suggests to the heart should not be more convincing to it than what [is suggested] by the Spirit of God. It is he who suggests all truth and secretly conveys it to us by a hidden inspiration. He uncovers the ear of the heart and speaks in

Ps 18:9[19:8]
Mt 18:9

Cf. Mt 18:9

a gentle whisper of the simplicity of pious devotion and of the mystery of faith, and his conversation is with the simple.* 'And he that is of God hears the words of God.'* It was not flesh and blood, not the wisdom of the flesh nor the bodily senses[18] that revealed to Peter the mystery of faith, but the heavenly Father who is in heaven.*

Pr 3:32
Jn 8:47

Mt 16:17

Our faith, then, is based on truth and has its beginning and its foundation[19] in the God of truth himself, to whom is said, 'The beginning of your words is truth'.* God does not deceive, for he is supreme Truth; nor is he deceived, who is supreme Wisdom; nor is he weakened who is supreme Power. All that he says or proclaims will be done. For him, to do something is as easy as saying that it be so. As he has determined, so shall it be,* and all his intentions shall stand.* If he has decreed it, who can deny it? Our faith, therefore, should be based on certainty: it does not wander about in conjectures, it does not waver as if [dealing] with something doubtful, nor does it hesitate as if [concerned with] something uncertain. It does not falter, does not vacillate, does not fluctuate, but stands upon a steadfast rock, on a foundation which none can change,[20] [the foundation] which is Christ Jesus.

Ps 118[119]:160

Is 14:24
Is 46:10

If faith is the knowledge of salvation, why should we not believe that it possesses certainty? 'I know', says Job, 'that my redeemer lives'.* 'I know', says Martha, 'that whatever you will ask of God, God will give it to you'.* And speaking of her brother, she says, 'I know that he will rise again in the resurrection on the last day'.* 'I know', says the apostle, 'whom I have believed, and I am certain'.* And speaking of Abraham, the same [apostle] says, 'He did not hesitate through mistrust, but was strengthened in faith, giving glory to

Jb 19:25

Jn 11:22

Jn 11:24
Rm 4:21–22

God, knowing that whatever God promised he is also able to perform'.\*

Is the conviction of faith therefore without certainty? Only someone who does not believe or whose belief is lukewarm will say this. Faith is based on supreme authority, truth, and certainty, and therefore by authority it excludes anything counterfeit, by truth it excludes error, and by certainty it excludes doubt. But whoever doubts irreverently is close to [being] one of the faithless.[21]

Thus, we see that it was from doubt that the sin of faithlessness and the crime of apostasy took their origin in mankind. When the Tempter approached the woman, he began with a question loaded with doubt: 'Why has God commanded you not to eat', etc.[22]\* This question, like the hissing [of a snake], disturbed the woman's soul, and she became proud and puffed up,[23] swollen with the venom of the serpent. So she hesitated, and soon her heart inclined to doubt, and she said, 'Perhaps it was so that we might not die'.\* The doubt she conceived in her mind she expressed in a doubtful word, and the word which God spoke she recalled in doubt, and a sort of trial was conducted in the woman's heart. The woman's proud reason sat in the seat of pestilence\* as the judge in the tribunal, and the word which God spoke is led into the centre [of the court] as the defendant. The accuser approaches and charges the defendant with being a liar and says: 'You shall never die'.\* It is just as if he had said: 'This word, this threat of God which threatens you with death, is false!'

Now the woman was not yet so fully persuaded by doubt as to fall, but she was wavering like a leaning wall and a tottering fence\* and still did not know whether to believe God's threat or the devil's suggestion. Meanwhile she considered the tree in question, and saw that it was good to eat and fair to the eyes and beautiful to behold.* Its alluring appearance made it wholly effective as a witness on behalf of the accuser; no sign of death appeared in it, so she could not deduce from this that what the accuser said was false or what God said was not. Added to this was [the fact] that the woman naturally loved life, which the serpent was promising, and, equally, had no love for death, which God was threatening. And having experienced life but never having experienced death, she preferred to follow that to which love and experience were drawing her. And so, conquered at last, she stretched forth her hand to iniquity.* So she was seduced, first [being brought] to doubt and [then] being led from doubt to unfaithfulness until she believed that what God had proclaimed was false. Beginning with desire and ending with consent, she was so convinced that she presumed [to do] what God had forbidden.[24]

All the while, proud reason was sitting in the tribunal, and delivered the woman from the fear of death. It did not justify God in his words but by a proud judgement convicted him of being a liar. Thus the woman transferred to the glory of the Tempter that honor of faith which should have been shown to the words of God, believing the former and not believing God. By the side of proud reason sat proud will, which renounced the honor of obedience to God and, through disobedience, subjected itself willingly to the Tempter. In the woman, therefore, reason was corrupted by pride, for she doubted whether God's word could be trusted.[25] But it is wicked to doubt the words of God and impious not to accede to his instructions.

Gn 3:6

Ps 54:21[55:20]

Created in the image and likeness of God in the judgement of his reason and the freedom of his will, man should naturally and justly conform to God in these things and be subject to him, so that he might always be willing to submit to him from whom he derived his being. He should so humble his reason before him as to believe all his words and so [humble] his will as to obey all his precepts. It is the pious devotion of faith which humbles reason in man and obedience [which humbles] his will. The pride of human reason which rejects pious devotion and knows not how to humble itself to faith is a culpable blindness of the heart and hateful to God, since it refuses to believe that which is beyond its understanding.

When the Lord gave light to the man born blind, the Pharisees, who did not believe, were made more blind, and their eyes were darkened that they might not see.* The Lord directed his explanation of this new and great miracle against them[26] and said: 'I came into this world for judgement, that those who do not see may see, and those who see may become blind.'* [In other words] that those who do not see because of pride may see by the grace of humility, and those that see through pride may not see by the removal of grace. But after saying this, he adds, 'If you were blind, you would not have sin; but because you say, "We see," your sin remains'.*

Not to see great things in oneself and to be devoutly ignorant of things we are not permitted to know is a good blindness. In [the realm of] heavenly mysteries and divine sacraments, therefore, every impious doubt should be banished far from our heart, and all inquisitive questionings should be restrained, so that faith, which possesses the conviction of truth, should also possess a devout ignorance.

## Tractate I

The wisdom of God is incomprehensible and cannot be confined within the narrow limits of human reason.

In this sacrament, therefore, the whole of human reason should be humbled under the pious devotion of faith. Such a thing was right and proper, for the course of our restoration required that the image of God, which had been deformed by the pride of reason, should be reformed through the humility of reason in this sacrament of our redemption. Thus, by humbling the whole of his reason to God, man may believe of this sacrament that which the Lord ordained to be believed, when he said: *This is my body.** Mt 26:26

Let us believe this firmly, let us believe it without any doubt, let us confess it faithfully. If it appears impossible according to human reason or unbelievable according to human wisdom, let it remain ever true and certain in the conviction of faith because of our reverence for the divine word. Let man have faith in[27] God rather than himself. Let him have faith in God lest God should not have faith in him. Let him trust his spirit to God so that his spirit be faithful to God.* Let him trust his reason to God and deny himself, and as he hears from God so let him judge, following him who says, 'As I hear, so I judge'.* Cf. Ps 77:8[78:7]

Jn 5:30

In himself, Christ presented us with a twofold example from which we can profit: in his humility of judgement and his humility of will. Of his humility of judgement it is written, 'As I hear, so I judge',* Ibid. and through the Prophet he says, 'His judgement was taken away in humility'.* Of his humility of Is 53:8 in Ac 8:33 will he says, 'I came not to do my own will, but the will of him that sent me'.* Jn 6:38

Neither the being of Christ nor his works derive from himself,[28] but from the Father, as he himself says, 'I cannot of myself do anything'.* As the Son's being is from the Father, so it is from the Father that he possesses judgement and the will to work, although in these things he is the equal of the Father. Man, therefore, who does not derive his being from himself but who was made by God, should learn from this to judge nothing from himself, but from God, to will nothing from himself, and to perform no works from himself, especially with regard to those works which engender salvation, or in which he works with God to bring it about.²⁹

This sacrifice which we are now discussing is not only a sacrament which sanctifies us, but it contains in itself an example which we should imitate. It is a sacrament through the mystery of faith and an example of the way we should live. As a sacrament [it brings about] the humbling of our will, and the sacrament benefits those who imitate the example. Those who do not imitate the example, the sacrament does not benefit.

The way we should live, however, is not only set forth in this sacrifice, but was already pointed out in an earlier prefigurement of this sacrifice. In the law of Moses, one is commanded to offer up each year on the tenth day of the seventh month a victim whose flesh is burned outside the camp and whose blood is carried into the sanctuary.* As the Apostle says, 'The bodies of those animals whose blood is brought into the sanctuary are burned outside the camp'.* The day on which the animal in question is offered up is called the Day of Atonement, and in referring to this day the Scripture adds, 'Every soul that does not mortify itself on this day shall perish from among his people'.*³⁰

In what way is a day of mortification a day of

atonement? Is it that mortification is atonement? We should ask instead in what way mortification is *not* atonement, if every soul that does not mortify itself on this day shall perish. It is certainly better to mortify oneself on this day than to perish from among [God's] people. 'The bodies of those animals whose blood is brought into the sanctuary are burned outside the camp.'* The souls of those who are not willing to mortify themselves here below with discipline[31] cannot be accepted into heaven, but when a soul is received into heaven, it is then that the blood is brought into the sanctuary. In holy Scripture, the soul is often symbolized by blood, and Scripture itself makes no secret of the reason for this symbolism, saying, 'The soul of all flesh is in the blood'.* Thus, the Lord symbolizes the soul by blood when he says to that watchman of the house of Israel who fails to inform the sinner of his sin, 'I will require his blood from your hand'.*

Heb 13:11

Lv 17:11

Ezk 3:18

No one is exempt from the necessity of christian discipline; no one is excused. No condition, no sex, no age, no rank, no dignity, no power. Every soul that does not mortify itself on that day will perish. This agrees with what is written in the psalm: 'Embrace discipline, lest at any time the Lord be angry, and you perish from the just way'.* Whoever does not embrace discipline will certainly perish. Thus, the Apostle says, 'If you are without discipline, then you are bastards'.* You are not of Christ, but of the devil, who is an adulterer and no [true] husband.

Ps 2:12

Heb 12:8

Through discipline we share the sufferings of Christ, just as through mercy we share those of our neighbour. It is always kind to show that compassion[32] which stems from mercy, though we cannot always bestow it because of our own personal indigence.

Sometimes, therefore, it exists only in our will, but anyone who has not the wherewithal for these works of mercy is excused them. The shared sufferings, the compassion, of discipline, however, should not be measured by mere will but should be borne for Christ in the actual and real experience of mortification by those who profess the name Christian. For since we all offend in many ways,* no one is exempt from sin, and no one, therefore, can be free from punishment. Everyone who stumbles because of sin deserves punishment. But anyone who deserves punishment and does not undergo it is like a man who turns to deceit by reneging a debt. Then, just as in civil judgements, when those expert in law have determined that damages be doubled in cases where debts are reneged, so it is in divine judgements, except that those sentenced by God are not sentenced to twice the amount [of the debt], but to the punishment of eternal death, [hidden] from the face of God and the glory of his majesty.* And to disregard penitence is a sort of reneging on the debt of punishment. Because of penitence, God disregards the sins of man,* but man disregards penitence! From this latter sort of disregard is born dissension, and in due course eternal enmity comes into being under the cloak of hidden hatred and continues indefinitely.

We are the debtors of Christ who has taken upon himself all that we owe and has paid [it] for us, as he himself says, 'I paid the debt which I did not contract'.* But he demands from us the like of that which he paid for us, and who is able to avoid it?[33] A vast amount of suffering was owed to God for the liberation of the human race, and as blessed Augustine says, we ought each of us to contribute to this amount until there are no more contributions to be made and God is paid [in full]; owners of fields or estates normally render to the state or the treasury a certain fixed payment, each according to the amount he possesses; in the same way we should render to a sort of state [treasury] the tax of suffering which we owe, each of us [giving] more or less in accordance with our resources and in conformity with our age, dignity, and rank.[34] What is more just than that man should suffer for Christ when Christ suffered for him? Hence the Apostle says, 'In my flesh I complete what is lacking in the sufferings of Christ.\* Therefore we are debtors, but not to the flesh to live according to the flesh. For if you live according to the flesh, you will die'.\*

Col 1:24

Rm 8:13

Notice how this sentence of death is aimed at those who live according to the flesh. But it is not yet implemented, since it is still possible to avoid it by penitence and discipline. But when it is implemented, there is no appeal which will be able to hold it back, nor can we evade it or elude it by any artifice[35] or subterfuge.

Because Christ suffered for us, if we live a life of voluptuous luxury and make every provision for the desires of the flesh,\* we should then not only be afraid, but ashamed. Is it not shameful, is it not ridiculous, if the Lord—and such a Lord—hangs upon the cross, hangs there for his servant, and the wicked servant, who is the one that deserves to be wounded, carries on in luxury? Is it not infamous, is it not scandalous, if Christ, hanging on the cross, says, 'I thirst',\* and our hearts are weighed down each day with intoxication and drunkenness?\* As the popular saying goes: In this game, the sides aren't equal! The passion of Christ is certainly not a game, or anything like a game. But we reckon our life to be

Rm 13:14

Jn 19:28
Lk 21:34

like a game, something arrayed and arranged for our amusement.

We still dwell in the world, as on a battlefield where Christ our Lord has been killed. Anyone who leaves this field without a wound or a swelling or a bruise can reckon on no repute. 'By his bruises we are healed.'* The Lord has been killed for us on the field of battle, and if we escape unharmed, our bodies healthy and whole, are we not judged guilty of treason to Christ and guilty of his death? Those who brought about his death were also guilty of his death, and so, too, those who agreed to it, and also their accomplices who crucified him. But in a certain way, anyone who in himself annuls the power of the death of Christ by his wicked life is guilty of his death. For although he does not take away the fact that Christ died, he nevertheless acts in such a way that for him Christ died in vain. For him the death of Christ does not effect salvation, and for such a person, who refuses to carry his own cross and thereby destroys himself, the cross of the Saviour is of no advantage. If the cross of Christ, which we are charged to carry, stands opposed to sensual pleasure, and sensual pleasure [stands opposed] to the cross, how can those who love sensual pleasure avoid being judged as persecutors of the cross? Of these, the Apostle says: 'They are enemies of the cross of Christ. Their end is destruction, their God is their stomach, and they glory in their shame, their minds being set on earthly things.'*

These, as we have said, are guilty of the death of Christ, not as those who actually brought it about, or their supporters or accomplices, but as those who scorn his death, who annul in themselves the sacrament of his dispensation and invalidate the intention of the Most High. They make themselves unworthy of heavenly blessing and ineffable grace, and carrying on in voluptuous luxury, they jeer at the mystery of the cross. They trample underfoot the Son of God and say[36] that the blood of the testament, by which they were sanctified, is unclean, and they offer insults to the Spirit of Grace.* A life [lived] according to the flesh is an affront to God, a reproach to the cross, and an overwhelming insult to the whole Trinity. It is an affront to the Father, for the Son is trampled underfoot; it is an affront to the Son, for his blood, as it were, is made unclean; it is an affront to the Spirit, for grace is scorned.[37]

    Heb 10:29

You priests of the Lord, beware of the sensual pleasures of the flesh and the vain way of life of the world. Honor your ministry, you who shine as lights in the world.* Pursue righteousness, embrace discipline.* You were bought with a great price, so glorify and bear God in your body.* carrying [with you] the mortification of Jesus.* Show yourselves in all things as ministers of God.* Bear in your body the marks of Jesus,* and that which brands you as a member of his army. [Live] in abstinence and continence, in chastity and sobriety, in patience and humility, and in all purity and holiness,* so that all who see you may know to whom you belong, and that the word of the prophet may be fulfilled in you: 'You shall be called the priests of the Lord, the ministers of our God'.* And again, 'All that see them shall know that these are the seed which the Lord has blessed'.*

    Ph 2:15
    Ps 2:12[11]
    1 Co 6:20
    2 Co 4:10
    2 Co 6:4
    Ga 6:17

    Cf. 1 Tm 2:15

    Is 61:6

    Is 61:9

'Priests of the Lord, bless the Lord!'* Bless him who has blessed us with every spiritual blessing in the heavens,* him who has blessed the house of Aaron.† Let God be sanctified in you so that in you he may

    Dn 3:84

    Eph 1:3
    †Ps 113[115]:12

appear as he truly is: holy, unstained, and undefiled.\* Do not let your conduct lead others to blaspheme his name, nor let your ministry be censured on your account.\* In the midst of a wicked and perverse people,\* let your way of life be such that those who see you say, 'Truly these are the priests of the Lord; truly these are the ministers of our God; truly these are the disciples of Jesus Christ, successors of the apostles; truly these are the seed which the Lord has blessed.'\*

Give heed to the dignity of the sacrament,[38] for its preparation and distribution have been committed to you. Because your hands have been given you to conduct such a venerable sacrifice, be sure they are clean from all the filth of unclean gifts,[39] lest you be counted among those in whose hands are iniquities, whose right hand is filled with gifts.\* Draw near the altar with your hands washed; approach with him who says, 'I will wash my hands among the innocent and go about your altar, O Lord'.\* Keep your mouth clean to taste the sweetness of the Lord,\* to receive the Eucharist, the living bread which came down from heaven.\*

The mouth of a priest should not be polluted with perjury, or with false testimony, or with lying, or with obscenities or idle chatter, or by speaking scurrilously of something which should not be sullied by such words, or by spreading scandal and slander about one's enemies. In the mouth of a priest should be the offering of thanks and the voice of praise, prayers, supplications, and appeals.\* From him should come no evil word, but only that word which is good, which shows to those who hear it the grace of edification, and which becomes that spoken by the Lord: 'I will bridle you with my praise, lest you perish'.\* Bridled by this praise, therefore, [the Psalmist] says, 'I will bless the Lord at all times; his praise will ever be in my mouth'.* The mouth is bridled with the praise of God lest it be opened wide with filth and disgrace through unbridled license of speech. The mouth which must touch the sacred banquet should not be foul and impure.

Ps 33:2[34:1]

Beloved brethren, let us hold most firmly and believe beyond doubt that the authority of God himself and of the holy Fathers directs us to believe in this sacred communion. In this sacrament is contained the power of our restoration and the price of our redemption. To exercise our faith, the truth is hidden, and the conduct and chastisement[40] of Christ is displayed as an example for our own lives. For this reason, when the Lord instituted this sacrifice and entrusted it to his disciples, he said: 'Do this in memory of me'.* Do that which I do; offer that which I offer; live in the way that I teach you. Take from this a model for living and for dying, [a model] which I entrust to you by my own example.

Lk 22:19

The effect of this sacrament on us is that Christ lives in us and we in him. Its effect in us is that just as Christ died for us, so, too, we die for Christ. All who die in Christ or for Christ, who fall asleep in pious devotion, have great grace laid upon them.* For them is promised and reserved the glory of resurrection, the restoration and salvation which is [obtained by] the worthy reception of this sacrament, by whose power God will reform our lowly body to be like his glorious body.* What do we have worthy to repay the Lord for so much grace bestowed upon us? How can we requite him for so much honor? It is futile to ask if he loves us, who, as a sign of his inestimable love, offers us in himself the bread of eternal life and the cup of everlasting salvation.[41]

2 M 12:45

Ph 3:21

It is only right, therefore, that as far as our human weakness allows, we should receive worthily and reverently so excellent a gift of God, so exceptional a favor, and guard it as the apple of our eye;* more, in fact, than as the apple of our eye: as our life, as our salvation,[42] as the hope and reality of our resurrection and glory.

However much we have sinned hitherto through neglecting reverence for so great a sacrament, let us atone for it in the future by being more exacting and exerting greater care, and let us make up for the faults of earlier days and of the life we once led by a more honorable resolution and a better intention, making the most of the time, because the days are evil.*

Dt 32:10, Ps 16[17]:8

Eph 5:16

## Notes to Tractate I

1. Title in PL 204:403-404. This first tractate seems to have been formed from what were originally two separate sermons—the one ending and the other beginning at n.37—and in certain manuscripts this is how they are presented. The two parts are separated by what appears now as Tractate XII (for details, see P. Guébin, 'Deux sermons inédits de Baldwin, archêveque de Canterbury 1184-1190', in *Journal of Theological Studies* O.S. 13 [1911-12] 571-574). I suspect that in the process of editing, part of both sermons has been lost, but it is impossible to say just how much. Both discourses, however, were obviously concerned with the same topic—the nature, distribution, and reception of the eucharist—and for this reason, I have retained the form of one single tractate in my translation. The second sermon is clearly that of a bishop or archbishop addressing his priests, and while I suspect that this is probably true of the first sermon as well, the internal evidence is not quite as conclusive. For further material on Baldwin's understanding of the nature and importance of the eucharist, see my 'Baldwin of Ford and the Sacrament of the Altar', due to be published soon by Cistercian Publications.

2. Baldwin has in mind 1 Co 6:20 and other similar pauline ideas. The conception of the eucharist as a re-enactment of the sacrifice of calvary dates from the early patristic period.

3. PL 204: 403B suggests that we add here, 'that which is hidden is the true body and blood of Christ', but there appears to be no manuscript justification for this.

4. Baldwin also used this term in his *De sacramento altaris*, and included there a defence of its usage (see PL 204: 662C-D [SC 1481]). For a full account of its development, see DThC 5: 1287-1293. By the latter part of the twelfth century, the term was in widespread use.

5. As Thomas observes (35/30-31, n. 1), the word *fides* means both 'faithfulness/fidelity' (as in Ps 32[33]:4) and 'faith/belief' (as in Heb 11:6). We may compare the ideas in this paragraph with Baldwin's comments in Tr. IX.1, n. 13.

6. *Dispensatio* is here the Latin equivalent of the Greek *oikonomia*, 'economy', i.e. God's plan and design for the world. See Eph 3:9.

7. PL 405C omits *datus*.

8. Baldwin's exegesis demands 'the Son' rather than 'a son' in this quotation of Is 9:6.

9. Hab 3:18 according to the Vulgate. 'Jesus' is here being used in its etymological sense of 'saviour'. The O.L. rendering was much clearer: 'gaudebo super Deo salutari [or salvatore] meo' (see Jerome, *Commentaria in Abacuc* II [in Hab 3:18]: PL 25: 1335C-D).

10. *Ecce quantum nos amat Jesus*. Thomas (35/37, n. 1) compares Bernard, SC 17.7; PL 183: 858C; (SBO 1:102): 'Quomodo me amas, Deus meus, amor meus! Quomodo me amas . . . .'. The idea is certainly similar, but we cannot say more than that.

11. *In incorruptione* renders the Greek *en aphtharsia* and should be translated (as in the RSV) by some such phrase as 'with undying love'. It is eminently possible, however, that Baldwin understood it to mean something like 'without corrupt thoughts'.

12. Thomas (35/43, n. 1) admits ignorance as to the source of this text. It is, in fact, the O.L. version of Is 25:1 which Baldwin may well have found in Jerome's

*Commentariorum in Isaiam Prophetam* VIII (in Is 25:1); PL 24: 289A: 'consilium antiquum verum fiat'.

13. The passage from 'being led by faith' to 'the powers of God' has been omitted in PL 407A by homoioteleuton.

14. *Cui semper subest, cum voluerit, posse.*

15. In nearly all cases, I have rendered *pietas* by 'pious devotion', although it is not a satisfactory term. *Pietas* indicates an inner attitude and consequent conduct which involves duty, devotion, affection, gratitude, loyalty, and love. It is therefore our dutiful conduct with regard to God and the things which are God's which, because it arises from a heart truly turned to God in love, devotion, and gratitude, is both natural and a joy to perform.

16. *Benignissimus Jesus.*

17. *Superscriptio.* The term here would seem to mean 'appearance' or 'distinguishing characteristics', even though the dictionaries do not give this meaning.

18. *Sensus animalis,* i.e. the physiological, as distinct from the spiritual, senses. *Animalis* is the Latin equivalent of the Greek *psychikos* (see DLF, s.v. *animalis*).

19. PL 408A omits *et fundamentum.*

20. Thomas (35/48) has *mutare;* PL 408B has *revocare,* 'which no-one can take away'.

21. For a similar argument that faith is also true knowledge (*scientia*), see Baldwin's CF, 584A–C.

22. The 'etc.' is in the text.

23. The verb is *tumescere,* 'to swell with venom or excitement or pride'. Hence my 'proud and puffed up'.

24. For a similar account of the unfortunate events in Eden, see CF, 626B–D.

25. PL 409C has *de fide sermonis Dei dubitavit;* Thomas (35/54) omits *Dei. Fides* here means 'fidelity' or 'trustworthiness' (see n. 5 above).

26. *At Dominus novitatem miraculi tanti contra eos interpretans* . . . PL 409D substitutes *intentans* for *interpretans.*

27. The verb is *credere.* This would normally be rendered as 'believe', but it also means 'have faith or trust in' (as in Ps 77:8, which is echoed here).

28. Lit. 'Christ is not from himself and does not effect things from himself'. The same construction occurs elsewhere.

29. *Nil a se velle, nil a se operari, in iis maxime quae ad salutem operantur, vel cooperantur.* On the significance of *operari*, see Tr. v, n. 5.

30. PL 410D is quite different here, and substitutes for this last sentence: 'The day of mortification is the day of atonement from sin'.

31. *Disciplina.* This is an important term for Baldwin and it comprises a number of meanings. Blaise (DLF, s.v.) gives six such, of which two are of particular importance: (a) *disciplina* as the regular discipline of the monastic / ascetic life; and (b) *disciplina* as correction or penitential chastisement. It is this second meaning which B. has in mind here. See also n. 40 below.

32. Etymologically, compassion means "suffering with someone, shared suffering", and not just feeling sorry for him.

33. *Quis poterit ei extorquere?* PL 411D has *ea* for *ei.*

34. Baldwin's source here is Augustine, *Enarratio in Psalmo* 61.4; PL 36: 731.

## Notes to Tractate I

35. Thomas (35/68) has *nulla arte*; PL 412B reads *occulta arte*.
36. PL 413A, influenced by the Vulgate, has *ducunt*. Baldwin however, wrote *dicunt* (see 35/72, n. 1).
37. See n. 1 above.
38. For *sacramenti*, PL 413C has *sacerdotii*. Thomas (35/76) gives *sacramenti* in the latin text (which is correct), but translates as if it were *sacerdotii*.
39. Baldwin may have been thinking of priests who charged fees for the sacraments. This was quite contrary to canon law, but was certainly done on occasion. In the thirteenth century, for example, the clergy at Bristol were charging two pence for each baptism (see J. R. H. Moorman, *Church Life in England in the Thirteenth Century* [Cambridge, 1955] 128, n. 6).
40. Once again, the word is *disciplina*, but here it involves Christ's disciplined and ascetic life as well as the sufferings he willingly accepted. Hence my 'conduct and chastisement'.
41. A formula from the liturgy.
42. PL 414D omits *sicut salutem nostram*.

# TRACTATE II
## ON THE CORRUPT WAY OF LIFE OF THE CLERGY AND PEOPLE[1]

**S**EE HOW DANGEROUS are these times in which we live, and how corrupt and abominable the sons of men have become in all their endeavors!* The earth is full of iniquity, and just as all flesh had corrupted its way* in the days of Noah, so too [it is] at this present time. In those days, before the waters of the flood came over the earth, they were preceded by a spiritual flood in the dissipated manners of mankind and in human immorality was prefigured the manner of that just retribution which was to come. Torrents of iniquity have overflowed,* and those who are in the flood of many waters have not come near God.* Thus, the depths have overwhelmed them, and they have sunk into the deep as a stone.*

While the abyss of sins called upon the abyss of God's judgements* and its clamor entered the ears† of the Lord God of Hosts, the fountains of the great deep were broken and the flood-gates of heaven were opened,* and the Lord blotted out flesh from the face of the earth. [Then] he placed in the clouds the bow of his covenant,* so that mankind might no more fear the waters of the flood. But this does not mean there is nothing left to fear: for when God bent his bow and made it ready,* he gave a sign to those who feared him so that they might flee from before his bow.* In the recollection of that judgement which is past is rooted the dread of that which

*Margin notes:*
Ps 13[14]:1
Gn 6:12

Ps 17:5[18:4]
Ps 31[32]:6

Ex 15:5

Ps 41:8[42:7]
†Ps 17:7[18:6]

Gn 7:11

Gn 9:13

Ps 7:13[12]

Ps 59:6[60:4]

is to come, and with the bow which God placed in the clouds there appears, in all its many colors, the terrible sign of judgement by water and fire. From judgement by water we are pardoned; but terrible is the expectation of judgement and the rage of fire which shall consume his adversaries.* Heb 10:27

See how it is that even now human conduct reveals in advance the manner of the judgement to come. The fire of cupidity and lust and malice has been kindled in the midst of the people and everywhere ravages² all who dwell on earth, as if the flaming destruction of the world had even now drawn nigh. When it arrives, the punishment will be modelled on the sin, and what the nature of the sin now is, so will be the nature of the punishment. [Thus], since the life of the wicked is [one] of fire, fire will be their punishment. [But] since the life of the just is also fire, fire will be their glory. For now the just burn with the fire of divine love, the fire which the Lord came to spread on the earth, but which he also wishes to see kindled.* Lk 12:49

There is now a fire in Sion, but there will be a furnace of fire in Jerusalem.* The just shall indeed burn in the future, but they will burn like the Seraphim.³ They will blaze like the sun in the sight of the Lord* and will shine in the brightness of the saints.* Such shall be the glory of those who, like bright and flaming lamps, burn within with [the fire of] charity and outwardly shine as an example to others.

Is 31:9

Mt 13:43
Ps 109[110]:3

The wicked too shall burn in the future, but in a different way. Of them, the Prophet said to the Lord, 'You shall make them as an oven of fire in the time of your anger'.* Even now they burn, those of whom it is said, 'They are all adulterers; their hearts Ps 20:10[19:9] are like an oven'.\* And the Psalmist says of the wicked: 'Fire has fallen upon them, and they shall not see the sun'.\* The fire with which they burn gives no illumination, but only darkness, so much that it prevents them from seeing the sun. Thus, in the last days, moaning within themselves in anguish of spirit, they shall say, 'The light of justice has not shone upon us, and the sun has not risen upon us'.[4]

The signs which shall precede the day of judgement will also be modelled on our present conduct, and the things which will come to pass in reality[5] may now be seen in us spiritually. It is written that 'the sun shall be turned into darkness and the moon into blood before the great and terrible day of the Lord shall come.'[6]\* What the sun and moon are in the sky [corresponds] in the church of God to the order of prelates[7] and the life of those who are subject to them, and also to ecclesiastical authority and secular power. The moon is inferior to the sun and shines not of itself but from the sun. So too the life of those in their charge[8] is inferior to the life of the prelates by whom they should be enkindled and enlightened. For to the latter it is said: 'You are the light of the world'.\*

But in those prelates who are ignorant and in error, who are blind and leaders of the blind,\* the sun is changed into darkness; and therefore in the life of those subject to them the moon is changed into blood[9]\* — into the blood, that is, of corruption and cruelty. See how the charity of many grows cold and iniquity abounds!\* 'The blood has risen from the pool as far as the bridles of the horses',\* as far as the guides and leaders[10] of the people, and there is blood and more blood, murder upon murder.[11]

## Tractate II

The laity do not find in us that which they should imitate; they find that which they would rather persecute. They persecute us with lies; they persecute us with injury, invective, and taunts. And they even persecute us with swords.

Not long ago the fury of our persecutors wounded us in the head.[12] They have persecuted to the death that man of the Lord Christ, most blessed Thomas, our bishop, for his noble defence of the freedom of the Church. And if we can believe what has been spread abroad as the reason for this deed, something which troubles the conscience of many, it was our undisciplined life which spawned so great an evil and kindled so great a hatred. A certain man did not regard us as ministers of Christ and dispensers of the mysteries of God;* but he shall bear the judgement of God, whoever that man may be.[13]

1 Co 4:1

Perhaps we appeared unworthy of those ancient privileges which, for the peace and freedom of the clergy, were granted us by the favor of the roman pontiffs and the noble kings of old. We were indeed unworthy! If only it were otherwise! But according to our merits we were totally unworthy! Yet in any priest at all, the priestly ministry is always holy and the priestly sacrament honorable.[14]

There comes to our mind now that time when Doeg the Idumean slew with the sword eighty-five priests vested with the ephod.* Remember those days of old and [remember] too the blood of Zachariah, the son of Barachiah, who was slain between the temple and the altar.[15]* In our times, too, there are many notable cases of sacrilegious cruelty, but when compared with this single deed, the enormity of a host of crimes is set at nought. God knows what things the enemy has done wickedly in the

1 S 22:18

Mt 23:35

sanctuary!* All the wickedness of our times—even though there is now so much of it—has been absolved by this one single act. One single act—but in that one act there is [contained] a multitude of crimes! For carefully cultivated wickedness, cunningly contriving at its own ruin, intended that there be nothing lacking from perfect villainy, and brought the whole business of wickedness to its consummation in an extremity of malice.

But if we consider it a likely view that it was our disordered and undisciplined way of life which was responsible for such an evil deed, what can we do but call upon the Lord our God until he have mercy upon us?* He is compassionate and full of mercy.† What is more beneficial and what more honorable than to recall our life to order and discipline and to show ourselves in all things as ministers of God,* so that those who persecute us and speak against us as evildoers may see our good way of life* and themselves be led by our example to penitence?

If the light itself is darkness, how great will the darkness be?* If we still walk in the works of darkness, we, who were appointed in the Church of God that our life might enlighten others by our good works, then is it surprising if those who are subject to us, unknowing and ignorant, [also] walk blindly in darkness and, by our example, become yet more blind?

Will their blood not be required from our hands?* And that most blessed martyr who, for us, laid down his life, will he not lay a charge against us? Will the voice of his blood not cry out against us from the earth,* and will we not all be found guilty before the judgement seat of a severe judge? Did he not die for our faults? And was it not through our faults that he died? For if they did not provide the [actual] cause of his death, they were responsible for its happening. If we continue in sin—as may well be the case—he will no longer be [our] advocate for justice, no longer an intercessor for our pardon, but an accuser and witness for our punishment. In the evils which we suffer by the just judgement of God, we have no right to rage at anyone save ourselves. We have deserved worse and are not yet suffering what we really deserve.

We are justly to blame—and it redounds to our peril—that the secular power has arrogated ecclesiastical jurisdiction;[16] that it is not governed by ecclesiastical authority; that it neither uses nor trusts to the council of the Church but resists it; that the sword of Peter is blunted and the keys of Peter are not reckoned with; that the sacraments of the Church are scorned; that the holy and terrible name of God—with no thought of perjury—is taken in vain; that the respect due to inviolable churches is not given and the honor due to ecclesiastics not shown; and that the venerable name of holy religion is brought to scorn. All these things, and many more like them, are laid at our door and blamed on our sins. Our conduct and our iniquities have brought them upon us. But God has the power whenever he will to free the bride whom he loves[17] from the hands of those who persecute her. He is a little angered,* for it is we who have encouraged wickedness. The [secular] power seems to be striving to subject the Church to itself lest it be itself subject, but what does Scripture say? 'The multitude of nations', it says, 'fighting against Ariel shall be as the dream of a vision by night.'*

Today there are things happening on earth which are both bewildering and extraordinary. Contrary

2 M 7:33

Is 29:7

to [the natural] order of things, the moon is exalted over the sun and does not remain in her place. But what does Scripture say? 'The sun has been raised, and the moon has remained in her order.'[18] May the sun [indeed] be raised and recalled to its own place; may the priestly life return to what it should be, ordered and disciplined. Then the moon, too, will remain in her order. Then the life of those subject to us will be ordered and disciplined, content within its bounds.

What is more fitting for those who have entered [holy] Orders[19] to live an ordered life? What an abuse it would be, both factually and verbally, if those who are spoken of as being in Orders were found to be in disorder. When the prophet says the moon remained in its ordered place, he implies that the moon, which is inferior to the sun, does indeed have an order. But if order and discipline are demanded in the life of those in their charge, how much more so in the life of the prelates? The latter, clearly, should do everything in an ordered manner and, by their judgements, order the conduct of others. They are the throne of God on which God sits and hands down his judgements, that throne of which the Father, speaking of the Son, says: 'His throne is like the sun in my sight'.* And there is added, 'and as the moon, perfect for ever'.

By this order, God will bring to perfection the glory of the just. For the prelates and those who have led perfect lives[20] the throne of God will be like the sun, far more glorious than the moon and far superior [to it]. And for those in their charge and those who are now less than perfect, the moon will [also] be for ever perfect, but perfect within its own order. May God lead us to this glory, each of us in his own order, he who is above all things for every blessed. Amen.*

Ps 88:38[89:35]

Rm 9:5

Notes to Tractate II 75

1. Title as in PL 415–416. For a discussion of the nature of this tractate and its date, see n. 12 below.
2. *Depopulator* in Thomas' text (35/90) is a typographical error for *depopulatur*.
3. Seraphim, etymologically, means "the burning ones". Cf. Isidore, *Liber Etymologiarum* VII, v, 24; PL 82: 273D–274A.
4. Ws 5, 6 in the Vulgate reads *sol intelligentiae*, but Baldwin omits the second word.
5. *Visibiliter*.
6. Jl 2, 31 in the Vulgate reads *horribilis*; Baldwin substitutes *terribilis*.
7. *Ordo rectorum*. *Rector*, in medieval usage, was a word of wide meaning, but it normally referred to a bishop.
8. *Vita subditorum*. Lit. 'the life of those who are subject to them'.
9. Baldwin changes the future *convertetur* of Jl 2:31 to the present *convertitur*.
10. Once again, *rectores*, which I have rendered as 'guides and leaders'.
11. *Sanguis sanguinem tetigit* is a quotation from Ho 4, 2. I have given both a literal and (following the RSV) a meaningful translation.
12. Baldwin is referring to Thomas Becket, and his *in capite* may perhaps be understood in three ways: (i) the body of the Church has been wounded in its head; (ii) the head of the Church has been wounded; (iii) the head of the Church has been wounded in the head, for it was well known that when Thomas was martyred, William Tracy's first blow cut into the crown of his head, and Richard Brito completed the murder by slicing off the top of his skull. Baldwin says this occurred 'not long ago' (*nuper*), but it is difficult to say precisely how long before he wrote. Becket was killed at the very *end of* 1170, and at that time Baldwin was a monk at Ford. This sermon, however, is unquestionably addressed to clerics (perhaps bishops and / or suffragan bishops — see n. 7 above), not to monks, and the person delivering it is unquestionably a high ecclesiastic. In other words, Baldwin is either Bishop of Worcester (as Thomas thinks [34/85]) or Archbishop of Canterbury (which is the opinion of Beryl Smalley; see *The Becket Conflict and the Schools* [Totowa, N.J., 1973] 219 — and also that of the present writer): since he was elevated to the former see in 1180 and to the latter in 1184, the events he narrates must have taken place at least a decade earlier. It is possible, of course, that we have here a later sermon incorporating earlier material (see Smalley, 219, n. 11), although this is not my own view. Baldwin also touches on Becket's martyrdom (without mentioning him by name) in his earlier *De sacramento altaris*, written while he was still at Ford (see Smalley, 218–219 for a brief discussion).
13. Baldwin is referring (cautiously!) to Henry II, who was still very much alive. He died in 1189, one year before Baldwin.
14. See also Tr. XII, n. 9.
15. A very apt biblical reference (Mt 23: 35), since Becket's murder did indeed take place close to an altar: he was martyred in Canterbury Cathedral, just by the massive pillar between the Chapel of St Benedict and the Lady Chapel. Ps 73[74]:3, which Baldwin quotes a little further on, also echoes this, as does his complaint that no respect is shown to inviolable (*sacrosanctus*) churches, nor any honor to ecclesiastics.
16. As far as Becket was concerned, this was what Henry was trying to do in 1164 at Clarendon.

17. *Quam sibi zelat.* We could also render it as 'whom he guards jealously for himself'.

18. This text does not occur in the Vulgate, but Thomas' suggestion (35/102-3, n. 1) that it is from an O.L. version of Joshua is incorrect. It is indeed O.L., but it is Habakkuk, not Joshua. Baldwin may well have found it in Jerome's *Commentaria in Abacuc* II (in Hab 3:11); PL 25:1323C.

19. Baldwin is playing on the word *ordinatus*, 'ordained / in orders'.

20. Lit. 'the prelates and the perfect'. *Perfectus*, in medieval usage, can refer not only to one who has achieved perfection, but to one who is devoting himself wholly to its achievement. Thus, when the later writer Uthred of Boldon, on the authority of pseudo-Dionysius, refers to monks as *ordo perfectorum*, he is describing them in relative rather than absolute terms. For Uthred, see W. A. Pantin, 'Two Treatises of Uthred of Boldon on the Monastic Life', in R. W. Hunt *et al.*, *Studies in Medieval History Presented to F. M. Powicke* (Oxford, 1948) 363-385.

# TRACTATE III
# ON THE LOVE OF GOD[1]

*You shall love the Lord your God with all your heart, and with all your soul, and with all your strength, and with all your mind.* \*

Mt 22:37

WE MAY BE DISTURBED—and it would not be unjust to say that we should be disturbed—when we consider the purpose of this accumulation of words, this earnest injunction which is so loving, so accurate, so exact, so extensive, and yet one single commandment. It is one single commandment, not several, and of it is written: 'This is the first and greatest commandment'. \*

Mt 22:38

Although it says 'You shall love the Lord your God with all your heart', then, as if this were not enough, there is added 'and with all your soul', and then, as if what has been said still does not suffice, there is added 'and with all your strength'; and finally, as though all these words were not enough, there is added 'and with all your mind'.

What is the intention of all this? Was it idly and to no purpose that these things were so carefully written down? Anyone who believes this believes wrongly! If no leaf falls from the tree save by the decision of the Father, how much more is the word of God—and most especially this word, the first and greatest among the words of his commandments—

spoken by the decision of God, so that not a jot or a tittle should be taken away?*

We should therefore make a real effort to inquire into this, and investigate with the greatest care what it is that God willed to be commanded and written so carefully. No quest is more profitable, nor any discovery more useful, provided that those who seek and find do what is commanded.

It would seem that it is because of the hardness of our hearts that God took such care to insist on this commandment, and by commanding it [repeatedly], as it were, to drill it into us really deeply. It is like driving a nail into hard wood: normally, the hardness of the wood prevents the whole nail from going in all at once, and we therefore drive it in with blow after blow until the whole [nail] has gone in and we consider it driven home. This injunction is a sort of nail which must be driven into our hearts; for if, as Solomon said, the words of the wise are like goads and like nails deeply fixed,* how much more is the word of God a goad and a nail, when it is living and effective, and more penetrating than any two-edged sword?* Thus, because God wanted to pierce our hearts through and through, and penetrate them completely with this nail of his divine word and divine love, he says: 'You shall love the Lord your God with all your heart'; and driving it in further, he adds, 'and with all your soul'; and to make it enter yet more deeply he adds, 'and with all your strength'; and to make it reach all the way to the utmost depths, he adds finally, 'and with all your mind'. Such a commandment exceeds all measure, for he wants us to exceed all measure in putting it into practice.*

But we may also see that there is another possible explanation for the [four-fold] division of this one commandment: because the love of the world occupies our whole heart and fills up all its chambers, the love of the world must be cast out from our whole heart. Only then shall the Prince of this world be cast out* and the love of God enter in to claim for itself all our heart. Only then shall God be known in all the most secret places of our heart and all the ends of the earth remember the Lord and turn to him.* Only so shall God possess all our heart and the heart [possess] God, so that we can say with the Prophet, 'God of my heart, and God, my portion for ever'!*

Jn 12:31

Ps 21:28[22:27]

Ps 72[73]:26

## THAT IN THIS PRESENT LIFE GOD IS NOT LOVED PERFECTLY

Because of the condition of this present life, God is only known imperfectly and in part,* and in just the same way, he is loved only imperfectly and incompletely. If we compare our knowledge of God in this present life—however great it may be—with that full and complete knowledge of God when God will be seen in his glory,* when he will show us his face and we shall be saved,* it is like [comparing] the morning light entering a house through the narrowest of cracks with the sun in its midday splendor, shining in its full strength.* The same is true of the sort of love for God we can have in this present life. It is like a tiny spark of fire beside that great flame of love with which the just shall blaze in Jerusalem among the ranks of the Seraphim.² There is now a fire in Sion, but there will be a furnace of fire in Jerusalem.*

1 Co 13:9

Ps 101:17[102:16]
Ps 79:4[80:3]

Rev 1:16

Is 31:9

In the meantime, you should love God with your whole heart in accordance with the measure of your imperfection. But how can this be with your *whole* heart? How is this possible when your whole heart is not yet wholly yours, but is torn apart by strangers? This is why a certain man, amidst other lamentations, complained that 'My thoughts are dispersed; my heart is tormented'.\* And another said: 'My iniquities overwhelmed me, and I could not see. They are more than the hairs of my head, and my heart has forsaken me.'\* Forsaken by their heart, they are forsaken, as if they were without a heart.

Meanwhile, we do not have a whole heart with which to love God. Neither do we have a heart with which to adore him,³ so that [through this adoration] our heart might be restored to loving him. David, therefore, says in one place: 'Your servant has found his heart that he might pray to you with this prayer'.\*

Speaking for myself, I do not find my heart when I come to pray. Where, then, is it? Or rather, where is it not?⁴ When I look for where it is, I can find no place where it is not! It dashes away and flies back; it sallies forth, scampers about, and hurries back again. When it returns it does not stay; when restrained, it is not detained; and when I try to grasp it, it slithers out from my hands as if it were greased!

O man, if you should feel this in your heart—and because you are a man you certainly feel it to some degree—you have in yourself your own proof that you do not yet love God perfectly with your whole heart. I mean according to that measure of perfection in which he wants you to love him.

Yet if you love God in truth and offer your heart to God as much as you possibly can, then in giving it to God you make it your own. Or, more accurately, he to whom you give it makes it not your own, and unless he makes it not your own,⁵ it cannot be your own! Thus, the more of your heart you give to him, the more he makes it your own.

## Tractate III

If you could unwaveringly direct to him all your thoughts, all your affections, and all your intentions, and hold and maintain them unswervingly, even burning within yourself, in all your marrow, with the fire of love, then indeed you might be able to love God more perfectly with all your heart. But because our human weakness does not permit this, then if you cannot love as much as you should, as much as you are obliged to love, love as much as you can, as much as is in your power, as much as you are capable.[6] [In so doing], you begin to love God here below with your whole heart—so far as it is now your own—so that in the end you may love him with your whole heart[7] more perfectly, when [your heart], which is not yet wholly yours, is more perfectly your own.

You should not wish to imitate an unjust debtor who, if he does not have enough to repay his debt completely, refuses to pay as much as he has, as if he were no more guilty in paying nothing at all than in paying only in part. God is a kind-hearted creditor and pours out his mercy on anyone who pays as much as he can so he may be able [to pay] more.

### THAT GOD SHOULD BE LOVED WITH ALL OUR HEART IN HIS BLESSINGS[8]

The four divisions of this commandment introduce to us the four main feelings[9] of love or its four forms. But although we speak of these feelings as a specific group of four, they actually contain in themselves innumerable different forms and divisions of feeling. God should be loved in his blessings with all our heart, loved in his promises with all our soul, loved in his judgements with all our power, and loved in his commandments with all our mind. By these four things—that is, blessings, promises, judgements, and commandments—the four feelings of divine love are formed in us by the inspiration of God. Just as in our present life God is known in his creatures in a mirror and a riddle,* until he be known more fully in himself, as he is, so too God is loved in this present life in his blessings and the other things we have mentioned above, until he be loved more fully and perfectly as if in himself.

Among the blessings of God, some are the blessings of creation, others of restoration, and others of day-to-day consolation. The blessings of creation are that we were created in the image and likeness of God, that in him we live and move and have our being and are his offspring,* and that by his gift we have a soul and body and all the senses of soul and body in their full number and completeness. Whatever good things we possess as a result of our creation, these we receive by God's generosity, and all these good things of ours are nothing but gifts of God.

The blessings of restoration are the sacrament[10] of the incarnation, the mystery of the passion of Christ, and all the sacraments which Christ took upon himself for us or which he instituted for us to receive. Such are the sacrament of the body and blood of Christ, the sacrament of baptism, and all the other sacraments of the Church by which the merciful God has bestowed grace and power for the remission of sinners and the salvation of believers.

The blessings of everyday consolation are those which the Father of mercies and the God of all consolation, who consoles us in all our tribulation,* accords us in his mercy day by day. Our Father knows all that we need, we, I say, his unjust servants who, by his condescension, are yet his children. From our Father himself we receive [the power] to desire, to ask, and to hope.[11] From him we can look for relief from all our sufferings, support in all our needs, and the remedy for all our infirmities. Who else shall we look to for all these things, if not him? 'Where does my help come from?' asks the prophet. 'My help is from the Lord, who made heaven and earth.'\*   Ps 120:2[121:1-2]

See how the Lord has done great things for us!\* He overwhelms us with the multitude of his blessings and by his blessings strives to wrest from us our love. Surely God should be loved with our whole heart because of these great and manifold blessings! It is only right and proper and just that we should give [our heart] to him if he himself thinks fit to ask for it. And he *has* thought it fit! 'Give me your heart',\* he says to man! He who asks you to give him your heart wants to be loved from the heart. God wants our whole heart for himself, that it may draw back from the love of the world and wordly things and turn to him, that in him, before all else, it may take its pleasure, and whatever is displeasing to [God] may be wholly displeasing [to it]. But what is displeasing to God is wickedness and vanity, for he loathes wickedness and despises vanity. This is why the prophet says, 'You detest all those who commit wickedness',\* and again, 'You detest all who care about useless vanities'.\*   Ps 125[126]:3

Pr 23:26

Ps 5:7[5]
Ps 30:7[31:6]

The love of God, then, begins from a jointly-held hatred and contempt. But it is God's will that that which he hates or despises should be equally hated and despised by us. As long as we love that which God hates, we are not at peace with God; but if we find ourselves in accord with God in hating evil, then we love God from the heart.¹² We love God from the heart if we remember both the good which we have received from God and the evil which we have committed against God, if we return thanks for the good and do penance for the evil, and if we are reconciled to God by returning from discord to concord.¹³ This is the first degree of love: the conversion of the heart from evil to good, from vanity to verity, from the things which displease God to the things which please him.

The prophet, therefore, wishing to disparage the things which God hates, says, 'Incline my heart to your testimonies and not to covetousness'.* And the Apostle shows how his heart has turned to God through his contempt for vanity by saying, 'Whatever gain I had, I counted loss for the sake of Christ. Indeed, I count everything as loss for the excellent knowledge of Jesus Christ our Lord. For him I have suffered the loss of all things, and I count them as dung, that I may gain Christ.'*

When we read 'You shall love the Lord your God with all your heart', the word 'heart' can indicate this first feeling of divine love. And rightly so. Through this we begin to enter into accord with God and to give our heart to God.¹⁴ He showed us the grace of his blessings, but he also makes demands on us, lest we repay his grace with injury and sin against him who is our benefactor. If we detest with our whole heart the evil which he hates, then, in accordance with our imperfection, we love God with our whole heart. This is why the prophet says: 'You who love the Lord, hate evil!'*

*Ps 118[119]:36*

*Ph 3:7–8*

*Ps 96[97]:10*

## Tractate III

### THAT GOD SHOULD BE LOVED WITH ALL OUR SOUL IN HIS PROMISES

God should be loved with all our soul in his promises, for he has [already] given us great things and has promised us yet greater. He has promised us rest from labor, freedom from servitude, security from fear, alleviation from suffering, resurrection from the dead — and in the resurrection, fullness of joy, a supreme and unfailing joy. Finally, he has promised us himself, as he promised to our fathers, that he would give himself to us.*     Lk 1:73

Great and inestimable, therefore, are the promises of God, and for these and in these he wants us to love him with a certain type and measure[15] [of love]. If you ask what measure, this measure of love is a burning desire for what he has promised. This measure has a measure beyond my comprehension; it is rather without measure,[16] for the promises of God surpass every desire. What is surpassed is exceeded: its size is limited, and its limits give its measure. But however much we may desire the promise of God, we desire it less than we should, for there is no possibility of our desiring worthily that which is beyond all desire! Thus, if there is a measure to holy desire in what it *can* be, there is none in what it *should* be, but however much progress it makes, it ought to make more. In a certain way, therefore, there is no measure to burning desire, since there can never be too much of it.

In other things impatience should normally be reproved, but when we are waiting for such a great promise, burning impatience at its delay is something to be praised. The more one loves and the more one desires, the more one is tormented with impatience at any delay, for the hope that is deferred torments my soul.\*

The bride, therefore, desiring her desire to be commended to God by the merits and prayers of blessed souls and of heavenly powers, says, 'I adjure you, daughters of Jerusalem, if you find my beloved, tell him that I am sick with love'.\* And the Psalmist, as if unable to bear the delay in patience, says: 'As the heart desires the fountains of water, so my soul desires you, O God. My soul has thirsted for God, the living fountain.¹⁷ When shall I come and appear before the face of God?'\* Paul, too, as if burning with impatience with this same desire, says: 'I am hard pressed between two things: my desire is to die and be with Christ, for that is something far better; but to remain in the flesh is necessary on your account'.\* Yet this same Paul, who is now so impatient that he prefers death to being kept in suspense by [continued] delay, says in another place: 'We wait for it with patience'.\*

So we see in a marvellous way the patient impatience of this holy and burning desire. The just suffer torments in having to wait, but they are long-suffering and do not complain; and while enduring this anguish indefatigably, they retain an unshaken hope and bravely endure any adversities.

It is this feeling of holy desire which can be understood by the word 'soul' when it says 'You shall love with all your soul'. And there is a good reason for this. The soul is a spirit, and by the inspiration of the Holy Spirit it continually desires and sighs until it be refreshed in him for whom it aspires.¹⁸ The saints, therefore, very often mention [the word] 'soul' when expressing their desires. This is why the prophet says, 'For you my soul has thirsted';\* and again he says, 'My soul faints with desire for the courts of the Lord'.* And another prophet says, 'Your name, O Lord, and the memory of you are the desire of my soul. My soul desired you in the night, and my spirit [sought you] within myself.*

Ps 83:3[84:2]

Is 26:9

THAT GOD SHOULD BE LOVED WITH ALL
OUR STRENGTH IN HIS JUDGEMENTS

God should be loved in his judgements with all our strength. To judge God's judgements is difficult, for the judgements of God are a great abyss.* Nevertheless, it is clear that when the prophet says to the Lord, 'Look upon me and be merciful to me, according to the judgement of them that love your name',* he is referring to one [sort of] judgement, and when the same prophet says, 'Do not enter into judgement with your servant',* he is referring to another [sort of] judgement.

Ps 35:7[36:6]

Ps 118[119]:132

Ps 142[143]:2

In that judgement by which those already in the fire are condemned, no one loves God, but no one loves himself there either. In this present life, however, God administers his judgements in various ways, both on those he reproves and on those he has chosen. Sometimes, in a marvellous manner, he conceals his mercy and anger from them, and at other times he shows them forth in such a way that what is [actually] anger appears to be mercy and what is really mercy appears to be anger. This is why the prophet says, 'Who is wise and will take heed to these things? Who will understand the mercies of the Lord?'* And referring to anger, he says to God, 'Who knows the power of your anger?'*

Ps 106[107]:43

Ps 89[90]:11

By his hidden judgement, God allows some of the wicked their will and abandons them to their heart's desires so that they might continue in their wicked conduct. He raises up his enemies and honors them; day by day he heaps more and more good things upon them and does not chastise them with [other] men.\* In so doing, he adds iniquity to their iniquity,† so that those who are unclean may remain unclean†† until their iniquity be brought to its full measure. In this [type of] judgement, God hides his anger under the form of what appears to be mercy from those who transform his mercy into judgement, so that their prosperity may become their destruction and they perish as they truly deserve, just as those who do not love God. This is why it is written: 'The prosperity of fools shall destroy them'.\* Yet fools rejoice in their destruction! They do not know what he who is terrible in his counsels over the sons of men\* intends for them, and they do not understand the deep thoughts of God, [those thoughts] of which it is written: 'How great are your works, O Lord; your thoughts are exceedingly deep! The foolish man will not know these things, nor will the fool understand them'.\* But when the sinners spring up like grass and all the workers of iniquity appear so that they may perish for ever and ever,\* then shall they understand what the Most High intends for them! Such is the outcome of that hidden judgement of God in which God hides his anger from those who do not share the troubles of men, who will not be chastised with [other] men.[19]\*

There are, however, other wicked people who *are* chastised by God here below. But in their case, the chastisements do not cleanse them because they blaspheme and complain in their impatience, and neither show reverence to him who chastises them nor accept his correction.[20] Because they do not love God in God's judgements, these people, through their

Ps 72[73]:5
†Ps 68:28[69:27]
††Rev 22:11

Pr 1:32

Ps 65[66]:5

Ps 91:7[92:6]

Ps 91:8[92:7]

Ps 72[73]:5

impatience at his judgement, make that judgement worse in that they go from torments [here] to torments [in the next world].

But when the good are chastised by God, some of them love God in his chastisements, and others love the chastisements themselves for the sake of God. The former glorify God and praise him *when* they are chastised, the latter *because* they are chastised.[21] The former, who are patient in tribulation,* love God in his judgements; the latter, who rejoice in tribulation, accept his judgements joyfully as if they were blessings and rejoice in them. Of these it is written, 'The daughters of Judah rejoiced because of your judgements, O Lord'.* By 'daughters', therefore, we are right in understanding those souls who acknowledge God, who always glorify God in adversity, and who accuse themselves, saying: 'All that you have done to us, Lord, you have done in true judgement, for we have sinned against you and have not obeyed your commandments. But give glory to your name, and do with us according to the multitude of your mercies.'[22]

There are others who so love the judgements of God that they do not wait for the correction of the Father but judge and punish themselves. Each day they look for retribution for those daily sins which human infirmity cannot avoid. Of such as these the Apostle says, 'If we would judge ourselves, we would not be judged'.* Whoever judges himself and punishes himself as a criminal is at one and the same time the accused, the judge, and the executioner.[23] [He is] a just judge, for he prosecutes the guilty; and because he is himself the guilty party, he justly suffers; and while he justly prosecutes himself, he hates his own soul and [thus] preserves it for eternal life.*

Rm 12:12

Ps 96[97]:8

1 Co 11:31

Jn 12:25

In his judgements God tries and instructs those he has chosen in being patient; he trains them to endure their sufferings and strengthens them with hope. 'Tribulation brings about patience, patience trial, and trial hope. And hope does not disappoint us.'* Because of this, the prophet says to God, 'I have great hope in your judgements',* indicating that by undergoing the judgements of God in patience and by loving them, he is established not in just any sort of hope, but in a firmer and more certain sort, and confident of a greater glory. The certainty of hope and the greatness of glory lighten the weight of tribulation so that it may be borne more composedly, or even loved. But as the Apostle says, 'The sufferings of this present time are not worth comparing with the glory to come, which will be revealed in us'.* And again: 'That which is at present passing and trivial in our tribulation produces for us, beyond all measure, an eternal weight of glory'.*

Someone who says to the Lord, 'Your judgements are delightful',* knows how worthy of love are God's judgements. And again he says, 'The judgements of the Lord are true, justified in themselves. They are more to be desired than gold and many precious stones and sweeter than honey and the honeycomb.'* By these words we see that all the pleasure which comes from possessing gold and silver and all the sweetness of this present life—even if it be like honey and the honeycomb—is less than the delight with which God's judgements become sweet for the soul that desires God above all things. To such [a soul], all its sufferings are as nought, and it counts it all joy when it meets with various temptations.* 'How great is the greatness of your sweetness, O Lord, which you have hidden for them that love you!'\* Great indeed! I cannot say how great! You are sweet in your judgements—but not yet for someone who says, 'I am afraid of your judgements'!\*  Ps 30:20[31:19]

Ps 118[119]:120

## That God should be loved with all our mind in his commandments

The mind is what rules in a person and holds the highest and principal place. Just as the father of a family regulates everything in the house according to his decision, arranging what needs to be done, commanding the servants, and making judgements on everything, wishing to be heeded and obeyed by all in all things, so the vigorous activity[24] of the mind should rule every movement and sense of body and soul according to its decision. It should order them, judge them, and take care that it is obeyed in all things.

But just as the mind knows itself to be superior to everything beneath it, so it should remember that of necessity it has a strict obligation to be obedient to God. The obedience which it demands from its inferiors it accords most justly and fairly to him who is superior to it. But woe to that man who has not obeyed God! The punishment of his disobedience will be the triumph over him of death itself!

Death, however, is as hateful as it is terrible, and because it is intimately linked to disobedience, disobedience itself deserves to be hated just as much as death. It was through the sin of disobedience that death came into this world. But if disobedience is just as hateful as death since death arises from it, why should we not love obedience as much as life, since life arises from obedience and life continues in it? It is obedience which submits to God and his will, and life is in his will.[25]\*

Ps 29:6[30:5]

The charity of God and obedience are bound each to each with an unbreakable bond and in no way separated from each other. The Lord shows us that there cannot be charity without obedience when he says, 'If anyone loves me, he will keep my word';* that is to say, he will observe my commandments, and in observing them, he will obey me. And he also shows us that there cannot be obedience without charity when he says, 'He who does not love me does not keep my words'.* If, then, he who loves obeys, and he who does not love does not obey, it follows that just as there cannot be charity without obedience, neither can there be obedience without charity.

<sub>Jn 14:23</sub>

<sub>Jn 14:24</sub>

Through charity, obedience sees God in his commandment, and through the commandment, charity directs obedience to God. Through the commandment God reveals his will, and charity enjoins obedience to the commandment. But whoever truly loves God also loves his commandment. For just as it is impossible for someone to love God and not to love his will, so one cannot love him and not love his commandments as well, since it is in them that his will is revealed and made known.

The love of obedience, therefore, is always joined to the love of God, just as the latter is always joined to the love of his will and the love of his commandments. Whoever loves the commandment of God and his will also loves obedience [and we can prove this in the following way:] God's will is that what he commands be done, and when he commands that it be done, his will is that he be obeyed. Thus, whoever loves God's will, which he commands to be done, loves to be commanded. But no one loves to be commanded unless he also loves to obey. If, then, there cannot be obedience to God without charity (that is, without the love of God), and if the love of God cannot exist without the love of his will, which he commands to be done, and if [the love of his will] cannot exist without the love of his commandment, nor the love of his commandment without the love of obedience, what can we conclude but that there cannot be obedience to God without both the love of obedience and the love of the divine commandment to which obedience is due?[26]

Let us look into this a little further and see if it is indeed the case. First of all, let us consider what the Psalmist means by these words which refer to the love of God's commandments: 'I meditated', he says, 'on your commandments which I loved',* 'and I lifted up my hands to your commandments which I loved',* 'and I shall strive in your statutes'.†[27] He shows [us here] that there are three ways in which he loves God's commandments: by meditation, by lifting up his hands — that is, by practical work[28] — and by striving.[29]

We should love the commandments of God by meditating [on them] in accordance with this [saying]: 'Think always on the things which the Lord has commanded'.* In meditation, God's commandments become sweet, for we consider how beneficial they are, how upright, how faithful, and how they are established for ever and ever, made in truth and equity.*

There are some, however, who find them sweet and agreeable in meditation, but because they are lazy in putting them into practice, find them bitter and burdensome in action. This laziness is banished

Ps 118[119]:47

Ps 118[119]:48
†*Ibid.*

Si 3:22

Ps 110[111]:8

by him who says, 'I lifted up my hands to your commandments which I loved'.*

Again, there are a considerable number who seem to love God's commandments and to delight in them both in meditation and in action, but who are found to be lacking in courage and constancy when it comes to striving. This is banished by him who says, 'I shall strive in your statutes'.* There is a sort of striving [involved] both in carrying out God's commandments and in meditating on them, but here by 'striving' we understand something which struggles against any difficulty — whether it be from temptation or persecution or adversity — which tries in some way to divert us from the righteousness of God's commandments. The love of God's commandments, therefore, finds its perfection in the love of meditation, of action, and of striving.

The love of obedience, however, proceeds from the love of the commandments, and anyone who does not love the commandments does not love obedience. What, then, shall we say? Are there not many who keep the commandments but who do not really want to be commanded, wishing instead that the commandments be abolished? Are there not many who do not fornicate and do not steal and do not attack their enemies but who really wish that God had not commanded these things, that they did not exist? Truly, there are many who wish that God had commanded nothing concerning these things, but who, nevertheless, refrain from [doing] them because he commanded that they should not be done. They fear him who so commanded, lest he punish them for doing something which he has forbidden.

## Tractate III

People like this appear to keep God's commandments and to obey God [but] without loving obedience, and if this is so, then not everyone who is obedient loves obedience and not everyone who keeps God's commandments loves them. How, then, is obedience the inseparable companion of charity? And how can it be true that 'He who does not love me does not keep my words'?* Jn 14:24

We must consider the fact that one sort of obedience can be distinguished from another by one's intention and one's attitude.[30] According to one's intention, obedience can be either true or counterfeit. True [obedience] is in the Truth—that is, in God—and guarantees the hope of reward; but counterfeit [obedience] only pretends to submit to God, and as a result of cupidity, it places the hope of its efforts outside the Truth. [Similarly], according to one's attitude, there is an obedience which is forced and another which is voluntary. It is fear which exacts the former, but passionate love which urges on the latter.

If we consider both attitude and intention in combination, then [we see] there can be a type of obedience which is both forced and true, [an obedience], that is, which is produced by fear of God and which is directed to God. This sort of obedience sometimes involves more fear and less love and, in other cases, more love and less fear, but it always derives something from both, for just as there is never a forced [obedience] without fear, so there is never a true [obedience] without love.

There is also a type of obedience which is both forced and counterfeit. This is produced by fear alone and is not directed to God. So too there is a type of obedience which is both voluntary and counterfeit, such as that of hypocrites. But there is also a type of obedience both voluntary and true, which arises from charity and which, through charity, stretches out toward God. It is this which God looks for,[31] and this that he loves; it is this that he commends by his commandment and his example; and as it is this that he loves, so it is this that he rewards.

But in the case of obedience which is forced and true, although it does not have the [full] freedom of charity because of the attitude of fear which drags it into doing what it does not want [to do], yet it has something of the freedom of charity because of the intention by which it directs itself [to do] what it does wish [to do]. Just as it is aware of its unwilling inclination, it also willingly brings into play its intention.[32] This type of obedience, therefore, is not always reproved but is to some extent approved. If someone is restrained from sin by fear of punishment, he avoids the punishment he deserves because he does not commit the sin which deserves the punishment, and because he directs his intention to God, he deserves something from God in whom he puts his hope. So long as he is restrained from sin by the fear of God, he shows his respect for the fear of God, and in a certain way he dedicates his fear to God and honors God in so doing.

In all fairness and justice, however, it is the obedience which is voluntary and true which should really be shown to God. Just as a rational creature should subject himself to his Creator so that he might will the things which [God] wills simply because He wills it, he should also, in addition to this, will that [God] wills whatever it is that he wills. Let me explain more clearly: if I will what God wills, but not because God wills it, then my will,

## Tractate III

because it is so much my own, is not yet formed in God's will. If, however, I will what God wills *because* he wills it, then my will has God as its origin and cause and is [consequently] good. But this is especially true if it is my will that [God] wills what he wills. If, however, my will were that he should *not* will what he wills, then however much I might will what he [wills] for the sole reason that he [wills it], I do not yet will it with all my will, because my will is that he should *not* will it, so that I need not will it either.

For example, if I love my enemy because God has so commanded and so wills, then in a certain way what pleases God also pleases me because it pleases God. Nevertheless, it does not please me in every way, since I do not yet love my enemy freely. In fact, I do violence to myself and divide myself against myself: part of me is willing, because loving one's enemies is a good thing and merits a great[33] reward, and part of me is unwilling, because it is difficult to forget an injury one has received and to stop oneself from grumbling about it. And although I may have no intention of seeking revenge in any way, and although my heart is ready to show kindness [to my enemy] when he asks for it or needs it, yet if my heart still whispers and murmurs secretly that I wish God had not commanded this and did not wish us to love our enemies, then I do not yet will fully and perfectly what God commands. But the extent to which obedience falls short of perfection is also the extent to which charity [falls short] of perfection, and if both charity and obedience are to be perfect, then whatever someone realizes he should do to please God, this he should be pleased to do. The reason it should please him is because it is pleasing to God, and its purpose is that God be pleased with him. There is but one purpose for both obedience and charity: to please God—but [only] in those things which are pleasing to God.

I have added this last [provision] because the wicked [also] want to please God, but in things which are pleasing to them and displeasing to God. Thus, there are many who do not love God but who believe that they love God and think that they want to please God. They think about those blessings and promises by which God pleases them, but they give no thought to the things in which they want to please God—the very things, in fact, in which God is displeased with them! They judge charity, not by the virtue of obedience, but by their own personal opinion.[34]

Obedience, however, is the companion of charity, and just as it struggles against a person's own self-will, so it always relies on God's will. And in that first and foremost standard of justice, that form of equity—namely, the will of God—the will of the rational creature is so formed that it still remains its own self, but because it has its source in God according to prevenient grace and strives towards God according to the direction of its intention, it is not unjust to speak of it also as the will of God. No one can derive from his own self the ability to be good, but only from him who says, 'Without me you can do nothing';* and in just the same way, he cannot will what is good except through him who works in you that you might will and accomplish, according to his good will.* When we speak of the power of God, we mean not only that which is in God and which is God, but also that which is given to man by God and which is in man; and in the same way, when we speak of the will of God, we mean both that which is in God and which is God and also that which is in man—not, indeed, to the extent [that it derives] from man, but [to the extent] that it is from God. And in addition to all this, we also speak of the will of God [in referring to] whatever he wills be done by man—any act of righteousness or mercy, for example. The full meaning of the will of God, therefore, is, firstly, the will of God which does the commanding; secondly, the will of God in the person whom God commands; and thirdly, the will of God which God commands be done.[35] Authority appertains to the first; service to the second; and to the third, the proof of love.[36]

Obedience, therefore, comprises nothing but the love of God, for it directs itself to the will of God from the will of God through the will of God and returns to the will of God. The will of God which is in God works the will of God in man by the will of God in the commandment because of the will of God in God! The will of God in God, therefore, is the beginning and end of obedience, for someone who obeys in charity yearns for God as for his goal, and it was God who inspired him in the beginning. Inspired by God and yearning for God, he finds in God eternal rest from the labor which he frames in his commandment.*                       Ps 93[94]:20

## NOTES TO TRACTATE III

1. Title as in PL 417–418. The nature and content of this important tractate would seem to indicate that it dates from Baldwin's years as abbot of Ford.
2. For the etymology of *seraphim*, see Tr. II n. 3.
3. PL 420B has *ad orandum*; Thomas (35/120) reads *ad adorandum*, which is correct.
4. Thomas (35/122, n. 1) compares this with William of St Thierry, Med 3.4 (PL 180:212A): 'Where are you, Lord, where are you? And where, Lord, are you not?' (CF 3:103). The expression is indeed similar, but the context is quite different.
5. Thomas (35/122) omits an essential *non*. The text should read: *nisi ille fecerit non esse tuum* (as in PL 420C).
6. This is a Bernardine idea: see E. Gilson (trans. A. H. C. Downes), *The Mystical Theology of St Bernard* (London, 1940) 36.
7. PL 420D omits 'so far as it is now your own . . . your whole heart' by hom.
8. The term is *beneficia*, 'blessings, favors, kindnesses, benefits'.
9. *Affectiones*. Baldwin usually speaks of *affectus amoris*, not *affectio amoris*, but both words are very difficult to translate. *Affectiones* could be rendered by feelings, affections, types, movements, forms, or manifestations, depending on the context. See also n. 30 below for a further translation. *Affectus*, likewise, covers a wide range of ideas, but in this translation of the tractates we have normally rendered it by 'disposition' or 'inclination', and have provided the Latin wherever it occurs.
10. In the twelfth century, the term *sacramentum* was used in a much broader sense than it is today. As in the early church, 'everything which could be called a "mystery" was to Latin Christians a "sacrament"' (J. F. Bethune-Baker, *An Introduction to the Early History of Christian Doctrine* [London, 1903] 376). For Augustine, for example, a *sacramentum* was simply the visible sign of a sacred thing, whether or not the gift of grace was attached to it. Baldwin's view is not essentially different from this.
11. PL 421C (incorrectly) reads *orare* for *sperare*.
12. Baldwin is playing on words here: being in accord (*concors*) with God means being of one heart (*cor*) with God. We then love God from the heart (*corde*). He continues in this vein in the next sentence: 'remember' is *recordari*, 'to bring back to the heart'.
13. From *discordia* to *concordia*. Baldwin is still playing on the word *cor* 'heart'.
14. *Per hunc incipimus Deo concordare, et cor nostrum Deo dare.* Cf. nn. 12 and 13.
15. I have rendered *modus* here as 'type and measure' since the whole of this paragraph, deeply indebted to Bernard, plays on these two meanings of the word.
16. Baldwin is echoing the beginning of Bernard's *De diligendo Deo* I.l (see CF 13:93).
17. Baldwin substitutes *fontem* for the Vulgate *fortem*.
18. In this sentence, Baldwin plays on the root SPIR-: *spiritus . . . Spiritus . . . suspirat . . . respiret . . . adspirat.*
19. PL 424C has *flagellantur*; Thomas's text (35/144) follows the Vulgate version of Ps 72:5 and reads *flagellabuntur*.
20. *Disciplina*. See Tr. I, nn. 31, 40.
21. The contrast is between *in flagellis* and *de flagellis*.
22. As Thomas indicates (35/147 n. 1), we have here a liturgical amalgam of Dn 3, 31, 29, 42.

## Notes to Tractate III

23. *Minister judicis*.
24. *Vigor*.
25. There is a longer discussion on the ideas expressed in this paragraph in Tr. x.
26. Baldwin's argument here is logical, but complex. Expressed symbolically, what he is saying is: if A then B; if B then C; if C then D; if D then E; therefore, if A, then E and D.
27. For the Vulgate *exercebar* (which is imperfect), Baldwin substitutes the future *exercebor*.
28. *Operatio*.
29. *Exercitatio*. Baldwin explains what he means a little further on.
30. Lit. 'by one's *intentio* and one's *affectio*'. On the difficulty of translating *affectio*, see n. 9 above.
31. Or 'It is this which God demands'. The verb is *requirere*.
32. Lit. 'For just as it perceives its *affectio* unwillingly, so it directs its *intentio* willingly'.
33. PL 428C omits *magna*.
34. Lit. 'by the opinion of their own wisdom'.
35. This is a paraphrase of Baldwin's very concise Latin: *Est ergo voluntas Dei, et quae mandat, et cui mandat, et quam mandat fieri*.
36. *Experimentum amoris*. I.e. it is by one's obedience in doing the will of God which he commands be done that one demonstrates one's love for him.

## TRACTATE IV
## ON THE TWOFOLD RESURRECTION
## WHICH IS OBTAINED BY
## PERSEVERANCE IN OBEDIENCE[1]

Ps 107:2-3[108:1-2]
*My heart is ready, O God, my heart is ready; I will sing and give praise in my glory. Arise, psaltery and harp! I will arise at dawn!\**

WHAT OBEDIENCE can bring about, where it goes, and where it leads, what its goal is, and what its fruit is, is revealed to us by the glory of the Lord's resurrection. The fruit of obedience is resurrection and life through the obedience of Christ who is the resurrection and the life.\*

Jn 11:25

Christ died but once and only once was raised. One unique resurrection corresponded to one unique death. But for us, a single resurrection is not enough. We are so utterly cast down by the debt of a double death, we are brought so low, that we cannot find contentment[2] by a single resurrection.

OF THE TWOFOLD RESURRECTION.[3]

Rev 20:6
A twofold resurrection is necessary for us: a first [resurrection] and a second. 'Blessed is he who shares in the first resurrection.'\* The first resurrection is partial; it is of the soul rather than the body. Yet in a certain way it applies to the body too, but because the latter is imperfect, it is only in part,[4] and that

which is imperfect always lacks something. 'But when that which is perfect is come, that which is in part shall be put away.'* (1 Co 13:10) The second resurrection will involve absolute perfection in which nothing whatever will be lacking.

These two resurrections are distinguished [from each other] in the words of the Lord. [First of all] he says, 'The hour is coming, and now is, when the dead will hear the voice of the Son of God, and those that hear it shall live'.* (Jn 5:25) As compared with eternity, this present life is like an hour. The dead are those who, through disobedience, are separated from God, who is the life of the soul. But because there is accorded us a time for repentance⁵ in the hour of this present life, those who hear the voice of the Lord in obedience will live. They will be raised from death to a good life and raised once more to the life of the blessed.⁶ Thus [the Lord] goes on to refer to the second resurrection: 'The hour is coming when all who are in the tombs will hear the voice of the Son of God'.* (Jn 5:28) This will be the hour when the Lord will come down from heaven with the voice of the archangel and the trumpet of God,* (1 Th 4:15) and he will give to his voice the voice of power.* (Ps 67:34[68:33]) Then those who have done good will come forth to the resurrection of life; but those who have done evil, to the resurrection of judgement.* (Jn 5:29)

For the good, who are raised to eternal life, there will be in the future a resurrection of life. But there will also be a resurrection of judgement for the wicked. They have no part in the first resurrection, for in the present hour they do not rise up to judge themselves. 'The wicked do not rise again in judgement; nor sinners in the council of the just.'⁷* (Ps 1:5) The wicked are those who do not believe, and whoever does not believe is already judged.* As for the sinners, even though they believe, they have no part in the first resurrection, for they live abandoned lives and do not rise again in the council of the just.

What, then, is this council of the just?⁸ Listen to the prophet speaking to the Lord: 'Your commandments are my council!'* We therefore have little choice!⁹ We must judge ourselves. In no way can we avoid judgement! We either judge ourselves here and are therefore [judged] more leniently, or else judged in the future by a wrathful God and therefore more severely! But what does the Apostle say? 'If we would judge ourselves, we would not be judged by the Lord!'* The Lord will not render judgement twice for the same offence. The resurrection of life, therefore, is the second resurrection. But we see that the resurrection of judgement is neither first nor second: it is not the first, for nothing follows it, and not the second, for nothing precedes it.¹⁰

Both forms of our resurrection, the first and the second, have as their cause, their form, their model, and their sacrament, the resurrection of Christ. It is by faith in the resurrection of Christ and by imitating it that we are reformed, justified, sanctified, and raised from the dead, so that being dead to sin, we might live in righteousness.* We walk in newness of life,* waiting to be adopted as children of God, [waiting for] the redemption of our body.* In the second resurrection Christ will reform our lowly body and conform it to his body of glory.*

The first resurrection begins with obedience and finds its perfection in perseverance. The second begins with glory and is established in eternity. Whoever perseveres in obedience to the end will

## Tractate IV

persevere in glory for ever, for, in a certain way, perseverance and eternity are similar. Just as eternity is a sort of perseverance of glory, so perseverance is a sort of eternity of obedience. 'For whoever perseveres to the end will be saved.'*

Mt 10:22

It is perseverance which is the glory, the perfection, and, as it were, the virtue of all the virtues. Now charity is also a virtue[11] which is much praised — a virtue, indeed, which deserves much praise for it is the life and virtue of the other virtues — but the virtue of charity is patience, and the virtue of patience is perseverance. Charity without patience is not true charity but an imitation, and imitation charity flourishes in good times but collapses in adversity. Patience without perseverance is inconstant and feeble; it is born in adversity, but it weakens in the course of time, and with prolonged effort it succumbs. But perseverance neither flourishes, nor falls, nor weakens, nor succumbs. It is as if all the other virtues were running in a race, but that which takes the prize is the straight course of perseverance.*

1 Co 9:24

Obedience which perseveres to the end experiences in the first resurrection as much as it truly deserves and in the second will experience the reward which it has earned. In the first, it strives for [the goal] which it wants to reach; in the second, it reaches [the goal] for which it earlier strove.

### Of the Obedience of Christ

It was Christ himself who taught this sequence of obedience, perseverance, and glory. When he was in the bosom of the Father, he knew the advantages of obedience and perseverance in obedience and wanted us to know them. He therefore reflected and resolved in his heart to subject himself to the yoke of obedience, to assume the habit of humility, to garb himself in sackcloth, to cover his soul with fasting, to take for his vestment a garment of goat-hair,* to give himself up to abuse, to commit himself to obedience, and to persevere in obedience to his death.

    Ps 68:12[69:11]

What he determined, he did. And just as Abraham left his homeland, his kindred, and his father's house for the land which God had promised him, as he left it all in obedience to the voice of God, so too the Son of God went forth from the highest heaven and his Father's house into the land which his Father had promised him when he said, 'Ask of me, and I will give you the nations for your inheritance and the uttermost parts of the earth for your possession'.*

    Ps 2:8

When he came into the world he was clothed in a seamless garment. It was woven [in a single piece] from top to bottom and was given to him by his mother, who wove it with the hand of Wisdom and the finger of God. It was a robe which his Father had prepared for him, but [a robe in which] his mother also cooperated. She was a strong woman, who put out her hand to strong things, and her fingers took hold of the spindle.* She sought wool and flax* and from the choicest material, in a new way, with new skills, made a new garment, a unique product, the like of which no-one on earth can make.

    Pr 31:19
    Pr 31:13

When Jesus had assumed this garment, it was as if he were girded for total obedience and filled with zest and zeal for his complete submission to humility, and then he said to the Father, 'My heart is ready, O God, my heart is ready!'*

    Ps 107:2[108:1]

He said that his heart was ready, but he did not state what it was ready for, and so the phrase, though twice occurring, appears incomplete. The doubling of the phrase, however, is a confirmation of obedience, and the incompleteness of the phrase is a manifestation of perfect obedience. In promising obedience, he bears witness that his[12] heart is completely ready and shows us that there is nothing for which it is not prepared. It is as if he says, 'Father, command what you will! If there is anything you want me to do, my heart is ready. If there is anything you want me to suffer, my heart is ready. If you want me to be scourged, behold! I am ready for the scourges!* If you want me to keep your commandments, I am ready, and I am not troubled in keeping your commandments.'*

Ps 37:18[38:17]

Ps 118[119]:16

This was not the case with Peter, when he said, 'I am ready to go with you to prison and to death'.* But Christ was a rock more steadfast in obedience than Peter[13] and he became obedient to the Father to his death.* 'His heart is ready to hope in the Lord: his heart is strengthened; he will not be moved until he looks down upon his enemies.'*

Lk 22:33

Ph 2:8

Ps 111:7–8[112:8]

After he had declared his obedience, Jesus revealed to us his glory, saying, 'I will sing and give praise in my glory; arise, psaltery and harp!'* The psaltery and harp [symbolize] the joy and exultation of his glorious resurrection, and the song and the psalm [symbolize] praise and thanksgiving for this same glory. Christ will sing in his glory. Now Christ, as the Apostle says, is the power of God and the wisdom of God,* but the Wisdom of God speaks of the Father thus: 'Before he made anything I was with him forming all things. I was delighted every day, playing before him at all times.'* What a vision! What sweet and ineffable joy! In heaven to see the Son of God playing before the Father and to hear him singing—there, where sing the stars of the morning

Ps 107:2–3[108:1–2]

1 Co 1:24

Pr 8:23, 30

and all the sons of God shout for joy!* Who of the faithful would not clap his hands in the hope of such a blessed vision, would not dance in his heart, would not raise his voice in exultation?*

Jesus sings in his glory. But to whom does he sing, and what does he sing? He sings to the Father, he sings to the angels, and he will also sing to us.

To the Father he sings eternal eulogies of praise, psalms of triumph and psalms of exaltation, and a new song, the song of songs, which none can sing save Jesus alone: 'I will extol you, O Lord, for you have sustained me'.* And he sings this: 'For me you have turned my mourning into joy. You have torn up my sack-cloth and have surrounded me with gladness, so that my glory may sing to you, and I may feel no remorse. O Lord my God, I will give praise to you for ever.'*

To the angels he will sing: 'Rejoice, Jerusalem! Celebrate a feast-day, all you that love her!'* One great angel, falling like lightning from heaven,* caused great ruin and drew in his train[14] a third part of the stars.* But Christ, in rising from the dead, will fill up the ruins,* rebuild the walls of Jerusalem,† and complete the number of its citizens. Then there will be joy and exultation among the angels, for if they rejoice over one sinner who is penitent,* how much more [will they rejoice] over the thousands upon thousands who will join them and be like them? 'For the chariot of God is attended by tens of thousands, thousands of them that rejoice.'*

Finally, Jesus will sing to us. He will sing a song of joy, a song of delight, saying, 'Come, you blessed of my father, possess the kingdom prepared for you from the foundation of the world'.* In the ears of those that hear it, this utterance will be like a song, a melody sung in sweet and delightful tones. Oh, if only he would let us hear such a voice! If only it would caress our ears! If only it would come to us! If only it applied to us,[15] so that we would never be unworthy of hearing such a wonderful song.[16]

In the meantime, [we pray] that the voice of Jesus inviting us to him may grow strong in our hearts. Even now he sings his invitation, saying, 'If anyone will come after me, let him deny himself, and take up his cross, and follow me'.\* The author of life invites us to life: he calls us from labor to rest, singing ceaselessly, 'Come to me all you who labor and are burdened, and I will refresh you'.\* All who hear this voice shall live\* — even if they are dead. This is the voice[17] that could say but once, 'Lazarus, come forth!',\* and immediately raise from the earth a man dead and buried for four days. Woe to those who are found to be more deaf than a man four days dead when the Lord calls to us: 'Come to me, all you who labor', etc.

Mt 16:24

Mt 11:28
Jn 11:25

Jn 11:43

Let us cry to each other and exhort [each other] by our mutual example, 'Come, let us praise the Lord with joy! Come, let us adore and fall down before God, and weep before the Lord that made us';\* 'And let him who hears, say "Come!"'\* [Inspired] by the singing of Jesus, let us also sing in the ways of the Lord, for great is the glory of the Lord.\*

Ps 94[95]:1, 6
Rev 22:17

Ps 137[138]:5

### OF THE SPIRITUAL HARP[18]

Christ, in rising from the dead, awakes the psaltery and harp. He wakes them for himself, and he wakes them for us as well. How could we hear the psaltery and harp unless he awakened them? Whatever we are within is our own doing;[19] it is lamentable and a matter for mourning and sorrow. Since the time of

By Adam's transgression our harp has been turned to mourning; joy is eclipsed in our heart, and it is lamentation, not song, which befits our misery. Like the children of the exile in the midst of Babylon, we have hung up our instruments.* 'I shall go to the gates of hell':* such is the voice of man in the condition of his first birth.[20] But if we are raised in Christ, then in the first resurrection, glory is given to us, and psaltery and harp are awakened.

Ps 136:2[137:1]
Is 38:10

On a harp there are many strings arranged in a certain order, and by the harpists' skill they are so modulated and tuned that when the harp is sounded there is one concordant sound from many notes, one sweet consonance, one melodious harmony. But if it should happen that one note is somewhat out of tune,[21] if it sounds out separately and disturbs the concord of the others and disrupts the harmony, the harpist immediately brings into play his tuning-key[22] and skillfully corrects it. He either sharpens it or flattens it until harmony is restored and the string which was previously out of tune is once more in accord with the others. The harpist, therefore, is always careful to watch out for this, so that we do not hear any discord or dissonance which could offend our ears.

This also applies to our conduct with regard to each other. The senses of the body and the senses of the heart which [we have] within us are just like the strings of a harp. The senses of the heart are like the limbs of our body, and the way in which we use and move the one is similar to the way in which we use and move the other. In the heart there are different thoughts and affections and intentions, different ideas and different opinions, different wishes and different desires, and it is these which, in us, are either dissonant or consonant, either in disagreement

## Tractate IV

or agreement, either discordant or concordant. At the dawn[23] of our resurrection—at the beginning, that is, of our conversion from the vain ways of the world—all these begin to be ordered within us and arranged in their places by the laws of holy obedience, the exercise of daily discipline, and the rule of reason. And if it should happen that something disordered or undisciplined suddenly breaks out—either from the resurgence of an old habit or because of our weak human condition—we immediately correct it with the tuning-key of penitence and discipline so that everything within us is [once again] composed, tranquil, and harmonious. All is then obedient to reason alone, until there is spiritual harmony and spiritual joy, peace and joy in the Holy Spirit,* when the flesh is subjected in obedience to the Spirit, as in the spiritual harp. The joyous harmony and harmonious joy is the music of harpers playing on their harps.* 

Rm 14:17

Rev 14:2

If someone strives for peace in others while not being at peace in himself, he does not yet play his own harp, even though he seems to play on the harp of others. But if he is not in accord with himself, with whom can he be in accord? With whom can he be in harmony, if he is at variance with himself, inconsistent with himself, always quarrelling with himself, and always contrary to himself? With whom can he be at peace if he is always disturbed and unquiet, like the raging of the sea which is never at rest?* 'There is no peace for the wicked, says the Lord.'* None of the wicked, therefore, plays upon this harp, but the sound of rejoicing and salvation is in the dwellings of the just.* This is the rejoicing of the just, to whom is said, 'Rejoice in the Lord, you just!'† and 'Give praise on the harp'.*

Is 57:20
Is 48:22

Ps 117[118]:15
†Ps 32[33]:1
Ps 32[33]:2

But why does it say elsewhere, 'Sing praise to the Lord on the harp, on the harp'?*[24] What is the

Ps 97[98]:5

meaning of this repetition? Is it because one harp [represents] our own individual conduct, and the other our mutual interaction, one with another? Indeed it is! There are many strings on a harp, and they are not all tuned to the same note, but it is possible to combine a number of them in concord and harmony to produce, as it were, one single sound. Similarly, all of us together are like a harp, each of us separate, but each [responding] to each, as string responds to string. And as often as one of us applies himself with holy zeal and sets an example to another, or, through some service of charity and humility, shows himself worthy of love,[25] it is like one string responding to another in the playing of a harp.

No instrument you can think of can produce a more joyous and delightful melody than the sweet and pleasing fellowship [we can enjoy] in the company of the holy assembly. [A fellowship] in which, in Christ and for Christ, each in turn strives to attune himself to the other and in which, to preserve its peace, each adapts himself in all things to the actions of others in humility and patience. Here is no one puffed up with pride, no one consumed with envy, no outbursts of anger, no quarrels or discord, no murmurs of impatience.[26] We do not find here perverse distrust, and nothing shameful is ever mentioned. 'Behold', said the Prophet, 'how good and how pleasant it is for brethren to dwell together in unity.'*

Those who think that there is more pleasure [to be found] in the vanity of the world than in the truth of Christ are clearly and completely wrong. 'Let them rejoice and be glad', said the Lord, 'who are well pleased with my justice.'* If anyone experiences this, he will not deny it, but man shall say: the just shall receive the fruit of their works.* Ps 57[58]:11

The entirety of the reward due to the just for keeping God's commandments is not, however, reserved for the future. On the contrary. 'In keeping them there is a great reward. For the commands of the Lord are right, rejoicing hearts',* and 'at your right hand there are delights for evermore'.* His right hand is liberal and generous; it bestows such pleasures as the world does not know and gives a peace which the world cannot give.²⁷ But only to those who do not love the world.*  Ps 18:12, 9[19:11, 8] Ps 15[16]:11 1 Jn 2:15

See how it is that now, even now in this present time, [although only] in part, we see clearly how good it is and how joyful, how useful and beneficial, how sweet and how delightful, for brethren to dwell together in unity.* Those whom the love of Christ has gathered together as one love each other mutually, and each obeys the other in turn. And if they are awakened daily to the love of God by the examples and encouragements they give each other, if they serve God with one accord, and with one heart sing eternal praises to him with chosen lip,* if all desire the same and are all averse to the same, if all feel the same and have the same understanding, if they have one heart and one soul, are they not a spiritual harp, and do they not rejoice in God and in themselves? 'Blessed is the people that knows this jubilation!'*²⁸ Ps 132[133]:1 Zeph 3:9 Ps 88:16[89:15]

### Of the Spiritual Psaltery

At the dawn of our resurrection, Christ awakes for us not only the harp, but also the psaltery. And even though I have here spoken first of the harp, which seemed to me to need some discussion, it is the psaltery [which he awakes] first. 'Awake', he says, 'psaltery and harp.'* As Father Augustine tells us, the sound-board of the psaltery is on the top, whereas that of the harp is on the bottom.²⁹ The harp, as we have already shown, is that joyful harmony [which we have] either within ourselves or with our brethren. The psaltery is peace and harmony with God and in God. Of this peace the Apostle says, 'Since we are justified by faith, let us have peace with God'.* By the sin of disobedience man began to be at odds both with God and with himself, and by the just judgement of God, he who did not want peace with God did not find peace in himself. As it is written, 'You have set me against you, and I am become a burden to myself'.* Man, therefore, who did not wish to be united with God, is divided in himself, for disobedience separates the soul from God and is the death of the soul. But in the first resurrection that death is swallowed up in victory,* for it is by obedience that the soul is restored to life and united with God.

The soul, therefore, occupies a sort of middle position between God and the flesh; it is united to God above itself and united to the flesh below itself. The former union can be dissolved by the will but not by force; the latter can be dissolved by force, but not by the will. The soul cannot leave the body, even if it wants to, unless it has been wrenched away by the force of some tremendous pain, but in the case of a soul which is more perfectly united with God, there is no force, no violence, no intensity of pain which can bring about a separation. 'Who shall separate us from the love of Christ?' says the Apostle. 'For I am sure that neither death, nor life, nor angels, nor principalities, nor powers, nor things present, nor things to come, nor might, nor height, nor depth, nor any other creature shall be able to separate us from the charity of God.'* All of these things, or even any one of them, had the power to separate Paul's soul from his body, but not all of them together [could separate it] from the charity of God.

My beloved brethren, you who are so zealous for God, see how strong is this union, how it cannot be broken by any cause, save only the will of the soul itself. 'He who is joined to the Lord is one spirit [with him].'*

It is written that the soul of Jonathan was joined to the soul of David, and Jonathan loved him as his own soul.* David and Jonathan made a covenant, and Jonathan stripped himself of the garment he was wearing and gave it to David, and the rest of his garments too, even his sword and his bow and his girdle.* If Christ is the true David, why then do we not see in Jonathan, the friend of David, one who truly emulates[30] Christ? He abandoned all for the sake of God and even gave his garments to him with whom he joined himself.* This was the sign of the covenant he made with David. But was Christ ignorant of the way to make a covenant? Is it not he who, through the Prophet, says to certain people, 'I will make their work in truth, and I will make a perpetual covenant with them'?* The soul of Jonathan was joined, was 'glued', to the soul of David – and with what glue but the glue of love?[31] By the glue of charity the soul of a just person is so glued to God as to be joined to him inseparably. This is why the Psalmist says: 'It is good for me to be joined to my God'.*

Rm 8:35, 38-39

1 Co 6:17

1 S 18:1

1 S 18:3-4

2 Tm 2:4

Is 61:8

Ps 72[73]:28

The same [Psalmist], however, considers both the union of soul and body and also that of the soul and God. Of the former he says, 'My soul has cleaved to the floor',* and of the latter he says to God, 'My soul has cleaved to you'.* The flesh is the floor of this house of clay in which we dwell, we who have an earthly foundation. The soul cleaves to this foundation by inclination, but if it is too attached, it becomes subjected to it and dies. It becomes so far separated from God that it holds no longer the middle place, but the lowest of all, as if it were now buried in the earth and entombed beneath the floor. Thus, after the Prophet said, 'My soul has cleaved to the floor', he added, 'Give me life according to your word!'*

[The soul] receives life, however, only if it is subjected to God and not the flesh. One who is just, therefore, can truly say: 'My soul has cleaved to you'.* It has cleaved to you and preferred you to itself; it has neglected itself for you, so that it may love you more than itself. But it is not for its own sake that it loves you like this; it is for your sake that it loves itself![32] O Lord, God of my salvation,* this I pray: draw me after you in such a way* that my soul may cleave to you!

This union of the soul and God is far closer than the other [union]; it is much more binding and, as it were, much more inward, for God is in the soul and the soul is in God. The soul is also in the flesh, but the flesh is not in the soul. The soul is certainly in the flesh, and in the flesh it lives and senses. But the flesh is not in the soul. It does not live in it, and it does not sense in it, even though it receives from it its capacity for living and sensing. It is the soul which gives life to the body and bestows upon it movement and sensation. By movement, it carries out its tasks and attends to itself by using the body to do what it wants. By sensation, it is able to perceive pleasures and sufferings, either painfully or pleasurably. For the five senses of the body, each in its own individual way, have a knowledge of sensible objects and are brought into play in experiencing pain or pleasure. But whereas the flesh and the soul have their own individual delights and discomforts, which they feel in themselves either pleasurably or painfully, they rejoice together and suffer together at the changing course of things, both good and bad. The soul is consumed with misery at the things which the flesh suffers in anguish and is overjoyed at those which give the flesh delight and pleasure. But when, as often happens, the soul feels a sense of delight at the unlawful pleasures of the flesh, it becomes jealous of its own integrity and separates itself from them by the restraint of reason. In a marvellous manner, it wills in a certain way, or wants to will, what it does not fully will because of its disapproval; and when the desires of the flesh are contrary to those of the spirit, and those of the spirit to the flesh, then, in some extraordinary way which cannot be explained, the soul, as it were, is divided against itself: it wants to satisfy the will of the spirit and wants just as much to satisfy the will of the flesh. It is troubled, therefore, and tormented within itself. It longs to carry out the will of the flesh and yet withholds its approval or consent. It loves the flesh so much that it grieves over its vicissitudes, and it is troubled when its will — which it is not itself willing to carry out — is not satisfied.

## Of the Five Spiritual Senses[33]

When it is wonderfully united to God by the love of obedience, the soul lives and senses in him and by him, and it draws a sort of analogy with the things it knows through the bodily senses. Thus, by the grace of a most inward inspiration, it senses God within itself and touches him spiritually by faith, smells him by hope, tastes him by charity, hears him by obedience, and sees him by contemplation.

## Of Spiritual Touch

Touch refers to faith, for it is faith which grasps things.[34] Thus, the woman in the Gospel who was suffering from a flow of blood believed that she would be cured if she touched but the hem of Jesus' garment. She may not have known that she symbolized the touch of faith, but when, in her belief, she touched it, the Lord said, 'Who touched me?' And when his disciples were astonished that Jesus, who was so hedged in by the crowd, said that he had been touched, he added, 'Somebody touched me'.\*

Lk 8:45-46

And when he had been raised from the dead, he said to Mary, 'Do not touch me, for I am not yet ascended to my Father'.\* It was not the spiritual touch that he forbade, but the corporeal, for if Mary had touched the man and therefore, because she put too much faith in the corporeal touch, did not believe that Jesus was the equal of the Father, the spiritual touch [of faith] would have been hindered by the corporeal. In [her] heart, Jesus had not yet ascended to equality with the Father, since she did not yet believe that he was indeed his equal. If, in her heart, Jesus had already ascended to the Father,

Jn 20:17

## Tractate IV

then there is no doubt that Mary, at that moment, would have touched Jesus with the hand of faith. But because it was after this that Mary touched Jesus spiritually, he forbade that touch which could have hindered or weakened faith. Nevertheless, his refusal to let her touch him was not absolute. It was deferred until the time of his visible or spiritual ascension, so that Mary would then know herself that she truly touched Jesus when, by the hand of faith, she began to comprehend his divinity and his equality with the Father. For the touch of faith not only apprehends the humanity of Christ, but by handling it reverently,* it also comprehends the whole of his divinity.   Cf. 1 Jn 1:1

It was not unusual for Mary to touch Jesus, nor was she aware of having recently offended Christ in some way so that [as a result] she should believe that he had forbidden her such a familiar approach. But when he said to Mary 'Do not touch me', he did not say it in the same way as was said to certain others, 'Do not touch my anointed!'35* The pursuit of   Cf. Ps 104[105]:15
malice is one thing, and the service which stems from devotion another.

In Mary the sinner, we sinners find a double consolation, both when she was permitted to touch Jesus and when she was forbidden to touch him. Do not despair of forgiveness! It is true that we have sinned much36 and in many things we all offend,*   Jm 3:2
but Mary sinned [too], and yet Jesus permits her to touch him and admits her to the grace of [his] friendship. See how this raises our hopes! It was not granted us to see Christ in the flesh or to handle him with our hands,* but yet we need not despair. To   1 Jn 1:1
Thomas he said: 'Blessed are they that have not seen and have believed';* and to Mary too he said: 'Touch   Jn 20:29

me not'.* See how this also raises our hopes and offers us an abundance of consolation! The touch which he permitted Thomas has the power to dispel doubt and establish faith in the resurrection, but the touch which he forbade Mary also, in a certain way, provides consolation for us, because it was not granted us to touch Jesus either. To the former he gave permission since it was necessary for someone who did not yet believe; to the latter, permission was refused, since it was unnecessary for someone who already believed. Even then Mary believed in the resurrection. What she did not believe in was the glory of Jesus in his equality with the Father, a glory which would be declared to the world by his wonderful ascension. But because she was being led from faith to faith,* she was then told of the glory of the ascension, so that she who was [already] aware of the resurrection would know in advance of the ascension yet to come. For Mary, therefore, the bodily touch — that with which she touches the feet of Jesus* — is not necessary; but when Jesus said to the women, 'I give you greeting',* Mary was given permission to touch him for a certain mysterious reason. The touch which was required of her was the spiritual [touch], that with which she touches his head — in other words, his incomprehensible divinity in which he is the equal of the Father in all things.

It is clear from all that we have so far said that the spiritual touch refers to faith. It is one of the five senses by which the soul is united with God and perceives God. The soul perceives God in five ways and in five ways is perceived by God. There is therefore a total of ten ways, for the ten-stringed psaltery is provided with ten strings. This is the delightful

## Tractate IV

psaltery which accompanies the harp,* [the psaltery] which Christ raised up with himself when he rose from the dead, saying, 'Awake, psaltery and harp! I will arise at dawn.'*

The soul perceives God, as we have said, by touching him with the hand of faith, and God perceives the soul by touching it with the hand of various graces. He touches it, for instance, [in moving it] to tearful penitence,³⁷ and he lays low the swelling of pride as though it were a mountain.* This is why it is written: 'Touch the mountains, and they shall smoke'.* The smoke which is sweetest to the Lord [rises] from a contrite and humble heart,* but it is a smoke which is bitter to the eyes and wrings from them tears of remorse. [God] touches the place of the leprosy to heal it,* he touches and caresses the head with manifold consolations, he touches the eyes to enlighten them, he touches the cheeks to make them rosy, he touches the neck to make it like jewels,* he touches the breasts so that they will not be dry and without milk, and he puts his hand through the opening that our heart may be moved.* Finally, the bridegroom touches the whole of the bride with the sort of freedom of those who are married; he talks with her, he joins himself to her with kisses, he clasps her in his embrace. But yet his touch is the purest [of touches] and purifies by its touch, and whatever he touches is kept wholly chaste, inviolate, and untouched. For the bridegroom is full of zeal* for the bride to whom he has betrothed himself in faith, as it is written: 'I will betroth you to me for ever. I will betroth you to me in justice and judgement, in mercy and commiseration. I will betroth you to me in faith.'*

Ps 80:3[81:2]

Ps 107:3[108:2]

Is 40:4

Ps 143[144]:5
Ps 50:18[51:17]

2 K 5:11

Sg 1:9

Sg 5:4

1 K 19:10

Ho 2:19-20

## Of the Spiritual Sense of Smell

It is also through [the sense of] smell that the soul perceives God and is perceived by God. It smells the sweetness of God[38] by hope and by longing for God. This is the hope that his promise will be fulfilled, as the blossom is fulfilled in the fruit, for the scent of the blossom is the hope and expectation of the fruit. In hope we await the promises of God, which are fragrant as perfumes and sweetly redolent. In the midst of the afflictions of this present life we breathe in the fragrance of his promises for our comfort, and by their fragrance we are drawn to persevere to the end unremittingly. Otherwise we might wander from the path and be diverted from our proposed undertaking.

This is why the bride says to the bridegroom: 'Draw me after you; we will run to the odor of your perfumes'.* The bride scents the virtues of the bridegroom as if they were precious perfumes, but she scents them in the hope of imitating them. Since she is stimulated by the example of the bridegroom, she hopes in some way to follow the tracks which he leaves. But she does not presume to follow him in this way by herself, as if by her own power. She perceives the fragrance by which she knows he is present, and in the hope that he will come to her aid, she says, 'Draw me after you; we will run to the odor of your perfumes'.

If we offer [ourselves] as a living sacrifice, pleasing to God, in an odor of sweetness,* if we burn the frankincense of devotion or the incense of pure prayer on the glowing coals of charity in the censer of our hearts, if the smoke of the perfumes ascends before the face of God,* then he smells the sweetest

of savors,* and perceives the devotion of a soul    Gn 8:21
which burns in itself with holy desire, a devotion
which enables the soul in its turn to perceive him.³⁹

### Of the Spiritual Sense of Taste

It is through love, as if through taste, that [the
soul] perceives and is perceived. Christ says, 'My
food is to do the will of my Father',* and he shows    Jn 4:34
us elsewhere what the will of his Father is: 'This is
the will of the Father who sent me—that I should
lose nothing of all that he has given me'.* It is clear    Jn 6:39
from this that God is fed and refreshed by his love
of our salvation, and when the soul tastes the sweet-
ness of God,* it is this love which feeds and refreshes    Ps 33:9[34:8]
it.

### Of the Spiritual Sense of Hearing

It is through hearing that God perceives and is
perceived when he hears and is heard. But he is
heard through obedience,⁴⁰ for if he is obeyed, then
he hears and grants our prayers and supplications,
petitions, wishes, and desires.

We say to God, 'Hear my words, O Lord',* and    Ps 5:2
God says to us, 'Listen to the words of my mouth'.*    Ps 77 [78]:1
If you hear God, God hears you; but if you do not
hear him, he does not grant [your prayers]. This is
why it is written: 'If anyone refuses to hear the Law,
his prayer shall be an abomination'.*    Pr 28:9

### Of the Spiritual Sense of Sight

It is through sight that God perceives and is perceived. It is said of the just, 'The eyes of the Lord
are upon the just',* and the just man says, 'My eyes    Ps 33:16[34:15]
are always [turned] towards the Lord'.* The wicked,    Ps 24[25]:15

however, walk in darkness\* and do not see God, and of them it is written: 'They have not put God before their eyes'.\* 'But the eyes of the Lord see the good and the evil wherever they are.'\* They gaze upon the just with a tender and caressing glance, but to the wicked he says, 'My eyes are upon you for evil, and not for good'.

As we have shown already, the spiritual harp is constructed from the senses of the body and the senses of the soul, mutually harmonized through the obedience of the flesh subject to the spirit. [Similarly], the ten-stringed spiritual psaltery is constructed from the five spiritual senses by which the soul senses God and consents to God[41] and the five ways in which God perceives the soul spiritually. When God touches the five upper strings on the psaltery, he sings praises to the soul; and when the soul touches the five lower [strings], it sings praises to God, delighting God and finding its delight in God.

God touches the psaltery when he breathes his grace upon it. He is the Breath of Life[42] and breathes where he will, and the soul hears his voice.\* Then, so as to make the lower string respond to the upper string, [the soul] returns thanks for the grace it has received,[43] touching him who touches it, scenting him who scents it, tasting him who tastes it, hearing and contemplating him who hears and contemplates it.

But it is God who comes first to us and sings to us the first song. [It is God] who, accompanied by measured harmonies, like a harpist playing his harp, says, 'Let your voice sound in my ears, for your voice is sweet'.\* God works [in us] both to will and to accomplish,\* and by moving the soul inwardly so

## Tractate IV

that it believes and hopes and loves and obeys, he enables it always to see him whom it loves and perceive him who perceives it; in other words, [the soul is so moved] that it can always give its consent to the will of God.[44]

It is not, therefore, to no purpose, not without reason, that the Psalmist five times repeats [his invitation] to sing praises to God. 'Sing praises to our God', he says, 'sing praises. Sing praises to our King, sing praises. God is the king of all the earth, sing praises wisely.'\*      Ps 46[47]:6-7

There is also a specific reason for his adding at the end [the word] 'wisely'. 'The fear of the Lord is the beginning of wisdom.'\* Someone who sings praises    Ps 110[111]:10 wisely is someone who rejoices in the Lord, but who always fears the danger of falling. 'For blessed is the man that is always fearful'.\* This is why the      Pr 28:14 Prophet says: 'Let my heart rejoice so that it may fear your name',\* and again, 'Love the Lord with      Ps 85[86]:11 fear, and rejoice in him with trembling'.\* Thus,      Ps 2:11 although it is proper for the soul to perceive God through fear, this fear should not separate it from the five spiritual senses which we discussed earlier. It is united with each and regulates and maintains the overall spiritual harmony so that it does not relapse into the danger of discord through carelessness and laxity.

Let us return now to the text with which we began. It is the voice of Christ professing obedience and offering service to God his Father: 'My heart is ready, O God; my heart is ready'. We may see in this repetition a two-fold obedience: that of the soul subjected to God and that of flesh humbled even to the shame of the cross. But what follows is the voice of Christ rejoicing in the glory of his resurrection: 'I will sing and give praise in my glory. Arise, psaltery and harp!' Christ had a double glory and a double joy: the glory of the soul (which is the psaltery on which he plays) and the glory of the flesh (which is the harp with which he sings), and he therefore praises God on the ten-stringed psaltery and with his singing upon the harp.

For us who have been raised with Christ, this same saying[45] can be applied both to our first resurrection and our second. It is the voice of someone who repents, who returns to obedience and promises obedience: 'My heart is ready, O God; my heart is ready'. It is ready to perform good works, ready to sustain the wicked, ready to begin, ready to persevere, ready for the obedience of the soul which should be in your service, O God; ready for the obedience of the flesh which should be subject to the spirit.

Those who are obedient and serve God are given a double joy in accordance with their double obedience: [the joy which comes] from the obedience and peace of the flesh with regard to the spirit (which is called the harp) and [that which comes] from the peace and obedience of the spirit with regard to God (which is called the psaltery). With these spiritual instruments, man is justified by God through penitence, and since he is raised from death to life, he sings and gives praise in his glory: 'I will sing', he says, 'and give praise in my glory'.

The first resurrection has its glory: the glory of the flesh and the glory of the soul. Let us consult the Apostle on each of these glories. Of the present glory of the flesh he says, 'God forbid that I should glory, except in the cross of our Lord Jesus Christ',\* and again, 'If I must glory, I will glory in the things that concern my infirmity'.\* But of the glory of the

## Tractate IV

soul he says, 'Our glory is the testimony of our conscience',* and again, 'We glory in the hope of our adoption as children of God'.⁴⁶*

2 Co 1:12
Cf. Rm 5:2

The second resurrection will also have its glory: the glory of the soul in the vision of God, when it shall see God in his glory and the glory of the flesh in its incorruption, when what is corruptible shall put on incorruption and what is mortal shall put on immortality.* Each of the saints will have a double vestment. They will be clothed in white and hold psaltery and harp. They will sing and give praise in their glory, singing together eternal praises to God. Their mouth shall be filled with gladness and their tongue with joy,* to the praise and honor of our Lord Jesus Christ, who is above all things,
God, for ever blessed.
Amen.*

1 Co 15:54

Ps 125[126]:2

Rm 9:5

## NOTES TO TRACTATE IV

1. Title as in PL 429–430. It is fairly certain that this tractate dates from Baldwin's years at Ford. The brief allusions to the nature and benefits of the common life (see nn. 26 and 28) are elaborated at length in Tr. xv.
2. Thomas (36/16) reads *contenti esse;* PL 429C has *beati esse.*
3. This subtitle occurs in the manuscripts, but not in PL.
4. Thomas's text (36/18) accidentally omits *ex parte est.* PL 429C is correct here.
5. An expression borrowed from the liturgy. See Thomas 36/19, n. 2.
6. The second half of this sentence has been omitted in PL 429D by hom.
7. Ps 1, 5 with the tense of *resurgere* changed from future (*resurgent*) to present (*resurgunt*).
8. Baldwin is playing on words here: *consilium* means both council / assembly and counsel / advice.
9. Lit. 'Our situation is straitened'.
10. I.e. the resurrection of judgement may take one of two forms: (a) if we judge ourselves, we will not be judged by God (judgement is not followed by judgement); or (b) if we do not judge ourselves, God will judge us (judgement is not preceded by judgement). But in neither case are there two judgements.
11. PL 431A omits *virtus.*
12. For *cor suum,* PL 432A reads *cor meum.*
13. There is a play on words here: *Petrus* 'Peter' is linked with *petra* 'a rock', as in Mt 16:18.
14. Lit. 'His tail drew the third part of the stars' (Rv 12:4). The text is referring to the seven-headed, ten-horned dragon.
15. Or 'if only it reached us'. The verb is *pertinere.*
16. Lit. 'May we not deserve to be separated from such a good hearing'.
17. Thomas (36/36) has *vox una;* PL 433B reads *vox tua.*
18. PL 433C (incorrectly) has *creatura* instead of *cithara.* See Thomas 36/38, n. 1.
19. Lit. 'Whatever is in us is from us'.
20. I.e. his natural birth. The second birth, in which we are raised in Christ (= the first resurrection), is baptism.
21. *Raucius.*
22. The text reads *plectrum,* but it is difficult to see how it could be referring to a plectrum in the normally accepted sense. The medieval *cithara,* unlike the *psalterium,* was played with the fingers, not a plectrum, and in any case, in neither instrument was a plectrum used to adjust the tension of the strings. A T-shaped tuning-key, however, appears in a remarkable number of portrayals of medieval harps and harpers, and it may well be that Baldwin's comments in this paragraph reflect the fact that medieval harpers had great difficulty in keeping their instruments in tune. Since the strings at this time were of animal gut, this is not surprising. For an illustration of a tuning-key being used on a ten-stringed *cithara,* see D. Munrow, *Instruments of the Middle Ages and Renaissance* (Oxford, 1976) 21.
23. This is an allusion to the basic text of Baldwin's sermon, 'I will arise at dawn'.
24. The PL text (434C) is corrupt here.
25. Lit. 'renders himself loveable'.

26. This same passage appears word for word in Baldwin's fifteenth tractate: see Tr. xv, n. 18.
27. A liturgical phrase deriving from Jn 14:27.
28. Once again, similar ideas and similar expressions may be found in Tractate xv: see Tr. xv, n. 18.
29. See Augustine, *Enarratio in Psalmum* 56. 16 (PL 36:671–672) and *Enarratio in Ps.* 32. II. I. 5 (PL 36:280–281).
30. *Verus Christi aemulator.* An *aemulator Christi* is someone who zealously imitates Christ: see Tr. x, n. 2.
31. The idea of *gluten amoris / dilectionis* occurs fairly frequently in twelfth-century spiritual writings. We also find it in Augustine (*Confessiones* IV. x. 15; PL 32:700), but here, Baldwin is echoing the biblical text of 1 S 18: 1 'Anima Ionathae *conglutinata* est animae David' ('The soul of Jonathan was knit to the soul of David' in RSV).
32. Baldwin is thinking of the fourth degree of love in Bernard's *De diligendo Deo* x. 27. See CF 13:119–120.
33. This subtitle is omitted in PL 437BC.
34. The verb is *comprehendere*, 'to grasp, seize, take hold of', either physically or mentally.
35. Ps 104[105]:15 reads literally, 'Touch not my christs *(christos meos)*'. *Christus* is here being used with its etymological meaning of 'annointed'.
36. A phrase from the liturgy. See Thomas 36/63, n . 1.
37. There are three variant readings here: (a) following MS Troyes 876: *Tamquam ad lacrimosam poenitentiam* . . . (see Thomas 36/66); (b) following MS Troyes 433: *Tangit cor ad lacrimosam poenitentiam* . . . (see Thomas 36/67, n. 2); and (c) following PL 438D: *Tangit tamquam ad lacrymosam poenitentiam* . . . .
38. PL 439B omits *Dei*.
39. Lit. 'by which he too is perceived'.
40. 'To hear' *(audire)* is linked etymologically with 'to obey' *(obedire = ob-audire)*.
41. The association of *sentire* and *consentire* occurs a number of times in Baldwin. See Tr. IV, n. 44; Tr. VI, n. 35; and Tr. IX / iv, n. 5.
42. The Latin simply has *Spiritus est* (Jn 4: 24), but I have rendered it as 'Breath of Life' so as to bring out Baldwin's play on words.
43. A play on words impossible to render satisfactorily into English: 'having received grace *(gratia)*, one returns thanks *(gratia)*'.
44. Baldwin's thought is less logical in English than it is in Latin. Once again, there is a play on words: . . . *sentientem sentiens, hoc est voluntati Dei semper consentiens.* Cf. n. 41 above.
45. Thomas (36/80) has *ipsa vox*; PL 441B reads *prima vox*.
46. Rm 5:2 actually reads 'Gloriamur in spe *gloriae* filiorum Dei'. Baldwin has borrowed his *adoptionis* from Rm 8:15.

# TRACTATE V
# ON THE REST WHICH CHRIST HAS SOUGHT AND PREPARED FOR HIMSELF AND FOR US[1]

*In all these things I sought rest, and I will abide in the inheritance of the Lord. Then the Creator of all things commanded and spoke to me.[2] And he that made me rested in my tabernacle, and he said to me, 'Let your dwelling be in Jacob and your inheritance in Israel, and take root in my elect.'\**

Si 24:11-13

W E SEE in [the twenty-fourth chapter of the book of] Ecclesiasticus the Wisdom of God, in whom all things are renewed and restored, declaring and relating certain of his mighty achievements, wonderful and marvelous, and then adding [the words], 'In all these things I sought rest'.

Christ is the power of God and the wisdom of God. But God is a certain supreme peace and supreme rest, for he is always the same, always immutable and unchanging. With him there is no change,\* since he is not changed from what he was, nor any shadow of variation,\* since he will not be changed from what he is. Variation, indeed, is the changeable condition of a changeable thing, and it cannot in any way be applied to God. He is not affected by the rise and fall of different passions nor found to be subject to a succession of variations. Just as he is

Jm 1:17

Ibid.

always that which he is, so he always remains the same.³

He is therefore always stable and at rest, and he who cannot be at variance with himself has no need to seek rest within himself. But yet⁴ he says, 'In all these things I sought rest'. For whom, then, has he sought rest? For himself, or for us? Or is it rather both for himself and for us? This is clearly the case. In everything God has done for us since the creation, he sought rest for himself in us and [rest] for us in him. Everything which he created or founded or made for man was done to glorify man in him or to glorify himself in man and to enable each of them to find that rest which is sought in so many ways, God pleasing man in all things, and man displeasing God in nothing.

If we consider the course of time from creation [onwards], we find that sometimes God effects things but does not labor;⁵ sometimes he labors but does not effect things; and sometimes he effects things by laboring or labors by effecting them. In creating the world, God effects something but does not labor, and on the seventh day [therefore] he does not rest from labor but from effecting things. In this he has provided us with an illustration of how, before sin [came into the world], he effected things without labor and afterwards rested. For this reason he placed man in Paradise to effect things in it and to preserve it.\* After [the advent of] sin, however, God labors in the perverse conduct of men but effects nothing, since he is not the maker, but the hater, of wickedness. Thus, through Isaiah, he condemns the deeds of certain wicked men, even though they seem to have been done in his honor: 'I am weary with the labor of enduring them'.\* And

Gn 2:15

Is 1:14

elsewhere, through the same prophet, 'You have served me with your sins and have caused me weary labor with your iniquities'.*

But in coming into the world, God both effects things and labors. He effects salvation in the midst of the earth,* and he labors even to death, and through [his death] he brings about the end of his own labors and equally [the end] of ours.

[On the one hand], therefore, there is the labor of enduring our sins and [on the other] the labor of suffering on account of our sins. God rests from the labor of endurance when he brings about in us what is taught through the prophet: 'Cease to act perversely',* for at our conversion[6] we begin to be humbled under the mighty hand of God,* to be at peace with the Lord, and to tremble at his words. In this way, he too rests in us, as he himself bears witness, saying, 'Upon whom shall my spirit rest, but on one who is humble and at peace, and who trembles at my words?'* And we rest in him, as he says again, 'Learn from me, for I am gentle and humble of heart, and you shall find rest for your souls'.* God rests from the labor of suffering, as he himself says: 'In peace will I sleep and rest in him who is ever the same'.* And we too shall rest from our labors after death: 'Blessed are the dead who die in the Lord. Now and from henceforth, says the Spirit, may they rest from their labors.'*

'In all these things I sought rest.'[7] It is as if he says, 'In all my works I have sought rest for myself: for myself in all, and for all in me, to the full extent of my capacity.' 'For God wants everyone to be saved and to come to the knowledge of the truth.'*

But although he says to all, 'Come to me all you that labor and are burdened',* it is not in all that he finds rest. He finds rest in those who were known in advance as belonging to the Lord's inheritance, and he therefore adds, 'I shall abide in the inheritance of the Lord'.* 'Blessed is the nation where God is the Lord, the people whom he has chosen for his inheritance.'* This inheritance is that of which it is written, 'The Lord has chosen Sion; he has chosen it for his dwelling. Here will I dwell for I have chosen it. This is my rest for ever and ever.'*     Si 24:11

   Ps 32[33]:12

   Ps 131[132]:13–14

This is the inheritance which the Father gave to [the Son] when he asked him for it. He said to him, 'Ask of me, and I will give you the nations as your inheritance and the uttermost parts of the earth for your possession'.* But the Son's request was to lift up his hands on the cross and to utter this prayer: 'Let my prayer be directed as incense in your sight, and the lifting up of my hands as evening sacrifice'.* Thus, by the Father's command and injunction, the Son gained for himself the possession of this inheritance by his blood. Therefore he now says, 'Then the Creator of all things commanded and spoke to me'.* [The word] 'then' refers to time, not to eternity, and it is as if he says, 'When the time is fulfilled, and I gain the inheritance in which I have remained, long⁸ awaiting and desiring it, then I said, "Behold, I come."'* It is then that the Creator of all things commanded and spoke to me. He commanded me as a servant, as one less than he according to humanity, and he spoke to me as a son, as his equal according to divinity.

   Ps 2:8

   Ps 140[141]:2

   Si 24:12

   Ps 39:8[40:7]

Just what he commanded, however, or what he said is not clearly stated but must be deduced from what follows. The same thing occurs elsewhere. When it says, [for example], 'Command your strength, O God,'* there is no statement of what he     Ps 67:29[68:28] wished to command of his strength (that is, of Christ), but we understand from what follows that [he wanted] to confirm what he has already effected in us. And in another place, when we read, 'He spoke, and they were made; he commanded, and they were created',* what he said and what he commanded is shown from the context but is not plainly stated. In the same way, then, we understand [from the passage we are at present discussing] that God the Father, Creator of All, commanded and said to Christ that he should be created after the manner of men. This is why he says through Isaiah, 'Let justice spring up together: I the Lord have created him'.*

Pss 32[33]:9, 148:5

Is 45:8

Furthermore, in order to make known to us the nature of this command, the Son himself makes mention in this same passage of the Father, the Creator of all, saying of him, 'He that made me rested in my tabernacle'. It is as if he said, 'By so commanding me, the Creator of all created me and rested within me'. [God] also says of him, 'This is my beloved Son, in whom I am well pleased'.* By his tabernacle he means the humanity he assumed, [the tabernacle] in which he fought so valiantly and vanquished the powers of the air,[9] the tabernacle in which the Father himself also rested, since God was in Christ, reconciling the world to himself.* The Father rested in the Son to establish the beginning of the rest he desires and afterwards to perfect the rest he desires through the mystery of the incarnation.

Mt 3:17

2 Co 5:19

The way in which the Son himself should prepare his rest in his inheritance is made clear to us when he says, 'And he said to me, "Let your dwelling be in Jacob and your inheritance in Israel, and take root in my elect."' The Son [thereby] shows us that there are three things which the Father has said to him and enjoined upon him, and, if you like, we can relate these three things to [the passage] we quoted earlier: 'Then he commanded and spoke to me'. In this passage we have only a brief allusion to the incarnation, but we are now told more precisely what it was that his Father commanded and said to him. And even though this earlier passage does contain the two phrases 'he commanded' and 'and he said', the reference is so brief and fleeting that he now repeats 'and he said' to reveal exactly what was said and what was commanded with regard to the preparation of his rest in his inheritance.[10]

Thus, there are three [virtues], faith, hope, and charity, and by them the hearts of the elect are prepared for Christ to rest in them. And to these three [virtues] correspond very neatly the three expressions [from the verse we are at present discussing]: 'your dwelling', 'your inheritance', and 'your root'.

'Your dwelling' appertains to faith; as the Apostle says, 'May he grant you, according to the riches of his glory, to be strengthened by his spirit with might in the inner man, so that Christ may dwell by faith in your hearts'.\* 'Your inheritance' corresponds to hope, since an inheritance which is promised is not yet seen, not yet possessed in actuality, but only held in hope. The inheritance of the just is Christ, and meanwhile [in their time on earth], they inherit in hope him to whom the Father says, 'Make your inheritance in Israel', which is the same as saying, 'Become the inheritance of Israel'. And he adds, 'Take root in my elect', which corresponds to charity. This is why the Apostle says, 'being rooted in charity'.\*

By these three virtues God prepares for himself rest in his inheritance and in the people whom he

Eph 3:17

Ibid.

has chosen for his inheritance.* 'The portion of the Lord is his people, and Jacob the lot of his inheritance.'* Therefore, have faith and hope and charity, and you will be of the house of Jacob, of the people of Israel, of the number of the elect, and Christ will dwell in you, and you will have him as your inheritance. He will take root[11] in you so as to remain in you forever, and he will rest in you as in his inheritance.

'In all these things I sought rest.'* The Wisdom of God, which works all in all things,[12] is Christ, who works in us. For the most part he works without our help, but sometimes, since we are God's helpers,* it seems that we assist him. With us he works in us what we, through him, work in him; and in the same way he speaks in us what we, through him, speak in him. Thus the works and words of the just are the works and words of Christ. This is why Peter says, 'If anyone speaks, [let him speak] as the words of God. If anyone ministers, [let him do it] as by the power which God administers.'* If any right thoughts are suggested to our heart or [right] words to our mouth, they are God's and not ours—or if they are ours in some way, they do not [derive] totally from us. He knew this who said, 'Such is the confidence we have through Christ to God. Not that we are sufficient of ourselves to think that anything comes from ourselves: our sufficiency is from God.'* So too the Psalmist says, 'In God I will praise my words'.* And when he says, 'There is no speech in my tongue',* it is as if he says, 'It is not in my tongue but rather in God that I bring forth words worthy [of him]'. Whenever we bring forth something worthy of him, it is he himself who speaks, and it is by his gift that [such words] are brought forth. 'Do you seek a proof', asks the Apostle, 'that it is Christ who speaks in me?'* It is Christ, therefore, who speaks in his saints, Christ who works in his saints, as it is written, 'Lord, you will give us peace, for you have worked all our works for us'.* And the Apostle says, 'He works in you to will and to accomplish, according to his good will'.*

2 Co 13:3

Is 26:12

Ph 2:13

This passage, 'In all these things I sought rest', therefore, applies in such a way to Christ, working and speaking in all the just, that it also applies to all the just themselves, and it applies to all the just in such a way that it applies no less to Christ! When a just man seeks rest for himself, Christ also seeks rest for himself in that just man, having first given him the power to seek his rest in Christ.

Rest, wherever it may be [found], is something much craved and desired. All entreat it in their prayers; all long for it, both good and bad; all desire it and yearn for it; it is sought by everyone in his toil. Everyone engaged in study, every skilled artisan, every manual worker—all of them—, in accordance with the desire they seek, strive for rest and aim for rest, although their searches do not always lead them to it. Those who are involved with farming, those occupied with the pursuit of arms, those concerned with the world of business, all those, in short, who are engaged in any of the many different sorts of study and labor and busy themselves with them—all of them, in all these things, yearn for rest and seek for rest. They strive for anything which they think will please them and in which they may rest with pleasure. All a man's work and equally all his leisure, all his activities and all his free time are turned to this end and look to this goal.

A rest which is [too] extended often turns into boredom, and after the boredom of inactivity, we want to rest all over again by busying ourselves with labor. In this way we seek rest even when we flee it! We seek it in our labor, through our labor, and after our labor, but for those who do not enter the path which leads to its attainment, there is no end to their labor, no rest from their searching. The wicked, therefore, seek rest in all these things, but they do not find rest. 'Grief and misfortune are in their ways, and the way of peace they have not known.'* [Ps 13(14):3]

The just man, however, also seeks rest in all these things, but in order to find it, he first finds where rest may be found and says, 'In all these things I sought rest', etc. Here is rest! Here, in the inheritance of the Lord, where the just man determines to remain for his repose. And what is the inheritance of the Lord but the communion of the saints, of which it is written, 'The portion of the Lord is his people; Jacob is the lot of his inheritance.'* [Dt 32:9]

To someone determined to remain within the Lord's inheritance, God himself, full of compassion for the things he created, goes forth to meet him, as to one returning from the paths of error. He receives the runaway servant who has returned to him, subjects him to his lord, and then, to enable him to find rest through obedience, enjoins on him a command. [The text], therefore, says, 'Then the Creator of all things commanded and said to me,' and what he commanded and what he said follows soon afterwards.

At this point, however, there is interposed another [passage] which reads, 'He that made me rested in my tabernacle'. The great hope of the just man is to find the rest he seeks, for in the very first moment of his conversion to God, God, being pleased with his intention [to live] a better life, rests in the heart of his convert so as to make his convert rest in him.[13] It is impossible for anyone to rest in God unless God rests in him and unless the Spirit of the Lord rests upon him. Therefore he now[14] says, 'He that made me rested in my tabernacle', that is, in me, as if in a tabernacle. The voice of the Son himself tells us that the just man is like God's dwelling-place: 'My Father will love him', he says, 'and we will come to him and make our dwelling with him'.* Or again, 'He rested in my tabernacle' means [that he rested] in my heart, for the just man dwells in the tabernacle of his heart where God also dwells. But the wicked, who do not dwell within themselves in this way,[15] are exiles from their own heart. They are therefore called back to their heart through the prophet saying, 'Return, you transgressors, to the heart!'*

Jn 14:23

Is 46:8

'He that made me rested in my tabernacle.' There can be no doubt that this passage, which applies to each and every one of the just, applies in a special way to the most blessed Mother of God. In her womb she bore her God and the Creator of all and she therefore claims this saying for herself with a unique right and says, 'He that made me rested in my tabernacle'. 'For a man is born in her, and the Most High himself has created him.'*

Ps 86[87]:5

When someone who is just has turned to God, God, by grace, dwells and rests within him, so that by receiving his commands with reverence and being obedient to him, he might, through obedience, be worthy to rest [in God]. The rest we desire is prepared by obedience to his commands, and it is attained by the merit of obedience after the labor which God has framed in his commandment.* To find rest, therefore, he is told,¹⁶ 'Let your dwelling be in Jacob', in the people, that is, whom I have loved. 'For I have loved Jacob but have hated Esau.'* It is just as if he says, 'Live your life among the good, and let your dwelling be with the just'. There is no rest among the wicked; as it is written, 'Judah has removed her dwelling-place because of her affliction, and because of the greatness of her bondage she has dwelt among the nations and has found no rest.'*¹⁷ And of some it is written, 'They were mingled among the nations and learned their works and served their idols, and it became a stumbling-block to them.'* We should therefore flee the company of the wicked—always with the soul, though not always with the body; always by our different way of life, but not always by removing ourselves physically.¹⁸ For it often happens that when good and wicked are living together communally, the wicked are reformed, and the good become better and purer. The lily springs up among thorns,* and the just man grows among the wicked like a lily. He is pricked by the spines and suffers tribulation at the hands of the wicked, just as Jacob [did] at the hands of Esau, the innocent [afflicted] by the guilty, the just by the unjust. But yet, so far as he is able, he is at peace with everyone* so that he may say, 'I was at peace with them that hated peace'.*

In a metalworker's workshop, a file is essential. [It is used] to scrape the rust from iron until it becomes gleaming and polished. The same is true of a wicked man who lives his life as part of a community. Even though he injures himself and seeks to injure others, those he persecutes he also 'files' and purifies.

What then? Does the just man who says, 'I have

dwelt with the inhabitants of Cedar', also dwell in Jacob? Indeed, he does, with the soul if not with the body, for he walks simply, as did Jacob. Jacob was a simple man, but nonetheless astute,[19] so astute that he supplanted Esau [once] by purchasing his birthright and supplanted him a second time by robbing him of his blessing. But [these actions were] not unjust! The blessing was lawfully due to him, and Esau despised his birthright, for he went away thinking little of the fact that he had sold it. Since he was born first, he hastened to his inheritance in the beginning, and he was therefore without a blessing at the end.* 'When he wanted to inherit the blessing, he was rejected; he found no place for repentance, even though he sought it with tears.'*

Ps 119[120]:5

Gn 25:27, Pr 10:4

Pr 20:21

Heb 12:17

If, then, a person acts in all things with simplicity so as to injure no one and [acts] in all things astutely so as not to injure himself, if he is neither supplanted by anyone nor cheated of his right, such a person is Jacob, and to the best of his ability, he preserves unharmed and unimpaired the laws and customs of fraternal fellowship.

A peaceable way of life in the midst of our brethren is, therefore, recommended for us, and although [such a life] may be less pleasant for the good [who dwell] among the wicked, it is often more useful. But for the good [who dwell] among the good, it is both useful and full of delight. There is nothing in human life better than mutual love nor anything sweeter than holy fellowship. To love and be loved is a sweet exchange, the joy of one's whole life,[20] the recompense of blessedness. What can be lacking in the sweetness of this good and pleasant dwelling,* [this place] where God dwells and where he rests? 'God is in his holy place, God, who makes those

Cf. Ps 132[133]:1

who share the common life to dwell in his house.'²¹\*

    The unity of the religious life is a symbol and in some ways an expression of that celestial fellowship in which, through the communion of love, things which are particular to each separate individual are found to be common to all.²² Here indeed is the merit, but there is the reward; here is the figure, there is the truth, although the figure itself is not without truth. Here our rest is begun, there it is perfected. Perfect rest cannot be found in this place of affliction, this place of pilgrimage. For us, the fullness of rest is not to be found outside our inheritance.

    [The text], therefore, adds, 'Let your inheritance be in Israel'. Jacob himself is Israel. He is himself the inheritance of the Lord, and the Lord is his inheritance. Esau is a malicious man who hates his brother, and if any one of the just supplants Esau, so that in his sight anyone malicious is brought to nothing,\* he is himself Jacob. Whoever is 'strong against God'²³ and acts courageously, whoever holds firm to God²⁴ and always sees God in his fear, his desire, his hope, and his intention, this man is Israel.²⁵

    But Jacob, just as Israel, is himself the inheritance of the Lord. It is written of Israel, 'Israel is the work of my hands and my inheritance',²⁶ and of Jacob, 'He has chosen for us his inheritance, the beauty of Jacob whom he has loved'.\* 'He has chosen', he says, 'for us', for it is we who profit from what he has chosen. He has chosen for us,²⁷ but it is his inheritance that he has chosen. And what is this inheritance but the beauty of Jacob whom he has loved? The beauty of Jacob is the form of faith and righteousness which Jacob shows as being proposed for all, as being something which all should imitate. He consented to dwell for a time in Egypt, but he did not want to remain there after he had died. He wanted instead to be carried to the land which had been promised him, and he [thereby] indicates that his inheritance should be sought, not in Egypt-in the world, that is—nor in this life, but [at death], when God will give sleep to his beloved.\*  Ps 126[127]:2

The inheritance of Israel is none other than that of which the prophet says, 'O Lord, [you are] my portion',\* and 'The Lord is the portion of my inheritance'.\* But as for Esau and those lovers of the world whom he symbolizes, because of the food of base desires and because of a single meal, once [eaten] and soon finished, they despise and lose the right to their inheritance. Of them it is written, 'They set at nought the desirable land'.\* But Jacob despised this food, astutely acquired the birthright, and thereby inherited the blessing as well.  Ps 118[119]:57  Ps 15[16]:5  Ps 105[106]:24

This inheritance is gained by the love of God. Outside this inheritance rest is sought in vain. To them that seek it, therefore, it is said, 'Let your inheritance be in Israel', that is, 'Strive and struggle to have your inheritance in Israel, not in Egypt; not among the nations who do not know God, but among the people of God'.[28]

Those who seek rest, then, should seek only the inheritance of Israel, and since it is the one who perseveres to the end who will be saved\*, [they should seek it] with perseverance. There is added, therefore, 'Take root in my elect'. Just as cupidity is the root of all evil, so charity is the root of all good.[29] Of the former it is said, 'I have seen a fool strongly rooted, and I cursed his beauty immediately'.\* Anyone who prefers the things of this world to those of eternity is a fool, and he is certainly strongly rooted—but only in his own estimation and that of  Mt 10:22  Jb 5:3

those like him! 'They trust in their own strength and glory in the multitude of their riches',* and 'They have called happy the people that have these things'.* But [God] says, 'I cursed his beauty immediately', and with this the Psalmist agrees: 'God will destroy you for ever. He will pluck you out and remove you from your dwelling place, and your root from the land of the living.'*

Therefore, lest love of God slip back into lust for the world through inconstancy of soul, and the love of your neighbor degenerate into hatred or contempt for your neighbor because he has pestered you with unjust actions, it is rightly said to someone who loves God and his neighbor, 'Take root in my elect'. By these words, we are taught to fix our roots immovably in both these forms of love and to persevere to the end, so that one day we may be able to say, 'I took root in an honorable people'.*

The people of the just, however, are designated in three ways and, as it were, by three names: 'in Jacob', 'in Israel', and 'in my elect':[30] Jacob according to the simple astuteness in which he walks simply, supplanting every attempt [to move him from his path] so that he will not himself be supplanted and lose his right; Israel when he is so strong that he can hold even God in check[31] and so blessed that he sees him; his elect because he is loved first while he himself has not yet loved.[32] He is loved and elected for the rest which God has prepared for him, [the rest] which will be bestowed upon him at its proper time and which will find its perfection in a threefold joy: in the communion of a most blessed fellowship; in the vision of God's divine majesty; and in the immutability of unending eternity. This is why it is written, 'They will receive double in their land, everlasting joy will be theirs'.* The love of one's neighbor corresponds to the first [of these forms of] joy; the love of God to the second; and to the third, the constancy of persevering, that is, of loving even to the end.

Is 61:7

Let us therefore love our neighbor, either in God if he is good or for the sake of God if he is wicked. Let us love him so that we may thereby dwell in Jacob—in other words, that we may remain in the communion of the just and always be far from the communion of the wicked, so that when we live among them or with them, we may never be [counted as one] of them. The law of this dwelling in Jacob is the love of our neighbor, and by this [love], fraternal unity is preserved among the just so that it may lead to communion in the celestial fellowship. Let us love God with all our heart and with all our soul. Our inheritance will then be in Israel, and we will seek no other inheritance but the vision of God himself, for he swore to Abraham our Father that he would grant it to us.* Let us persevere in the love of God and our neighbor to the end, so that there will be no end to our eternal rest in the kingdom of God.

Lk 1:73

OF THE THREE FORMS OF DISQUIET

Let us consider now the three forms of disquiet which hinder the rest we long for. They continually trouble us and force us to think of them nearly all of the time. We are disquieted [firstly] by the evil of time, that is, by the everchanging character of earthly existence;[33] [secondly] by the evil of the heart, that is, of our own cupidity; and [thirdly] by the evil of man, that is, by the wickedness of others.[34] O evil upon evil! The second upon the first, and the third upon the second! 'Sufficient for the day is the evil thereof!'* The evil of time has [already] sufficed to make us miserable enough, but the perversity of others and our own iniquity oppress us beyond all measure, and our misery is more than enough. Did I say that we are miserable? Say rather that we are in the very depths of misery, completely and utterly miserable!

Where shall I escape such great and manifold miseries? Where shall I turn to find rest? In all [these] things I sought rest, but that which I sought everywhere, I found nowhere. O rest, where are you, and where shall I find you? I know that I will not find you unless you come to me. O Lord God, you alone are the repose of souls, and there is no peace for us from all this misery save through you and in you. As for me, [when I sought] to find rest in you, I turned to your inheritance in which you are at rest, and I said, 'I shall abide in the inheritance of the Lord'. This I said with my mind's resolve, my heart's desire, and the vow of my profession. Grant me now that I may say, 'He that made me rested in my tabernacle'. Build in me your tabernacle and rest in me, that I may rest in you. For this is your rest: to effect our rest. Work therefore in me, that I may love you before all things and above all things, that I may desire nothing apart from you, nothing at all, save only you or for your sake. Thus will I find peace, and in my heart will be rest from evil cupidity, from the evil of my heart, and from all the cares—so many, so wicked, so bitter—which devour my heart like birds with bitterest bite.*

What blessedness I could claim—or rather, [what blessedness] I would feel in my heart—if I flamed with desire for you alone and, burning and yearning, could with the prophet say, 'What have I in heaven, and what do I desire on earth but you?'* And if I could say this, why not add immediately and joyously, 'Away! Away! all these vain cares of mine, and all my worries, for man is disquieted in vain.* Away with my anxieties! Give place to my peace and my rest! For you are the God of my heart, and God is my portion for ever!'*

O Lord God, repose of souls, if you grant me rest from evil cupidity, which is the root of all evil, how can another's wickedness injure me once I am not ruled by my own iniquity? If Esau says, 'I will kill my brother',* if he persecutes Jacob and drives him across the Jordan with [only] his staff,* leaving behind his father and mother and homeland, [if he forces him] to ask of and hope in God alone for food to eat and a garment to cover him, and to be exiled and to be a servant for the course of so many years so far from his own borders, even then, what can he really do to Jacob?³⁵ For you are his strong helper, O God of Jacob.*

Strengthen me, O God, in your love and in the love of my neighbor whom you have directed me to love for your sake. Strengthen me, I beseech you, that for your sake I may be able to love even those who hate me. And if my enemy is my brother and I am truly afraid of him, [grant] that I may not hate him in any way but may strive to appease his anger with gifts,³⁶ returning good for evil, so as to calm his rage and find favor with him, leading him to love me by my submission, so that from being my enemy he may become my friend, never conquered by evil but conquering evil with good. And if so forceful a love grows strong within me, then, through you the whole course of human wickedness will cause me no disquiet.

Ps 72:24[73:25]

Ps 38:7[39:6]

Ps 72[73]:26

Gn 27:41
Gn 32:10

Ps 45:8[46:7],
Is 17:10

But as for the evil of time, when will that cease? How long will that endure? While we are enslaved by time, subject to this mutability, there will be no peace for us from its evils. The righteousness of the perfect cannot free them from this disquiet [which stems] from time until every imperfection of this mortality is destroyed by death. Yet by the power of your charity, O Lord, in those whom you have perfectly justified, there is even now, here in this present time, peace from the evil of man and from the evil of the heart, for justice and peace have kissed.* But the evil of time has not yet ceased, and for the just, that is quite sufficient. But for the wicked, there is yet more evil to come.³⁷

When the wicked seek for things which are vain and needless and harmful, they make their own chains heavier, and to the evil of the day, to the misery of our common infirmity and our common needs, they add the misery of an evil will, of their concern with things needless and harmful. To seek what we need to alleviate our common misery is [already] onerous and burdensome and wretched, but to wear oneself out in affliction of body and spirit* for things which are useless and harmful is to heap misery upon misery.

This misery [which results] from self-will is more of a burden to those who take more delight in self-will, for [self-will] itself is something we all need and is therefore common to good and bad alike.³⁸ It endures for the whole course of time until the end, so that in it we might be exercised in your love, O Lord, and persevere until the end. But when the evil of time has, with time itself, ceased, you will crown our perseverance in love with the perseverance of eternity, and those who fail in these times [while waiting] for that time will then rest in you fully and unchangeably and never more fail. 'For you are always the self-same, and your years will not fail.'\*     Ps 101:28[102:27]

Finally, O Lord, I beseech you to hear this little prayer of mine, so profitable for me, and no difficulty for you. Hear me, and do not refuse me.\* This is     1 K 2:16
my prayer: Do not set my portion with those to whom you swore in your wrath and said, 'They shall not enter my rest',\* but 'Let me rest in the     Ps 94[95]:11
day of tribulation, and go up to our people who are girded'.\* Say to my soul on the day of my death, 'Rest
in peace'.³⁹ Amen.     Hab 3:16

150                    *Spiritual Tractates*

## NOTES TO TRACTATE V

1. Title as in PL 441-442. This treatise also dates from Baldwin's time at Ford, and, as in Tr. IV, there is a brief discussion of the common life (n. 22) which is elaborated in Tr. XV.
2. To understand Baldwin's exegesis, the phrase *et dixit mihi* must be translated in this way. At this point, we are only told that the Creator said something; we are not yet told what he said.
3. *Sic semper est ut semel est.*
4. Thomas (36/94) has *et tamen*; PL 441D (incorrectly) reads *iterum*.
5. The contrast here is between *operare* and *laborare*, but to render these verbs as 'to work' and 'to labor' fails to bring out the difference between them. Hence my translation (see also n. 12 below). The principle is actually augustinian: for Augustine, as John Burnaby points out in his *Amor Dei. A Study of the Religion of St Augustine* (London, 1938) 57, *labor* 'does not mean "work", which he never disparages, – there was work in Paradise! – but "toil" which is for him indisputably one of the world's evils'.
6. Baldwin is using *conversio* here to refer to one's entry into the monastic life. See DLF s.v. *conversio* #6.
7. Thomas (36/98) omits the *itaque* which appears in PL 443B.
8. PL 443D omits *diu*.
9. I.e. the demons. See Eph 2:2.
10. This is an awkward passage in Latin, and I have paraphrased it to bring out the sense. A literal translation would be: 'Having mentioned his incarnation in a parenthesis (*interpositio*), he now finally adds what it was that the Father commanded and said to him. And although above he said both, viz., "he commanded" and "and he said", nevertheless, because of the parenthesis, he repeats "and he said" in order to reveal what was said to him, or commanded, for the preparation of his rest in his inheritance'.
11. Thomas (36/106) reads *mittet*; PL 445A has *mitte*.
12. In this passage, 'to work' (*operare*) is to be taken in the same sense as in the passage at n. 5 above.
13. For Baldwin (and his confrères) a 'convert' meant, literally, someone who had turned again to God, and most especially someone who had done this by entering monastic life. See also n. 6 above.
14. PL 446C omits *nunc*.
15. Lit. 'the wicked who do not remain *apud se*'.
16. Thomas (36/118) has *dicitur ergo*; PL 447A reads *dicitur ergo ei*.
17. The passage from 'as it is written . . .' to '. . . has found no rest' has been omitted in PL 447A by hom.
18. Lit. 'but not always by corporeal separation'.
19. In describing Jacob as *simplex* but *prudens*, Baldwin is echoing Mt 10:16, 'Be wise (*prudens*) as serpents and simple as doves', but in the circumstances, *prudens* is better rendered as 'astute' than 'wise'.
20. Thomas (36/122) reads *totius vitae*; PL 447D (incorrectly) has *fons vitae*.

## Notes to Tractate V

21. Ps 67:6-7 (Vulgate) actually reads 'God [is] in his holy place; God, who makes men of one manner (*unius moris*) to dwell in a house', but since Baldwin is referring to the common life of a monastic community, I have amended the verse a little in order to make this clearer.

22. The ideas expressed in this last sentence are elaborated at considerable length in Tr. xv.

23. This is the etymological meaning of Israel (= Jacob) according to Gn 32:28.

24. *Deum sustinens*. This is an allusion to Jacob's wrestling-match with the angel, when the latter 'did not prevail against Jacob' (Gn 32:25). *Sustinere*, however, not only means 'to hold in check', but also 'to hold onto in hope', i.e. to await, to yearn for (see, for example, Ps 32[33]:20).

25. The correct meaning of Israel is given at n. 23 above, but a popular and false etymology, deriving from Philo, is to be found in Ambrose, Augustine, and other canonical authorities. E.g. Augustine, *Enarratio in Ps.* 75, 2; PL 36:958.

26. According to the Vulgate text of Is 19:25, Israel is certainly God's inheritance, but the work of his hands is actually the Assyrian. There is, however, liturgical authority for attributing both phrases to Israel (see Thomas 36/127, n. 3).

27. *Nobis elegit* has been omitted from PL 448B by hom.

28. Thomas (36/128) has *in populo Dei*; PL 448D reads *in populo Israel*.

29. Baldwin is quoting Augustine, *Enarratio in Ps.* 90.1.8; PL 37:1154 (and elsewhere).

30. The subject of the sentence is actually 'the people of the just'.

31. See n. 24 above.

32. Baldwin is echoing 1 Jn 4:19 (an important text for the Cistercians) and playing on words: he is his elect (*electus*) because he was loved (*dilectus*) first.

33. Lit. 'the evil of time, that is, of all this mutability'.

34. PL 449D omits this third form of *malitia*.

35. Lit. 'What can he [do] against Jacob?' Jacob's inner purity guards him against Esau's malice.

36. As Jacob sought to appease Esau (see Gn 32:20).

37. *Quod autem amplius est, a malo est, et malorum est.*

38. Self-will (*voluntas propria*) is self-centered or egocentric will. To a certain extent, this is essential—after all, we must use our will to keep alive—but the more we concern ourselves with self-will, the more we alienate ourselves from God. God's will and self-will vary in inverse proportion. For a useful discussion, see Gilson, *Mystical Theology of St Bernard*, 55-58.

39. A liturgical phrase from the office for the dead.

# TRACTATE VI
# ON THE POWER OF
# THE WORD OF GOD[1]

*The Word of God is living and effective, more piercing than any two-edged sword, reaching to the division of soul and spirit, of joints and marrow, and a discerner of the thoughts and intentions of the heart. No creature is hidden from his sight, but all are open and laid bare to the eyes of him with whom we have to do.\**

Heb 4:12–13

WHAT GREATNESS OF POWER, what wealth of wisdom in the Word of God is shown by these words of the Apostle to those that seek Christ, who is himself the word, the power, and the wisdom of God.\* In the beginning, this word was with God, coeternal with him; in his time he was revealed to the prophets,[2] proclaimed by them, and received humbly in the faith of his believing people.

1 Co 1:24

We have, therefore, the word in the Father, the word in the mouth, and the word in the heart.[3] The word in the mouth is the expression of the word which is in the Father and also the expression of the word which is in the heart of man. The word in the heart of man is either the understanding of the word or faith in the word or the love of the word when the word is either understood or believed or loved. When these three are united in one heart so that the word of God is at one and the same time understood, believed, and loved, then Christ, who is the word of the Father and of whom the Father himself says, 'My heart has uttered a good word',* dwells in [the heart] by faith. And with wonderful condescension he who is God in the heart of the Father descends even to the heart of man and is there conceived and formed in a new way, as the Apostle says to the Galatians: 'My little children, with whom I am again in labor, until Christ be formed in you'.*

Ps 44:2[45:1]

Ga 4:19

When Christ is proclaimed, we hear the word of God. That is to say, we understand it and therefore believe it (for faith comes from hearing*) and therefore love it. There can be no love of the word without faith in the word, nor faith in the word without hearing the word; for whoever loves believes and, by an inward revelation of the Spirit who breathes where he will, whoever believes hears the words, as it is written, 'You hear his voice'.* [This is true] whether [we hear it] outwardly as a result of someone's preaching or inwardly as a result of the Spirit telling us the same things, for unless he is there to teach us inwardly, the tongue of the preacher labors in vain.

Rm 10:17

Jn 3:8

Our understanding should be employed in two ways, either with regard to the beginning of faith or to its end, for when the word is proclaimed, then unless we understand it in some way, we do not believe it. It is this understanding, inspired by the Spirit, which is called 'hearing', and the Apostle [refers to it when he says]: 'Faith comes by hearing'.* The same apostle also shows us that 'hearing' can be interpreted as 'understanding' when he says, 'He that speaks in tongues speaks not to men but to God, for no one hears him',* that is, no one understands

Rm 10:17

1 Co 14:2

him If someone speaks a foreign language to people who do not understand it, then as far as they are concerned, he is a barbarian, and since they do not understand him, they are not edified.* Understanding, therefore, is essential to the beginning of faith, that we may understand what is being proclaimed and what we should believe.

There is another [sort of] understanding which applies to the end of faith, to its consummation, and it is said of this that 'Unless you believe, you will not understand'.[4] Although it seems that this refers to future knowledge, there is no doubt that we can also understand it [as referring] to the progress of faith in those who have exercised their senses* to achieve a more comprehensive knowledge of the reason for faith,[5] those who are always ready to give an answer to all who ask the reason for the faith and hope which is in us.*

The word of God, with which the words of my sermon are concerned, is living, and the Father granted to him that he should have life in himself as [the Father] has life in himself.* On this account, he is not only living, but life; as he says of himself, 'I am the way, the truth, and the life'.* Because he is life, he lives in such a way that he is able to give life, for as the Father raises up the dead and gives them life, so the Son also gives life to whom he will.* He gives life when he calls a corpse from the tomb and says, 'Lazarus, come forth!'* When this word is proclaimed, the voice of him who proclaims it gives to the voice which is heard outwardly the voice of power* which is heard inwardly, and it is by this [voice] that life is given to the dead and the children of Abraham raised up from these stones.[6] This word, therefore, is living in the heart of the Father, living in the mouth of him who proclaims it, and living in the heart of him who believes and loves it.

Just as this word is living, there is no doubt that it is also effective.* It is, in fact, an all-powerful word. When it said, 'Let there be light',* then immediately it was light. When it said, 'Let there be lights [in the firmament of the heavens]',* then immediately the lights appeared. Whatever it said should come to be came to be without the slightest delay. This word runs swiftly,* and in the course of its swiftness there suddenly appeared the lights of the heavens, the vast reaches of the earth, and the depths of the seas. With this word, nothing is impossible.* It is effective in the creation of things, effective in governing the world, effective in redeeming the world. Is there anything more effective, anything more powerful? 'Who shall declare its powers? Who shall set forth all its praises?'* It is effective in operation; it is effective when it is proclaimed; 'it shall not return in vain, but shall prosper in everything it was sent to do'.*

It is effective and more piercing than any two-edged sword when it is believed and loved, for what is impossible to him who believes,* and what is difficult for him who loves?[7] When this word speaks, its words transfix the heart like the sharp arrows of the mighty.* They enter in like nails hammered home* and enter so deep that they pierce our inmost parts. This word is more piercing than any two-edged sword; it cuts more effectively than any strength or power; it is more subtle than any human sagacity or shrewdness; it is more acute than all the subtleties of human wisdom and all our learned words. But the power which lies in strength is also a two-edged sword, and the acuity of reason is again a

Cf. Heb 4:12
Gn 1:3

Gn 1:4

Ps 147:15

Lk 1:37

Ps 105[106]:2

Is 55:11

Mk 9:22

Ps 119[120]:4
Qo 12:12

two-edged sword, and so too the subtlety of our [learned] words.

If anyone asks [why we say this about] strength or power, the reason is obvious. There are two powers by which this world is governed: royal power, and priestly dignity;⁸ and of these it is written: 'See, here are two swords'.* The king bears a sword, but the most that this sword can do is shown us by the Lord when he says, 'Do not fear those who kill the body and are not able to kill the soul',* and again, 'Do not be afraid of those who kill the body and after that have no more that they can do'.* This sword has two edges and cuts with both. It cuts the body and kills it, and although it also cuts the soul by the amount of pain [it causes], yet it does not kill it. By the pain [it inflicts] it can separate it from the body, but it cannot separate it from its life, which is hidden in God.* It dissolves the union of body and soul, but it does not dissolve the union of the soul and God. 'Who shall separate us from the charity of Christ?' says the Apostle. 'Shall tribulation or distress or famine or nakedness or danger or the sword?'* It is as if he had said, 'Certainly not the sword!' This sword can do much, but it cannot go that far.

More piercing, therefore, than this sword which cannot [separate the soul and God] is that word which has been entrusted to the power of the Church, [the word] which can destroy both body and soul in hell-fire!* For those in authority in the Church also have a sword in the power of the word of God. Is it not written that 'Two-edged swords are in their hands'?* Is it not written that 'A sword is in their lips; who has heard?'* And if it is said of the wicked that 'Their tongue is a sharp sword',* how much more of a sword is the tongue of Peter, a sword which is twice as sharp!

In addition to this, the penetrating insights of human genius and the human senses, together with the subtlety of our words, are also a two-edged sword, [a sword] of most subtle discernment,[9] which makes a division between the true and the false, the good and the bad, the honest and the dishonest, and all the other opposites which are subject to its shrewd and skillful investigations. From this there derives the whole of worldly philosophy and human wisdom.

The latter, however, being ignorant of the limits to which it could go, has dared to attempt an examination of the things above it, things to which it could never attain if left to itself. It has busied itself with arduous and abstruse investigations into the nature of God, the origin of the world, the condition of the soul, and the quality of righteousness and blessedness, and [in so doing] has been able neither to find the way of truth nor to attain to the wisdom of God which is hidden in mystery.* The Wisdom of God, therefore, says, 'I will destroy the wisdom of the wise, and the prudence of the prudent I will reject',* and again, 'I will catch the wise in their own craftiness'.* And the prophet [says]: 'The wicked have told me fables, but they are not your law, O Lord'.* Whatever elaborate investigations the wise of this world attempt, and however subtle they may be, the more they disagree with the word of God, the more they differ from the truth. They are like fables which contain in themselves nothing but error and vanity.

The word of God, however, is truth and is like a two-edged sword, a two-edged sword more piercing

1 Co 2:7

1 Co 1:19
1 Co 3:19

Ps 118[119]:85

than any other. It examines all things—even the depths of God—with a discernment as subtle as it is true. When we think of a two-edged sword, therefore [we may think of it in terms] of either power or wisdom, but the word of God, who can do all things and who examines all things, is more piercing [than any sword], for he is the power of God and the wisdom of God.

<sub>1 Co 12:6</sub> Since this word works all in all* in a wonderful way, it also works in a still more wonderful way in the hearts of the saints; [it does so] by the effect of its grace—through fear and love, that is, and the other holy virtues—as if [it had spoken to the heart] certain secret words. [In this way] it shows them its power and its wisdom, piercing all their inmost parts and reaching to the division of soul and spirit.

To elucidate this more clearly, we should note that [the words] 'soul' and 'spirit' are used in three ways: according to nature, according to sin, and according to grace. They are used with reference to nature when they are understood in accordance with what they are naturally, or what they have naturally, what they have from the beginning of their creation. So when it says, 'The first man, Adam, was made a living soul',* or 'The rational soul and the flesh make one person',[10] we take this as referring to the soul according to nature. [Similarly], when it says, 'Who knows a man's thoughts, but the spirit of a man that is in him?'* we understand this to refer to the spirit according to its essential nature. But when it says, 'Whoever hates his soul in this world keeps it to eternal life',* this is understood of the soul not only according to nature but also according to sin. And when it says, 'He remembered that they are flesh; a spirit that goes and does not

1 Co 12:6

1 Co 15:45

1 Co 2:11

Jn 12:25

return',* this is to be understood of the spirit according to sin. When it says, 'Whoever loves iniquity hates his own soul',* we should understand that [the psalmist] is not [speaking of] a hatred of sin, but of nature or grace. When it says, 'The Lord keep you from all evil, may the Lord preserve your soul',* soul is here to be understood according to nature and grace. And when it says, 'If by the spirit you put to death the deeds of the flesh, you shall live',* this is to be understood according to grace.

Although in their essential nature soul and spirit are the same, they are sometimes regarded as different and distinguished [from each other]. Such is the case with the Apostle when he says: 'May God himself sanctify you in all things, so that your spirit and soul and body may be preserved sound and blameless at the coming of our Lord Jesus Christ'.* And [the same is true] in the passage we are at present discussing: 'Reaching to the division of soul and spirit'. Here we see that soul and spirit are united as two distinct things, and this union, therefore, seems to be in need of some sort of distinction. And as far as I can see, the spirit pertains to the better and more worthy part, since it lives its life for God. As for the soul (which is itself also spirit), when it lives well it lives for God, in accordance with the saying of the prophet, 'My soul shall live for him',* and this is the life of grace. When it lives wickedly, it lives for itself, for it is a slave at the beck and call of self-will, and this is what the life of sin is.

There is still the life of nature [to be considered], that which the soul provides for the body so that its members can perform their duties, [the life] which supplies motion and sensation. Life according to nature is common to both the good and the wicked;

Ps 77[78]:39

Ps 10:6[11:5]

Ps 120[121]:7

Rm 8:13

1 Th 5:23

Ps 21:31[22:29]

life according to sin is only usual for the wicked; life according to grace, by which we cleave to God, appertains only to the good.

In the passage we are discussing, it is not inappropriate to take [the word] soul in accordance with the life of grace, [the life] by which we cleave to God, since it is written that 'Whoever cleaves to God is one spirit [with him]'.* Nor is it unsuitable to take [the word] soul in this passage as referring either to temporal life, by which we live naturally, the good as well as the wicked, or to a sinful and undisciplined life, which is lived in wickedness by the wicked alone.

This passage, therefore, where the word of God is said to be living and effective, and more piercing than any two-edged sword, and to reach to the division between soul and spirit, suggests to us that there are two sorts of martyrs: those who are slaughtered for Christ in the flesh and those in whom the will and desires of the flesh are in opposition to the spirit.*

When the flesh is slaughtered, when it is killed by the sword of the persecutor, does not the living word of God, through the love and fear of God, reach to the division of soul and spirit? Does not Christ say, 'I lay down my soul for my sheep'!* And does he not say, 'Into your hands I commend my spirit'?* And when Stephen, the first martyr, laid down his soul for his friends, did he not say, 'Lord Jesus, receive my spirit'?* Does Paul not say, 'Bonds and afflictions wait for me, but I fear none of these things, and I do not count my soul more precious than myself'.* He said 'myself' to indicate the spirit which cleaved to God and 'soul' to indicate the temporal life which he despised for the sake of God.

## Tractate VI

This is the soul of which it is said, 'Do not be anxious about your soul, about what you should eat',* and again, 'Is not the soul more than food?'*

Mt 6:25
Ibid.

Thus, when the sword of the persecutor mangles the bodies of martyrs and divides and sunders their members, the sword of the spirit, which is the word of God, makes an inner division between soul and spirit. The fear or love of God is greatly strengthened inwardly, and for the sake of confessing the truth or the defence of justice, it remains steadfast and immoveable to the point that it despises [the temporal life of] the soul.

It is a similar situation – though not one of equal glory – in spiritual combat, when we resist the flesh whose desires are contrary to the spirit and renounce our self-will. Whoever lays aside the pride of self-will lays down his soul for God. This is the soul of which it is written, 'Whoever does not hate his soul cannot be my disciple.'* You see how the word of God is more piercing than any two-edged sword and can reach to the division of soul and spirit.

Lk 14:26

There are certain desires and intentions[11] which cling to the soul only weakly and superficially: they lack deep roots and are like the hair on our body, which can easily and painlessly be shaved off with a razor. Yet when we renounce such desires as these for God's sake, God rewards us for this with no mean recompense, for not a hair of your head shall perish.*

Lk 21:18

There are others, however, which are deeply rooted and cling much more firmly, and it is wholly impossible – or at least very difficult – to cut them off without blood and pain. Thus, just as a visible sword, which the hand can wield, inflicts a painful wound and a wounding pain when it cuts and divides things which are joined together, so too the sword of the spirit cuts with both edges—here through love, there through fear—and divides up all the things which our love embraces[12] as if [it, too, were dividing] things which are joined together; it uses its power to despise what it loved [at one level] so as not to lose what it loves more.

Anyone who loves God also loves his own flesh, [the flesh] which no one has ever hated.\* The love of a just man embraces both of these [loves], but not to the same extent, since the more he loves God, the less [he loves] the flesh. Thus, when he is threatened by a persecutor, he despises the life of the flesh so as not to lose the life which is hidden in Christ.\* But when we give up our concern with preserving the body through the love or fear of God, it is like breaking off a limb which is very tightly attached, and we suffer great pain. The same is true of self-will. By our desire—though not by our consent—we embrace both this and God in our love, and when we cut it off for the sake of God, the sword of the spirit divides up things which are joined together and inflicts a very painful wound.

### Of the Way in which the Soul is Divided Asunder

As we have noted earlier, this sword reaches to the division of soul and spirit and divides from one another the soul (which is natural or carnal life) and the spirit (which is spiritual life). But this sword also reaches to the divisions within the soul itself and, in a similar way, even to the divisions within the spirit, but I think that [for the moment] we should say more about the divisions of the soul.

The soul is a certain simple nature, indivisible in

*Margin notes:* Eph 5:29 ; Cf. Col 1 3:3

## Tractate VI

its essence, united with each individual body in a personal unity, a single [soul] with a single [body], one with one, and thus, as is rightly said, the unique with the unique. But when this soul, according to God, loves someone it knows it should love for the sake of God, it unites itself by the disposition of charity[13] to the one to whom it joins itself in charity, and thus, by these feelings of love,[14] it becomes divided in itself:* it lives not only in its own body, [the body] to which it is personally united, but in a certain way it divides its life and feeling off from itself [and shares them] with those to whom it joins itself in love.

Thus, it feels not only the good and evil things which pertain to itself alone, but by rejoicing with others and suffering with them, it also feels what they feel and makes their feelings its own. The sword of the spirit, therefore, does not only cut with the pain of one's own personal suffering, but also with the pain that one suffers with someone else. And it can happen that the pain we suffer with another is more severe than our own suffering. It is often the case [for example] that a mother who suffers with her son when he is ill suffers more than the son himself suffers. It is love that does this, [love] which transfers to itself the sufferings of another, [love which seeks] to increase these sufferings so that it may itself suffer more than the other suffers, [love] which sometimes seeks to suffer alone, so that the other will not suffer at all.

In its compassion and fellow-suffering, the soul which suffers with another is in a certain way divided from itself and in itself. When the one it loves suffers, it gives itself up to him, it pours itself out from itself,[15] so as to share his suffering with him. By this

Cf. 1 Co 7:34

willingness to suffer with him, it unites itself to him so that it may suffer in his place; it pours itself into him by its desire to suffer with him[16] and somehow manages to become part of him. It is as if it were living with him whose pain it feels.

Thus, when old Simeon had delivered his prophecy about Christ by saying, 'Behold, this [child] is set for the fall and rise of many in Israel, and for a sign which shall be spoken against', he immediately spoke to the Blessed Virgin and added, 'And a sword shall pierce your own soul'.* That is, a sword shall pierce your soul, as if it were his.[17] But we can also understand it in this way: a sword shall pierce your own soul, that is, your own personal soul. Speaking in this way, as do certain holy doctors [of the Church], the Apostle says, 'With fear and trembling work out your own salvation',[18]* that is, your own personal salvation.

Now just as the Mother of God loved more than all the others and was loved more than all of them, so she suffered with her son when he was dying as if, in truth, it was she herself who suffered. The greatness of her suffering [matched] the greatness of her love, for she loved her son more than herself, and therefore, feeling his pain within herself, she endured in her own soul[19] the wounds he received on his body. For her, the suffering and passion of Christ was martyrdom, for the flesh of Christ was in a certain way her own flesh; his flesh [had come] from her flesh, but the flesh which Christ had assumed from her she loved more in Christ than in herself. But the more she loved it, the more she suffered, and suffered more in her soul than a martyr in his body. She therefore shines forth with a special sort of glorious martyrdom. There were certainly other martyrs who consummated their martyrdom with their own deaths, but she, from her own flesh, supplied the flesh which would suffer for the salvation of the world, and during the suffering of Christ — and by reason of this suffering — her soul underwent such violent pain that her martyrdom, as it were, was consummated in that of Christ, and one could believe that she, after Christ, deserved the supreme glory of martyrdom.

A FURTHER [DISCUSSION] ON THE DIVISION OF SPIRIT AND SOUL IN MARY

There is something else which we should consider at this point, since it pertains to the division of soul and spirit. When the Mother of God realized that the salvation of the world would be brought about by the death of her only-begotten son, she wished for his death but also suffered because of it. She wished for it for the sake of her own salvation as well as ours, but she suffered because she was a mother, the mother of Christ's weakness, and herself weak. The sword of the Spirit, therefore, made a division between the sadness of her soul and the joy of her spirit which rejoiced in God her Saviour.\* Lk 1:47
This is the sword which divides father and son, brother and brother, husband and wife, friend and friend, soul and spirit, soul and soul, spirit and spirit, love and love, hate and hate, love and hate, peace and peace, war and war, peace and war. 'I came not to send peace', says the Lord, 'but the sword'.\* Mt 10:34

Who can know all the divisions of soul and spirit which lovers who are wounded by charity must needs feel in themselves, a number so great that even they cannot count them? The divisions of soul and body are many and various, and just as the word of God touches the heart in many different ways, so there are many different ways in which it reaches to the division of soul and spirit.

### OF THE WAY IN WHICH THE SPIRIT IS DIVIDED ASUNDER

What we have said already concerning the way in which the soul is divided asunder can itself lead us to an estimation of the way the spirit is divided asunder, but I would like to glance at the division of the spirit [a little further] so as to give the wise an opportunity to become yet wiser.\*

God is spirit,\* and he who cleaves to God is one spirit [with him].\* But since the human spirit is totally divided and dispersed within itself, it can only be collected together and united by joining itself to God, who is one and simple. Yet even when it joins itself to God, it divides itself up, for in seeking to join itself to him and be joined to him more closely, it joins itself to him in a whole variety of different ways.[20] But who is capable [of enumerating these]? Who can count every single rapturous outpouring[21] of awe, wonder, amazement, meditation, or contemplation? Who can count all the pricks of his conscience, the joys of devotion, the bursts of rejoicing, the extent of his yearning, his sobs and his sighs, his burning desires, and earnest prayers? Only he who counts the days of the world and the drops of rain,\* he alone, can comprehend and count them! The mind which is fixed in the love of God is subject to countless loving passions and is drawn [to God] in countless ways; but although its affections interchange and alternate in a marvellous manner,

## Tractate VI

its love still remains constant and immoveable. When it changes within itself in so many different ways, it is certainly divided [in its approach] *to* God, but it is not divided *from* God. Nor is it separated from itself since its love remains constant in all its various forms. The sword of the spirit, therefore, reaches to the division of the spirit.

When this sword persecutes the old man [in us], it is not satisfied with just killing him: it slices up whomever it kills, cuts him to pieces, and reaches to the division of joints and marrow, until the body of sin is totally destroyed. So it was that the sword of Samuel did not only kill the obese Agag but cut him to pieces.* We should examine with the greatest care, therefore, how this sword divides the joints and then how it reaches to the division of the marrow.

1 S 15:32–33

Whether we consider the life of a sinner sin by sin —limb by limb, as it were—or bring them all together at once before the eyes of the heart, we find that there are both joints and marrow. Just as one body is composed of a multitude of interconnected members, so a life which is totally wicked [is composed] of a multitude of sins. The joints of the members are the connecting-points of the [various different] sections, for sin is joined to sin either by the movement of self-will or the severity of God's judgement.

A person who sins and who thinks to remain in sin by living wickedly commits certain sins, and then [commits] further [sins] as a result of others: some [he commits] to pave the way for others to follow; others to hide or excuse or defend what he has already done. [He commits] some after pausing to weigh up the matter carefully; others by a sudden impulse of his will, as when a temptation presents itself or there appears an opportunity too good to be missed.

The connections between these sins, whether they are a result of premeditation or a chance opportunity, are like the joints of our limbs, and just as in the case of the body, they make it possible for the life of the sinner to develop and grow and increase until his iniquity is complete. But in accordance with what these sins demand and deserve, and as a result of the just decree of divine judgement, the sinner who scorns repentance and resists the divine will is left for a while to his own will and allowed to fall from sin to sin, since the cause of his later transgressions is his neglect in repenting of his earlier ones. And when iniquity is added to iniquity, it comes to the point that the sinner is excluded both from justice and from the kingdom. This is why it is written, 'Add iniquity to their iniquity, and let them not come into your justice. Let them be blotted out of the book of the living, and with the just let them not be written.'* Such is the end of those who despise the riches of God's goodness†. By their piling up of sin upon sin, they horde up for themselves the wrath of God, until the wrath of God is revealed from heaven upon all unrighteousness.*

Penitence, therefore, should not be neglected, for by it the living and effective word of God, through the fear [it inspires] of a terrible and dreadful judgement, severs the joints of our old life, the ligaments of our former conduct, like the joints of a body. It reaches so far into the division of the joints that all the bonds of sin are broken, and there is no link by which any one sin is joined to any other. This is why the prophet says, 'Break the bonds of wickedness; loose the burdens which weigh you down'.*

*Ps 68:28–29 [69:27–28]*

†Rm 2:4

Rm 1:18

Is 58:6

## Tractate VI

The word of God, therefore, divides the joints when, through the contrition[22] of our heart, it breaks into pieces all that we have wickedly joined together in our perverse way of life, just as [the Lord] tears to pieces a calf of Lebanon.* [It divides the joints] when it tears apart all the things which stick together so tenaciously, when it rips off from their joints all the limbs of the old man and leaves no member unseparated or unsevered from its joints. These are the members which are listed by the Apostle when he says, 'Mortify your earthly members: immorality, impurity, lust, evil concupiscence, and covetousness'.*

Ps 28:5[29:6]

Col 3:5

Although a single sin is only one member of the body of sin* or of the body of the old man, it is also possible to refer to each [sin] itself as a body, since each is brought to perfection in its various parts just as a body is completed by its joints. The Lord shows us that we can refer to sin as a body when he says, 'If your eye is evil, your whole body will be evil'.[23]* It is not unreasonable to apply this to the sinner's whole life, for if someone lives only for himself and for his own advantage, and considers only himself in deciding how he should live, we can understand [this whole life] to be wholly dark. On the other hand, it is also correct to believe that this [passage] can refer to one particular sin, for, when one's purpose in doing something is perverted by the vice of error or wickedness, even what seems to be done rightly is reckoned among the works of darkness.

Rm 6:6

Cf. Mt 6:23

This body [of sin] has its joints sundered and divided when the whole mass of sin is smashed to bits by the testimony of a trustworthy conscience, when the quality, quantity, form, and cause of sin, together with everything that accompanies it, is, as it were, impeached before God, when our whole heart is shaken within itself by everything that arouses shame or fear, when it is inflamed with the love of God in the hope of forgiveness and is brought contrite to God as a burnt-offering, bit by bit, as a sacrifice cut in pieces. The sword of the spirit, therefore, reaches to the division of the joints and reaches even the division of the marrow.

The marrow supplies the bones with nourishment, and in the whole of the body we can find nothing more inward than the marrow. The marrow of the body, therefore, is whatever is deepest in our thoughts, our affections, and our works. But what lies deeper in our desire than that which we desire most of all? What lies deeper in our hope than that which we hope for beyond all else?[24] What lies deeper in our love than that which we love most of all? What lies deeper in all the thoughts and affections of our heart than that which occupies the highest place in our affections and our thoughts? But since I am speaking of sins, the thing which we seek, the thing which lies deepest, seems to me to be none other than the pleasure which sin provides. At the beginning of sin, in its course, or at its end, the sinner craves and desires nought but this one thing: the pleasure which he feels, or which he hopes to feel, by sinning. It is true that one often seems to enjoy sinning for reasons other than pleasure, but the motive of pleasure must always be there, either directly or indirectly.[25] Sometimes, too, one enjoys sinning when there is no immediate pleasure,[26] but one never enjoys sinning without intending that such pleasure should arise! What, then, lies deeper in sin than pleasure? What is more worthy of being

## Tractate VI

called the marrow of sin? In every sin it is sought above all else, even if it is not found.

Let us now turn our discussion from sin to righteousness. What is more worthy to be called the marrow of righteousness than the fat which lies deep within it, that innermost pleasure which righteousness brings?

### OF THE THREE TYPES OF FAT WHICH PERTAIN TO THE GOOD

If we consider the bodies of healthy animals and the kinds of fat we find in them, there appears [first of all] a sort of external fat which adheres to the flesh, and then another [sort of] fat which is internal and adheres to the vital organs, something which is usually called the soft fat or tallow, and finally another [sort of] fat which fills the bones: this is entirely fat, and it is this which is the marrow.

In the first stages of righteousness, the soul of the just also has a certain sort of fatness insofar as it finds its delight in the law of God;* but [this fat], as it were, adheres to the flesh, for having been weighed down by the former habits of the flesh, it is not yet free to aspire to the perfection of righteousness. When it has climbed a few steps [along the path] of righteousness, it begins to feel that it has now made some headway in its progress, and it desires to be filled with that internal fat which adheres to the vital organs. We are shown that this is so by him who says, 'Let my soul be filled with tallow and fatness'.* Certainly it desires to be filled with tallow, to be fattened so completely within itself that its burnt-offering might be fat;* [to be filled and fattened] until it attains the perfection of righteousness and finds the plenitude of its pleasure in the love of [God].

Rm 7:22

Ps 62:6[63:5]

Ps 19:4[20:3]

Then, as if it were fattened to the very marrow, it can say, 'I will offer up to you burnt-offerings full of marrow'.\*

There are certain of the just who use this world\* in such a way that they prefer to be without things which are unlawful and forbidden rather than to have them, but with regard to things which are lawful, they prefer having them to being without them. Thus, they use the things which are permitted them by [God's] indulgence and have wives, possessions, and the other things granted to human weakness, things which may be used—if one wishes to use them—without endangering one's salvation.

There are others who, to some extent, wish to do without the things which are permitted, insofar as they do not wish to have either a wife or possessions.[27]

But there are others who, in striving for perfection, renounce everything which is permitted, as far as this is possible for human weakness. These, in accordance with the counsel of the Apostle, have food and [clothes] to cover them, and with these they are content.\* They are as much fatter [and richer] in spiritual goods as they are found to be thinner [and poorer], for the sake of God, in the goods of this world.

Righteousness, therefore, has external fatness, internal tallow, and marrow; the more interior it is, the more profound it is, and the more perfect it is.

From another point of view, it is possible to refer to the pleasure of righteousness as the marrow not only in the case of those who are perfect in righteousness, but also in the case of those who are beginners in righteousness, or making progress in it. For there is no righteousness so insignificant or so meagre that it does not have joined to it some degree of fortitude—a degree proportionate to its insignificance—and in this fortitude [it finds] its pleasure, as marrow [is found] in the bones.

### OF THE THREE TYPES OF FAT WHICH PERTAIN TO THE WICKED

Iniquity also has its fat, its tallow, and its marrow in those who are fattened with the love and abundance of worldly things, those who are rebellious and puffed up with pride, who give little obedience to God, those who grow fatter and fatter with their ever-increasing iniquity, their intemperate use of the things they have in over-abundance, and their voluptuous habits. Then, as both their pride and their practice of vice increase, they are fattened by their very love of iniquity until finally, as if completely bloated with the fat of presumption, they are so proud of themselves that they openly scorn God. They are so swollen that they forsake God their maker and abandon the God who is their salvation, as it is written, 'The beloved grew fat and rebellious; he grew fat and swollen and gross',* and again, 'They have shut themselves up in their fat; their mouth has spoken pride'.* And once again, 'Their iniquity has come forth, as though from fatness; they have passed into the affection of the heart. They have thought and spoken wickedness; they have spoken iniquity on high'.* So it is that iniquity begins, as it were, on the surface of the heart, then little by little enters insidiously into its interior, until finally the marrow of iniquity becomes like the oil in his bones.*

Dt 32:15

Ps 16[17]:10

Ps 72[73]:7-8

Ps 108[109]:18

In the soul, there is something which craves evil,[28] something which consents to it so as to bring about that which is craved, and something which moves

Rm 6:13

the bodily members as instruments of iniquity to sin* so as to complete the act in accordance with the wish expressed by our craving and our consent.

In this same soul, there is also something which finds pleasure in this action—the action, that is, which it craves to do, to which it consents, and into which it moves itself [in such a way] that the body also moves with it in its service so as to bring about that which pleases it, since the object of all this is pleasure. Thus, there is something in the soul which is in command of all these and to which they provide pleasure.[29] First [we have] craving, then consent, then the movement [from intention] into action, and then the final goal: the pleasure that the action [produces].

When all four of these give us pleasure at the same time—craving, consent, movement into action, and the action which results from the movement—the reason why they please us and the goal [to which they aim] is the pleasure which is sought and coveted in the action. There are therefore five things: craving, consent, movement into action, the action which results from the movement, and the pleasure produced by the action. But only four of these are found in the soul: craving, consent, the movement into action, and the pleasure produced by the action. The action itself is not in the soul, but by the power and will of the soul, the body, by a voluntary movement, uses itself to act externally for the sake of that pleasure which it seeks either in this very action or as a result of it. I say 'as a result of it' so as to include all those actions which do not themselves, perhaps, give us pleasure, but which are done to bring about something else which will give us pleasure.

When these three together—craving, consent, and the movement into action—give us pleasure because of the action or because of the pleasure which the action produces, we can see that it is not the action with which they are associated alone that gives us pleasure, but these three [factors] which precede it also please us because of the pleasure brought about by the action [which they produce]. Craving, therefore, has its pleasure, since craving itself pleases us.

## That the Craving for Wickedness is not under Our Control

One often comes across people who crave for things to which they are wholly averse and totally opposed; they feel a craving for many sorts of wickedness, but they do not consent to them.[30] But although it is granted to such as these to restrain themselves from going further, they cannot stop [the craving] from arising or command it to keep quiet. The craving for wickedness is not within man's control, for when it is quiet, it does not rise up by his decision, and when it has arisen, he cannot quieten it or even stop it from increasing further.

For this reason, the just man—although he has been freed by the Lord\* and released from the yoke of sin—is not yet free to the extent that he is not yet completely freed from concupiscence of the flesh which stirs him in its craving for wickedness. He is free, in fact, to the same degree that he has evil concupiscence in his power, [the power] by which, through the grace of God by whom he has been freely justified, he can stop himself from going so far as to give his consent to the act. Such is the grace given to someone who has been justified. But although he

\* 1 Co 7:22

has been justified, although he has been established in this freedom with the help of God's grace and is able thereby to refuse his consent when he is tempted by concupiscence, he cannot—as we have said before—stop concupiscence from rising up before he is stirred with unlawful craving. Nor is it in his power to stop it increasing in any way, nor to quieten it immediately. The grace of such power is not yet granted to man, even though he be justified. But by disciplining himself long and assiduously, it is possible for a just man to obtain the grace by which this concupiscence rises up but rarely, increases to only a small extent, and dies away more swiftly.

In the case of the sinner who is a servant of sin because he consents to sin, the more he desires concupiscence to be stirred within him—even when it is not actually stirred—the more firmly is he bound by the bonds of his servitude. There are some who have sunk so deep into iniquity that they carefully think up ways to invite sin and deliberately encourage it so as to satisfy their will. Their desire is to bring about a condition of habitual depravity, even when they are not disposed to sin.[31] They are so well trained in sin[32] that they want to sin even when they cannot sin. So pleasing to them is evil concupiscence and its stirrings—evil craving, that is, or its disposition [to evil][33]—that far from wishing such things were absent, they desire them to increase more and more in themselves; this is the very depth of iniquity. Concupiscence is the cause and the beginning of the sin which follows it, just as pleasure is the goal at which the craving for sin and consent to it are aimed. Concupiscence is as hateful as death, for it leads to death through the pleasures of sin; as it is written, 'When concupiscence has conceived, it brings forth sin. But sin, when it is full-grown, brings forth death'.* Jm 1:15

The just, therefore, justly hate concupiscence as they do death, and they justly fight against it with all their power and all the warfare of spiritual discipline, so that even if they cannot totally eradicate it, they can at least weaken it. The more the just hate this concupiscence, the more they love righteousness. The less there is of concupiscence of the flesh whose desires are contrary to the spirit,* the more there is of concupiscence of the spirit whose desires are contrary to the flesh. Just as unrighteousness begins from concupiscence of the flesh, so righteousness takes its origin from concupiscence of the spirit. Thus, to hate the concupiscence of the flesh and to love the concupiscence of the spirit is [already] a form of righteousness, and without this no one can be righteous or just—neither he that begins, nor he that makes progress, nor he that achieves perfection. The more progress he makes and the closer he comes to perfection, the more he hates the one and loves the other. Ga 5:17

THAT THERE ARE THREE THINGS WHICH PERFECT THE PLEASURE WHICH COMES FROM CONCUPISCENCE OF THE SPIRIT

There are three things which bring to perfection this love and this hatred: the desire for righteousness, the resolve, and their execution. Desire on its own, which lacks resolve and execution, is a useless desire. When it touches a sinner's heart, it goads him for a moment, but when he is tempted, it is so fickle that it vanishes away. Of such a kind, perhaps, was the desire of Balaam the soothsayer, for when he considered the tabernacle of Jacob he was goaded to say, 'Let my soul die the death of the just, and my end be like theirs'.* Many are the criminals and profligates and malefactors who have this sort of desire; for a moment, they are goaded to righteousness, but because they condemn themselves by returning to their sins, it is all in vain.

There are others who have the desire for righteousness together with the resolve [to pursue] a better life, but they postpone that which they intend for a long while and either set no time limit to this delay or set yet a further time limit when the last has expired, and then when the second time limit has arrived, they take the opportunity to set a further limit and thereby seek [to provide themselves with] a delay which has no limit at all. But should their scheme be interrupted by death,[34] then neither their desire nor their resolve [to pursue] this postponed righteousness will free them from the punishment due to unrighteousness. Thus it is essential that those who desire the life of righteousness and who are resolved [to pursue it] should put their desire and their resolve into execution. It is one thing to intend to go all the way to Jerusalem and show on one's face that one is already going there,* and quite another to have an idle desire to make the journey and then, by endlessly postponing it, never to set out.

The execution of our holy desire and holy resolve consists in our body and soul taking an active part in the combat of the concupiscence of the spirit and the concupiscence of the flesh, giving our consent to righteousness with the former and never permitting the latter to assent to unrighteousness. The desire and resolve for righteousness, together with their tireless pursuit, brings to perfection our holy hatred of concupiscence of the flesh, [that concupiscence] which, by its desire and resolve for wickedness, initiates unrighteousness and which has neither the desire nor the resolve for pursuing the good to its final goal.

But whereas the desire and resolve for wickedness is enough to make a person wicked, the desire and resolve for the good is not enough to make him good, although [it is true that] without these there is no one good and no one who is not wholly wicked. Those who have neither the resolve [to pursue] the good nor the desire for it love evil concupiscence beyond all measure, and it is not in their case as if they were led into this propensity for evil, this affection for it, by being tempted within themselves. They themselves, of their own accord, pass over into this affection apart from any temptations. Of such as these it is written, 'Their iniquity has come forth, as it were, from fatness; they have passed over into the affection of their heart',* and again, 'They were consumed with concupiscence in the desert'.* 

Ps 72[73]:7
Ps 105[106]:14

This concupiscence, then, unless it is resisted, first of all robs us of our consent to the good and then of our resolve [to pursue] the good and our desire for it, until [finally] it subjects to itself the whole of our will and the whole of our reason. There is then no movement or stirring of the will towards good, nor does the spark of reason,[35] the little light we have, reveal itself; the whole heart is hardened and darkened, and the lamp is extinguished in Israel.* When the will is not moved to desire the good, nor the reason moved by the resolve [to pursue] it, then concupiscence is the victor; it has subjected both to itself and celebrates a glorious triumph, [a triumph

Cf. 2 S 21:17

made] all the more glorious because neither [desire nor resolve] murmur or fight back.³⁶

If a person has been so utterly vanquished by victorious concupiscence, so blinded that he loves it, [then] it follows that he hates the concupiscence of the spirit which is directly opposed to it. He hates righteousness, he hates consenting to righteousness, he even hates to desire righteousness, he hates not desiring evil, he hates not consenting to evil concupiscence, he hates not sinning, he hates abandoning sin, he hates repentance, he hates the truth which refutes [his ideas], he hates the wisdom which suggests more profitable things to him, he hates the discipline [which leads] to peace, he hates the grace of God and comes little short of hating God himself. But if the course of his iniquity does indeed lead him to hate God for no cause,* then he descends ever lower and lower until he falls into the unforgivable sin, which shall be forgiven neither in this world nor in the world to come.* In this way evil concupiscence, victorious and dominant, hurls its slave down from sin to sin and leads him from a love of himself to a hatred of God, until the pit closes its mouth upon him.*

One cause of this great evil is the pleasure which sin [provides], the other is the concupiscence of sin, [our desire for it]. The former gives the reason *for* which [this evil arises]; the latter the means *by* which [it arises]. The latter initiates the matter, the former brings it to perfection. The latter, by its unlawful representations, leads us away from good and attracts us to evil; the former seizes what has been led away and attracted, and imprisons it. The latter precedes our consent to sin as its cause; the former follows it in succession.

## Tractate VI

### OF THE BODY AND SOUL OF THE OLD MAN

In a single human being there can be distinguished body and soul. In the body we can see flesh and bones, and in the bones, the marrow; but we believe that the power of moving the body is held by the soul. In just the same way [we see that] in putting together a single sin, our old man (which can be called with good reason the man of sin or the son of perdition)* has, for the flesh of sin, concupiscence. This accords with what the Apostle says: 'The desires of the flesh are contrary to those of the spirit'.* For its bones it has consent, for the strength of sin lies in consent, as the strength of the body [lies] in its bones, and for marrow, it has pleasure. For its soul it has that which is highest and most excellent in the mind, which presides over that which craves, that which consents, and also that which feels pleasure. Craving, consent, and pleasure can either please it or displease it, and without its connivance, craving is not led to consent, the body is not moved into action, and the action [which results] from this movement, [the action] in which pleasure is so avidly sought, is not brought to fulfilment.

When the mind which presides over all is pleased by all and finds pleasure in all,[37] it does not feel pleasure only in the action, but apart from the pleasure [which comes] from the action, there is also the pleasure which the mind feels in craving and consent—but it feels pleasure in the craving only after it has given its consent. For if it finds no enjoyment in consenting, then it finds either no enjoyment or very little enjoyment in craving. But when it enjoys consenting, it also enjoys bringing [its

2 Th 2:3

Ga 5:17

intentions] to fulfilment. Thus, since all these three factors, desire, consent, and action, give pleasure to the mind, the mind finds pleasure in all three.³⁸

Now although it may appear that the pleasure found in craving pertains to craving itself rather than to consent—to the fat of the flesh, that is, rather than to the marrow of the bones—yet for this very reason we see that it can also refer to consent, since craving gives no pleasure whatever unless it is accompanied by consent. Thus, we find that it is not only the pleasure which comes from action which is [symbolized by] the marrow, but also the pleasure of craving, the pleasure of consenting, and every other pleasure which the mind experiences, for it is by the latter's command³⁹ that everything is arranged to procure for it its wicked pleasure. But since these forms of marrow are hidden so deep within bones which are themselves deeply hidden, who is the man or whose the sword that can divide them, save that of him who can crush the bones of sinners and break their horns?* He it is who humbles the proud to dust and ashes, who scatters the clouds like ashes, who sends forth his ice like morsels,* who, by his strength, brings out those that were bound, and likewise those that provoke him, that dwell in the tomb.* It is he who can waken the dead, he alone who has the power to change all these guilty pleasures into the bitterness of penitence, so that all those things which wickedly pleased us now displease us, until the body of sin is destroyed to its very marrow.

Ps 74:11[75:10]

Ps 147:16–17

Ps 67:7[68:6]

## Tractate VI

'And a Discerner of the Thoughts and Intentions of the Heart. No Creature is Hidden from his Sight, but All are Open and Laid Bare to the Eyes of Him with Whom We have to Do'

The Lord knows the thoughts and intentions of our heart: there is no doubt that in himself [he knows] all of them, but in us he knows those whose nature he makes us perceive by the grace of discernment.[40] The spirit in man does not know all that is in man, and when it feels his thoughts, either giving or refusing them its consent, what it feels does not always correspond to reality. When someone looks at the things in front of the eyes of his mind, he does not see them accurately because his eyes are darkened. So it often happens that when another person or the tempter does something which has every appearance of piety, his own thought judges it worthy of the reward of virtue, although in the eyes of God it certainly deserves no such thing.[41] There exist certain imitations both of true virtues and of vices which delude the eyes of the heart and which so beguile the keen-eyed mind with their illusions that what is really not good may have every appearance of being good, and what is really not wicked may have every appearance of being wicked. This is a part of our misery and our ignorance: we have much to suffer and much to fear! Thus it is written: 'There are ways which seem right to men, but their end leads to hell'.[42]

To avoid this danger, blessed John gives us this advice: 'Test the spirits to see whether they be of God'.* But who can test whether the spirits are from God save he who is granted by God [the grace of] discernment of spirits, who can thereby examine with accuracy and true judgement spiritual thoughts, affections, and intentions? Discernment is the mother of the virtues,[43] and it is essential for every individual, whether it be for governing the lives of others or the direction and correction of one's own [life]. But the only word that can introduce this into our senses is that living and effective [word] who is the discerner of the thoughts and intentions of the heart. This word organizes our life in accordance with a certain, specific pattern and directs it towards a certain, specific end. By being thus organized in this way, we ought always to love God in all that we plan to do, so that all that we do is done according to him and also for his sake. Do you want to know what I mean by 'according to him' and 'for his sake'? Listen, [and I will explain] both: [firstly] the whole of our life should be organized according to the pattern [laid down] by God's commandments,[44] [and secondly] every one of our actions should be directed to the end of God's promises. We are not permitted to do other than what [God] commands or permits or advises; nor should we hope for anything other than what he has promised, simply because he has promised it. Our righteousness is formed by God's commands and counsel; our hopes are raised by the truth of his promises. Our thought about what we will do is upright if it is ruled by God's command; our intention is devout if it is directed simply to him. It is in this way that the whole body of our life

*1 Jn 4:1*

or of any one of our actions will finally be full of light, provided that our eye is simple.* And the eye is both an eye and simple because it sees what it should do by means of upright thought, and by means of its devout intention, it does simply what it should not do with duplicity. Upright thought does not admit error; devout intention excludes deception. This, therefore, is true discernment: the union of upright thought and devout intention. But do not be surprised if I refer to discernment as union when [the word] discernment itself implies division.⁴⁵ This union does, in fact, involve division: whoever unites these two things divides the light from the darkness. Error and deception are dark; righteousness and pious devotion are light in the Lord.

Mt 6:22

But a person who tries to divide upright thought according to God from devout intention for the sake of God when he is choosing what he should do and the goal for which he should hope has an eye which is partly blind, and therefore he either walks in darkness or does not know where he is going.* Whoever acts wickedly walks in darkness, and whoever does not direct his steps to God does not know where he is going. We should not commit wicked deeds for the sake of God, nor should we perform good actions without God in mind. A vain intention corrupts a work of devotion, and a devout intention does not excuse a work of iniquity.

Jn 12:35

Everything, therefore, should be done in the light of discernment, as if it were in God and before God, for no creature is hidden from his sight:* nothing corporeal, nothing animal, nothing spiritual, nothing which God made for man or in

Heb 4:13

man, nothing which is made in man or by man in opposition to God. Whatever there is in man – part of which man sees and part of which he does not – is revealed in its entirety to God. The human heart is a great abyss, and in its secret places all kinds of darkness are hidden. There are there creeping things without number,\* but God, who sees in secret† and brings to light the hidden things of darkness,†† sees all things, so that out of many hearts thoughts might be revealed.\* Nothing, whether visible or invisible, escapes him, for all are open and laid bare to his eyes.\* There are many things which are now hidden and concealed by mysterious silences and policies, fabrications and deceptions, trickery and deceit, cunning words and deeds, subterfuges and excuses, simulations and dissimulations. But there is nothing covered which shall not be revealed.\* All that is now so skillfully concealed will be stripped of its covering by that word with whom we have to do.⁴⁶ It is to him that we should render account, an account to which is credited the whole course and conduct of our life.

The Lord is so attentive to the ways of each and every individual and counts their steps so [carefully] that neither the most insignificant thought nor the most inconsequential word which serves to demean us remains unexamined. What, then, can I say to defend myself? What excuse can I offer on my own behalf? All that I can do is to say with the prophet, 'You have understood my thoughts from far off; my path and my line you have searched out. You have foreseen all my ways, and there is no speech in my tongue.'\* O good Jesus, I am inadequate to render account; accept, then, my prayer as my account,

and do not enter into judgement with your
servant, for in your sight there
is no one living who shall
be justified.* Ps 142[143]:2

## NOTES TO TRACTATE VI

1. This is a title of convenience, and does not occur in the manuscripts. In the course of this lengthy tractate, Baldwin sometimes uses the term *sermo*, and sometimes *verbum*, for 'word', and it is not always possible to distinguish between them in English translation. In addition to this, when he speaks of the 'word' he often implies two things at the same time: the word of God in scripture and the word of God as Christ. It is important to bear this in mind when reading the text. Finally, both *sermo* and *verbum* can signify rather more in Latin than 'word' in English, and Baldwin is therefore able to play upon words (literally!) in ways which are impossible to render satisfactorily in translation. The tractate most probably dates from Baldwin's years at Ford.

2. Thomas (37/22) has *prophetis*; PL 451B (incorrectly) reads *apostolis*.

3. This threefold division of the word is also to be found in SA 766 C-D (SCh 94:556–558).

4. This is the O.L. version of Is 7:9; Baldwin's source for it was most probably Augustine (e.g. *De Trinitate* xv. II. 2; PL 42:1058, *Sermo* 272; PL 38:1246). This text appears elsewhere in Baldwin's writings (e.g. SA 703B [SC 93:300]).

5. A full explanation of what Baldwin understood by *ratio fidei* would be out of place here, but his approach on the whole was extremely cautious and conservative, and is well exemplified by the following passage from SA 653B–C (SCh 93:116): 'We cannot give a reason for everything that the ancients have handed down, but in those things they have transmitted which are not contrary to reason, the very authority of the ancients should be sufficient reason for us. Our very faith, without which it is impossible to please God, relies more on authority than human reason. So when Peter tells us that we should give a reason to all who ask for the faith and hope which are in us, I cannot think of any better reason to give for our faith than the authority of Scripture or the authority of the ancients – at least, of those ancients who have not been found to be in error on any point of faith, and whom we know have pleased God by virtue of [their faith]'.

6. Since this is based on Mt 3:9, the reading *laudibus* in PL 452D is an error for *lapidibus*.

7. Thomas suggests that this idea has its roots in Augustine (see 37/33, n. 1, and 40 / 134, n. 1, citing *De bono viduitatis* XXI. 26; PL 40; 448, and *Sermo* 70. III. 3; PL 38: 444), but although the principle is the same, the actual source of the expression is Cicero, *Orator*, x. 33. Bernard also quotes it (see Palm I. 2; PL 183: 255C [SBOp 5:44]), and it would seem to have been a phrase which was fairly well known at the time.

8. Thomas (37/32–34) has *sacerdotalis dignitas*; PL 453C reads *sacerdotalis auctoritas*.

9. This follows the reading of MS Troyes 433 which Thomas prefers (see 37/36): *tamquam gladius anceps subtilissime quasi per discretionem dividit* . . . PL 454B substitutes *subtilissimi corporis* for *subtilissime quasi*. Discernment (*discretio*) is of considerable importance for Baldwin (and many other twelfth-century writers) and he elaborates on it in the final section of this present treatise. Cf. also nn. 43 and 45 below.

10. A phrase from the Athanasian Creed.

11. Lit. 'certain wills (*quaedam voluntates*)'.

## Notes to Tractate VI

12. *Quae communiter amantur.*
13. *Per affectum caritatis.*
14. *Per affectiones amoris.*
15. *Se illi indulget et se transfundit extra se. Transfudit* in Thomas's text (37/54) is merely a typographical error.
16. *Per affectum condolendi.*
17. This only becomes intelligible when we consider the peculiar Latin rendering of Lk 2:35: *et tuam ipsius animam pertransibit gladius.* It is, in fact, a literal translation of the Greek, but what is in Greek a perfectly sound construction does not work in Latin. The *ipsius*, then, may be understood in two ways: (a) 'your soul, of himself', i.e. your soul, as if it were Christ's soul; or (b) 'your soul of itself', i.e. your very own soul. The latter, of course, is what the Greek says, and which Baldwin here prefers.
18. Baldwin is quoting Ph 2:12 in the O.L. version which appears in a number of patristic writers. E.g. Augustine, *Epistola* 157, IV. 29 (PL 33:688), *De sancta virginitate* xxxviii . 39 (PL 40:419).
19. Both here and in the phrase 'suffered more in her soul' a few lines further on, the term is *mens*.
20. This is a fairly loose translation of the Latin in order to bring out the meaning.
21. *Excessus.* This is a very important term, but it is clear that in the present context, Baldwin is using it fairly broadly. We may contrast Tr. VIII, n. 18.
22. *Contritio* is derived from *contero* which means 'to grind up' or 'separate into small pieces'. A contrite heart, therefore, is a heart which is broken up or divided into pieces.
23. Mt 6:23 with a second *nequam* substituted for the Vulgate *tenebrosum*.
24. PL 460D omits *maxime*.
25. A loose translation to bring out the sense.
26. PL 460D omits *nulla* in *cum nulla adest delectatio*.
27. The whole of this sentence has been omitted in PL 461C.
28. *Quod malum appetit.* Baldwin's name for this factor is normally *appetitus*, and thus accords with early scholastic usage.
29. As is clear from his later comments, Baldwin is referring to the *mens*. See n. 37 below.
30. Baldwin's argument centers around *sentire* and *consentire* (cf. Tr. IV, nn. 41, 44) and he provides a detailed explanation of what he means later in this present tractate.
31. *Qua desiderant consuetae turpitudinis effectum, et tunc cum nullum habent affectum.*
32. Thomas (37/84) reads *acuant*; PL 463C has *amant*.
33. *Appetitus malus, vel affectus.*
34. PL 464B omits *morte*.
35. *Scintilla rationis.* A well-known term deriving from Augustine, *De civitate Dei* XXII, 24, 2; PL 41, 789. It is this 'spark' which distinguishes man from the animals, and characterises us as created in the image of God.
36. PL 464D omits the last part of this sentence.
37. See n. 29 above.
38. This is an explanatory rendering. The Latin simply says, 'that which all these please finds its pleasure in all these'.

39. Thomas (37/96) reads *nutu*; PL 466A (incorrectly) has *motu*.
40. As Baldwin explains in his CF 597C, '[God] is said to know when he makes us know'. It is an augustinian idea.
41. This is a fairly loose translation to bring out the meaning.
42. This curious text appears to be based on the O.L. version of Pr 16:25 (which Baldwin could have found in Ambrose, Jerome, or even the *Rule of St Benedict* [RB 7, 21]), but it also shows traces of Pr 14:12 which, in the O.L., is very similar.
43. Baldwin is here echoing RB 64, 19.
44. PL 466D omits the whole of this first point.
45. *Discretio* derives from *discerno* 'to separate, divide', and hence, 'to distinguish, discern'.
46. A play on words which cannot be rendered satisfactorily into English: . . . *suis tegumentis nudabit sermo ad quem nobis sermo*.

# TRACTATE VII
# ON THE ANGELIC SALUTATION[1]

*Hail, full of grace, the Lord is with you;
Blessed are you among women.*\*     Lk 1:28

THE MATTER OF OUR SALVATION begins with a salutation,[2] and the commencement of our reconciliation is consecrated by a proclamation of peace. The herald of salvation and messenger[3] of peace was sent from God and came to the Virgin, and this lover of virginity greeted her with a strange new greeting — [a greeting] which had never been heard from eternity until that moment — and thus conferred upon her at one and the same time both the favor of a new greeting and the acclaim of a new commendation. For a woman to be greeted by an angel is indeed new and rare! Although Hagar and the wife of Manoah enjoyed seeing an angel and speaking with him, the angel did not greet them.\*  Gn 21:17, Jg 13:9–20
But now a woman is greeted by an angel. Now the time draws near when women may be greeted by the Lord himself, saying to them, 'All hail'!\*    Mt 28:9

The Virgin reflected on what manner of greeting this might be.\* Let us, too, reflect upon it as best    Lk 1:29
we can and consider its nature. It is not the sort of greeting [you give to someone you meet] on the road, but a greeting which leads [us] back to [our] homeland. 'Greet no one on the road',\* says the    Lk 10:4
Lord.

If someone deliberately flatters you and fawns on you and agrees with everything you say to ingratiate himself with you in vain things, or makes a great show of his friendship for you, or sings your praises — this is one who greets you on the road. Beware of him! Beware of those who give you this sort of greeting.[4] And woe to you if you become the slave of such a one! Woe to you if those who seek your soul rule over you!* Do not be enamoured of greetings in the market-place.* Let the testimony of your conscience be enough for you,* and the faithful witness in heaven,* to whom you should say, 'With you is my praise in a great church'.*

Ps 69:3[70:2]
Mt 23:7
2 Co 1:12
Ps 88:38[89:37]
Ps 21:26[22:25]

We [need to] distinguish two sorts of greeting because there are two distinct sorts of salvation. There is a vain salvation, of which it is written, 'Vain is the salvation of man',* and there is a true salvation, of which it is written, 'Hear me in the truth of your salvation'.* But this [angelic] greeting [which we are now discussing], whether it be a yearning prayer for a salvation much desired or the proclamation of salvation given and received, does not proffer false friendship on the part of him who gives the greeting, nor does it proclaim false praise of the Virgin. But just as virginity is always dear to the angels, so the praises he utters of the Virgin are truly sincere, and he begins by praising her fullness of grace, saying 'Hail, full of grace!' O saving greeting, spoken by the angel, instructing us in how we should greet the Virgin. O joy of the heart, sweetness to the mouth, seasoning of love! What place can there be for anger where there is fullness of grace? For fullness of grace renders the [first] sin void and restores nature. It was sin which corrupted nature and gave rise to anger, but God, in his anger,

Ps 59:13[60:12]

Ps 68:14[69:13]

has not suppressed his mercies.* He has poured out grace and turned away his anger. That sex which he condemned and cursed⁵ in the first woman, he now, in the blessed Virgin, fills with the grace of his blessing and the oil of his mercy. This is the cruse of oil;* this is the vessel of Gideon filled with dew;† this is the golden jar containing the manna of surpassing sweetness which rained down from heaven.* Who can conceive the nature and the abundance of the grace which filled her who is named first among women, who alone is called full of grace, who gave birth to the only-begotten Son, full of grace and truth?*

We read that Stephen, the first martyr, was filled with grace⁶ and strength,* but we believe that [the Virgin] was still more full of grace in accordance with her greater capacity to receive it. She could contain in both her heart and mind him who was the author of grace, him who is so great and so immense that the whole world cannot contain him.⁷

We have heard that when blessed Elizabeth was filled with the Holy Spirit,* she recognized a greater grace in the Virgin and was amazed that she visited and greeted her. 'How is it', she said, 'that the mother of my Lord should come to me?'* Since she had been greeted herself, she was right to greet her through whom salvation had to be imparted, for in this way she rendered thanks to God, who gives salvation to kings* and who commands the saving of Jacob.* For [Mary] was full of grace, in good measure, pressed down, shaken together, and running over,* for the reason that through her the grace of God might abound in us. God chose her in advance in a unique way and accorded her the grace of being endowed with a triple grace – the grace of beauty,

Ps 76:10[77:9]

1 K 17:12
†Jg 6:38
Heb 9:4

Jn 1:14

Ac 6:8

Lk 1:41

Lk 1:43

Ps 143[144]:10
Ps 43:5[44:4]

Lk 6:38

the grace of favor, and the grace of honor—so that she should be made beautiful, gracious, and glorious.

### OF THE TRIPLE GRACE OF BEAUTY, FAVOR, AND HONOR[8]

The grace of beauty shines out in an attractive face, and according to the definition of blessed Augustine, an attractive face is regularly formed, with a good color and a cheerful expression.[9] The regularity of the features, their proportion, uniformity, composition, and the way in which the corresponding parts are arranged and matched, plays no small part in beauty. Eyes which are different or unequal, or a distorted visage, or lips which do not meet properly are displeasing, and if any part [of the face] differs from its corresponding part by its deformity or irregularity, it detracts from the beauty of the whole. Any part which is greater or less than it should be or is out of proportion with its corresponding part disfigures the grace of beauty.

The praise of true beauty belongs to the mind rather than the body. Yet in a certain way it belongs to the body as well, for it often happens that what a chaste heart conceives inwardly is manifested outwardly and becomingly through the agency of the body. But whatever is not born from purity of heart shows its impurity, since all the glory of the king's daughter comes from within.* Yet not all her glory [remains] within! It often comes forth from her inmost [parts] and glorifies outwardly the King of Glory* who is in heaven.

Ps 44:14[45:13]

Ps 23[24]:7 ff

This interior beauty, however, [also] loves regularity and balance.[10] For where there is no cause for irregularity, irregularity is always unseemly. If you judge what is good and evil in yourself in one way and in your neighbor in another, then your two eyes are not the same. If you are proud before God but humble before men, the two sides of your face are out of proportion. If you speak well of your neighbor to his face and denigrate him behind his back, or if you praise God in prosperity but grumble in adversity, your two lips are ill-matched. The whole of this deformity stems from the sin of pride, which always loves imbalance and irregularity in our conduct, just as humility restores the balance to things unbalanced.

In the case of the Virgin, we are looking for the precise way in which the features of her face are proportioned, for [her face] is so attractive and so praiseworthy that a more attractive or more praiseworthy cannot be found among all the daughters of Sion.* And in what better way can we speak of the regularity of her features than in the balance of humility and honor, of condescension and dignity? It is written, 'The greater you are, the more you should humble yourself in all things'.* If you stand out from the crowd, become one of the crowd; if you are always in command, do not think it beneath you to be subservient.

Consider yourself, and consider your Master. And [consider too] the occasion on which he confesses that he is the Master—truly so, since that is what he is.* Consider what he said and what he did. 'I have not come', he says, 'to be served, but to serve.'* And he explained what he meant like this: 'Whoever is the leader, let him become as the servant; and whoever is greater among you, let him become as the younger'.* So much for what he said. Do you know what he did? He humbled himself at the very feet of his own disciples! Who was it who did this?

Sg 3:11

Si 3:20

Jn 13:13
Mt 20:28

Lk 22:26

| | |
|---|---|
| Is 66:1, Ps 109[110]:2 | He for whom the earth is a footstool for his feet.\* |
| Rv 1:17 | He who says, 'I am the first and the last':\* the first in dignity, the last in humility. He has given us an |
| 1 P 2:21 | example, therefore, that we may follow in his steps\* |
| Ps 131[132]:7 | and worship in the place where his feet have stood.\* |
| Ps 94[95]:6 | Come, let us worship and fall down before God;\* |
| Gn 16:9 | let us humble ourselves beneath him and with him,\* |
| Ps 33:19[34:18] | for he will save the humble of spirit,\* those, that is, |
| Jn 4:23 | who worship in spirit and in virtue.\* The place of worship is the virtue of humility. Here his feet stood. How did they stand? In humility he came, and in humility he persevered. He emptied himself and took the form of a servant, and on behalf of his servants, the Lord endured the shame of the cross |
| Ph 2:7–8 | and became obedient to the Father even to death.\* What is the height of humility, if not this? How beautiful is this balance of the highest dignity and the highest humility! |
| | O faithful soul, if you are guarded against pride by this example, and thus, through humility, follow in your Master's footsteps, then to you is said, 'How beautiful are your steps in sandals, O prince's |
| Sg 7:2 | daughter'.\* 'Listen, daughter, and incline your ear, that you might be humble, and the king will greatly |
| Ps 44:11–12 [45:10–11] | desire your beauty'.\* Who is the king but he who alone is king? If you incline your ear to him, if you humble yourself, he will find you desirable and more than desirable and worthy of his love, and the more you [humble yourself], the greater you will be. The more you humble yourself, the more you magnify the Lord. |
| | She, therefore, who we believe humbled herself so much more than any other that she was to that extent more worthy, she who alone says, 'My soul |
| Lk 1:46 | magnifies the Lord',\* she magnified him more who |

had herself been more magnified and raised to such eminence that she alone can say, 'He who is mighty has done great things for me';* and having been magnified more, she magnified God more because she humbled herself more and bore witness herself to her own humility, saying humbly, 'He has regarded the humility of his handmaid'.* Elizabeth, too, was a witness, for when the Mother of God visited her, she extolled equally her happiness, her dignity, and, in that great dignity, her humility. For great humility in great dignity is always admirable, and so too [is] great humility in great power, or great humility in wisdom, eloquence, or virtue. In a word, in anything great, great humility is the balancing feature. It arranges and orders the face and conforms and regulates everything so that all the various parts are in harmony.

Lk 1:49

Lk 1:48

## OF THE GRACE OF BEAUTY

The grace of color, both of whiteness and rosiness, adorns the grace of beauty. Color means propriety, but there are two forms of propriety: propriety which stems from chastity and propriety which stems from modesty.¹¹ Chastity and modesty are the white lily and the red rose. Chastity bestows upon the face its whiteness; modesty bathes the cheeks in its redness. Modesty is the guardian of chastity as well as its glory and adornment. Each of the senses of body and mind has its chastity and its modesty. There is a chastity of the eyes and a modesty of the eyes; there is a chastity of the ears and a modesty of the ears; and with each of the senses, modesty is normally the companion of chastity. The senses are considered chaste when they are uncorrupted. This is why the Apostle says,

'As the serpent seduced Eve by his cunning, I am afraid that your senses may be corrupted and fall from the simplicity which is in Christ'.* There is a holy modesty which blushes at shameful things; there is a holy chastity which preserves itself unstained. There was a man who said, 'I made a covenant with my eyes that I would not so much as think about a woman'.* See how chaste were his eyes! But if someone looks at a woman and lusts after her,* his eye is nothing but shameless, and an eye with no shame is the messenger of a mind with no shame. Corruption of the senses and shamelessness go together hand in hand. Integrity of the senses is the seal of chastity.

The integrity of the Virgin, however, and the chastity of her mind and body were such that she was wholly virgin, wholly undefiled, wholly unstained, in none of her senses corrupt, in none of her senses impure. She blushed at all things shameful; she condemned all things wicked; she desired all things seemly; she abominated all things dishonorable. The perfection of virginity is the inviolate integrity of all one's senses, and every detraction from this integrity is a sort of deflowering of virginity. This is the radiant color, the whiteness of chastity combined with the rosiness of modesty, which shines on the face of the Virgin and adds to the grace of her beauty. She was so radiantly colored, therefore, with chastity as well as modesty, that in her was realized that which is written, 'A holy and chaste woman has a double beauty'.[12]

'Full of grace.'[13] Her cheerful expression further added to her grace, and her face was gladdened with the oil of exultation.* With total devotion and the full fervor of charity, she offered herself to God in an odor of sweetness. More than all the daughters of Sion who rejoice in their king,* her spirit rejoiced in God her saviour.* See the beauty of her face: how the grace of regularity formed it, how the grace of whiteness and rosiness illumined it; how the grace of cheerfulness gladdened it. Yet not only is her face beautiful, but she is wholly beautiful, and he who found in her his joy bears witness to this when he says, 'You are wholly beautiful, my love, and in you there is no stain'.* See how full is the grace of her beauty!

Cf. Ps 149:2
Lk 1:47

Sg 4:7

### Of the Grace of Favor

No less than this is the grace of favor. She is loved and praised and honored by all. For men and for angels, she is, after God, the first [object of] love and praise and honor. The whole church of the saints proclaims her praises: 'The daughters of Sion saw her and declared her most blessed; the queens and concubines praised her'.* Nor does she herself pass over in silence this grace of such great favor: 'All generations', she says, 'will call me blessed.'*

Sg 6:8

Lk 1:48

### Of the Grace of Honor

It is not in my power to tell you how great was the grace of honor bestowed upon her. Everything in her is worthy of praise. Whatever is hers alone, whatever she shares in common—both extol her with special praise. Even the things she has in common she has in a unique way, for whatever she shares with others, she herself possesses more than all others in a manner surpassing all excellence. She remains unique, therefore, even in the things in which she is not unique! She is chaste, she is humble, she is sweet and kind. And although there are others [who have] similar virtues, they do not [have them] in the same way, or to the same extent. She surpasses all, and in all things she is the Mistress of the World, the Queen of Heaven, of men, and of angels, the Mother of God and his daughter, his sister, and his bride, his friend, and his neighbor. She is his mother by her fertile virginity, daughter by the grace of adoption, sister by the grace of communion, bride by the trust of betrothal, friend by the exchange of love, neighbor in being near to him in likeness.[14] She is more lovable than all, more honorable than all,[15] beautiful beyond beauty, gracious beyond grace, glorious beyond glory.[16]

'The Lord is with you.'[17] But is there any special glory in her being told, 'The Lord is with you'? After all, the angel said to Gideon, 'The Lord is with you, O strongest of men'.\* And the Psalmist says, 'The Lord of hosts is with us',\* and Christ says to us, 'Behold, I am with you always, even to the end of the world'.\* And Isaiah says of Christ, 'They shall call his name Emmanuel, God with us'.\* But he had prefaced what he was going to say with 'Behold, a virgin shall conceive and bear a son, and they shall call his name Emmanuel'. How could he come to us to be with us unless he comes to the Virgin? To her he came first so as to be with her and in her and from her, so that through her he should be in us, since he is the God of Jacob, our protector.\* For the reason that the God of Jacob took our nature from her was so that he might always be with us, saying, 'My delight is to be with the children of men'.\*

But if God's delight is being with the children of men, can you imagine his delight in being with her who is his alone, whom he chose in advance to

Jg 6:12
Ps 45:8[46:7]

Mt 28:20
Is 7:14

Ibid.

Ps 45:12[46:11]

Pr 8:31

administer such delight? That he is with us, therefore, sharing in our nature and sharing with us his grace that we may be sons and heirs of God, brothers and joint-heirs of Jesus Christ,\* is the great gift and great good which, after God, we owe in a unique way[18] to her to whom was said in a unique way, 'The Lord is with you'.      Rm 8:17

Having been made the agent and collaborator in the divine plan, she gave us the salvation of the world, for she brought forth for us the Saviour who is himself the world's salvation.[19] She could not, however, do this alone, and therefore she offered her service, revealed her role as mediator, and brought forth in our midst the Mediator who could indeed bring it about, and it is for this reason that she was rightly told, 'The Lord is with you'. You are to effect a sublime work; through you the salvation of the world is to be achieved, and the rod of the oppressor is to be broken, as it was in the day of Midian.\* That for which you have been chosen surpasses all human power and wisdom, but the Lord is with you, and for him nothing is impossible.\* Thus, when Gideon was about to free the children of Israel from Midian, he was told, 'The Lord is with you, O strongest of men'. Strength is mentioned here specifically because it was a work which demanded strength, and strength was given by God himself, who is a strong helper.\* [Similarly], in the work of our salvation, [a work] which begins from fullness of grace and is consummated in fullness of grace, fullness of grace is specifically mentioned, and praise is ascribed to the Author of grace who, with the cooperation of the Virgin, is revealed as the author of this work.

Is 9:4

Lk 1:37

Ps 70[71]:7

## The Blessing of the Virgin

God is the author of all such benefits, but after him, praise is due first to the Virgin, who deserves to be blessed by all.[20] For this reason the angel said to her, 'Blessed are you among women',* as also Elizabeth said, 'Blessed are you among women'.* Eve, through pride and the sign of disobedience, brought down on herself a curse, and through her we are subject to the [same] curse. Pride deserves a curse, for God resists the proud but gives grace to the humble.* This is why it is written, 'Pride is the beginning of all sin. Whoever clings to it will be filled with curses.'* Mary, however, humbled herself and deserved a blessing. Let us consider, as best we may, the extent to which she humbled herself and how much she was blessed.

There is one sort of humility which comes from a command, another which comes from deliberation, another which comes from an example, another which comes from a resolution or vow, and another which comes from a curse. A command imposes an obligation, deliberation arouses free will, an example provokes emulation, a holy resolution or vow increases devotion, and a curse induces confusion. Humility which comes from deliberation is better than that which comes from a command. We are *commanded* not to rob others; we are *instructed* to abandon even what is ours. The former is more necessary, but the latter is the greater good. The former is more general [in its application]; the latter is more rigorous.

Humility which comes from an example, without a command and without deliberation, is clearly far removed from puffed-up pride and arrogant disdain.

It is a mark of great humility, without any pressure or persuasion to esteem someone who is acting rightly more than oneself and to hold in contempt nothing worthy of imitation.

It often happens, however, that without command, deliberation, or example, the mind, by a hidden impulse, realizes that there is something good to be done and adopts it as a resolution or a vow. This is a wonderful [sort of] humility, for it is truly a great virtue to renounce our common liberty and submit ourselves to holy necessity.[21]

Sometimes, however, something which we realize is acceptable to God is found to be shameful among men and subject to a curse. Some, therefore, who are conquered by the fear of confusion, are often ashamed of their efforts in trying to reach perfection, and so long as they fear the tongues of men, they flee from the good things they so earnestly desire. Others, however, are so zealous for righteousness and holiness, and esteem them so highly, that they despise human curses and abuse. They count it glorious to suffer insults for the name of Christ* and esteem the reproach of Christ greater riches than the treasure of the Egyptians.* With this sort of humility, the less it fears the curses of men for the sake of God, the more abundant before God is the grace of blessing it deserves. Christ did not neglect this sort of humility, for in wishing to satisfy every [demand of] justice,* he was made a curse for us, as it is written, 'Cursed is he that hangs on a tree'.* But the way in which he was made a curse is shown us by [the Apostle], who says, 'He was rejected by men certainly, but chosen by God'.* And this too applies to him: 'They will curse, and you will bless'.*

Ac 5:41

Heb 11:26

Mt 3:15

Dt 21:23, Ga 3:13

1 P 2:4
Ps 108[109]:28

In the light of all we have said, let us consider the nature of the Virgin's humility. She dedicated her virginity [to God] not by a command of the Law [of Moses], but under the curse of that Law, for any woman who did not leave offspring in Israel was considered cursed. If God also said to those he blessed at the creation, 'Increase and multiply',* and gave them the grace of fertility as a blessing, surely she who has no part in fertility has no part in blessing? If fertility is a blessing, how can barrenness be other than a curse? And what is more barren, more infertile, more unfruitful than virginity? Nothing whatever—[provided we are talking about the time] *before* a virgin is made fertile! For fertile virginity is actually the most fruitful thing there is. The holiness of virginity is above the Law, since no law required it as a command; but when the Lord said, 'Whoever is able to receive this, let him receive it',* he *advised* it for those who wanted to achieve the perfection described in the Gospels.[22] The same is true of the Apostle: 'Concerning virgins', he says, 'I have no command of the Lord, but I do have advice.'*

No command of the Law, therefore, preceded this resolution of the Virgin; nor, as some would think, did any advice from the Law or example from the Law—although when I speak of an example,[23] I am thinking of women rather than men. In the case of Elijah and Jeremiah and Daniel, we consider that they did preserve the purity of their virginity, but among women, either before the Law or under the Law, I can think of no example of virginity preserved and dedicated to God.

The fact that the daughter of Jephthah obtained a delay of two months to bewail her virginity* may be interpreted in a number of ways, for the Scripture does not indicate her intention in doing this. But if the reason she bewailed her virginity was that she was sterile and without fruit and could not leave offspring in Israel, then this thought in her mind and profusion of tears are far removed from a resolution of holy virginity! Yet it seems that she had a more noble reason [than this] — and whatever it was is known to him who examines the heart*—since she said to her Father, 'My father, if you have opened your mouth to the Lord, do with me whatever you have promised, since he has granted you revenge and vengeance upon your enemies'.²⁴*

Pr 24:12

Cf. Jg 11:36

How, then, could our Virgin really think that her virginity would be pleasing to God when [virginity itself] is as much the subject of a curse as it is nigh to barrenness? On the other hand, she could have read in Isaiah, 'Let not the eunuch say, "Behold I am a dry tree!" For the Lord says to the eunuchs, "In my house and within my walls I will give them a place and a name better than sons and daughters."'* Or she could have read, 'Behold a virgin shall conceive and bear a son, and they shall call his name Emmanuel'.* Since the honor of a name better than sons and daughters was promised to the eunuchs — that is, to the virgins — and since it was foretold²⁵ that the Saviour of the World would be born from a virgin, then by the suggestion of the same Spirit that inspired the prophet who said this, the Virgin (for whom was reserved the honor of being the virgin who would conceive God and give him birth) could have realized by divine inspiration that her virginity would be wholly pleasing and wholly dear to God. So whether she was instructed as to the merit of her virginity by the revelation of a prophet or whether it was through divine inspiration that

Is 56:3-5

Is 7:14

she became so thoroughly apprised of it within herself, she fell in love with virginity, and the virginity she embraced she offered to God in an odor of sweetness and dedicated it [to him] and despised the shame of the curse.

But [in her case], to that virginity which had hitherto been barren was added fertility, and instead of the curse she despised she found the grace of a blessing. For other [women], the curse brought iniquity in conception, pain in childbirth, and, for some, barrenness without fruit. She, however, conceived without sin, gave birth without pain, and brought forth fruit from virginity. What kind of fruit? A fruit in all ways unique, a fruit more precious than any fruit of marriage.

What is the fruit of marriage but the whole posterity of Adam, this whole multitude of the children of men? They are the offspring of the conjugal union of our first parents and are born of fornication.\* The entire fruit of the union of the flesh has been condemned in advance, for it has sprung from an evil tree and is contaminated by its corrupt roots. An evil tree brings forth evil fruit.\* What is this evil tree, you ask? It is evil concupiscence, concupiscence of the flesh, which drags with it all who are engendered according to the law of the flesh, all who are begotten by the transmission of sin. This is the original evil in us, the seed-bed of evils, the leaven which has corrupted the whole lump,\* the beginning and end of our common condemnation.

It was fitting, however, that this original evil, so calamitous and deadly, should be remedied by an original good, something associated with man's first condition, enduring after the first transgression and

Jn 8:41

Mt 7:17

1 Co 5:6, Ga 5:9

the consequent law of natal corruption, and still to be found in those born now.[26]

God, in fact, tempered his sentence against sinful man in such a way that although nature was contaminated by its corruption,[27] it was on the one hand aware of the evil which it deserved but on the other was redolent[28] of the good which it [still] possessed. As a result of the sin of disobedience, therefore, corrupt procreation brought upon those who were born the law of disobedience—the corruption, that is, of concupiscence—but despite this, the [nature of our] earliest condition preserved in those who were born a certain integrity of incorruption. For every virgin born is accompanied by her virginity from the time she comes forth from the womb through all her growing years, and she retains the grace and flower of incorruption until the flesh, by failing to restrain the impulse of concupiscence, becomes corrupted and destroys the name of integrity and corrupts the flower of vernal virginity. Nevertheless, that which is lost in the union of man and woman when they mate is partly restored to a child at birth. But the virginity and integrity common to all who are born is lauded and praised as virtue most especially in those who preserve with the integrity of the flesh the chastity of their mind; and if we have virginity of the flesh without chastity of mind, then although this does not of itself deserve reproach or censure, it still does not warrant the commendation of true virtue.

The virginity of this blessed Lady, however, is praised as virtuous in a unique way, for she who deserved to be told, 'Blessed are you among women', obtained a unique grace of blessing. Blessed indeed!

First because she was exempt from the common curse, then because she was delivered from a just indictment, and finally—and this is most important—because she turned away the condemnation due [to humankind]. All other women, whether bearing or barren, are bound by the general curse, but [the Virgin], by grace, was excepted from this, for the share of blessing she received was such that it freed her alone from the general misfortune and set her forth as exempt. This is what we have called her exemption from the general curse.

It would have been possible for sinful man to plead that his sin was due to the woman, and he could have said, 'It is through you, accursed woman, you who deserve to be cursed, that I too am cursed! It is through you that I am cast out of Paradise, through you that I have lost all these goods, through you that I have found all these evils. Woe to you, for it is your fault that I must say, woe to me!' No woman could reply one single word to this. She could only be covered with confusion and confounded with consternation. This is why the whole female species could have been detested and deserve nothing but universal reproach. Such indeed was the case before the birth of the Virgin. But things now are very different! Women now have someone who can reply. In the blessed Virgin they have someone who can oppose this reproach, and it is this which we have called her deliverance from a just indictment. From this indictment the Virgin herself stands free, and by her merit she has delivered others. It was she who brought forth the Saviour of the world who destroyed death\* and turned away the condemnation due to us, and it is to her, therefore, after God, that we owe everything:

2 Tm 1:10

that we are freed from the curse and blessed with all manner of spiritual blessings in the heavens.* Thus, as she is ever blessed before God, so too she should be ever blessed by us.

Eph 1:3

### BLESSED IS THE FRUIT OF YOUR WOMB

Every day we devoutly use this angelic salutation, just as it was given to us, to greet the most blessed Virgin, but we normally add to it [the phrase]: 'and blessed is the fruit of your womb'. It was Elizabeth who added this closing passage, for after she had been greeted by the Virgin, she repeated, as it were, the end of the angel's greeting and went on to add [these further words]: 'Blessed are you among women, and blessed is the fruit of your womb'. This is the fruit of which Isaiah says, 'In that day the shoot of the Lord will be magnificent and glorious, and the fruit of the earth will be high'.* What is this fruit but holy Israel, which is also itself the seed of Abraham, the shoot of the Lord, the flower which climbs from the root of Jesse, the fruit of life in which we share? Blessed indeed in the seed, and blessed in the shoot, blessed in the flower, blessed in the gift, and blessed, finally, in the giving of thanks and in the proclamation [of praise].

Is 4:2

Christ, the seed of Abraham, was descended from the seed of David according to the flesh.* But if the Virgin, who was pledged to Joseph of the house of David, was herself of the seed of David, and if Christ was born of woman,* from whom he was born without seed—'of the seed of David', that is, 'without seed'[29]—why, then, do we not devoutly believe that Christ was [wholly] descended from the seed of David? [The reason is to be found in the phrase] 'without seed'. Why does it say this? Because

Rm 1:3

Ga 4:4

the Virgin was found to be with child by the Holy Spirit,* because she conceived in a marvellous way and took nothing from the normal processes of reproduction.³⁰ She provided from herself the substance³¹ of the flesh [of Christ], and in taking flesh from her, he remained undefiled.

This, therefore, is the blessing of the seed: that he was under no obligation to sin and that in his birth no trace of iniquity was transferred or contracted. He took the form of a servant,* but not that of a slave, and he was innocent of sin in his birth. He alone, therefore, he who acquits the guilty and makes them free, [he alone] is free with a true, innate, and natural freedom.³² To this blessing, which is freedom from sin, there is added the blessing of the shoot: the fullness of grace and of perfect righteousness. He alone among men is found to be perfect in all good since he is free from all evil. To him was the Spirit given without measure* so that he alone could fulfill all righteousness.* Compared with this, all the righteousness of the saints is found to be but a trifle, for none is holy as the Lord is [holy].* Our own righteousness is barely adequate even for ourselves, but his righteousness is sufficient for all nations, as it is written, 'As the earth brings forth her shoot, and the garden causes her seed to sprout forth, so shall the Lord God make righteousness spring forth and praise before all nations.'*

This, then, is the shoot of righteousness, and when it has grown with blessing, it is adorned with the flower of glory. And what measure of glory? A greater measure than we can conceive—or rather, in a measure wholly beyond our comprehension. The flower climbs up from the root of Jesse. How high [does it climb]? Surely to the highest point of all, for

## Tractate VII

Jesus Christ is in the glory of God the Father.* His magnificence is raised above the heavens,* so that the shoot of the Lord may be magnificent and glorious, and the fruit of the earth be high.*

But what fruit is there for us in this fruit? The fruit of blessing, surely, [which comes] from this blessed fruit! From this seed, this shoot, this flower, the fruit of blessing comes forth and reaches all the way to us. First, as if in the seed, through the grace of forgiveness; then, as though in the shoot, through increasing righteousness; and finally in the flower, through the hope and attainment of glory.

For being blessed by God and in God—so that God, that is, may be glorified in him—he is also a blessing for us, so that we too, being blessed by him, may be glorified in him. Through the promise made to Abraham, God gave him the blessing of all nations, so that in the gift of blessing he should himself be a blessing for us and that for this gift he should be ever blessed by us in the offering up of thanks and in the proclamation of praise. May the name of his majesty, therefore, be for ever blessed and the whole earth be full of his majesty. May it be so! May it be so!*

Ph 2:11
Ps 8:2[1]
Is 4:2

Ps 71[72]:19

## NOTES TO TRACTATE VII

1. Title as in PL 467-468. The tractate would seem to date from the days of Baldwin's abbacy. For an excellent account of the development of the theology of Mary in the Middle Ages (a development to which Bernard of Clairvaux made important contributions), see J. Pelikan, *The Christian Tradition, III: The Growth of Medieval Theology* (Chicago, 1978) 160-174.

2. In Latin (and French) the close relationship, both phonologically and etymologically, between *salus* 'salvation' and *salutatio* 'greeting, salutation' makes possible certain puns and word-plays which are not always apparent in English. There are a number of these in this tractate, but any attempt to render them literally produces a form of English which, though theoretically correct, is appallingly pedantic. *O salutatio salutifera*, for example, which occurs a little further on, could be rendered as 'O salutiferous salutation', but if anyone speaks like that, he has my sympathy.

3. *Angelus* means both an angel and a messenger.

4. Lit. 'Beware those who say to you "Hail"'.

5. Lit. 'condemned with a sentence of cursing'.

6. Thomas (37/122) has *gratia*; PL 469B reads *gratiae*.

7. A phrase borrowed from the liturgy. See Thomas 37/123, n. 1.

8. PL 469C has *Of the Triple Grace of God*, and another of the manuscripts used by Thomas has *Of the Triple Grace of Beauty*. See Thomas 37/124, n. 1.

9. Cf. Augustine, *De civitate Dei* XXII. 19. 2 (PL 41:781).

10. Lit. 'equality of comparable parts'.

11. Baldwin's terms—*pudor, pudicitia, verecundia*—are not easy to distinguish in translation. All three, for example, could be rendered by 'decency' or 'modesty'. The context, however, seems to suggest 'chastity' for *pudicitia* and 'modesty' for *verecundia*.

12. Si 26:19, which reads literally: 'A holy and chaste woman [has] grace upon grace'.

13. PL 472A (and certain of the manuscripts) provide these echoes of Baldwin's main text (there is another example at n. 17 below). MS Troyes 433 does not contain them, and Thomas prefers to omit them, remarking—rightly—that if they are section-headings, they are somewhat peculiarly placed (see Thomas 37/113). It is possible, however, that they are not section-headings, but simply asides from a preacher who was recapitulating his text and reminding his congregation of how far he had progressed in his exegesis.

14. This is an augustinian (and ultimately platonic) idea well known in the Middle Ages. 'We do not draw near to God in space (for he is everywhere and not contained in any space), nor do we draw apart from him in space. To draw near to him is to become like him; to withdraw from him is to become unlike him' (Augustine, *Enarratio in Ps.* 34.II.6; PL 36:337).

15. Thomas (37/138) reads *omnibus amabilior, omnibus honorabilior*; PL 472D has *omnibus pulchrior, omnibus amabilior*.

16. *Superspeciosa, supergratiosa, supergloriosa*. For these terms, Baldwin is almost certainly indebted to Anselm, *Oratio* 54; PL 158:960C.

17. See n. 13 above.

18. *Post Deum singulariter debemus, cui* has been omitted in PL 473A by hom.
19. The last part of this sentence has been omitted in PL 473A by hom.
20. Thomas (37/144) has *in omnibus*; PL 473C reads *ab omnibus*.
21. To appreciate Baldwin's point here it is necessary to recall Bernard's teaching on *libertas* and *necessitas*. We all have a body (whether we like it or not) and this body imposes certain demands upon us: it needs to be fed, for example, and cared for. This we may call 'natural necessity', and it is a necessary form of carnal love. We also possess free-will, and, if we may quote Gilson, 'a voluntary agent is able to accept such and such a thing or to refuse it, to say yes or no, and this in virtue of the sole fact that he is gifted with a will. It is this natural liberty, inherent in the very essence of volition, that is called "freedom from necessity"—*libertas a necessitate*' (*Mystical Theology of St Bernard*, 47). Baldwin takes this idea one stage further: this 'natural' or 'common liberty' may be renounced in favor of a total submission to the will of God, and in this case, by our own voluntary decision, we are no longer a free agent. The demands laid upon ourselves by ourselves bring us once again into the realm of constraint and *necessitas*, but in this case it is 'holy necessity' and not 'natural necessity.' And paradoxically, of course, it is this holy necessity which is true freedom.
22. Lit. 'No law made it a command, but evangelical perfection formed it as a *consilium*, the Lord saying, 'Whoever is able, etc."' *Consilium* is 'advice' when it comes from another, and 'deliberation' (as we have rendered it above) when it takes place in oneself. This is the second form of humility—*humilitas sub consilio*—as it applies to the Virgin.
23. PL 474D, *quod de mulieribus*, should read *quod de exemplo dixi de mulieribus* as in Thomas's text (37/150).
24. Jg 11:36 with *vindicta* substituted for the Vulgate *victoria*.
25. *Praenutiatus* in Thomas (37/152) is simply a typographical error for *praenuntiatus*.
26. This is a fairly loose translation to bring out the sense.
27. Thomas (37/156) has *vitio suo corrupta*; PL 476A omits *suo*.
28. Thomas (37/156) has *redoleret*; PL 476A reads *recoleret*.
29. 'Of the seed of David' is a quotation from Jn 7:42. 'Without seed' (*sine semine*), as Thomas indicates (37/162, n. 1), is liturgical and occurs in the antiphon *O admirabile commercium* for vespers of the feast of the Purification.
30. Lit. 'accepting nothing *a gignente*'.
31. *Substantia* in Thomas (37/162) is a typographical error for *substantiam*..
32. Lit. 'it is an innate and true freedom (*genuina libertas*) and a truly free condition of being free-born (*libera ingenuitas*) with which he alone is free'. PL 477C reads *gemina* for *genuina*.

# TRACTATE VIII
# ON THE WOUND OF LOVE
# WHICH THE BRIDE INFLICTS UPON
# THE BRIDEGROOM[1]

*You have wounded my heart, my sister, my spouse, you have wounded my heart with one of your eyes and a single hair of your neck.* *

Sg 4:9

THERE ARE MANY WAYS in which God displays his charity towards us: now by deeds, now by words, now by blessings, now by promises, now by caresses and words of encouragement, now by certain mental representations [which are aroused by external phenomena].[2] By mental representations I mean the specific forms and dispositions of love—whether given or received, natural, social, or chaste—which are aroused in our mind when the latter is stimulated by the various external phenomena naturally suited to it. Thus, as a result of this stimulation and by being consciously aware of these forms of love, our mind might always be consciously aware of God, whom we should love with all our mind* and who should always be present in our memory.[3]

Mt 22:37

Natural love is that by which all living things, not only human beings, love those of their own nature. They feel within themselves the force of love and, by a sort of natural instinct, consent to the laws of love. There is also social love, and by this, as a result of their own choice, they live together socially when they agree to dwell together. And there is also chaste love, which strengthens and adorns marriage.⁴

The eagle, therefore, loves when she is concerned for her young,⁵ and so too the hen loves when she gathers her chicks beneath her wings;* she stretches forth both her wings and her tenderness and is weakened by the greatness of her love. A father loves the sweet children born to him, and a mother cannot forget the offspring of her womb.* And as for brother and sister, when they each speak or hear the sweet name of their relationship, they awake loving affection in each other⁶. Friends are joined by a bond of friendship which cannot be broken, and bride and bridegroom lay aside their affection for their own homes and families to devote themselves to chaste embraces and the delights of love.

Yet more intense than all these is the love of Christ: more profound, more inward, more incisive, more penetrating, more compassionate, more sweet, more steadfast, more fervent. We can compare its power with every other love, but no comparison can surpass it, nor equal it, nor express to the full [its intensity]. Yet Christ is not ashamed to be compared to an eagle or a hen, and by this very fact he demonstrates his marvellous charity, his marvellous humility, and the wonderful sweetness of both of these [virtues]. He is a father when he says, 'From this time call me "my father", for you are the guide of my youth,'* and 'You will call me father and will not cease to walk after me'.* No mother is more tender than he⁷ when he says, 'As a mother comforts her children, so shall I comfort you'.* He is a brother when he says, 'My sister is an enclosed

Lk 13:34

Is 49:15

Jr 3:4
Jr 3:19
Is 66:13

garden'* and 'Go to my brothers'.† He is a friend when he says, 'You are wholly beautiful, my friend',†† and when it is said of him, 'Such is my beloved, and he is my friend'.* He is a bridegroom when he says, 'The bridegroom will rejoice over the bride, and your God will rejoice over you'.*

But when he says, 'You have wounded my heart, my sister, my spouse',* he is then both brother and bridegroom. When he calls her his sister, he points to the communion of nature and grace, and it is this which is the transaction of love: he assumed nature, and he communicated grace. When he calls her his bride, he points to the trust [implicit] in a betrothal and the sacrament[8] of an unbreakable union.

But why does it say of her whom he calls sister and bride that she has wounded the heart of her brother and bridegroom? Does it mean that love also has its wounds? It does indeed, but there are some wounds which offer healing and others which bring death. What wounds are more mortal than those sustained by the very author of death, wounded with the spear of envy and the sword of pain? Of him it is written, 'You have humbled the proud one like someone mortally wounded'.* But he is not the only one to be so wounded: through him many others have also been wounded and have died, and of them it is written, '[They are] like the dead who sleep in the sepulchers, whom you remember no more'.* But the wounds with which the bride is wounded—the wound of love and the wound of pain—are wounds which bring healing, and the wounds of the bridegroom—which are also wounds of love and pain—bring greater healing still. Of the wound of pain the bride says, 'They struck me and wounded me',* and of the wound of love she says,

'I am wounded by charity'.⁹ And if we may serve the truth by introducing into so sacred and reverent a matter the opinion of a distinguished poet,\* then he too is a witness to the wound of love:

Virgil

> *But the queen, long since suffering the sharp*
> *pains [of love],*
> *Nourishes a wound in her veins, and is*
> *consumed by an invisible flame.*¹⁰

We are also told that the two old judges in Daniel 'were both wounded with the love of her'\*—of Susanna, that is—but this does not refer to holy love. Holy love is much more effective in its capacity to wound and much more powerful. Let us, then, consider the way in which the bridegroom announces that his heart has been wounded by his sister and spouse. He does not say it only once but repeats it a second time: 'You have wounded my heart, my sister, my spouse; you have wounded my heart.'\* It is surely because he loved us with so much charity, even when we were dead in our sins,\* that he wanted life for us and death for himself. This is why he was wounded and hung upon the cross; this is how the wounds of us sinners are healed; this is how we have received salvation! His desire for our salvation, therefore, and his desire to die for our salvation comprise two wounds: one of love and one of pain, although both of them are really [wounds] of love. For in both cases, the desire arises from a love which preceded that of the bride, so that when she had been loved first in this way, she could love him who loved her and preserve herself unstained for him in the perfect purity¹¹ of holy love and holy fear.

Dn 13:10

Sg 4:9

Eph 2:4

[Our text] then says that the heart of the bridegroom was wounded by a single eye and a single hair of her neck, as if it were he who was lured into love by their beauty, he who loved her [so much] when she was ugly that he himself made her beautiful. But [in fact, the reference to] the beauty of these things makes it clear that it was the bride who was chosen by love. The whole loving intention [of the bridegroom] was directed to the end that she whom he loved so much before he made her beautiful should be made beautiful, and thus, when he considers the ways in which he made her beautiful, he says that his heart has been wounded by the enormity of his love. [In this way] the bride and bridegroom wound themselves with mutual wounds, but whereas the bridegroom inflicts no wound unless he is wounded [first], the bride wounds him when she herself is not yet wounded.

But if, as he says, the bride is wholly beautiful, why is the bridegroom only wounded by one of her eyes and a single hair of her neck? Why not by the whole of her beauty? He certainly loves all of her and praises all of her—her cheeks and lips, breasts, hips, and everything else—why, then, is he not wounded by the beauty of her cheeks and lips and all the other wonderful things? Why is he wounded by the beauty of just one of her eyes and a single hair of her neck, like someone snared by love? Is it because [her eyes and hair] shine with a certain unique grace of beauty and please him more than all the rest? This is indeed the case, and because they please him more than everything else, the whole [of the bride] is pleasing to him. In what way, then, are these [especially pleasing]? [It is because they represent] the purity of holy love and the purity of holy fear: by one of her eyes we understand the former and by a single hair of her neck, the latter.

## Tractate VIII

In the [book of the] prophet Zechariah it says of the vessel of wickedness (which is cupidity or the love of the world) that 'this is their eye in all the earth'.\* This eye gazes at the earth and not at heaven; at the world and not at God; at transitory things, not those which are eternal; at visible things and not those invisible. Nor can it do so since it is unclean and darkened. But when the love of God is perfect and undivided, it is an eye which is simple[12] and pure. It is striking in its beauty and striking, too, in the wonderful acuity with which it contemplates not the things which can be seen but those which are unseen. This is the countenance of Rachel who is described [as having] a beautiful face and an attractive appearance.\* It is the eye with which Mary sees the better part, [the part] which she chose and which will not be taken from her.\* And although this eye does not exist alone but is actually one of two, it is in truth one, for since it is intent on one thing alone, there is only one thing it loves and one thing it cares about.

The bride also has another eye, but with this one she does not now contemplate the beauty of the bridegroom. Instead, she sinks deep into herself, unwillingly rather than willingly, and sees herself destitute and miserable, open to a multitude of needs and infirmities, not only from herself but from others as if from herself. From these [arise] her preoccupation with the demands of everyday life, her agitation of mind, anxiety of heart, and affliction of spirit. This is why the mind is divided up among dozens of different things and busy with a whole multitude of different matters, and this is why Martha is worried and troubled over many things. Mary's name was called only once because she had chosen

Zc 5:6

Gn 24:16

Lk 10:42

one thing once and for all, and that alone was necessary.* But since Martha was worried and troubled with the concerns of the present and with providing for the future, she was addressed twice as 'Martha, Martha'.*¹³ There are indeed many things which must be considered, many things which must be provided for, all sorts of needs for ourselves and our fellows, and although it is impossible to fulfill every demand laid upon us, we must at least attend to those which, in all honesty, are right and proper.¹⁴ Thus, since this eye considers earthly things, how can it avoid being sullied with the dust of earthly thoughts? How can it be other than troubled?

It is not this eye, therefore, whose beauty wounds the bridegroom, but that one eye which sees the bridegroom alone and which abhors all other things that it might be joined to him. For if a man leaves his father and mother to be joined to his wife,* how much more should the bride of Christ despise and leave everything to be joined to her bridegroom? But in what better way can she cleave to him than by the eye? Where there is love, there too is the eye.¹⁵ It is the eye which usually guides us to love and entices us into it, for it [is the eye which] can see and be seen. It arouses love by its beauty and declares it with secret signs. When I speak of its beauty, [I mean] a faithful and true [beauty], not one which is spurious and artificial. Someone who colors her eyes with cosmetics feigns a beauty which she does not have, and the eye of intention which is colored¹⁶ with a lie is colored in vain before the eyes of God. He takes no pleasure in make-believe virtues, but truth he always loves, since he is himself the Truth. The signs made with the eyes are also sometimes false, as we read of certain people, 'They

## Tractate VIII

have hated me without cause and make signs with their eyes'.\* But truly, God is not mocked!†     Ps 34:19[35:20]
    †Ga 6:8

By means of these signs, the eye arouses love when it turns towards the same person time and time again, or when it stares fixedly, or when it candidly puts on a certain feigned expression.[17]

The bridegroom, however, loves the eye [of the bride] when it is turned from him as well as when it is continually turned towards him. Does it surprise you that I said, 'when it is turned away from him'? Listen to what he says to the bride: 'Turn away your eyes from me, for they have made me flee away.'\* If one is in the rapture of contemplation[18] and the unfathomable God is sought in an unfathomable way beyond the permitted bounds, then it is good to turn away the eyes. Otherwise, it is he who will hasten away and say, 'Turn away your eyes'; it is he who will warn us with [the voice of] Wisdom: 'Do not seek the things that are too high for you, and do not search into things above your ability.'\*     Sg 6:4

    Si 3:22

At other times, however, the bridegroom does not love to see the eye [of the bride] turned away from him; he loves instead to see it turned again towards him. For it often happens that when someone is in distress and calls upon God, he lifts up his eyes to God, but when he is freed from his troubles and is relaxed and unconcerned, he looks elsewhere and turns away his eyes from the Lord. But the Lord immediately beats him with the rod of discipline,\* and when he has been chastised, he looks back [to God] and wants [God] to look upon him, saying, 'Look upon me and have mercy on me'.\* In another psalm, therefore, [the following line] appears a number of times: 'And they cried to the Lord     Pr 22:15

    Ps 24[25]:16

in their distress, and many times did he deliver them'.¹⁹

It is often the case, however, that the just are obviously not freed from the troubles which at present beset them. 'They were tortured', it says, 'and did not receive deliverance, so that they might find a better resurrection.'* They often despise worldly consolation so much that they do not want to be freed, although it is also true that since they are confident that God will provide something better for them, they often want it but do not hope for it. Or it may be that they were persecuted when they were faint-hearted and that after continual prayer they still fail to get what they prayed for. Then, little by little, their hope wavers and weakens as if he who could free them does not want to do so. This is why [the psalmist] says, 'My eyes are weakened because of wickedness',* and 'My eyes have failed while I hope in my God'.* Thus, when hope fails, the eye turns away; when hope is restored, the eye quickly returns.

All this, [however], should only be said of the hope of temporal consolation or liberation, which, for various reasons, makes headway one minute and falls back the next. But the hope of eternal salvation is not like this. Amid the greatest dangers and all sorts of temptations, it remains unmoved. Not to desire this salvation is forbidden; nor must we ever despair of it. This eye, therefore, is immovably fixed and never turns away [its gaze]. It remains for ever fastened on that from which it is never unfastened. This is why the Prophet [says], 'My eyes are ever on the Lord'.* Do not be concerned that it says 'eyes' in the plural here, whereas the heart of the bridegroom is wounded by one single eye. [The reference to] one eye is because there is one love wholly directed on one thing, but in one love there are many diverse affections, and these, by desiring and hoping in many different ways, direct it to that one end on which the eye is irrevocably fixed.

The eye adopts its feigned expression[20] when it is not opened fully but is closed, little by little,[21] with a covert and sort of furtive look, and conveys a secret understanding with no more than a hint.[22] Holy love can also give certain hints appropriate to it, but these are different from those of which it is written, 'The daughters of Sion are haughty and have walked with stretched-out necks, their eyes hinting [at improper things]'.\* [The hints of holy love] are mysterious and aware of holy propriety, and with them the bride and bridegroom exchange meaning glances and intimations.[23] She wills or does not will [to respond] to his hints as he himself wills her to will or not to will. The bridegroom gives her a meaning glance when he suggests his will to her in a secret way; he gives her a sign when he grants her prayers and supplications. The bride gives him a meaning glance when she obeys God's commands imposed upon her. She gives him a sign when, by means of a secret intention, she sees in his secret good works — as if it were something just between the two of them — him by whom alone she longs to be seen. She gives him a sign when, in the humility of prayer, she gives him a secret and reverent hint of her desire.

Do not be surprised if we say that the eye 'feigns'\* a certain expression in signifying this love which we are now discussing, when there is nothing feigned\* in holy love. [The word] *fingere* does not always [refer to] imitating and falsifying, but sometimes to

Is 3:16

*fingi*

*fictus*

constructing or forming or disguising, and it is in these ways—by constructing, that is, and forming and disguising—that we find and perceive that God 'feigns' things. Thus, it is written, 'Jesus appeared* to be going further,'* and 'He who has formed† the hearts of every one of them,'* and 'He who formed† the eye, does he not see?,'* and 'You who frame† labor in the commandment.'*²⁴

*finxit*
Lk 24:28
†*finxit*
*Ps 32:15[33:14]
†*finxit*
*Ps 93[94]:9
†*fingis*
*Ps 93[94]:20

## OF ONE OF HER EYES AND ONE OF THE HAIRS OF HER NECK

'You have wounded my heart', he says, 'with one of your eyes and a single hair of your neck.' It is as if the bridegroom surveys the bride from all directions and sees that she pleases him on both sides, both in front and behind, and on both sides her unity is revealed: [at the front] by one of her eyes and [at the back] by a single hair of her head.

Listen now to how this single hair is arranged. From the top of the head, the hair falls in different directions: some of it falls to the front, some to the back of the head, and some to the ears and shoulders. And in the case of women who normally take care of their hair, they comb it, part it in the middle from the top of the head to the brow, and arrange it becomingly in two attractive waves. These they then draw back over the ears to the neck and shoulders and entwine them together there to form a single [plait of] hair. In this way, they make one hair from many hairs and bind it all up in a single knot.²⁵ If this were not so, their hair would lie loose in disorder, unkempt and untidy, streaming here and streaming there and quite unbecoming. Such is the skill with which [women] who think on worldy things, who are concerned with pleasing those who look at them, groom and bedeck themselves.

So, too, the bride of Christ does not neglect to care for her hair. She wants to be pleasing in his eyes, and he does not find pleasure in just any sort of hair. On the contrary, it is written, 'God will break the heads of his enemies: the hairy crown of those that walk in their sins'.* And in Isaiah, 'The Lord will make bald the crown of the head of the daughters of Sion, and the Lord will strip them of their hair',* and a little further on, he threatens baldness in the place of curled hair.* And the Apostle [says], 'Not with braided hair'.*

Ps 67:22[68:21]

Is 3:17
Is 3:24
1 Tm 2:9

But contrary to this, the holiness and sanctification of the Nazarites and the strength of Samson lies in their hair. Thus, the profound thoughts of holy resolutions and affections are divided into four parts from the highest point of the mind[26] (that is, from the knowledge of God) and are separated out by the comb of discernment.[27] The part which falls to the front pertains to things which are good and eternal; that which looks behind pertains to things which are bad and eternal; and the parts which are divided to the right and left pertain to things good and temporal and bad and temporal respectively. The bridegroom makes it clear that these hairs are pleasing to his eyes, for he says, 'Take away from my eyes the evil of your thoughts'.* And again it is written, 'The holy spirit of discipline will flee from the deceitful and will withdraw from thoughts that are without understanding'.* [But] he guarantees the safety of those whom he has chosen when he says, 'A hair of your head shall not perish'.* All the hairs of their head are numbered,* for the Most High takes care of them.*

Is 1:16

Ws 1:5

Lk 21:18
Mt 10:30
Ws 5:16

In the case of the bride, however, all her hair is drawn back to her neck, and it is there that [we find] the yoke of obedience. It is bound together in a

single plait with the knot of fear, for we should always think to obey [God] in all things in the fear of God, as it is written, 'Whatever God has commanded, think on them always',* and 'Fear God and keep his commandments: this is the whole duty of mankind'.* The single plait at her neck, therefore, [represents] the unity and harmony of her thoughts under the yoke of obedience. It is gathered together into one by the fear of God and so bound together that it cannot be loosed. This is that holy fear which endures for ever and ever;* it is not that which charity casts out,* but that which preserves humility and strengthens charity. This fear gathers together whatever is scattered; it unites whatever is dispersed; it drives out whatever is evil; it nourishes whatever is good, and when it has nourished it, protects it. In a word, it makes the heart pure and clean and tries to guard it with every possible protection. The first form of protection [ensures] that nothing evil appears in one's actions. The second, that no evil word proceeds from one's mouth; the third, that nothing evil remains in the heart which would offend the eyes of the bridegroom. This is how the heart of the bridegroom is wounded, and this is how the bride is praised, for the woman that fears the Lord shall be praised.* Therefore, O Lord, grant that we may possess forever both the fear and love of your holy name.[28]
Amen.

Si 3:22

Qo 12:13

Ps 18:10[19:9]
1 Jn 4:18

Pr 31:30

1. Title as in PL 477-478. The tractate most probably dates from Baldwin's years at Ford.
2. The Latin simply reads *similitudinibus rerum* 'likenesses of things', but I would defend my explanatory rendering here on two grounds: firstly, Baldwin's own explanation of what he means; and secondly, I suspect that in using this phrase, Baldwin is echoing Augustine, *Confessiones* x.viii.14 (PL 32:785) where *similitudines rerum* refers to all the various mental representations or images stored in the great *thesaurus memoriae*, the treasury of memory.
3. These last two sentences are an explanatory rendering of a very tricky paragraph. A glance at the Latin text will show that a literal translation is of little use. As Thomas points out (38/17, n. 1), both Bernard (Div 10, 2; PL 183: 568A-C; SBO 6/1: 122) and William of St Thierry (Nat am xvii-xviii; PL 184:391B-C) have divisions of love which partly correspond to that of Baldwin (Bernard uses *amor socialis* and *amor generalis*; William has *amor socialis* and *amor naturalis*; *amor castus* occurs a number of times in Bernard), but there is no obvious relationship between their descriptions and that of our author.
4. *Conjugum* in Thomas (38/18) is simply a typographical error for *conjugium*.
5. *Amat igitur aquila desiderans super pullos suos*. This derives from one of the O.L. versions of Dt 32:11 (cf. Jerome, *Commentaria in Isaiam Prophetam* xviii [in Is 66:13-14]; PL 24:662A). The Vulgate has *volitans* for *desiderans*, and this is the reading which appears in PL 478D.
6. Thomas (38/18) reads *mutuos*; PL 478D has *mortuos*, which makes no sense at all.
7. Lit. '. . . more abundant than the bowels of maternal devotion'.
8. On the wide use of the term *sacramentum* in the twelfth century, see Tr. iii, n. 10
9. *Vulnerata caritate ego sum*. Thomas' suggestion that this quotation derives from a phrase (*caritate vulneratus*) in the cistercian liturgy of the Feast of St Bernard (see 38/23, n. 1) is incorrect. It is actually the O.L. version of Sg 2:5 and 5:8 (Vulg. *amore langueo*) and appears, for example, in Ambrose, *Expositio in Ps* 118, *sermo* 15.39; PL 15:1424A, and Bernard, Ep 42.11: PL 182:818B (SBO 7:109).
10. Virgil, *Aeneid*, iv, 1-2.
11. Thomas (38/24) reads *puritate*; PL 480A has *veritate*.
12. Baldwin is echoing Mt 6:22, and there is an explanation of what he means by an *oculus simplex* towards the end of Tr. vi.
13. These last two sentences are a fairly loose translation. See also Tr. x/ii, n. 3 for a similar exegesis of Lk 10:41.
14. This is a paraphrase of Baldwin's very concise Latin: *nec undecumque potest, sed unde licet, unde honestissime decet*.
15. *Ubi amor, ibi oculus*. It is possible, as Thomas suggests (40/144, n. 1), that Baldwin is here quoting Richard of St Victor, *Benjamin Minor* xiii (PL 196: 10A). On the other hand, the same expression is to be found elsewhere (e.g. in Adam of Perseigne, *Letter* ix; PL 211:596D [*Ep.* v in PL 211]; SCh 66:160; CF 21:135), and Thierry of Chartres tells us quite straightforwardly that it was a proverbial saying (see B. Hauréau, *Notices et extraits de quelques manuscrits latins de la Bibliothèque Nationale*

[Paris, 1890] 1:53). We cannot be sure, therefore, that Richard was Baldwin's source. See further, H. Walther, *Lateinische Sprichwörter und Sentenzen des Mittelalters* (Göttingen, 1967) 5:431, #32036.
  16. Thomas (38/32) reads *coloratur*; PL 481B has *roboratur*.
  17. *Aut sine fraude fingitur.* Baldwin explains what he means a little later on (see n. 22), and also offers some useful comments on the very real difficulty of translating *fingere* (see n. 24).
  18. *Excessus contemplationis.* This is what *excessus* normally means in the spiritual writings of the twelfth century. It can, however, have a rather more general application. Cf. Tr. VI, n. 21.
  19. This is a composite quotation: the first half is Ps 106: 6, 13, 19, 28, and the second half is Ps 105:43 (Vulgate).
  20. Thomas (38/36) has *fingitur*; PL 482B has *figitur*.
  21. PL 482C omits *paulatim*.
  22. Baldwin seems to be describing some sort of slow wink; the sort of gesture, laden with illicit promise, which would be characteristic of a medieval Mae West.
  23. *Quibus sponsa innuit et annuit sponso innuenti et annuenti.*
  24. All the verbal forms cited here—*fingi, fictus, finxit, fingis*—derive from *fingere*, and *fingere* can mean to touch, handle, form, frame, feign, fashion, shape, mould, construct, alter, change, teach, train, invent, devise, dissemble, or disguise.
  25. Thomas' text (38/40) reads *in uno modo* and is, for once, incorrect. We should read *in uno nodo* with PL 483A. In actual fact, after about 1120, it was usual for ladies of higher rank to wear their hair in two very long plaits, bound with ribbons, and reaching sometimes below the knees (see N. Bradfield, *Historical Costumes of England from the Eleventh to the Twentieth Century* [London, 1970³] 21; R. Corson, *Fashions in Hair* [London, 1965] 105-106). Many single women, however, preferred to wear their hair dressed in a plain knot or a single braid. Towards the end of the twelfth century, the long-hanging plaits began to go out of fashion, and the braids were often worn coiled around the head or in coils over the ears.
  26. *Vertex mentis.* This is synonymous with *apex mentis, principale mentis*, etc., and designates the highest point of the soul. It always remains in contact with the divine world (the world of the Platonic Ideas) and is our immediate link with God. Hence Baldwin explains that the *vertex mentis* is *cognitio Dei.* For some further examples of its use in the twelfth century, see R. Javelet, 'Thomas Gallus et Richard de Saint-Victor, mystiques', in RTAM 29 (1962) 219-220.
  27. *Discretio.* See further Tr. VI, nn. 9, 43, 45.
  28. Thomas (38/45, n. 1) identifies this last sentence as part of the liturgy for the Feast of the Holy Name of Jesus.

BALDWIN OF FORD

SPIRITUAL TRACTATES

VOLUME TWO

# VOLUME TWO

# TABLE OF CONTENTS

**VOLUME TWO**

| | |
|---|---|
| Tractate IX / i: *On the Beatitudes in the Gospel* | 7 |
| Tractate IX / ii: *On the Meek* | 26 |
| Tractate IX / iii: *On Those Who Mourn* | 47 |
| Tractate IX / iv: *On Those Who Hunger and Thirst for Righteousness* | 67 |
| Tractate X / i: *On the Seal of the Love of God* | 74 |
| Tractate X / ii: *On Human Misery and Want Which Results from Sin* | 85 |
| Tractate XI: *On the Crucifixion of Our Old Man* | 91 |
| Tractate XII: *An Exhortation to Priests* | 118 |
| Tractate XIII: *On the Love of God Poured Fourth in Our Hearts* | 131 |
| Tractate XIV: *On the Order of Charity* | 141 |
| Tractate XV: *On the Cenobitic or Common Life* | 156 |
| Tractate XVI: *In Praise of Perfect Monks* | 195 |
| Index of Principal Latin Words | 218 |
| Index of Proper Names | 220 |
| Systematic Index | 221 |

# TRACTATE IX
## ON THE BEATITUDES IN THE GOSPEL[1]

### TRACTATE IX/I
### ON THE POOR IN SPIRIT

*Blessed are the poor in spirit, for theirs is the kingdom of heaven.** Mt 5:3

THE PROMISES OF GOD are varied and diversified, depending upon the merits of the just and the different ways in which they manifest their righteousness.[2] For each [form of] righteousness, there is an appropriate recompense, and each separate virtue has its own particular praise and its own particular reward according to the dignity of its rank and its natural qualities. 'Let the poor see and rejoice.'* Let them see their role and the nature of their heritage, [a heritage] which is not earthly and perishable, but undefiled and incorruptible, reserved in heaven.* Let them see and rejoice for theirs is the kingdom of heaven.

Ps 68[69]:33

1 P 1:4

It is theirs, clearly, both to possess and to share: to possess it for themselves, that is, and to receive others with them, as it is written: 'Make friends for yourselves by means of unrighteous mammon, so that when it fails they may receive you into the eternal habitations'.* Here below the poor are received in the houses of the rich to be refreshed at their table like beggars and indigents, and in this way the needs

Lk 16:9

of the poor are filled from the abundance of the rich. [But] in the kingdom of heaven the rich will be received by the poor, and the indigence of the rich will be filled from the abundance of the poor. The righteousness of the rich will not be sufficient to obtain [for them] the kingdom of heaven, for the way to heaven is [the way of] poverty.

There are some who love this [poverty] for the sake of Christ. They are zealous in imitating the poverty of Christ, and theirs is the kingdom of heaven. There are others who do not love it but endure it patiently. In their case, they are purified in the furnace of poverty,* and when they have been proved [in this way], they too can enter the kingdom of heaven. But there are others who neither love poverty for its own sake nor endure it because of need, because they lack nothing. Yet for the sake of Christ they love the poor, readily bestowing [their goods upon them] and sharing [them with them]. They do not put their hope in the uncertainty of riches,* but in order to gain eternal life, they store up for themselves a treasure which is a good foundation for the future.* These, too, will enter the kingdom of heaven by the merit of poverty, for they are the recipients of a fruitful trade and exchange: in return for their comforting the poor, they receive from the poor.

But if all those who are good shall enter the kingdom of heaven—those who love poverty, those who endure it, and also those who offer comfort to the poor—how are we to explain the fact that the kingdom in which all should share is promised only to those who embrace voluntary poverty, who alone are judged to be 'poor in spirit'? [To understand] this, we must make a distinction: it is not said

*Margin:*
Is 48:10
1 Tm 6:17
1 Tm 6:19

of them, 'They *shall* enter the kingdom of heaven', but what seems to be something better: 'Theirs *is* the kingdom of heaven'. For since all who are blessed by God shall be blessed* and shall receive the kingdom of heaven which was prepared for them from the foundation of the world,* so we certainly believe that all of them will enter the kingdom of heaven. Nevertheless, there are some of whom it is specifically said, 'For such is the kingdom of heaven'.*

Gn 27:33

Mt 25:34

Mt 19:14

There is also another [point] which may strike us: whereas the other promises which form this series in the gospel³ are deferred for the future, this promise is not deferred by any delay at all. It is presented instead as if it had already happened, and it appears as the attainment of a present favor rather than the expectation of a future reward. The same formula is also applied to those who suffer persecution for righteousness' sake. In both cases the kingdom of heaven is stated to *be* theirs, as if there had been no postponement, no hindrance, and no delay, and the reward had already been given. The meek, however, are not yet told that they do possess the earth; they are told that they *shall* possess the earth. And [similarly] the merciful *shall* obtain mercy; those that mourn *shall* be comforted; those that hunger for righteousness *shall* be satisfied; the peacemakers *shall* be called the children of God; and the pure in heart *shall* see God. In all these cases, [the reference] is to the future, and it seems that we should seek some reason for this distinction. [The reason], perhaps, is that the two [forms of] righteousness whose reward is not postponed—the first, that is, and the last⁴—pertain to the perfect, to those who are tested in the furnace of poverty* or the fire of persecution as silver is tested* and smelted until it

Is 48:10
Ps 65:10[66:9]

becomes pure.⁵ It is these who build on a foundation of gold and silver and precious stones* and who, in departing this [life], do not carry with them either wood or hay or stubble* which burn up in them. As soon as they have gone from here, they fly together to heaven and suffer no delay in [entering] the kingdom, since theirs is the kingdom of heaven. By these virtues, those which are weak among the other virtues are purified (for all our righteous deeds are as the rag of a menstruous woman*), and it is clear that without them any good people we come across build to a certain extent on a foundation of wood, hay, and stubble. If they are to be saved, it is essential that these burn up in them — [and saved they will be], but only as through fire.* And even the pure in heart, those to whom is promised the vision of God, even they are also still in need of purification, for who can boast of having a chaste heart?

## OF THE [DIFFERENT FORMS OF] RIGHTEOUSNESS OF THE MARTYRS

There are two kinds of martyr, one in the flesh and the other in the spirit. It can be seen that they find their fulfillment in these two [different forms] of righteousness, and since all the just must suffer for Christ either in the flesh or in the spirit so as to acquire the glory of perfection, [it follows that] the perfection of the other virtues, when they too have reached their fulfillment, is to be justly attributed to these [two forms of suffering], since it is through them that they are perfected.

We will better understand who the poor in spirit are if we distinguish between two sorts of spirits, and we are given a chance to understand this more easily by the prophet, who says, 'The Lord is near to them that are of a contrite heart, and the humble in spirit shall be saved,'[6]\* and by the Apostle, who says, 'We have not received the spirit of this world, but the spirit which is of God'.\* By the spirit of this world it is not unreasonable to understand the prince of this world, he of whom the same Apostle spoke elsewhere 'When you were dead through the offences and sins in which you once walked, following the course of this world, following the prince of the power of the air, the spirit that is now at work in the children of unbelief.'\*

Cf. Ps 33:19 [34:18]

1 Co 2:12

Eph 2:1–2

When the spirit of this world breathes on the spirit of man, the latter is immediately puffed up and assimilated to the spirit which breathed upon it; for this reason, it can also be called the spirit of this world, for it lusts after the things of the world. This spirit is proud and vain, presumptuous, ambitious, always concerned with high things and despising those which are humble.\* But in the case of those who are led by the spirit of God,\* the more this spirit breathes on them, the less they are puffed up and the more they are humbled. Like the poor in spirit, they are not concerned with high things but are in accord with the humble.\*

Rm 12:16
Rm 18:14

Rm 12:16

The virtue of the poor in spirit, therefore, should be thought of both as a lack of spirit and an abundance of spirit. The less one has of his own spirit, the more the spirit of God abounds in him; and the greater the lack of his own spirit, the more abundant is his progress with regard to the spirit of God. If, then, we ask to which spirit [the expression] 'poor in spirit' refers, we see that it is more accurately understood of the spirit of God,[7] for it is this which makes poor and makes rich—which humbles, that is,[8] and which exalts.* Those he makes poorer he also makes richer,[9] and those [he makes] more humble, he makes more exalted—not according to the eminence of pride but according to the pinnacle of perfection.

Some, however, may think that the reason we say 'Blessed are the poor in spirit' is because [the poor] are deprived of spirit, as if they had but little spirit or were lacking in it—their own [spirit], that is, or [the spirit] of this world—just as those who have no material substance are spoken of as poor in material goods. This is a reasonable idea, and we do not object to it, but we can interpret it in such a way that it comes back to almost the same theory as that which [we put forward] above. Nevertheless, the first theory seems to be preferable, for I think that it is better to speak of the humble in spirit and the poor in spirit for the same reason. The humble in spirit are not described in this way because of deprivation, but because of possession, because of the spirit[10] they possess, that is, and not because of the spirit they lack. Those who make progress with regard to the spirit of God are lacking in their own spirit, and it is to them that the prophet refers when he says to the Lord, 'You will take away their spirit, and they will lack it and will return to their dust. You will send forth your spirit, and they will be created'.* When the north wind blows, there are no southern breezes; while the northern blast persists, there are no gentle sighs from the south.[11] This is why [Scripture] says: 'Arise, O north wind, and come, O south wind'.*

### Of the Human Spirit

There are three ways in which the human spirit becomes swollen and grandiose in itself, and there

are equally three ways in which it diminishes itself
and reduces this swelling. It becomes swollen by
vain opinion, vain hope, and vain cupidity, by all of
these three vanities. To be swollen and puffed up
is vanity, and whoever is swollen up is void and
empty* he is as full of nothing as he is full of the
wind of pride!

Gn 1:2

### Of False Opinion

There are three ways in which a person can be
swollen with vain opinion or, in other words, with
false opinion. Trusting[12] in himself through his
pride of spirit, he sometimes invents false [theories]
about God, sometimes feels pride in himself, and
sometimes finds occasion for dubious suspicions or
evil thoughts with regard to his neighbor.

To entertain a false opinion of God is exceedingly
dangerous. The things which are God's are secret
and concealed, and it is not permissible for them to
be tossed about by our untrustworthy human opinion. Nor are we permitted to believe anything
about God other than what he has deigned to reveal
about himself, since he himself is his own witness.
Insofar as his secrets were apprehended by the conviction of faith, he wanted us to have some knowledge of them, and since [the conviction of faith] is
confirmed by the testimony of the Scriptures and
founded on these grounds, it is settled and established
immovably. Holy Scripture is inspired by God.* In
it is prescribed for us the content of the faith,* and
whatever is sought beyond this will not be found.
Every human invention which opposes the pious
devotion of faith and its prescribed content should
be considered as presumption of spirit. But the only
thing which can cure presumption or swelling of
spirit is the humility of faith which blows away

2 Tm 3:16
2 Tm 1:13

whatever was inspired by the spirit of pride. [It is the latter] which is always opposed to God and which God, in giving his grace to the humble, always resists.\* 

It is humility of faith which claims first place in the virtue of the poor in spirit. It displays a worthy reverence for the words of God, putting in them its trust and finding in them its contentment. Anyone who possesses this perfectly does not trust in himself but trusts his spirit to God, so that God may find his spirit trustworthy.\* But God also trusts himself to him and entrusts to him, as to his faithful [subject], the mysteries of his intentions.[13] The spirit of man is formed by the spirit of God through the grace which the latter breathes into him, so that by putting his trust in the faithful God, who is faithful in all his words,\* he, too, may be faithful.

Then, when all impious and erroneous ideas have been eliminated from our heart by the spirit of God and we believe nothing false or unworthy about God, the Holy Spirit gives testimony to our spirit\* so that our spirit, for its part, might retain in itself nothing of itself. Instead, by renouncing itself and denying itself, it also comes to lack itself, lest it presume to entertain some opinion of God which [derives] from itself. Any opinion someone might have of God is sound if it [comes] from God, but not sound if it [comes] from man.[14] Lack of spirit, therefore, is good when it is lacking in its own opinions and dares [to say] of God nothing for which the spirit of God has not provided testimony in the words of God.[15] Thus, every time someone who is poor in spirit remembers God and finds his delight in this meditation, let him say, 'I remembered God, and I was delighted, and I became lacking in my spirit'.\*

## Of Vain Opinion

A person feels pride in himself when he attributes to himself the good things he has or appears to have, and when, being great in his own eyes, he supposes himself greater than he is and able to do more than he can. In the very same way, he feels pride in himself when he judges himself undeserving of the evils he suffers, or when he pretends not to have done the evil deeds he commits or excuses them or even thinks they should be praised and praises them himself.

He swells up with proud opinion against his neighbor when, in anger and because of his anger, he blames or condemns the evil deeds of the latter more severely [than they deserve] or when, through jealousy, he belittles his good deeds and so diminishes them. But just as the swelling of the spirit which results from [a false] judgement of oneself or one's neighbor is evil, so the lack of both of these swellings of the spirit is worthy of praise, and [it is this praise] which belongs to those who, through humility of spirit, are pleasing to God and displeasing to themselves.

## Of Vain Hope

The spirit of man swells up with vain hope when he is too sure of his own righteousness and puts great hope in the expectation of a divine reward which is more than his merits deserve. The spirit of man should lack this presumptuous hope in the expectation of a divine reward,[16] not from the violence of utter despair, nor from the timidity which comes from being distressed and afraid, but from the moderation of a hope which is mingled and tempered with fear. Hope without fear is a vain security; fear without hope is a dangerous[17] desolation. But if someone is so consumed with the sorrow which stems from fear that he despairs of salvation, if he judges himself worthy of punishment and unworthy of mercy, if he says, 'My iniquity is too great for me to deserve pardon',* then if such a person is proud, we may ask what sort of pride it is that appears to thrust his spirit[18] down into the lowest depths, not raise it up into the heights. And here is something else to convince us that we cannot[19] call him proud: [Scripture] says: 'Pride is the beginning of all sin'.*

A similar question arises with regard to timidity of spirit, of which the prophet says, 'I waited for him who saved me from timidity of spirit and from the storm'.* For since despair and timidity of spirit seem to be a corruption of humility—too great an abasement and an excessive humiliation—we may be surprised that what appears to be the opposite of pride pertains to pride. Or, if it does not pertain to it, then we may be equally surprised at how we can say that [pride] is the beginning of all sin. But since we do not propose to air these questions here, we will leave others to inquire as to whether such despair or timidity of spirit pertains to the sin of pride, or whether only to the punishment which pride deserves. We are concerned with the poor in spirit, and to them pertain neither the proud nor those who are timid or despairing in spirit—although the timid in spirit and those that despair should be distinguished from the proud.

### Of Vain Hope and Pride

A person who is proud and swollen up with vain hope is one who puts his trust in himself—in his power, that is, or his wisdom, or his eloquence, or his worldly substance, or his reputation, or his nobility, or the favor of men, or in some other grounds—rather than in God alone. He alone can deliver him in times of trouble, and he does not abandon those who put their hope in him. It is to him that the prophet says, 'O Lord of hosts, blessed is the man that trusts in you',* and 'O Lord, my hope from my youth',* and again, 'God of my help, my hope is in God'.* The hope which is humbly placed in God does not disappoint us,* for God is truth and deceives no one, but cursed be the man that trusts in man and relies upon the flesh!²⁰ Sometimes, when a person is able to deliver [someone from something], he does not want to do so; and sometimes, when he wants to, he cannot do it. But in God's case, just as he is always able, so too he always wills to save those who put their hope in him and not in themselves, those whose pride does not lead them to have presumptuous ideas either about God or about themselves. The prophet says, 'Those that trust in their own strength and glory in the multitude of their riches, no brother can redeem'.* See how those that trust in themselves and have presumptuous ideas about themselves are separated from the grace of redemption!

Ps 83[84]:13
Ps 70:5[71:4]
Ps 61[62]:8
Rm 5:5

Ps 48:7[49:6–7]

### Of Good and Evil Security²¹

There are some who find security in a vain hope, who heap sin upon sin and say, 'The mercies of the Lord are many'.* They delude themselves with regard to God's mercy, and the prouder they are, the more secure they feel, just as if they really had put their hope in [his mercy]. True security, however, is the fear of God, and it is this fear which makes [the soul] secure rather than swollen. Those who do not have it and who promise themselves the

1 Ch 21:13

mercy of God deceive themselves, and they will be disappointed in their expectation.* His mercy is promised to those who fear God and who cease from sin, not to those who feel secure in sinning.

Let us consult the testimony of the Scriptures on this matter. The prophet says, 'According to the height of the heaven above the earth, so he has strengthened his mercy towards them that fear him',* and 'As a father has compassion on his children, so the Lord has compassion on them that fear him'.* And in another place, 'His salvation is near to them that fear him'.* And the most blessed Mother of mercy says, 'His mercy is from generation to generation upon them that fear him'.*

See how the fear of God is conjoined with the mercy of God, so that we should not hope for the mercy of God without the fear of God. Just as fear without hope is dangerous and brings about despair, hope without fear is ruinous and leads to obstinacy. This is why it is written in the Law [of Moses]: 'You shall take neither the lower nor the upper mill-stone as a pledge'.* The upper millstone is hope and the lower, fear. Between the two is ground up everything we eat to keep us healthy. But one [stone] is useless without the other, and if one is taken as a pledge, the other on its own is of no value either to him that gives or to him that takes it. A pledge is taken as security because it makes us secure, and the Apostle informs us of the nature of this pledge when he says, 'It is God who has anointed us and put his seal upon us and given us the pledge of the Spirit in our hearts'.* This [he says] to the Corinthians. To the Ephesians [he says], 'You were sealed with the Holy Spirit of promise who is the pledge of our inheritance'.* The pledge, therefore, is the Holy Spirit who gives us true security in the conjoining of fear and holy hope. Without fear there is only a vain security; without hope there is no security at all. But in both of these together lies true security.

Hope should be restrained by the fear of God. In this way, the swelling of its presumptuousness is diminished, and it neither reduces itself to nothing in its vanity nor is it disappointed in its expectation.* It follows from this that the spirit of man advances to God by praying and hoping when he lacks a presumptuous hope in himself and can say with the prophet, 'I cried to the Lord with my voice; with my voice I made supplication to the Lord. In his sight I pour out my prayer, and before him I declare my trouble, for my spirit is lacking',* and again, 'Hear me speedily, O Lord, my spirit is lacking'.*

When the spirit of man is lacking because of his fear of God, he brooks no delay in God's granting [his prayer], but demands that it be granted speedily. Such a person has no hope in himself, or in his own power, or in his wisdom, or in his ability or astuteness, or in any of his faculties, but [his hope is] in God alone and in the things which are God's, simply because they *are* God's.

After God, we should put our hope in the good things we do—in faith, for example, or in works of righteousness and mercy—[but only] because they come from God. [In this way], even though these are our own good deeds, we remove from ourselves any confidence in ourselves and hold it out to him whose gifts they are. For with regard to these gifts of God, anyone who finds in himself the trust he should put in God offers an insult to God, and because the source on which we call for help is normally the source from which we hope for it,

Ps 118[119]:116

Ps 141:2-4[142:1-3]
Ps 142[143]:7

whoever hopes for help from himself calls on himself rather than on God. Such a person, therefore, cannot yet say, 'Hear me speedily, O Lord, my spirit is lacking'.*

## OF CUPIDITY OR PRIDE

Vain cupidity distends the soul in two ways: by the love of owning[22] or having what it actually possesses and by the desire to possess what it does not have. Desire itself, however, is really love, for if we desire [something], there is a certain way in which we love it. Just as charity is the love of God, so cupidity is the love of the world. Cupidity seeks its own [interests],* not those of Jesus Christ. Sometimes it seeks them through a love of worldly possessions, sometimes through the love of deceitful and transient sensual pleasures, sometimes through the love of domination, sometimes through the love of honor and ambition, and sometimes through the love of admiration, favor, and praise. These are the things which cupidity, in its pride, seeks insatiably in opposition to God, and these, too, are the things which charity, with its own sort of pride (so to speak), nobly despises for God's sake. For charity—if we may put it thus—does have its pride,[23] [but it is a pride] which nobly despises pride itself and anything which is proudly [arrayed] against God. This is why the apostles were told, 'You shall eat the riches of the nations, and you shall pride yourselves in their glory'.[24]*

To despise God for the sake of the things we should despise and to love the things we should despise more than God is a vile and shameworthy pride. But to despise the glory of the world for the sake of God is a noble pride. Yet it is more noble

## Tractate IX / I

still if we are shameless in despising shame itself for the sake of Christ, who had joy set before him but endured the cross and despised its shame.* It is better to be ashamed of the dignities and honors of this world than of the cross of Christ or the poverty of Christ or the humility of Christ. 'Whoever is ashamed of me and of my words', he says, 'of him will the Son of Man be ashamed when he comes in his majesty and [the majesty] of the Father and of the holy angels.'* 'The servant is not greater than his Lord.'* We should not be ashamed to do for Christ what he was not ashamed to do for us. Whoever is restrained by shame from imitating or emulating the humility of Christ still possesses something of his own spirit. This sort of shame is vain, and the further it retreats from humility, the nearer it comes to pride.

 We should judge holy poverty more from humility of soul than from a meagre inheritance. We should call the poor in spirit those who do not have big ideas rather than those who have little wealth. Those who feel proud and have proud thoughts[25] — even if they are poor in material things — belong less to the poor in spirit than those who actually have such things, but who [act] as if they did not have them.*

 Holy poverty, therefore, despises the world and worldly things. It renounces what it has, what it will have, and the very desire to have them. It restrains itself from every presumption of spirit and is so pleasing to God that he says, 'Blessed are the poor in spirit, for theirs is the kingdom of heaven'. Whoever is poor is so loved and cherished by God that he can boast of God's care for him and say, 'I am a beggar and a pauper. The Lord takes care of me.'* Though all honors and all riches were bestowed upon us,

Heb 12:2

Lk 9:26
Jn 13:16

1 Co 7:30

Ps 39:18[40:20]

what can equal this honor? Who dares to have such confidence in his wealth as to say, 'I have vast riches and all that I want. The Lord takes care of me'? The rich man is sufficient to himself, and since he seems to want for nothing, he does not need the Lord to take care of him.

The voice of the poor and the glory of the poor is this: 'Incline your ear, O Lord, and hear me, for I am needy and poor'.* If a poor man comes up to someone vastly rich and powerful and says, 'Incline your ear and hear me', who among his entourage will put up with this in patience? Will they not all drive him away with boos and hisses? Will he not be regarded as beneath contempt when the great man looks at him in his pride? Will he not order him thrown out of his house and expelled with insults? Who dares say to his lord, 'Incline your ear'? Who, then, dares[26] say it to the Lord of Lords?* Who but the poor and the poor in spirit? This is his cry: 'Give joy to the soul of your servant, O Lord, for to you I have lifted up my soul'.* If his mind is set on earthly things and not on those above,* he cannot say, 'To you, O Lord, I have lifted up my soul'. It is the poor in spirit, therefore, who lift up their soul to God. They do not degrade themselves with worldly things,[27] but desire and yearn and burn for those which are celestial. In [God] their life is hid with Christ;* on him [are fixed] their eyes and their love;[28] in him is their heart and their treasure.*

O happy poverty, whose reward is to be not only in the kingdom of heaven, but the very kingdom of heaven itself! O happy poverty, honored by God, though despised by the world! 'For he will spare the poor and the needy and will save the souls of the poor. Their names will be honorable in his sight.'*

## Tractate IX / I

O unhappy riches, to be changed for eternal need! O miserable happiness, to be paid for with eternal misfortune! When the rich man is buried in hell and the poor man rests in Abraham's bosom\* there will be no doubt as to their different condition! The rich man is tormented, burning and thirsty, and since he gave no comfort to the poor, he receives no comfort from the poor. He received his good things in his lifetime.\*

Lk 16:22–23

Lk 16:25

Yet the rich should not despair! They should consider that Abraham himself was a rich man, and it was in his bosom that Lazarus rested. But they should consider Abraham in such a way that they possess their riches as Abraham did. They should possess them with just cause; they should possess them to use them lawfully; they should possess them to show the grace of hospitality, as Abraham did. Finally, they should possess them to share them with the poor, not to keep for themselves, for it is [the poor] who will receive them into everlasting habitations.\* The salvation of the rich is the glory of the poor, for blessed are the poor in spirit,
for theirs is the kingdom
of heaven.

Lk 16:9

## NOTES TO TRACTATE IX / I

1. Title as in PL 483–484. There is no doubt that this long tractate comprises four separate sermons which form a related series. The first of them discusses the poor in spirit (the first beatitude); the second, the meek (the third beatitude); the third, those that mourn (the second beatitude); and the fourth, those that hunger and thirst after righteousness (the fourth beatitude). The juxtaposition of these four sermons to form one long tractate is obviously artificial, and does not occur in all the manuscripts (for further details, see the article by P. Guébin cited in Tr. I.n. 1). In our translation, therefore, we have presented them as four separate discourses. Whether Baldwin ever completed the series by speaking on the four remaining beatitudes is unknown. Considering the nature and content of all four discourses, there can be little doubt that they were delivered to a monastic congregation at the abbey of Ford.
2. Lit. 'according to the merits of the just and their righteousnesses' (*justificationes*).
3. Baldwin is referring to the series of the eight Beatitudes.
4. I.e. the righteousness which comes from the first beatitude (Mt 5:1) and that which comes from the last (Mt 5:10).
5. Not, as Thomas translates (38/65), 'they are completely consumed'. Baldwin is echoing Is 1:25: 'I will smelt away your dross until you become pure'.
6. Ps 33:19[34:18] with the Vulgate *salvabit* changed to *salvabuntur*. Thomas's text (38/66) reads *salvabit* by mistake.
7. A line of typescript has been accidentally omitted in Thomas's text: . . .*pronuntiantur (PL 486B: pronuntientur) pauperes dum spiritum Dei* should read . . .*pronuntiantur pauperes spiritu, rectius videtur intelligi secun / dum spiritum Dei* (Thomas 38/68).
8. *Id est* is omitted in PL 486B.
9. Thomas (38/69 n. 1) compares William of St Thierry, Cant PL 180, 510B (SC 82, 238; CF 6, 86): "The Spirit of wisdom, before enriching a man, is wont to make him poor of spirit; and before uplifting him, to humble him, that he may support the height of true perfection upon the foundation of true humility". The idea is certainly similar, but we cannot say more than that.
10. *Spiritum* should be added to Thomas's text (38/70), as in PL 486D.
11. The sudden appearance of this meteorological allegory may be a little startling to the modern reader. By the two winds, Baldwin means the two spirits—that of man and that of God—and is pointing out that they cannot both coexist at the same time in the same place. *Auster*, the south wind, as an allegory of the Holy Spirit is not uncommon in writings of the later patristic and medieval periods, and *aquilo*, the north wind, as an allegory of the spirit of man, although much rarer, is not without example.
12. The verb is *credere*, which means 'trust in' as well as 'believe'. See further Tr. 1, n. 27.
13. We may compare Baldwin's comments at the beginning of his first tractate. See Tr. 1, n. 5.
14. Here I have translated *pius* as 'sound'.
15. I.e. in Scripture.

16. There is an omission in Thomas's text (38/78). After . . . *supernae retributionis*, add *spem extendit*. *A praesumptione spei in exspectatione supernae retributionis.*
17. Thomas (38/78) reads *periculosae*; PL 488B has *perversae*.
18. 'Spirit' is *mens*.
19. PL 488B omits *non* in *ne non dicatur*.
20. The final phrase of Jr 17:5 reads literally: 'and makes flesh his arm' (i.e. his support).
21. We may compare with this section Baldwin's discussion of vain security in CF 604C-D.
22. Or 'using', or 'controlling', or even 'enjoying': the verb is *uti*.
23. Thomas (38/91 n. 1) compares William of St Thierry, Contemp VII. 15 (PL 184: 375D; SCh 61 *bis*: 100; CF 3:56): 'O the joy, the glory, the riches, the pride of it! For even wisdom has its own sort of pride when it says "Riches and honor are with me, proud strength and righteousness" (Pr 8:18)'. Baldwin, however, is talking about charity, not wisdom, even though they are closely related.
24. This is Is 61:6, but it is used as the canticle in the Third Nocturn of Vigils on feasts of the Apostles (See Thomas 38/91, n. 2).
25. PL 491A omits *superbe sapiunt et* after *nam qui*.
26. For *audiat* in Thomas (38/94) read *audeat* with PL 491C.
27. Lit. 'who do not lower their heart into the depths'.
28. Cf. Tr. VIII, n. 15.

# TRACTATE IX/II
# ON THE MEEK[1]

*Blessed are the meek, for they shall possess the earth.** — Mt 5:4

THE PROMISES OF GOD are varied and diversified, depending upon the merits of the just and the different ways in which they manifest their righteousness. For each [form of] righteousness, there is an appropriate recompense, and each separate virtue has its own particular praise and its own particular reward according to the dignity of its rank and its natural qualities.[2] The promise to the meek is that they shall possess the earth. The virtue of the meek is gentleness and docility,[3] so what the prophet says is true, 'The gentle shall inherit the earth'. If the meek are blessed, there is no doubt that the gentle are also blessed. Let those that are gentle hear this and rejoice!* Let them hear that they are blessed now—or will be so—and let them hear the reason for their blessedness: 'They shall possess the earth'. — Ps 36:29[37:30]; Ps 33:3[34:2]

There are some who fight and dispute for the earth, pitiless men who oppress and dominate the meek. Why are they not blessed if they possess the earth? [We should ask] rather in what possible way they can be blessed, if [one day] the earth will devour them! O earth, earth, earth,* how vainly do the sons of men love you! From the earth they are taken;* by the earth they are consumed; and what — Jr 22:29; Gn 3:19

are they themselves but earth? O sons of men, how long will you be dull of heart? Why do you love the vanity* of this world, where there is nothing but concupiscence of the flesh, concupiscence of the eyes, and the pride of life!* You that are born of earth, you sons of men,* know that no inheritance remains for us on earth, save only the earthly lump of our body, and that itself is earth from earth! (Ps 4:3; 1 Jn 2:16; Ps 48:3[49:2])

What, then, is the meaning of this promise, 'Blessed are the meek, for they shall possess the earth'? What does God mean by promising the earth to the meek when he promises to others the kingdom of heaven? 'Blessed are the poor in spirit, for theirs is the kingdom of heaven.'* Why does he who teaches us to despise the earth promise the earth? Is it not heaven that is promised to all the just and to sinners who do penance? This is why it is written, 'Do penance, for the kingdom of heaven is at hand'.* Does he not say to all those gathered on the right hand at the end [of the world], 'Come, you blessed of my Father, possess the kingdom prepared for you from the foundation of the world'?* Is the virtue of the meek so indifferent and of such little worth that its reward should be established [only] on earth? Let us listen instead to how much it is praised by the Lord, who in himself provided us with a guiding example of gentleness: 'Learn from me, for I am meek and humble of heart, and you will find rest for your souls.'* And he shows us where his Spirit may rest when he says, 'On whom shall my Spirit rest, but on him who is humble and peaceful and who trembles at my words?'⁴* If, then, the Spirit of God rests upon the gentle so that they might also rest in him and find rest for their souls, we are constrained more and (Mt 5:3; Mt 3:2, 4:17; Mt 25:34; Mt 11:29; Is 66:2(OL)) more to ask why it is that the Lord—who defends the gentle of the earth,* who guides the gentle in judgement and teaches the gentle his ways,* who arises in judgement to save all the gentle of the earth*—promises [only] the earth to [those that show] this virtue which is so much praised and which deserves so much.

Is 11:4
Ps 24:9[25:8]
Ps 75:10[76:9]

### THAT WE SHOULD DEPART FROM UR OF THE CHALDEANS

The Lord made promises to Abraham* and promised him the earth, saying, 'To you will I give the land⁵ of Canaan, the lot of your inheritance.'* And to lead him into this land which he had promised him he first led him out of the land in which he had made his dwelling, saying, 'Go forth from your country, and come into the land which I will show you'.* He led him out of the land of the Chaldeans, out of the place of his birth. By this example, we too are instructed to leave Ur of the Chaldeans, [to leave], that is, the fire of our vices, the place of our captivity. For it is our flesh, conceived in sin and subject to sin, which is the land of the Chaldeans and the place of our birth.

Cf. Ga 3:16
Ps 104[105]:11
Gn 12:1

Furthermore, since we belong to Christ, we are the descendants of Abraham, for those that are [his children] in spirit are held to be his true descendants, children of the promise, together with Isaac who was born of the promise.* When the Canaanites had been cast out from the promised land by the children of Israel, Abraham—in his descendants—dwelt there. But it was not by their own sword that [the Israelites] took possession of the land;* it was the Lord who cast out the pagans before them, divided and distributed their land for them by lot,

Rm 9:7–9

Ps 43:4[44:3]

and settled the tribes of Israel in their tents.* Ps 77:54-55[78:56]

OF THE THREEFOLD CONDITION OF OUR FLESH

The land of the Chaldeans, the land of Canaan, and the promised land denote the threefold condition of our flesh. Before our decision to be converted,[6] our flesh is the land of the Chaldeans which Abraham was commanded to leave. At the beginning of our conversion, when we have not yet subjugated our vices, it is the land of Canaan and still in the possession of the Canaanites, on whom the children of Israel have declared war. It is the promised land, possessed by the children of Israel, when we have expelled our vices and our flesh has been chastened by ascetic practices,[7] so chastened that sin does not reign in our mortal body.* The flesh has [then] been reduced to servitude and subjected to the spirit, not yielding its members to iniquity as instruments of iniquity, but yielding its members to holiness as instruments of righteousness.* The flesh is then the land of Canaan as it once was and is no longer possessed by the Canaanites. Its carnal desires have been expelled, and it is cleansed and possessed by the children of Israel. We still find a few scattered Canaanites dwelling there, but they are not in control, for it is possible [for us] to restrain fleshly inclinations[8] and refuse them our consent. This land, the former land of Canaan, is very different from the land of the Chaldeans. The Chaldeans remain in their land and are not cast out by the descendants of Abraham; instead, it is Abraham who is commanded to depart. There are some who are told, 'You shall die in your sin'.* They are the dwellers in the land of the Chaldeans, and from these Abraham departed

Rm 6:12

Rom 6:13

Jn 8:21

to cast out the Canaanites and possess the land flowing with milk and honey.

Consider, then, whether this is the land whose possession is promised to the meek. The virtue of the meek is gentleness and docility. But note that one's docility with regard to oneself is one thing, with regard to one's neighbor another, and with regard to God, something else again. Let us first consider the first mentioned.

### Of One's Gentleness and Docility with regard to Oneself

There are these three things in man: flesh, will, and reason; but for the moment we will talk about the flesh. The desires [of the flesh] are contrary to the spirit,* and to it belong not only the vices of the flesh but also the vices of the soul, [vices] like those which the Apostle describes, 'The works of the flesh are plain: immorality, impurity, immodesty, luxury, idolatry, sorcery, enmity, strife, jealousy, anger, quarrels, dissension, schism, envy, murder, drunkenness, carousing, and such like.'* You see how many vices of the soul are listed here—[vices] such as anger and envy—and how many vices of the flesh? Yet he calls all of them works of the flesh, and there can be no doubt that [he is referring to] that flesh whose desires are contrary to the spirit. Flesh, therefore, refers here to those inner cravings of ours in which reason plays no part,⁹ and midway between this flesh and reason, we find the will. [Will] is truly in the middle when it is in accord with reason, when reason is above it and commands it, and the flesh is below it and serves it. But if it is in accord with the flesh and not in accord with reason,

Ga 5:17

Ga 5:19-21

it is not then in command of the flesh but under [the control] of the flesh, and, contrary to custom, the mistress serves the maid in a shameful and wretched servitude. And when the flesh and the will agree among themselves but disagree with reason, the will refuses the yoke of obedience, like something wild and untamed, and is neither tamed by authority, quietened by counsel, nor mellowed by blandishments. Like a brash and contentious woman, it fights against reason, sometimes quarrelling, at other times grumbling, and in the house wherein she dwells there is no peace.

Since someone who walks in the way of the flesh and serves the passions of the flesh is ruled by sin in his mortal body, and since the kingdom of sin subscribes to the law of sin, so that the servant of sin is subject to it, how can we say that such a person possesses the earth of his body or [the land] of his heart? It is the earth, surely, which possesses him, for he has no freedom by which he might free himself or unfetter himself or shake off the things which burden and oppress him. He is swallowed up by the earth; he is like a person buried in the earth, among those who sleep in the sepulchers whom God remembers no more* — unless he who makes the earth tremble* should turn his gaze upon them.

Ps 87:5[88:4]
Ps 103:33[104:32]

If reason is abandoned by will and left alone, what can it do alone? 'Woe to him who is alone.'* But if the earth[10] is moved at the presence of the Lord* so that the will is aroused and is able to raise itself again, then when it begins to be in accord with reason, it is restored to its rank, its freedom, and its peace, and thereby to itself. It is restored to its rank when it is subjected to that which is superior to it and preferred to what is inferior. Then, through

Qo 4:10

Ps 113[114]:7

grace, it finds itself back in the place from which it willingly withdrew through sin. It is restored to freedom when on the one hand it accepts obedience [to reason] and is willing to show it and on the other imposes obedience [on the flesh] and then demands it as if it were law. [In this case], what [the will] does is not in accordance with the flesh, but what the flesh does is in accordance with [the will]; [the latter] forces the members [of the flesh] to be obedient to it in the service of pious devotion and salvation, in works of righteousness and mercy, and in everything which the authority of reason—with the agreement of the will—demands be done or endured and which we perform or achieve or accomplish.

If our members begin to act in accordance with their own [nature], then the will—with the agreement of reason—uses its freedom to oppose them so that they get nowhere. It orders them to find rest in themselves and be at peace.[11] It is now that the earth [of the flesh] begins to be possessed, for the humble soul is quiet, meek, and gentle. It agrees to be possessed by reason, so that [reason, in its turn] might possess the earth [of the flesh] and have it in its keeping. This possession of the earth is a sort of reward of gentleness and docility, and those who become gentle in the way we have described begin to be restored both to peace and to themselves and to be blessed in their peace, since peace is for people of good will.\*

Lk 2:14

At first, man is not in accord with reason. He retreats, as it were, from himself and begins to be robbed of the possession of his own land. [He begins] to be in exile within himself, just as if he were outside himself, in a strange land, in a land of forgetfulness, in the region of unlikeness.[12] But when he returns to his heart after his transgression,* he then finds himself near to himself, and he himself is returned to himself lest he be absent from himself. Then, just as in the Year of Jubilee, his possession is restored to him* so that he may rest under his own vine and under his own fig-tree* and possess the earth in peace, since he is meek.

Is 46:8

Lv 25:13
1 M 14:12

'Blessed are the meek, for they shall possess the land'. This is the land of promise, once the land of Canaan, which God promised to Abraham while he was still living in the land of the Chaldeans, in a strange land, where neither the Lord's song was sung nor the hymn of the songs of Sion.* This is the holy land, and here, when its senses and affections are set on spiritual things,¹³ the seed of Abraham dwells. Here, too,¹⁴ is the temple of the Lord, where God is adored and worshipped. The Apostle, therefore, says, 'Do you not know that your bodies are the temple of the Holy Spirit?'* and 'The temple of God – which you are – is holy'.*

Ps 136[137]:4

1 Co 6:15, 19
1 Co 3:17

The earth [of the flesh, however], is still not fully possessed, for we do not yet find in our will the perfection of gentleness and docility. Sometimes we struggle against reason, and sometimes the flesh struggles against us. The sort of things we do which are contrary to reason are the sort of things we experience through the flesh. If, however, the will is only partly subject to reason, then the flesh is only partly subject to [the will], and in part, therefore, it rails at it and contradicts it. These undisciplined movements of our heart or body are like the barking of dogs which annoy passersby more by their bark than by their bite. Their barks are certainly annoying and suspect, but it is their bites which cause [the real] damage. Their barks serve to make us watchful and cautious, for they do not always bark *at* us but sometimes bark *for* us. Things are arranged by God in this way so that we may walk cautiously and be roused to vigilance, lest some day, through a sense of false security, we fall asleep in death.\*

If dogs are barking round a house, is this not an indication that we do not possess the house in peace?\* And if there is a certain contrariness in our flesh, something contrary not only to reason but also to will, is this not an indication that we do not possess the earth [of our flesh]? Or, to be more accurate, we do possess it, but only to the extent possible for us at that particular moment; we do not yet [possess it] entirely, which is what we would like.

[Just as there are robbers on earth who rouse our dogs to barking,] so there are also robbers to be found in the kingdom of heaven, but they are arrested and either hanged or condemned to various tortures, so that through judgement and righteousness the kingdom is established in peace. Without righteousness there is no peace in the kingdom, no peace in the home, no peace in our heart, no peace in our flesh, no peace in our land. It is the righteous who shall inherit the land.\* If the land is possessed in righteousness, it is also possessed in peace, but without righteousness it is not possessed in peace. This is why it is written, 'Righteousness and peace have kissed'.\* We do not yet possess the land entirely (although we do possess it in a certain way), but we will possess it entirely when all the corruption of the flesh has been consumed by the glory of resurrection and when there will be no struggle of the will with the reason, nor of the flesh with the will, on any matter at all. Then the whole race of Canaan will have been driven from the land and the whole curse of Canaan taken from us. Canaan is cursed and subjected to servitude,* but creation itself will be freed from the servitude of corruption [and pass] into the freedom of the glory of the children of God.* Then shall the gentle inherit the land and delight in abundance of peace,* and those who now put their hope in the Lord and do good will dwell in that land and be fed with its riches.* That land will certainly be vastly rich and opulent, flowing with milk and honey,* for as a reward for past obedience, evil will have no place therein.

Gn 9:25

Rm 8:21
Ps 36[37]:11

Ps 36[37]:3

Ex 13:5

The virtue of docility, therefore, of a person with regard to himself consists of patience and obedience: first of the will to the reason and then of the flesh to the will. Sometimes reason imposes on the docile will certain hardships which it must endure, and [the will, in turn, imposes these] on the docile and conquered flesh. It is then that we have the virtue of patience, since these [hardships] are endured patiently.[15] And sometimes, [reason] enjoins certain good deeds which must be done, and it is then that we have the virtue of obedience, since these must be accomplished with humility. The reward of patience, therefore, (which is the milk of consolation) is being immune from evil, and the reward of obedience (which is honey) is the plenitude of all good.

## Of One's Gentleness and Docility with regard to One's Neighbor

'Blessed are the meek, for they shall possess the land.' The land promised to the meek is unquestionably the promised land, but it seems that the promised land can be understood symbolically in four ways. The first [way] relates to the whole number of the faithful, and here the promised land is the whole multitude of the faithful, united throughout the whole world in the righteousness of faith and obedience—[the virtues] in which Abraham pleased God*—and who will be united at the end in the bosom of Abraham. According to the Apostle, therefore, it was promised to Abraham that he would be the heir of the world,* since he would be the father of many nations.*

Cf. Heb 11:8

Rm 4:13
Rm 4:17, Gn 17:5

Seen as the personal hope of every individual, the promised land, in each person, is the land of his heart and body which is given to everyone as his possession and which will be possessed in peace through gentleness and docility.

Thirdly, the promised land is the land of the living.* There we find the fellowship of the blessed, there no one dies, and there, too, lies that Jerusalem whose participation is in the Self-same.[16] The uncircumcised and the unclean shall not pass through it,* and the Canaanites do not dwell there. Malevolent spirits are excluded from it and have neither part nor lot in the land of the saints.* The possession of this land is promised to those who are gentle and docile, for it is by gentleness and docility that we become part of the blessed fellowship.

Ps 26:13[27:15]

Is 52:1

Ac 8:21

Every holy fellowship achieves stability through peace, but peace is not preserved without gentleness and docility. A restive beast in a team does not pull, but only causes a disturbance, and in just the same way someone who lacks gentleness and docility[17] in a community of good men disturbs the peace, breaks the bond of friendship, bursts the chains of fellowship, disparages his neighbour, and welcomes slanders against him. Sometimes he fights and sometimes disputes, sometimes he grumbles, and sometimes he judges others with suspicious and questionable thoughts. He is like a stubborn and untamed bullock* and refuses to be yoked. His mind is swift to anger, his eye to envy, and his tongue to insults. He does not live sociably, but often separates himself from the society of his fellows by his own personal peculiarities. He is a bane to himself and a disturbance to others, and by his example gives no help in the matter of their common salvation but only breaks up the unity. He is a bad companion who obstructs the work in which they are all involved.

Jr 31:18

But just as the virtue of docility is always a stranger to all these evils, so it is always a friend and companion of peace. The special characteristic of this virtue is that it neither offers nor returns an injury — in other words, that it neither injures anyone for no cause, nor does it seek revenge. It is neither an enemy nor an avenger.* Both of these, the enemy and the avenger, are enemies of God, and he will destroy them, so that out of the mouth of infants and sucklings, he may perfect praise because of his enemies.* Who are the infants and sucklings? Who but the little ones, the humble, the simple, the meek, the docile, the patient, and those who do not overcome good with evil but overcome evil with good.*

Ps 8:3[2]

Ibid.

Rm 12:21

An infant is one who utters no word and a suckling one who sucks milk.[18] But listen to an infant speaking: 'I set a guard upon my mouth when the sinner stood against me'.* If he is cursed, he does not curse [in return], and if he is beaten, he does not utter threats.* When he is injured, he is silent and says, 'I became like a man who does not hear, who has no reproofs in his mouth'.* And to the sucklings it is said, 'Put away all malice and all guile and insincerity and all slander. Like newborn rational infants,

Ps 38[39]:2

1 P 2:23

Ps 37:15[38:14]

long for the pure milk so that by it you may grow up to salvation.'¹⁹*

With these the Lord is well pleased, and he will exalt those that are gentle and save them.* The 'land of the living',²⁰ surely, is the place where the most blessed fellowship of the elect is promised to those who are gentle and docile, to those who are now living sociably in the fellowship of the good, harming none and being patient [with all] and preserving the unity of the spirit in the bond of peace.* The peaceful possession of this land where the blessed fellowship is strengthened with peace is a worthy reward for the gentle and docile, for without gentleness peace cannot be preserved. The prophet, therefore, says to God, 'Let there be peace in your virtue'.* Which virtue O Lord? That, surely, whose example you displayed in yourself, when you said, 'Learn from me, for I am meek and humble of heart'?* In gentleness and docility, therefore, peace comes into being, and [in it] peace is preserved, so that at first we may possess our souls in patience* and soon afterwards pass over into the kingdom of peace. There, eternal rest is prepared for those at rest in themselves, and the abundance of your towers, O Lord, is [reserved] for the little ones and the humble.*

If, then, we seek an abundance of milk and honey, let us hasten our steps to this land. We have heard that it is a region which abounds in milk and honey, for as a reward for harming no one in the past, evil has no place therein, and as a reward for past patience it is full of all good. The gentleness and docility of a man with regard to his neighbor, therefore, clearly consists in doing him no harm and in being patient [with him, if he harms you] The reward of doing him no harm (which is the milk) is being immune from evil, and the reward of being patient (which is the honey) is the abundance of good.

### Of One's Gentleness and Docility with regard to God

If we consider the promised land in its fourth sense and take it to mean Christ, who is the fulfilment of the promises, then it is obviously difficult to give any reply to those who ask in what way the race of Canaan dwelt in the land. What place can there be for evil where the fullness of grace is dwelling?* Conceived by the Holy Spirit of the Virgin Mary, Christ is separated from sinners and made higher than the heavens,* and as he was full of all grace, so he was free from all sin. Yet the devout[21] inquirer may perhaps find an honest and satisfactory answer [to this question] if he stops disputing with himself and turns his attention devoutly to the unity of the head and body of Christ and to the nature of our mortality in [the incarnate] Christ.

Cf. Jn 1:14

Heb 7:26

[Christ] wished to be our head so as to show more deeply the love[22] by which he united himself to us, [a love which binds us] so tightly that we are like his own members. By means of this ineffable unity he transforms us into himself and thus pleads our cause before the Father when he says, 'Why have you forsaken me? Far from my salvation are the words of my sins.'* He speaks of our sins as if they were his own, and although it is we who are accountable for them, it is not we whom he will call to account.[23] Our [sins] they certainly were and had nothing to do with him who had no knowledge of wickedness himself, but in order to reconcile us to God he felt compassion for a misfortune in which

Ps 21:2[22:1]

he had no part in order to reconcile us to God. It was for our sake that [God] made him to be sin who knew no sin, so that in him we might become the righteousness of God.* Christ redeemed us from the curse of the Law and was himself made a curse for us, for it is written, 'Cursed is the man who hangs on a tree'.* But the curse is now ended, for we know that Christ has been raised from the dead and will never die again, and death shall no more have dominion over him.*

We do not think of the promised land, therefore, as the land from Dan to Beersheba, from the great River Euphrates to the river of Egypt, from sea to sea, from the river to the ends of the earth.* But we understand that the promises made to Abraham are fulfilled in Christ, and we say with the prophet, 'The Lord is the portion of my inheritance and of my cup. It is you who will restore my inheritance to me. The lines have fallen for me in pleasant places, for I have a goodly inheritance. I will bless the Lord, who has given me understanding.'* Our inheritance and our portion, therefore, are in Christ, and according to the nature which he assumed for us as part of the divine plan,[24] it is there that we find the promised land, the land of which it is said, 'Lord, you have blessed your land',* and of which it is written, 'Mercy and truth have met so that glory may dwell in our land'.*

In order to give this land to the gentle, the Lord himself, the very one who sits upon the cherubim,* came in gentleness and docility sitting upon an ass,* a gentle and docile animal,[25] obedient and patient in everything. In this, God showed us and proposed for us an example of gentleness, so that we too, in obedience and patience, might carry Christ seated upon us, the gentle upon the gentle. But what an embarrassment for us and what a disgrace! A dumb beast reproves our foolishness,* and as our teacher of docility we are given an ass! [And why?] So that by a stupid animal we, who are more stupid than it, might be taught wisdom! Woe to us, for we have wandered so far astray that we have become mindless in our folly. And the reason for this is clear: mankind, established in honor, failed to understand, and he is [now] compared to foolish beasts and is made like them.*

2 P 2:16

Ps 48:13, 21 [49:12, 20]

If only this example would produce in us a healthy and salutary embarrassment, so that it would not be said of us, 'The ox knows his owner and the ass his master's crib, but Israel has not known me'.* Let us therefore show our docility to God, for the Lord lifts up those who are docile.* He advised and instructed us [to put ourselves] under his yoke and his burden,* and thus, through obedience and patience, to become his docile [creatures], for it is in these two virtues, obedience and patience, that docility to God is shown. Obedience carries out the things we are instructed to do; patience bears the things which God imposes upon us and which we must endure. Obedience is not refractory, and patience does not complain. Obedience stands by the commandments; patience remains steadfast in judgement. Obedience is a yoke which is no yoke, for it banishes servitude and restores freedom. Patience is a burden which is no burden, for rather than loading us down, it lightens us. Through patience, the things which the impatient find burdensome are lightened, for patience is like a spiritual cart in which we can carry all our burdens with greater ease. All the plumes and feathers on a bird constitute a sort of burden, but yet they raise it up into the heavens, and in just the same way, patience enables us to rise above

Is 1:3

Ps 146[147]:6

Mt 11:29-30

tribulation and not to be crushed beneath it. All who become gentle under the yoke and burden of Christ find that God is also gentle with them. [He is gentle] even in his anger, with which he corrects transgressors here lest they be judged more harshly [hereafter]. This is why it is written, 'Gentleness is come upon us, and we shall be corrected'.*

Ps 89[90]:10

By these virtues—I am speaking of obedience and patience—those who are gentle carry the gentle Christ seated upon them and bear his weight. And what is their reward? 'Those that bear the weight of the Lord shall inherit the land,'[26]* the land flowing with milk and honey, where Christ, God and man, will be seen in his glory.* [He will be seen] with delight and joy in the glory of his glorified humanity, but with greater delight and greater joy in the glory of his glorious divinity. Those who look upon this glory will then overflow with milk and honey, for the streams of milk and honey will flow right to them. How else can they reach them unless they flow [to them]? Whatever delights they find in the contemplation of divinity face to face,[27] in [the contemplation] of Supreme Beauty and Supreme Sweetness, will be as sweet as honey. Then each of them will be told, 'You have found honey, eat until you can eat no more.'[28]* There they will be completely sated, when the vessels of mercy* are filled with the torrent of delight* and the servant is told, 'Enter into the joy of your Lord.'* Then he will be surrounded by joy; he will find himself in joy wherever he turns and find joy all about him and say, 'My inheritance is [sweeter] than honey and the honeycomb'.* It will then be good for him to eat a lot of honey, and when he contemplates the majesty [of God], he will not be overwhelmed by glory. In the

Ps 36[37]:9

Ps 101:17[102:16]

Pr 25:16
Rm 9:23
Ps 35:9[36:8]
Mt 25:21

Si 24:27

meantime, however, it is not good for him to eat a lot, for if he examines the majesty, he will be overwhelmed by glory.*²⁹ 'I will be filled', says the prophet, 'when your glory appears.'*

But from what source will they be filled, those who are to be filled? If they are to be filled with honey, where does the honey flow from? I filled them with honey, he says, out of the rock.* But the rock was Christ!* Honey, they say, is gathered from flowers which have been drenched with the dew of heaven, and some, therefore, speak of 'dewy drops of honey,'³⁰ as if it were made³¹ from the dew which falls on [the flowers]. This is why the poet says, 'Now I would speak of honey, which comes from the air, a heavenly gift,'³² [though we are not told] whether the dew grows sweet in the flowers or the flowers [grow sweet] from the dew or whether each affects the other.

If only we were flowers, the sort of flowers who are told, 'Put forth your blossoms, you flowers',* and of which it is said, 'Sustain me with flowers'!* If only the dew of Hermon, which falls upon Mount Sion,* would grow sweet in us and we in it and honey be made in us, the like of that which is found in the promised land! Then, by gaining a foretaste now, and a more plentiful foretaste later, we would taste and see the sweetness of the Lord,* and when we had experienced it, we would say, 'How great is the abundance of your sweetness, O Lord, which you have hidden for them that fear you and which you have wrought for them that put their hope in you!'*

It is not only honey which abounds in the promised land, but milk abounds there too. The source which produces the milk is the flesh, and with it a

Pr 25:27
Ps 16:15[17:16]

Ps 80[81]:17
1 Co 10:4

Si 39:19
Sg 2:5

Ps 132[133]:3

Is 33:9

Ps 30:20[31:21]

mother comforts her children. She nourishes them and gives them life, and if they have no milk they will have no life. It was for this reason that the Word was made flesh and dwelt among us,* so that we might drink of his milk and be filled from the breasts of his comfort.* Therefore it is said, 'As a mother comforts her children, so will I comfort you, and you will be comforted in Jerusalem.'* In that heavenly Jerusalem is the vision of peace,[33] and there, too, is the milk of comfort. Every delight which arises from the revealed glory of the Man-God in God will be a caress to those that look upon it; it will be like milk, nourishing them and giving them life, and without it they cannot have that life of which he who is Life itself says to the Father:

'This is eternal life: that they may know<br>
you, the only true God, and<br>
Jesus Christ, whom you<br>
have sent.'*

## Notes to Tractate IX / II

1. This is a title of convenience, and does not appear in the manuscripts. See Tr. IX/1, n. 1 for an explanation.
2. The beginning of this sermon is identical to that of Tr. IX/1.
3. The virtue of the meek is *mansuetudo*, which means both gentleness and docility (in the sense of being tractable or easily led). In some contexts the former translation is more apposite; in others, the latter. Sometimes, therefore, I have rendered it as 'gentle', sometimes as 'docile', and frequently as 'gentle and docile'.
4. Is 66:2 in an OL version. This verse, in varying forms, occurs fairly frequently in Latin patristic literature, but I would suggest that Baldwin's most likely source is Gregory the Great. The quotation of the verse *juxta vetustam translationem* in the *Moralia in Librum Job* IV. XLV. 78; PL 75: 724C (and elsewhere in Gregory) agrees word for word with Baldwin's rendering.
5. Once again, we have a minor difficulty in translation. *Terra* can mean the whole earth in a geographical sense, earth as one of the four elements, or a land or country. I have therefore used whichever rendering the context seems to demand.
6. Converted, that is, to the monastic life. See Tr. V, nn. 6, 13.
7. *Usu disciplinae castigata.* On *disciplina*, see Tr. 1 nn. 31, 40, and Tr. III n. 20.
8. *Carnalis affectus.*
9. Lit. 'that in us which desires irrationally'.
10. I.e. the earth of our bodies, or the flesh.
11. Thomas (38/113, n. 2) compares William of St Thierry, Med IV. 7 (PL 180: 216D–217B; CF 3:113–114), but the similarities are very general, and the idea that reason should rule our actions is a commonplace in the spiritual writings of the period.
12. *Regio dissimilitudinis.* There is a very large and important literature dealing with this expression, and I shall make no attempt to present a comprehensive bibliography here. For a useful discussion of its significance in Cistercian spirituality, see Gilson, *Mystical Theology of St Bernard*, chapter 2, and for a brief but excellent examination of its wider significance, see R. Javelet, *Image et ressemblance au douzieme siècle* (Paris, 1967) 1: 266–286.
13. *Secundum spirituales sensus et affectus.* Thomas (38/115) renders this simply as 'understood in a spiritual sense', but Baldwin implies rather more than that.
14. PL 495C omits *ubi est.*
15. In Latin, *patientia* normally implies the patient enduring of suffering. It derives from the verb *patior* 'to suffer, endure, undergo'.
16. This is a literal translation of the peculiar Latin of Ps 121:3: 'Jerusalem, quae aedificatur ut civitas, cujus participatio ejus in idipsum'. The RSV translates it as "Jerusalem, built as a city which is bound firmly together", but although this reflects the meaning of the Hebrew, it is not how Baldwin would have understood it. For him, the Self-Same is God, and the heavenly Jerusalem is what it is by participation in God's immutable being. Cf. Burnaby (*Amor Dei*, 189–190), who presents a brief discussion of Augustine's understanding of this same verse.
17. For *mansuetus* in Thomas's text (38/124), read *immansuetus* with PL 497A. Baldwin is referring, of course, to the problem of recalcitrant monks.
18. Baldwin is defining an infant (*infans*) and a suckling (*lactans*) according to their etymology. *Infans* derives from the negative prefix *in-* plus the defective verb *for* 'to speak'; *lactans* derives from *lacteo* 'to suck milk' (*lac*).

19. The Vulgate version of 1 P 2:1–2 reads: '. . .sicut modo geniti infantes, *rationabile, sine dolo lac concupiscite*'; Baldwin writes: '. . .sicut modo geniti infantes *rationabiles* sine dolo lac concupiscite'. PL 497C omits *sine dolo*.
20. Baldwin is referring back to the third interpretation of 'the promised land'.
21. *Plus*, in Thomas's text (38/130), is a typographical error for *pius*.
22. Thomas (38 / 132) reads *ut dilectionem altius commendaret*; PL 498B has *ut dilectis altius commendaret charitatem*.
23. In Thomas's text (38/132), *reputanda* should read *non reputanda* with PL 498C.
24. *Secundum dispensationem naturae*. On *dispensatio*, see Tr. 1, n. 6.
25. PL 499A omits *animal in* after *asinum*.
26. Ps 36, 9. We would normally translate *sustinentes Dominum* as 'those that wait for the Lord' or 'those that hope for the Lord', but in this case, *sustinere* must be translated literally. Cf. Tr. v. n. 24.
27. *In contemplata specie divinitatis. Species* is here used in the same way as in 2 Co 5:7.
28. Pr 25:16 would normally be translated: 'Eat only enough for you', but Baldwin's exegesis demands 'Eat until you are satiated'. The Latin can support either rendering.
29. There is a line omitted in Thomas's text. To the bottom of 38/140 add: *gloria. Interim vero non est bonum ei qui.*
30. *Roscida mella*. See Virgil, *Eclogae* IV, 30.
31. Thomas (38/142) reads *confecta*; PL 500B has *collecta*.
32. Virgil, *Georgica* IV, 1.
33. According to a multitude of patristic writers, *visio pacis* is the etymological meaning of Jerusalem. See, for example, Augustine, *Enarratio in Ps.* 9:12 (PL 36:122), *In Ps.* 50:22 (PL 36:598).

## TRACTATE IX/III
## ON THOSE WHO MOURN[1]

*Blessed are those that mourn, for they shall
be comforted.** Mt 5:5

THE WISDOM OF GOD and the wisdom of this world judge the value of things in different ways, and when they weigh in the balance the importance of things, they do not use the same standard.[2] Things which the wisdom of God counts worthy of rejection and contempt are held by the wisdom of the world to be of great value, and the wisdom of the world rejects in its own judgement the things which the wisdom of God judges to be great and precious.

The wisdom of God says, 'Blessed are the poor in spirit, for theirs is the kingdom of Heaven'.* The wisdom of the world says, 'Blessed are the rich, for now they have dominion in all the world'. The wisdom of God says, 'Blessed are the meek, for they shall possess the earth'.* The wisdom of the world says, 'Blessed are the warmongers and the pitiless, for they are [already] in possession of the earth'. The wisdom of God says, 'Blessed are those who mourn, for they shall be comforted'.* The wisdom of the world says, 'Blessed are those who laugh, for even now they are comforted'. The wisdom of the world approves and praises and loves the riches and laughter and joy of this present life, for they provide present comfort; it hates and despises poverty and grief,

Mt 5:3

Mt 5:5

Mt 5:4

for in them is present desolation. The wisdom of God judges the joys of this present life to be vain and harmful, for our vices feed on them and they are stumbling-blocks to salvation. But poverty and grief it commends and loves, for they purge our vices and are a preparation for endless bliss.

In this way, the wisdom of God and the wisdom of this world attack each other in their judgements. Each judges the other in turn, and each in turn is judged. The wisdom of this world is foolishness with God,* and the wisdom of God is foolishness with the world. To those that perish, the word of the cross is foolishness,* but in a certain way, the word of the cross is the word of poverty and grief, for poverty or grief is a sort of cross. The wisdom of God is justified by her children* and the children of light, but the children of this world are wiser in their generation than the children of light.* The children of this world, therefore, and the children of light reckon each other to be foolish and insane! The latter look to vanities and lying follies;* the former love to have as their light the foolishness of the preaching. It is through [this preaching] that God determined that those who believe should be saved,* and it is this which the sensual person does not comprehend. It is foolishness to him, and he cannot understand.*

This dispute between the wisdom of God and that of this world shakes the foundation of the faith in the hearts of many, and can become so powerful as to cause even the elect (if that be possible) to stumble.* This is why one of the just says, 'My feet had almost stumbled, and my steps had well nigh slipped, for when I saw the peace of sinners, I was jealous of the wicked'.* But when he realizes what their end will be,* he is amazed and says: 'How they are brought to desolation! They have suddenly ceased to be! They have perished because of their iniquity!'*

In the judgement of Solomon laughter is condemned and mourning is preferred to feasting. 'Laughter,' he says, 'I counted as error, and I said to joy, "Why are you vainly deceived?"'* And again, 'It is better to go to a house of mourning than to a house of feasting'.* Such [are the words] of Solomon, but there is one here greater than Solomon* who says, 'Blessed are those who mourn, for they shall be comforted.'

There are two sorts of mourning, one pertaining to vanity and the other to pious devotion.³ There are some who mourn for things they should not mourn for, and therefore, since their mourning is as vain as their faith,* they are the very ones for whom we should mourn. There are others, however, whose mourning is devout and leads to salvation,⁴ and because they mourn in this way, they will be blessed in the future; as the Lord himself told his disciples: 'Truly, truly I say to you that you will lament and weep, but the world will rejoice. You will be made sorrowful, but your sorrow will be turned into joy'.* And the Psalmist: 'Going, they went and wept, casting their seeds. But coming, they shall come with joyfulness, carrying their sheaves'.* This devout mourning is like a shower of heavenly grace which moistens our seeds, so that when the rain has fallen on them, they may spring forth to a richer harvest. This is the free rain which God has set aside for his inheritance.*

In this vale of tears* in which we are born, we have to hand a plentiful supply of reasons for mourning,

Ps 72[73]:17

Ps 72[73]:19

Qo 2:2

Qo 7:2
Mt 12:42

*pietas*

1 Co 15:17

Jn 16:20

Ps 125:7-8[126:7]

Ps 67:10[68:9]
Ps 83:7[84:6]

for everything that happens, whether it be inside us or outside us, nearly always gives us cause to mourn. Truly, we are altogether miserable! We were born in misery; we have been raised in misery to this very moment; henceforth we will live in misery; and at last in misery we will die! Inside ourselves we are full of misery, and outside ourselves misery surrounds us. This is why someone says, 'My soul is full of evils',* and 'Evils without number have surrounded me'.* What can we do amid all these evils but lament and weep and mourn, grieving over the evils we experience unceasingly and wishing for the good things which we do not yet experience? Or if it should happen that we experience just a taste⁵ of something good, it only serves to remind us of our misery, for our experience of it is rare and superficial and in no way complete. What, then, is the source of these mighty and manifold miseries? Nothing but the fact that we have sinned with our fathers and have acted unjustly and have wrought iniquity.* It is our conduct and our iniquities which have done this to us!

### OF THE FIRST REASON FOR MOURNING

It follows that the first reason for mourning is the evil deeds we have committed and the good deeds we have omitted. Who can number the evil deeds we have committed? 'My iniquities,' it says, 'are more than the hairs of my head.'* And who likewise can number the good deeds which we have lost? 'I thought upon the days of old,' it says, 'and I had in my mind the eternal years.'* We have lost both the one and the other! The days of old were [the days] when God created Adam good and blessed, and it was possible for him never to die. The eternal years were [the years] which would have been given to him if he had not sinned, and then it would never have been possible for him to die.⁶ This is what [we lost] in Adam. But [think what we have lost] in ourselves! How many good deeds we have stolen from ourselves! How many good deeds we could have done but did not do! How many years we have wasted in vain! Countless days have passed away when we did evil or did nothing, and they have dragged us along with them, sliding ever downwards.

O where are you, fountains of water? Where are you now, fountains of tears, that I might mourn for the things I have lost in my life and for what I have lost of my innocence! Would that the flood-gates of heaven were opened above me!\* Would that the fountains of the great deep would burst forth\* and a flood of mighty water overwhelm the land of my heart, so that all that dwells therein might perish, all those senses of mine which have been prone to evil from my youth!\* See how my days were consumed in vanity and my years in haste!\* Who will comfort me but one who is saddened as I am saddened, one who is himself penitent, who says, 'I labored in my lamentations'.\* The reason I rejoiced in worldly things, laughing and playing and praising their various attainments, was that I would not lament or labor, but now I have learned by my own experience that it was then, in fact, that I labored in my lamentations! The things which are judged to be of value here are really the things which should be exchanged for labor and lamentations, and those who value them are actually those whom they injure.⁷ This [realization] comes like night, late in falling on those who are late in lamenting, for 'We wearied ourselves in the way of iniquity and destruction and

Gn 7:11
Ibid.

Gn 8:21
Ps 77[78]:33

Ps 6:7[6]

walked along hard ways'.* There is a popular saying: 'This year's tears are last year's laughter'. When I walked where I wanted, doing the things which brought me lamentation—yet not with the intention of causing lamentation, but rather of avoiding it—then woe to me, for my thoughts and my wishes were a labor to me,* and I labored in my lamentations! Then I conceived sorrow and brought forth iniquity,* and therefore I will wash my bed [with tears],* the bed of my sorrow,† on which I lay sick and unclean, as a woman in labor is unclean. My bed of sorrow is my feeble flesh, my bad conscience, my sinful pleasures, and I should wash it in the secret silence of the night, when God, in secret,* sees each separate transgression.

And because I carry a conscience divided in two—now [thinking] on the wicked deeds I did and now on the good ones I might have done—I will wash the bed of my conscience in which I labor in sickness, the couch of my conscience where I threw myself down; I will water it with my tears that I may find rest. I will wash away the stains of my life; I will water the barrenness of my soul in the hope that it may sprout forth like ground watered by rain. For because of the evil deeds I did, neither my innocence (which is the evil I did not do) nor my conscience (which is the good I did) bears any fruit for me, and where I want to cast myself down and take my rest, there I find occasion for grief and a reason for tears. By means of the things in which I am corrupt, I corrupted the things in which I was not corrupt.[8] But what am I saying? Where am I not corrupted? Where am I incorrupt? For I often judge the incorrupt parts of me in such a way as actually to corrupt myself through them! When I am thinking about them, I say to myself: 'I am not as other men;* I am not like this one or that one; I am a very remarkable fellow, and he is not.' But when I judge myself as superior [in this way], I am often in doubt as to whether I should grieve more for the incorruption in me which puffs me up like this or for my sins which humble me when I think about them in fear.

### Of the Second Reason for Mourning

When, in mourning, I mourn for my sins and search for comfort by the medicine of penitence, there appears another reason for tears in the temptations which assault me and which I am not permitted to let in. They encompass and encircle me on every side, and there appears no way open for me to escape them. Thousands of temptations rise up in me: some above me, some within me, some around me, but all against me. When one leaves me, another immediately seizes me; when one yields, another takes its place, and in their midst there is no peace for my spirit. What I see, what I hear, what I do, what I think, what I wish, what I like, what I do not like—in short, whatever makes up my life is a temptation for me. As [the Scripture] says: 'The life of man upon earth is temptation'.⁹

Amid these temptations—so many, so evil, so troublesome, so confusing and inextricable, from which I cannot untangle myself—life is often a weariness to me, but when I search for comfort I find it less in the strength of the saints than in their weakness. I listen to Paul, so harried by temptations that he was forced to cry, 'Unhappy man that I am, who shall deliver me from this body of death?'* What comfort is provided for our weakness by

Lk 18:11

Rm 7:24

God's dispensation! For the weakness of the saints sometimes comforts us more than their strength. Their strength and virtue[10] kindles in us a desire [to imitate them], but it is their weakness that arouses our hope. Paul was told that 'Strength is perfected in weakness',* and he says of himself: 'When I am weak, then I am stronger'.* I too, then, can say: 'When Paul is weakened, I am stronger'. The weakness of Paul, therefore, helps me with myself. If only[11] his strength would help me with God, that he might deliver me from temptation,* my soul from death, my eyes from tears, and my feet from falling.*

### Of the Third Reason for Mourning

Besides the evils which stain our life and the evils which tempt us to sin, we are also beset by other things which purge us from sin. I am right to refer to them as 'other things', for the various temptations which we resist by refusing them our consent are one thing, and quite another thing are the various sufferings and tribulations which we have to endure and which thereby serve to discipline us. And although we are often tempted into sin by the very same things that discipline us by punishing us, what we fear in temptation is one thing, and what we suffer in tribulation is another. On the one hand we are talking about sin, and on the other, punishment.

These evils which here afflict us, however, also have their weariness and their tears. We have a witness in Elijah, who cast himself down in the shadow of a juniper tree and asked his soul if he might die: 'It is enough for me,' he said, 'take away my soul.'* We have another witness in Paul, who says, 'We were so utterly crushed that we were weary of life itself.* Jonah, too, is a witness when he says, 'I am angry enough to die'.* All these are speaking of the weariness [which these evils bring about], but there is also a man who tells us of lamentation and tears: 'The whole creation has been groaning in travail until now. And not only it, but we ourselves, who have the first-fruits of the spirit, we too groan within ourselves.'* And the Psalmist: 'You have rebuked me, and I am weak from the strength of your hand. You have corrected man for his iniquity.'* And speaking of tears he adds, 'Hear, O Lord, my prayer and my supplication: give ear to my tears'.*

2 Co 1:8
Jon 4:9

Rm 8:22–23

Ps 38[39]:11–12

Ps 38[39]:13

But if these tears pertain to every one of the just, is there not a contradiction in [the passage], 'They left the presence of the council, rejoicing that they were counted worthy to suffer reproach for the name of Jesus'?* And what of Paul's saying: 'Rejoicing in tribulation,'[12] and James: 'Count it all joy, my brothers, when you meet with various temptations'!* [The reason for these sayings is that] those who suffer in tribulation are the weak, whereas those who rejoice in tribulation are the perfect. For the latter, [tribulation] is [a proof] of their strength and virtue, but since even the perfect are not entirely without weakness (for their strength is perfected in weakness*), they also suffer as [a proof] of their weakness. Thus, in a wonderful way, God strengthens his saints through their weakness and humbles them through their strength. This is why the just man says, 'I ate ashes like bread and mingled my drink with tears'.* It is just as if he said, 'When I remember that I am dust and ashes, the memory of my weakness and my condition is my bread and my food, fortifying me and strengthening me. The drink of spiritual joy[13] makes me joyful, but it is not without

Ac 5:41

Jm 1:2

2 Co 12:9

Ps 101:10[102:9]

bitterness, for joy is tempered with sorrow.' If strength should be [totally] without weakness, then joy would be [totally] without sadness, but at the moment weakness has made progress toward strength — which is [the meaning of] 'I ate ashes like bread' — and the strong virtue of humility [has made progress] through weakness — which is [the meaning of] 'I mingled my drink with tears'. This is indeed as it should be, for a little wine is necessary for us because of our frequent weaknesses.* But if we drink wine intemperately, who will escape being drunk? Who will not have a headache? Who will not have the spirit of giddiness which the Lord mingled in the midst of the Egyptians?* It is wise, therefore, to mix our drink with tears, to temper our joy with sadness, and to humble our strength with weakness.

1 Tm 5:23

Is 19:14

### OF THE FOURTH REASON FOR MOURNING

If the things which now beset us are so grievous as to wring our tears from us, how much more should our tears be called forth by our terror at what is yet to come! [Our troubles] here are temporary; those to come are eternal. The former can always, with difficulty, somehow be endured; the latter cannot be endured at all! Who can dwell in devouring fire, and who shall dwell in everlasting flame?* Is it surprising, then, if we find grief in this fear? Is there anyone wise who does not want to extinguish with his tears the inextinguishable fire? 'Your wrath, O Lord, has come upon me,' says the just man, and he is here referring to the temporary punishment which now besets us, 'and your terrors have troubled me',* which refers to that eternal [punishment] which is yet more terrifying. 'The arrows of the

Is 33:14

Ps 87:17[88:16]

## Tractate IX / III

Lord are in me,' says blessed Job, 'and their rage drinks up my spirit. The terrors of the Lord wage war against me.'* In saying 'the arrows of the Lord are in me,' he means 'Your wrath has come upon me', and in saying 'the terrors of the Lord wage war against me,' he means 'Your terrors have troubled me'.

Jb 6:4

This reason for sorrow is implied by the Prophet when he says, 'I mingled my drink with tears because of your anger and indignation, for after you had raised me up, you threw me down.'* Consider what he means by being raised up and being thrown down. Man was made in the image and likeness of God, and as a result of this he is capable of reason and can therefore participate in blessedness. This is how he is raised up. But because he can be saved, he may also be condemned, and this is how he is thrown down. But since irrational animals cannot be saved, neither can they be condemned: since they are not destined to possess reason, they are not required to give reason [for their actions].

Ps 101:10–11
[102:9–10]

These four reasons for sorrow—the first [resulting] from our fear of the sins we have committed, the second from the danger of the temptations we suffer, the third from the weight of tribulation which now besets us, and the fourth from our terror at being judged and condemned—[these four reasons], although in a different order, are implied by the prophet [when he says]: 'The pains of death surrounded me, and the torrents of iniquity troubled me. The pains of hell encompassed me, and the snares of death laid hold of me.'* The pains of death are the pains which accompany death and also those which precede it, those which continually hasten [the coming of] death and which, like death's heralds,

Ps 17:5–6[18:4–5]

always announce it to us. For we carry in ourselves a sentence of death.* The torrents of iniquity are the assaults of sin which flood over us, and which, like torrents ever pouring over a precipice, drag us along with them. The nature of the pains of hell is clear from their very name, and the snares of death are those temptations which the tempter, like a man hunting birds or animals, uses to ensnare our souls.

These [four reasons can be seen as] four measures or four water-jars, and if we add to them two more, they become the six water-jars of stone, each holding two or three measures, which the Jews use in their purification.* The Jews are those who are penitent and who confess [their faults]. Their tears signify the purification of the Jews, and they are given tears in measure for their drink.* The reason why each separate water-jar contains two or three measures is because these sufferings, whether temporary or eternal, should arouse in us both fear and mourning because of the temptations we have permitted and the sins we have committed—sins which were acts of deliberate volition, and also, occasionally, simply a result of habit.¹⁴ And even if someone only intends to sin but is goaded by repentance and thus finds reason for mourning, this does not remove the two or three measures. For if we add up the craving, the consent, and the pleasure we get from consenting, the sum total remains the same.¹⁵ The stone of the water-jars [symbolizes] either the fact that our hearts are still as hard as stone, or otherwise the real firmness of that resolve for better things which is essential for those that mourn devoutly. Of our hardness of heart, the Lord says through the prophet, 'I will take away the heart of stone from your flesh,'* and of the firm [resolve] of our mind, it is said, 'I have set my face as a most hard rock'.*    Is 50:7

## Of the Fifth Reason for Mourning

These tears of ours which arise from the four reasons we have so far discussed, we always find to be either bitter or as tasteless as water. They stem from hatred, weariness, sorrow, or fear: from those things, in other words, which we find to be hateful, wearisome, sorrowful, or fearful. When [the Psalmist] said, 'Woe is me, for my exile is prolonged!',* it was these things which affected him. But just as these are [tears] which fall from a hatred of evil things, there are also other sweeter tears which well forth from a desire for good things. By good things, we now mean those which are spiritual and which give rise to good or those which are eternal and which give rise to blessedness. There is in us a desire for both of these goods, and each desire has its own tears. We are often goaded by a desire for the good which justifies us here in the world[16] and often by a desire for the good which makes us blessed in our homeland. Both have been promised us by God, and we should plead for them with tears and sighs too deep for words.* This is why the prophet says, 'You have set my tears in your sight according to your promise',* and 'When shall I come and appear before the face of God? My tears have been my bread day and night'.* If we are only beginners, our righteousness lies in our good intentions and the motives for our actions, but if we are more experienced, it lies in the habitual practice of good deeds.[17] But in both cases, [righteousness] hopes and desires and expects its reward, and therefore [we see once again why] each single water-jar contains two or three measures.[18]

Ps 119:5[120:4]

in via

Rm 8:26

Ps 55:9[56:8]

Ps 41[42]:2-3

All these tears—whether they flow from a weariness with evil or a desire for the good—can be shared by both the good and the wicked, for both the good and the wicked find themselves goaded by all these reasons [for lamentation]. The good weep, and the evil weep, but whereas [the weeping] of the good is healthy and leads to salvation,[19] that of the evil is useless. The Apostle testifies that when Esau wanted to inherit the blessing, he was rejected. He found no chance to repent, although he had sought it with tears.* After Judas had been led to repentance, he brought back the thirty pieces of silver,* and when Balaam was goaded to righteousness and said, 'Let my soul die the death of the just and my end be like theirs',* it was equally useless. It is possible, therefore, for the wicked to feel sorrow and fear for the wicked things which should arouse sorrow and fear, and also to desire and hope for spiritual and eternal goods. Their hope and desire for the one, and their sorrow and fear for the other, goad them to tears, but [their tears] are as fruitless as they are vain. It is not enough for anyone simply to mourn over evil and desire and hope for the good; in addition to this he must also forsake his sins, correct his errors, and apply himself to those good things which give rise to good. It is one thing to desire or hope for these goods and quite another to possess them. No one can be good solely by desiring or hoping for good things or by believing that he has them; it is only when he really has them that he is good. There are many who think that they really do have penitence and forgiveness of sins—things which can bring their wickedness to an end—or else they hope they can have them whenever they want, and the

Heb 12:17
Mt 27:3

Nb 23:10

same is true of charity, humility, and the other good things which make us good. But their hope is in vain, and their desire, their belief, and their heart is in vain.* Sometimes, therefore, they are goaded to righteousness, but it does them no good, just as the good are tempted to sin, and it does them no harm.

Ps 5:10[9]

[Consider] those who, in their pride, overestimate their merits and are thereby sure that God will judge them [favorably]. Do they not reckon themselves to be good? Of such it is written, 'A thousand shall fall at your side and ten thousand at your right hand'.* People like this, therefore, may abound with joy in their hope, and their tears may flow with the desires and yearnings and sobbings of their soul, but they still have no part in this promise: 'Blessed are those that mourn, for they shall be comforted'.

Ps 90[91]:7

### OF THE CHARACTERISTICS OF GOOD TEARS

The hope of the just, however, is founded on humility, and their desire on charity, and from these two — from charity and humility — the waters of holy tears are drawn as from the Saviour's fountains.* Someone who weeps devoutly is someone who is goaded [to do so] after he has sinned for the sake of his salvation. He is humbled in the fear of God and abhors iniquity, and he always grieves when he does something which he had no wish to do a second time. These are the devout tears of which the Psalmist says, 'My eyes have sent forth springs of water because they have not kept your law'.* Someone who weeps devoutly is someone who dissolves in desire and spiritual joy and flows and melts away in tears. When he remembers the things he desires he pours himself out within himself

Is 12:3

Ps 118[119]:136

in a wonderful way so that he can say, 'These are the things I remembered, and I poured out my soul within me. I shall go over into the place of the wonderful tabernacle, even to the house of God.'* She who was faint with love* experienced the sweetness of these tears, for she said, 'My soul melted when my beloved spoke'.* Well [might she say] 'when my beloved spoke', [firstly] because he is her beloved and [secondly] because he spoke. As soon as her beloved spoke to her, his words were more soothing than oil, but they are also darts.* How, then, could she not be soothed, how could she not dissolve and melt [in tears] at these words of his which she loves, for it is written, 'He will send forth his word and melt them; his Spirit will breathe upon them, and the waters will flow'.* Thus, when the beloved speaks and the Spirit breathes [upon them], those who love [him] melt away [in tears]. Their waters flow and water the garden of delights, and the south wind blows over it, so that its perfumes flow forth.* These tears are like drops of honey, for they drop down from heaven. They are the showers in which [the garden] shall spring up and rejoice,* the free rain which God has set aside for his inheritance.*

This rain, however, is often withheld from the just. When they have it they do not retain it, and when they want it, they do not obtain it. For often, when they are abandoned, when they are attacked by weakness and their strength is totally hidden, they are filled with bitterness and afflicted with weariness and pine away with evils.* They have a burning thirst, but the rains of heaven are withheld from them;* neither dew nor rain falls upon them,† and unless God comes to their aid, their soul soon begins to dwell in hell.* But should we be surprised if the just, as it were, descend for a moment into hell and there drink gall and wormwood? It is useful for them to know the place from which they may be delivered so that they may rejoice in their deliverance even more and glorify God for the abundance of their consolation. 'They descend,' he says, 'into the depths; their soul pined away with evils'* But will God forget to show mercy?* God forbid! The Spirit of the Lord is sweeter than honey,'* and when it breathes on the mind of the just, [it imbues them] with the hope and desire for his inheritance which is [sweeter] than honey and the honeycomb,* and it fills up all the inmost and secret places of the languishing soul with its inestimable sweetness. Then, from the grace of the inner sweetness and inward delight which comes upon us, everything bitter will be swallowed up in the joy of the heart, and rivers of tears will flow like streams of honey. When the mother of Jesus said, 'They have no wine,'* she suggested that the water of sorrow be changed into the wine of joy, but this occurred only after they had done as Jesus instructed, saying, 'Fill the water-jars with water'.* It is right that we should first of all fill the jars with water, for what this means is that we should saturate our hearts completely with abundant effusions of tears, make fitting reparation for the [sins] we have committed, and mourn sufficiently for the things we should mourn for. By doing this, we receive within ourselves the comfort of inner devotion and joy in the Holy Spirit and change the sorrow of our heart into gladness. As yet, however, we have not wept bitterly enough for the things we should mourn for, and as a consequence of this, we often feel a lack of devotion; and because we have not yet paid what we owe, it is only much

Ps 106[107]:26
Ps 76[77]:9
Si 24:27

Ps 18:11[19:10]

Jn 2:3

Jn 2:7

later that we obtain what we want. But when God gives us tears to drink in [full] measure, then, with the attainment of the good things we are so anxious to acquire, we will experience, in a whole variety of different ways, that our comfort there and then is the true comfort [promised us in this saying]: 'Blessed are those that mourn, for they shall be comforted'. This experience, however, is really a matter for the future, when God will wipe away all tears from the eyes of the saints,\* when our mouth shall be filled with gladness and our tongue with joy,\* to the praise and glory of our Lord Jesus Christ, who is above all things, God, forever blessed.\*
Amen.

Rv 21:4
Ps 125[126]:2

Rm 9:5

1. This is a title of convenience, and does not appear in the manuscripts (see Tr. IX/I, n. 1). There are a few obvious typographical errors in Thomas's edition of the text: 38/160 (503C), for *contre* read *contra*; 38/160 (503D), for *importumas* read *importunas*; 38/174 (504B), for *proprositi* read *propositi*; 38/186 (508C), for *bos* read *nos*.

2. *Et momenta rerum ad unius staterae momentum non ponderant*. There is probably an echo of Ws 11:23 here.

3. *Pietas* as 'pious devotion'. See Tr. I, n. 15.

4. They mourn *salubriter*, i.e. healthily, beneficially, in a way that brings about their spiritual health and salvation. See also n. 19.

5. *Modicum*. As Gilson points out, 'this word is often used by St Bernard to express the brevity of the mystic vision' (*Mystical Theology of St Bernard* 104, n. 146). Baldwin too is here referring to what he calls elsewhere the *excessus contemplationis* (see Tr. VIII, n. 18).

6. The background to Baldwin's thought here is to be found in Augustine. In his *De correptione et gratia* (and a number of other places), he contrasts (1) *posse non peccare* and *non posse peccare*; (2) *posse non mori* and *non posse mori*; and (3) *bonum posse non deserere* and *bonum non posse deserere* (*De correptione et gratia* 33; PL 44:936). In each case, the *posse non* ('possibility not to . . .') was rejected by Adam (and, in Adam, by us): he *did* sin, he *did* die, he *did* forsake the good. As a consequence of this, for Adam and for us, the *non posse* ('impossibility to . . .') does not apply; it is reserved for the saints in the life to come.

7. This is a fairly loose translation to bring out the sense.

8. Part of this sentence has been omitted in PL 503B by hom. For *nam per ea quibus corruptus non sum*, read *nam per ea quibus corruptus sum corrupi ea quibus corruptus non sum*.

9. This is an OL version of Jb 7:1 (see, for example, Jerome, *Dialogus adversus Pelagianos* II. 4; PL 23:539A). The Vulgate has: 'The life of man upon earth is warfare' (*militia*), which Baldwin quotes elsewhere.

10. In Latin, *virtus* means strength as well as virtue. The translation, therefore, depends upon the context.

11. Thomas (38/162) has *utinam*; PL 504A reads *ut*.

12. In all probability, Paul did not say this. The Vulgate text of Rm 12:12 reads 'Rejoicing in hope, patient in tribulation', and I know of no version or variant which reads 'rejoicing in tribulation'. Baldwin's memory seems to have played him false here.

13. Or 'the spiritual drink of joy'.

14. Lit. Sins 'which we did by will and by action, but also occasionally by habit'.

15. Baldwin's exegesis here is somewhat labored and not particularly easy to follow, but what he appears to be saying is this: in cases where we actually sin, the three measures are will, action, and habit (see n. 13 above), and in cases where we only intend to sin but do not actually commit the dead (lit. 'and if someone sins only by will' [and not by action]), the three measures are desire, consent, and pleasure (for a lengthy discussion of these three factors, see Tr.VI). But in both cases there are three measures involved. Each of these varieties of sin then produces (or should produce) a

further two measures: (1) fear and (2) lamentation, because of (1) suffering in this world and (2) suffering in the next. Every sin, therefore, is associated with two and/or three intimately related factors. See also n. 18 below.

16. *In via*, literally 'on the way'.

17. Lit. 'Our righteousness is in the *affectus* of a good will or in the *affectus* of action, as in the case of beginners, or in the practice of good habit, as in the case of the experienced'.

18. We are back with Baldwin's preposterous water-pots, and this passage (dealing with righteousness) counterbalances the passage we discussed at n. 15 above (dealing with sin). Once again, the three measures are will, action, and habit (see n. 17), and when utilised correctly, they can produce two different forms—two measures, that is—of righteousness (that of the beginners and that of the experienced). Both forms of righteousness are then, in turn, involved with three further measures: hope, desire, and expectation. Each form of righteousness, therefore, is associated with two and/or three intimately related factors.

19. Lit. 'The good weep *salubriter*'. See n. 4 above.

## TRACTATE IX/IV
## ON THOSE THAT HUNGER AND
## THIRST FOR RIGHTEOUSNESS[1]

*Blessed are those that hunger and thirst for righteousness, for they shall be filled.* \*      Mt 5:6

THERE ARE MANY who hunger for money rather than righteousness, and their only reason is that they want to be so filled up with it as to spend their days in prosperity.\*     Jb 21:13
Those who have an abundance of money are reckoned to be blessed, as it is written, 'They say that the people who have these things are blessed'.\*   Ps 143[144]:15
When he says 'they say,' he is not stating his own view but is referring to the opinion of others, for according to his own view he says, 'The rich have wanted and have suffered hunger'.\* They have   Ps 33:11[34:10]
wanted indeed, for what they have does not satisfy them, and they have certainly suffered hunger, since their appetite for what they do not have is insatiable. True satiety comes from righteousness, not from money. There is, however, a certain sort of satiety applicable to the rich since it is written: 'The fullness of the rich man will not allow him to sleep'.\* But   Qo 5:11
this fullness lies, in fact, not in putting an end to need but in using things to excess. It is the oppression of sickness, not the eradication of disease; it is the irritation of vice, not the fulfillment of desire. It is an empty satiety, therefore, and it does not refresh those who hunger [in this way] because

they are never satisfied. It is water from the well of Samaria, of which it is written, 'Whoever drinks of this water shall thirst again'.* 'He has filled the hungry with good things', it says, 'and the rich he has sent empty away.'*

Who are the hungry who are filled with good things, and who thereby are truly and fully satisfied? Who but those of whom it is written, 'Blessed are those who hunger and thirst for righteousness'! And what is this righteousness which satisfies us and makes us blessed but Christ, whom God made our wisdom and our righteousness?* He indeed is Wisdom who says, 'Those who eat me shall still hunger, and those who drink me shall still thirst'.* Christ was made our righteousness, justifying us freely, freely distributing righteousness, and through righteousness remaining in us, the giver of the gift with the gift. Our food is he who bestows righteousness, and our food is also the righteousness he bestows.

This is why he who fell and lost his righteousness bewailed his loss by saying, 'I forgot to eat my bread',* but because he strove to make reparation with penitence he added, 'I ate ashes as if they were bread'.* This is the food of the just, and only he who eats it hungers for it. We hunger for it by tasting it, and we taste it when we hunger for it; the more we taste it, the more we hunger for it; and the more it restores us, the sweeter it becomes. Its flavor, therefore, always attracts us, and when we taste it, our appetite grows larger and larger, and we never tire of its taste.[2]

Is it not true, then, that the love of righteousness is just as insatiable as the love of money? If this hunger becomes ever greater and stronger as a result of increasing righteousness, when will it end, and when will we find satiety? The prophet has an answer for us when he says, 'As for me, I will appear before your sight in righteousness; I shall be satisfied when your glory shall appear'.* Hunger,³ therefore, pertains to this present life and satiety to the future when those who hunger now will be filled. But who are those who hunger now? Does it mean everyone who *desires* righteousness? Or only those who *love* righteousness? It is one thing to desire something in some way, but quite another to love it; and although there is no love without desire, desire comes before love.

Ps 16:15[17:16]

There are many who are still wicked who want to be good and intend to be so, but they postpone the time of their repentance and delay the beginning of their conversion.⁴ They are bound and vanquished by the pleasures of sin and weighed down by the habit of sin, and they still love what they have no wish to love and do not yet possess that for which they yearn. They are goaded to righteousness, but embrace the delights of sin. They cleave to wickedness, but burn with the fire of desire for good. Their persistence in wickedness has more power to make them wicked than merely their fervent yearning for good to make them good.

On the other hand, when the good are tempted to sin, their persistence in goodness, by which they preserve their righteousness, has more power than that unbidden fire of the soul which makes them suddenly burn to do evil. The good always persist in goodness, but sometimes they burn to do good, and sometimes—without their consent—they burn to do evil. [The reason for this is that] there are two forms of concupiscence, both of which are to be found in the good as well as in the wicked: concupiscence of the flesh and concupiscence of the spirit, and they are mutually antagonistic. 'The desires of the flesh are contrary to the spirit, and the desires of the spirit are contrary to the flesh.'*

In the case of the good, concupiscence of the flesh provokes them to sin, but because they are governed by concupiscence of the spirit, it does not provoke them to the point that they consent to sin. In the same way, the wicked feel themselves goaded to righteousness but do not consent to it because they are governed by concupiscence of the flesh. The wicked, then, with their intention and desire for a better life, envy the good, and although this envy is itself a certain form of God's grace, it is the grace of an inner calling, not [the grace] of justification. We are justified and made righteous not simply by being disposed to it, but by actually consenting to it.⁵ 'What fellowship has righteousness with iniquity?'* says the Apostle. No one, therefore, consents to righteousness unless he refuses his consent to unrighteousness, unless he forsakes it and abandons it without delay. But whoever consents to righteousness now begins to love it. He now hungers for righteousness and now desires it worthily. He already possesses something of what he desires, but he desires to possess more. He has now set his foot upon the right path, and his desire is to be directed in it to its very end, saying, 'May my ways be directed to keep your righteous commandments'.* 'My soul,' said a just man, 'has longed to desire your righteous commandments at all times',* and it is to him that this saying now refers.

Even now he longs and desires, but since he is not content with the measure of his desire, he longs to desire more. He sighs for perfection and aspires to make progress, wishing to augment the goodness within him and persist in goodness at all times. Our progressive growth in righteousness, however, follows an ordered series of stages: we begin by consenting to it, then being disposed to it, then putting it into effect, then practising it, then making it habitual, and then reaping its fruit.[6] Righteousness begins with our consent to it, but when the mind has conceived a hatred of iniquity and has begun to consent to righteousness through its love of goodness, it becomes disposed to good works. And when this inner disposition is put into effect, it feels a delight in doing good and so strives to accustom itself to good works. After this [it strives] to strengthen this habitual action by perseverance.

In the course of this [progress], but most especially after it, it finds delight in partaking of the sweet fruit of righteousness, but the fruit of righteousness is not single. There is the fruit of the time to come, which is that satiety here promised us, and there is also the fruit of this present time, a certain foretaste of future sweetness which in the meantime we perceive in the delight [which comes] from righteousness. This is the delight of which it is said through the prophet, 'I found as much delight in the way of your testimonies as in all riches'.* But the satiety which is yet to come comprises two things much to be desired: eternal life and everlasting joy. Both of these are obtained and purchased by righteousness. Of the satiety of eternal life it is written, 'I will fill him with length of days,'* and there is no doubt that he is speaking of the just. Of the satiety of everlasting joy it is written, 'They shall be inebriated with the plenty of your house, and you shall

Ps 118[119]:14

Ps 90[91]:16

make them drink of the torrent of your pleasure',* and again, there can be no doubt that he is speaking of the just. Righteousness, therefore, which gives us life and joy, is food and drink. Since it offers us life and preserves it eternally (for righteousness is the acquisition of immortality⁷), it is food and the bread of life. Since it bestows joy and guards it for ever, it is drink and the wine of joy. Blessed are they, therefore, who hunger and thirst for righteousness, and blessed are they who desire to live and rejoice not in this world but in Christ. They shall obtain⁸ satiety when their desire is filled up with good things by our Lord Jesus Christ, who is above all things, God, forever blessed. Amen.*

## Notes to Tractate IX / IV

1. This is a title of convenience, and does not appear in the manuscripts (see Tr. IX/I, n. 1). This sermon on the fourth beatitude is very much shorter than the other three in the series, and it is possible that when the *corpus* of Baldwin's discourses was being arranged and edited, a certain amount of material was lost from the beginning. In its present form, the opening of the discourse is perhaps a little abrupt for Baldwin's style.

2. Lit. 'its taste can be continued without nausea'.

3. For *esuriens* in Thomas's text (38/190), read *esuries* with PL 509D.

4. *Conversio* is here being used generally (= 'conversion to a better life'), not specifically (= 'entry into the monastery'). Cf. Tr. v, nn. 6, 13; Tr. IX/II, n. 6.

5. Lit. 'Justification is not reckoned by *affectus* alone, but by consent'. Discussions of the psychological and spiritual importance of consent appear elsewhere in Baldwin: see Tr. IV, nn. 41, 44; Tr. VI, n. 30.

6. The Latin is here very concise: . . . *consensu, affectu, effectu, usu, habitu et fructu*.

7. This quotation derives from a variant reading of Ws 1:15. In a number of manuscripts of the Latin text (but not the Greek), there is added to the end of the verse which is given in the Vulgate: *injustitia autem mortis est acquisitio*. In certain other manuscripts this appears as: *justitia enim immortalitatis, injustitia autem mortis est acquisitio*. In this form it was known to a number of patristic writers, and it is this which forms the basis of Baldwin's quotation.

8. For *consequenter* in Thomas's text (38/198), read *consequentur* with PL 512A.

# TRACTATE X/I
## ON THE SEAL OF THE LOVE OF GOD[1]

*Set me as a seal upon your heart, as a seal upon your arm, for love is strong as death, and its demands[2] as hard as hell.* *

Sg 8:6

IN LOVING US and wanting to be loved, God fashioned a seal, and upon it was engraved the image of love. With this he sealed our heart clearly and firmly so that it received in itself a likeness of his image which was patterned on his image, a likeness which expressed his image by showing forth the same figure.[3]

[By the word] 'seal' you must understand on the one hand the one who does the sealing and on the other the one who is sealed. The Apostle [refers] to the one who seals when he says to the Romans, 'Abraham received the sign of circumcision, a seal of righteousness which he had by faith while he was still uncircumcised'.* And [he refers] to the one who is sealed[4] when he says to the Corinthians, 'You are the seal of my apostleship in the Lord'.* And to the angel who is sealed with the beauty of the divine likeness, it is said through the prophet, 'You were the seal who bore his likeness, full of wisdom and perfect in beauty. You were in the delights of the paradise of God.'*

Rm 4:11

1 Co 9:2

Ezk 28:12-13

Jn 6:27
Jn 10:36

Christ, however, both seals and is sealed, for on him has God the Father set his seal.* It is he whom the Father sanctified and sent into the world.* It is he whom the Father marked out from others by a unique grace, for it was fitting that we should have such a high priest, holy, blameless, unstained, separated from sinners, and exalted above the heavens.*     Heb 7:26

Through him, God has sealed us, as it is written, 'We have been sealed, O Lord, with the light of your countenance'.* He sealed us on the day of our creation when he formed us in his image and likeness.* He sealed us on the day of our redemption when he re-formed us according to his image.     Ps 4:7 / Gn 1:26-27

Iniquity and death caused a separation between God and man: God hates iniquity and man [hates] death. And as much as man hates death, so much does he love life. What is there in life sweeter than life itself? What is there more worthy of love? What is more bitter than death? What more hateful? What, then, is more detestable than iniquity, since it is through this that the enjoyment of life is lost to us and the necessity of dying imposed upon us? What can we love more than life, and most especially immortal life, and the God who promises it and bestows it upon us, the fount of life and life itself? But since it is written that righteousness is the acquisition of immortality,⁵ it follows that we should love righteousness no less than life. It is through [righteousness] that [life] is obtained, and immortal life is not preserved without it.

In a certain way, man was immortal from the beginning, for by preserving his righteousness it was possible for him not to die.⁶ To this extent—but only to this extent—he was like God. Now, however, being subject to death, he is like the foolish beasts;* in fact, since he is bound to sin and liable to be lost, he is worse off than they and is now as much lower than they as once he was more worthy.     Ps 48:13, 21 [49:12, 20]

Iniquity, therefore, is just as hateful as death; more hateful than death, in fact, for it is better to die than to sin. Sin is the sting of death,\* a sting which gives a mortal wound. The wages of sin is death,\* and the reward of iniquity is perdition. Sin is an affront to God and provokes his anger; in his condemnation of sin, the sentence of God is a sentence of death.

Sinful man is justly doomed to death, and having experienced the wrath of God in his many miseries, he could hardly hope for the love of God — or [could hope for] only the tiniest amount. His thoughts could only suggest to him that he say, 'If God so afflicts me, how can I believe he loves me? What good can I hope for from him who poured forth his displeasure upon me\* and did not spare me from death? If he loved me, he would not oppress me like this with his sentence; he would not hold back his mercy in his anger\* but would take away the displeasure which I have deserved. He would accord me forgiveness and absolve me from the debt of death.' Since God is angry with man and brings upon him a sentence of death, it certainly looks as if he hates him; but since he [also] suffered death to bring about the abolition of sin and death, it [also] looks as if he loves him!

Death, therefore, stands as a sign both of hatred and love: hatred against the sin which man committed and love for the nature which God created. Through the death which he brought upon man, God poured forth his displeasure and his wrath upon all nations, as it is written, 'I have trampled on them in my displeasure, and I have trodden them down in my wrath'.\* Through the death which he accepted for the sake of man, God poured forth his mercy and love upon all nations, as it is written, 'Our God is the God of salvation, and it is the Lord, the Lord, who brings about the end of death'.*   Ps 67:21[68:20]

Death, therefore, is both anger and mercy, judgement and kindness, condemnation and absolution, displeasure and reconciliation. God dispensed and furnished a remedy for our reparation in such a way that the rage of his displeasure was changed into the sacrament[7] of redemption and an aid to deliverance. This is why he says, 'My own arm brought me salvation, and my own displeasure aided me'.*   Is 63:5
In order, then, that every mouth be closed and the whole world be subject to God,* nobody should now say,   Rm 3:19
'God did not spare me from death. Therefore, he does not love me.' Instead, we should say in astonishment, 'To spare me, God did not spare himself from death. How great, therefore, is his love for me!'

If, then, we compare love and death, it is clear that love is as strong as death. Who can doubt the strength of death? What force, what power, what rank, what renown, what wisdom, what prudence, what art, what trickery can oppose it? It claims all men as its debtors; it exacts tribute from all; it overwhelms all; it spares none; it reigns everywhere on earth; it treats all equally; it commands all; and, itself unassailable, it assails all who assail its cities.*   Pr 16:32
All who sleep in the dust of the earth bear witness to this, and the very tombs of the dead testify to its truth. All the great rulers and kings and princes who have inspired terror in the land of the living have themselves experienced what death can do. All the wise of the world, who used to observe the stars of heaven and calculate months and days,* were suddenly   Is 47:13
forestalled [in their labors] by the onset of death and caught in their own craftiness.* In this we   Jb 5:13

see the double strength of death: it could capture all or snatch them away, and it could hold them all fast, and there was none who could deliver them out of its hand.*

But by the power of God's love for us, the chains by which death held us captive were broken, and, as a result, only for a short time could it hold fast to those whom, for a short time, it was allowed to assail. For Christ has risen, the first-fruits of those that sleep,* and by the sacrament[8] and example and testimony of his resurrection, and by the word of his promise, he strengthens the confidence we have in our own rising.

Strong is death, which can rob us of the gift of life. Strong is love, which can restore us to the enjoyment of a better life. Strong is death, which has the power to despoil us of this bodily vestment. Strong is love, which has the power to plunder the spoils of death and return them to us. Strong is death, which no one can resist. Strong is love, for it can triumph over [death] itself, make blunt its sting, soothe its strife, and confound its victory. There will come a time when we will scoff [at death], when we will say, 'Death, where is your sting? Death, where is your strife? Death, where is your victory?'*[9] Love is strong as death,† for the love of Christ is the death of death. Therefore, he says, 'O Death, I will be your death. O Hell, I will be your destruction!'*

The love with which we love Christ is also strong as death, for inasmuch as it is the extinction of our old life, the abolition of our vices, and an end to dead works, it is itself a sort of death. This love of ours for Christ is a sort of exchange—however unequal—of his love for us. It is a likeness [of his love] patterned on its image.¹⁰ He loved us first,* and by the example of that love which he offered to us, he was made a seal for us, [a seal] which enables us to be conformed to his image, laying aside the image of the earthly and bearing [instead] the image of the heavenly,* loving him as we are loved. In this he left us an example so that we might follow in his steps.*

This is why he says, 'Set me as a seal upon your heart'. It is as if he said, 'Love me as I love you. Have me in your mind, your memory, your desire, your yearning, your sighing, and your sobbing. Remember, mankind, how I made you, how I put you before all other creatures, how I ennobled you with such dignity, how I crowned you with glory and honor, how I made you only a little less than the angels, how I subjected all things under your feet.* Remember, too, not only the many things I made for you, but what harsh and undeserved things I endured for you, and see if you are not being unfair to me if you do not love me. Who loves you as I do? Who wants you to love them as I do?¹¹ Who created you, if not I? Who redeemed you, if not I? Who defended your life and underwent the danger of battle, if not I?

Therefore, to render me love for love, roll up your sleeves and set to work!¹² Set me as a seal upon your arm! Fight for me as I [fought] for you! Do not fawn on me with false flattery and say, 'Lord, I love you'. If you love me, show that you love me! Love me in deed and in truth, not with the word and the tongue.* Fighting for you, I conquered the world,* but the world and the prince of the world are still against you, and the flesh, too, is still against you. Fight them, then, for me—but still more for yourself! For it is you who are in danger! The

1 Jn 4:10

1 Co 15:49
1 P 2:21

Ps 8:6-8[5-6]

1 Jn 3:18
Jn 16:33

battle is for your soul and your salvation! You cannot be conquered, save by your own efforts; but you cannot conquer, save by mine. Rely not on yourself, therefore, but on me. You will not prevail against the enemy with your own sword, and your own arm will not save you. It is by my right hand, my arm, and the light of my countenance [that you will prevail].\* If you set me as a seal upon your arm, the victory will fall to you. Do not fight as if you were just beating the air, but chastise your body and bring it into subjection.\* Refrain from all things as one who strives for mastery.\*

If this seems hard for you, can you blame me?[13] I too kept to hard ways. If you want to emulate me, know that such emulation is as hard as hell.[14] It is fitting for you to drink the cup which I drank.\* I was thirsty, and I drank; I tasted death; I descended into hell. But I loosed the sorrows of hell and rose again.\* If, then, in wanting to imitate me and striving to emulate me, you feel as if you were oppressed and tormented in hell, it is this which I demand from you, this which I desire, this which I teach, this which I counsel. For by being tormented just a little as if you were in hell, you may avoid being tormented in hell for ever. Emulation is a sort of hell; it is just like the place of punishment. But it is the way which leads to the gate of the kingdom!

It is right for you to suffer these things and thereby enter into life. This is how the martyrs truly emulated me and now share the kingdom with me. But first, their bones and bodies were cast down on the earth by death and after death were treated with abuse, so that they say, 'Our bones are scattered by the side of hell'.\* See how they loved me! They wanted to follow me even to hell, although they had no wish to be swallowed up by hell.* If you suffer adversities and are therefore reckoned in the judgement of others to be a sinner and close to hell, you possess that which enables you to say with me, 'My soul is full of evils, and my life has come close to hell. I am reckoned among those that go down to the Pit.'*

Set me as a seal upon your heart that you may love me with all your strength. Set me upon your arm so that with all your love you may accomplish all that is pleasing to me. Set me upon your heart through the inner disposition of love. Set me upon your arm through the acts of love which you perform.[15] Take me as an example and a helper [in your struggle] to love purely and sincerely; an example and a helper [in your struggle] to act well and to suffer with fortitude. Set me upon your heart, upon all that you think, upon all that you love, upon all that arises from your heart. Thus, by setting aside all that is dear [to you], you may set me always before it and always love me more—not only [more] than whatever is outside you, but more than whatever is within you as well. In a word: more than yourself! In this way, you will love yourself for my sake, and not just myself for your sake. After [your love for] me, let your love for yourself hold the highest place in your heart, but let your love for me be yet higher! And since the proof of love is shown by deeds,[16] set me upon your arm. Fight and work for me in such a way that what you do [comes] from me. Let me be your hope, let me be your trust, let me be your strength, let me be your patience., Say to me, 'O Lord, my hope from my youth'.* Say to me, 'I will love you, O Lord, who are my strength'.* Say to me, 'You are my

Cf. Pr 1:12

Ps 87:3-4[88:2-3]

Gregory the Great,

Ps 70:5[71:4]
Ps 17[18]:1

patience, O Lord'.* Say to me, 'My God, [you are] my mercy'.* Do not make the flesh your arm,[17] but say to me, 'Be our arm in the morning and our salvation in the time of trouble'.*

With regard to the things within you, I demand the love of your heart; with regard to the things outside you, [I demand] that you emulate me. But in order to know whether your love be true, consider the strength of your soul, for [love] which is not as strong as death is not true love. First of all, consider my love for you and my death on your behalf. When I laid down my life for you, neither the malice or power of those who persecuted me, nor the violence of my death, wrested my life unwillingly from me. Charity itself urged me on, [charity] itself drove me, [charity] itself did me violence. What death could do in others, love could do in me, [love] which was followed by death. Consider what death can do to others and what love can do, and then you will realize that love is strong as death. Death divides those who are nearest and dearest and [breaks] the closest bonds; love, too, divides them, for whoever has left his house or brothers or sisters or father or mother or wife or children or lands for my name's sake will receive a hundredfold and inherit eternal life.* Death divides the soul and body; love, too, divides them, for whoever does not hate his own soul cannot be my disciple.*

As for emulating me in the things outside you, if [such emulation] is not harsh and difficult to bear,[18] it is obviously not true,[19] for someone who will not stay with me in adversity can [certainly] change in prosperity. Strength of soul, therefore, in separating [oneself] from one's affections is an internal sign and a sign of love. Tribulation which is harsh and difficult to bear is an external sign and a sign of emulation. Such are the signs impressed by the seal.

Lord, you say to me, 'Set me as a seal upon your heart', do then what you command! Where shall I find the power to set you upon my heart? How can *I* do this? Yet unless it were in some way possible—in such a way as if it were through you—you would not say to me, 'Set me'. What condescension on your part, O Lord! What honor, what freedom on mine, O Lord! For you do not scorn to be set by your servant upon the heart of your servant. You considered me so worthy and gave me free will so that I could reject whatever displeases you and choose the good which pleases you, and, by choosing the good, be pleasing to you and be united to you, participate in you, possess you within myself, and love you as you deserve, above myself.

Take from me, O Lord, my heart of stone. Take away my hardened heart. Take away my uncircumcised heart. Give me a new heart, a heart of flesh, a pure heart!\* You who purify the heart, you who love the pure heart, possess my heart and dwell within it, enclosing it and filling it, higher than what in me is highest, more inward than my most inward part. O form of beauty and seal of sanctity, seal my
  heart in your image, seal my heart under your
    mercy, O God of my heart, O God
      my portion for ever.\*
        Amen.

Cf. Ezk 11:19

Ps 72[73]:26

## NOTES TO TRACTATE X / I

1. There can be no doubt that Tr. x includes two distinct sermons, both of which were probably delivered to a monastic audience. The first is an exposition of Sg 8:6 (and for convenience, I have called it 'On the Seal of the Love of God'), and the second bears the title 'On Human Misery and Want which results from Sin' (see Tr. x/ii, n. 1). Certain manuscripts, in fact, do treat them as two separate discourses (for details, see the article by P. Guébin cited in Tr. i, n. 1). There is no doubt that the first sermon is complete, but I have grave doubts about the second. The ending is very abrupt for Baldwin's style, and just as I suspect that material has been lost from the beginning of Tr. ix/iv (see Tr. ix/iv, n. 1), I also suspect that material has been lost from the end of Tr. x/ii. Since the two sermons are obviously quite separate, I have presented them here as two separate treatises.
2. The Latin word is *aemulatio*, and it is usually rendered as 'jealousy' in this particular verse. It can also, however, mean emulation or zealous imitation in a positive sense (see Tr. iv, n. 30), and this is how Baldwin understands it. What he means, therefore, is 'Love is strong as death, and if we really try with all our zeal to imitate the love of Christ, then we will undergo trials and tribulations which are truly as hard as hell'.
3. The Latin is very concise: . . . *quo cor nostrum pressius signavit, ut coimaginatum similitudinem imaginis in se exciperet, et configuraliter exprimeret*. I suspect that Baldwin's terminology here may have been influenced by Hilary of Poitiers (*De Trinitate* viii. 45; PL 10:270A). See also n. 10 below.
4. Thomas (39/14) reads *designatur*; PL 511B has *quod signatur*.
5. See Tr. ix/iv, n. 7.
6. See Tr. ix/iii, n. 6.
7. See Tr. iii, n. 10 and Tr. viii n. 8.
8. *Ibid.*
9. Thomas (39/24) omits *ubi est mors aculeus tuus*; PL 513D omits *ubi est mors victoria tua*; *ubi est mors contentio tua* is common to both. Baldwin's original text actually contains all three phrases.
10. *Coimaginata similitudo*. See n. 3 above.
11. PL 514B omits this question.
12. Lit. 'Therefore, so that you may repay me an exchange of love, bare your arms, exercise your powers'.
13. Thomas (39/28) reads *causari*; PL 514C has *accusari*.
14. See n. 2 above.
15. Lit 'Set me upon your heart *per affectum amoris*; set me upon your arm *per effectum operationis*'.
16. As Thomas points out (39/33, n. 2), Baldwin is quoting Gregory the Great, *Homiliae in Evangelia* 30.1 (PL 76:1220C).
17. I.e. your support. See also Tr. ix/i n. 20.
18. The Latin simply has *durus*, but the word means hard, harsh, difficult to bear, cruel, lasting, and enduring.
19. The punctuation of this passage in PL 515D is obviously incorrect.
20. As Thomas indicates (39/35, n. 1), Baldwin is echoing Augustine, *Confessions* x.xxix. 40 (PL 32:796).

## TRACTATE X/II
## ON HUMAN MISERY AND WANT
## WHICH RESULTS FROM SIN[1]

**B**Y THE SIN OF DISOBEDIENCE, man separated himself from God and was therefore subjected to that most just punishment which his guilty condition deserved. By abandoning the unchangeable God, he also abandons himself within himself, and by gradually abandoning his own [powers], he becomes older and older and more and more feeble, until he is finally released by death, for something which grows old and feeble is near its end.\* By withdrawing from God, who is always one and the same, man is divided [from God] by the wrath of his countenance,\* but he is also divided within himself. He is not always one and the same to himself but is continually changing — now one thing and now another — and he fulfills that which is written: 'A fool is as changeable as the moon'.\* He differs and disagrees so much with himself and is so much in dissension and discord that far from being one single person to himself, it would be difficult to find two people who could be more contrary! He wants something and then does not want it, and the same person takes turns in hating and loving, doing something and deciding not to, approving something and then condemning it, searching for something and throwing it away, caring for something and then neglecting it. When he begins something, it often irks him to have begun it, and

Heb 8:13

Ps 54:22

Si 27:12

when he has finished it, he is sorry he did it. His wishes and desires, his endeavors and projects, his thoughts and affections and impulses, change in a multitude of ways as if they always displeased him, and by all these [changes] he himself is changed. Truly, 'a double-minded man is inconstant in all his ways'.\* What peace can there be for miserable man in such a welter of chopping and changing, [for someone] whose soul is so fickle and capricious? 'There is no peace for the wicked, says the Lord.'\* The perverse soul is contrary to both God and himself and is himself his own tormentor and his own torment. He is always demanding punishment from himself and always suffering it, and anyone who stands opposed to God in his sin and his guilt is like God's own instrument in exacting punishment.

See how the wicked are divided from God by the wrath of his countenance!\* They are so opposed to themselves that they are their own persecutors, and since they are as contrary to God as they are to themselves, they find no peace in their own will since they set themselves up against the will of God.

But is it only the wicked who are thus divided? What of the soul\*² of a just man who occupies himself with worldly things and busies himself with a whole multitude of concerns and is therefore less mindful of God [than he should be]? Is he not also divided? Is it not said to Martha, 'Martha, Martha, you are anxious and troubled about many things!'\* What purpose was there in saying her name twice? Was it not enough to say 'Martha' one single time without repeating it as 'Martha, Martha!' Or does the repetition mean that Martha was divided? 'Martha,' he says the first time, and then again, 'Martha'. It is surely a divided Martha, an anxious Martha, a troubled Martha; anxious to make provision for the future, troubled in attending to present needs. You are anxious and troubled about many things.³

Many indeed are the things which trouble us, for mankind in its misery has many needs. Misery and need always cling together, and anyone miserable is always in want. The needs of mankind are so many and so varied, so intricate and inextricable, that never at any time in his life can one be free of them. The tireless flux of time and things is always producing a new need and providing a new anxiety, and when one need disappears, another takes its place. One need draws another to it, and when the second follows and drives out the first, the second itself compels another to follow it. When one has arisen and been dealt with, another directly takes its place. It is like someone who borrows from one person to repay another: the way he frees himself [from one debt] is the way he binds himself [to a second]. And it is just the same for the whole of human life: when someone is released from the bondage of one need, he is bound by another, and the miserable man who is always striving to free himself is always struggling skilfully to bind himself! The ways of men are surely strewn with thorns! In this way, every time he flees from one need, he always bumps into another, and by continually seeking abundance so as to escape from need, he only finds [himself in] want.

As for the rich, who glory in the abundance of their riches,* they should only be aware of what the Scripture says, 'The rich have wanted and have suffered hunger'.* Those who possess much always want for much, and where there is great wealth, there too we find great numbers to consume it.

Ps 48:7[49:6]

Ps 33:11[34:10]

Those who extort from others against their will often unwillingly suffer the same thing, and those who take from others who are unwilling [to give] are often those who give unwillingly. There are some who have riches but do not distribute them, since they want to keep them to themselves so as never to be in want. But it is they themselves who are wanting! They are in want for what they have and equally so for what they do not have. They continually make their disease worse by the remedy [they apply], for those whose lust is insatiable can find no remedy for their need.

These needs which miserable and wretched people suffer are produced by the love of things which are themselves unnecessary. They seek comfort in a whole host of unnecessary things and do not find it. Yet one thing is necessary.\* One thing indeed is necessary, something without which nothing is necessary, one highest and common good. This one thing is enough for all, but without it, all the rest is not enough for even a single person. For this one thing, Peter abandoned all things so as to have all things in one thing, for if he lacked this one thing, he would have neither one thing nor all things! 'One thing,' says [the Psalmist], 'I have asked of the Lord; this will I seek.'\* Whoever seeks this one thing will not be deprived of any good.\* But whoever does not possess this one thing lacks himself, and since he lacks his mind, he is not in possession of his reason, nor is his own heart in his power. If a person lacks his mind he does not have himself. What, then, does he have? If he does not have himself, he does not have God, and it stands to reason, therefore, that the only thing he has is his sins!⁴

[Thus] it happens that by a wondrous judgement

of God, the wicked person who, in his own estimation, possesses much is actually empty in the very place where he seems to be full, and where he hopes for abundance, he suffers only want. The Scripture cannot be denied,* and it says of God, 'He has filled the hungry with good things and the rich he has sent empty away'.* And in another place, the Scripture says of the rich, 'They have slept their sleep, and no men have found any trace of their riches in their hands'.* If the rich sleep their sleep and dream that they have much in their hands, but in fact have no riches at all, if they are deluded by vain opinion⁵ and judge themselves happy when they are actually miserable, are they really in their right mind?⁶

Jn 10:35

Lk 1:53

Ps 75:6[76:5]

## NOTES TO TRACTATE X/II

1. See Tr. x/1, n. 1. This title appears in PL 516B, but is omitted in Thomas's edition of the text.
2. *Mens*; cf. IX/1, n. 18.
3. See also Tr. VIII, n. 13 for a similar exegesis of this passage.
4. I would suggest that the key to understanding this difficult passage lies in the Augustinian conception of the nature of human rationality. The distinguishing feature of the human creation is the 'spark of reason' (*scintilla rationis*: see Tr. VI, n. 35) which separates men and women from the animals and indicates that they alone were created in the image of God. But human rationality is what it is only by participation in God (or, from another point of view, by God's presence in the mind/soul), and the mind or *mens* (which is the seat of reason) is therefore in direct participatory contact with its Creator (see also Tr. VIII, n. 26). It follows, therefore, that being human, being rational, and 'possessing God' are ineluctably linked. If you do not possess God, you are neither truly rational (you do not have your mind/reason) nor truly human (you do not have yourself), and you cannot be truly human or truly rational unless you possess God.
5. There is a discussion of 'vain opinion' in Tr. IX/1.
6. On this very abrupt ending, see Tr. x/1, n. 1.

# TRACTATE XI
# ON THE CRUCIFIXION OF OUR OLD MAN[1]

On the Words of the Apostle: *Our old man was crucified with him so that the body of sin may be destroyed and we may serve sin no longer\**     Rm 6:6

### OF THE THREE CROSSES

CHRIST SUFFERED FOR US, leaving you an example that you should follow in his steps.'\* He suffered on the cross, so that by the mystery of the cross he might strengthen in us the virtue of patience.[2] It is right that we should suffer and thereby receive the due reward of our deeds.\* Christ, therefore, enjoined us to bear a cross ourselves, saying, 'If any one will come after me, let him deny himself and take up his cross and follow me.'\* Let him take up his own cross, he says, not mine, for there is a cross consecrated by the body of Christ, [a cross] which Christ alone ascended, [Christ] who alone is free among the dead.\* He was not in bondage to sin, nor was he bound by the debt of death, for in him he who had the power of death\* had no power at all.\* He was offered because it was his own will.\* The cross of Christ, therefore, is the cross of the innocent and the just. It was not he who was purified and justified through the cross, but he who, through the cross, purified and justified [others].

    1 P 2:21

    Lk 23:41

    Mt 16:24

    Ps 87:6[88:4]

    Heb 2:14
    Jn 14:30
    Is 53:7

There is also another cross, not that of the Man-God, but that of a guilty man, one who grumbles and does not suffer in patience. And there is yet another cross of a guilty man, but of one who was penitent and confessed and who was told, 'Today you will be with me in Paradise'.* There is no one absolved from the need to take up his cross, no one excused. The wicked bear their cross, for many are the scourges of the sinner.* And the good also bear their cross, for many are the afflictions of the just.*

The wicked sometimes bear their cross willingly, joyfully, and cheerfully, for in seeking and increasing and preserving the vanities which they love so vainly, they willingly undergo many great labors and many grievous afflictions.* But because they prefer to suffer for the world rather than for Christ, their patient suffering is worthless, and in the eyes of God they have nothing which can be called merit nor any hope of reward. 'Destruction and unhappiness are in their ways, and the ways of peace they have not known.'* These people could be happy if they would direct to the truth the arrangements they have made for [the pursuit of] vanity, but now, of their own free will, they are miserable, and the more they think themselves blessed, the more miserable they actually are! Because they believe themselves blessed, they make no attempt to avoid the misery which they willingly endure, just as Ephraim is a heifer who is taught to love treading out the corn.* In the hope of some worthless chaff, the heifer loves the labor of threshing. Rightly is this generation likened to the horse and the mule, senseless beasts who have no understanding!* Their jaws are bound fast with bit and bridle, for they do not come near to you, O God.* You will cast them down into the fire, and in their miseries they will not be able to stand.\* They run from misery to misery and merit torment on torment. 'You, O Lord, will preserve us, and keep us from this generation for ever.'\*

Sometimes the wicked bear their cross because they are forced to do so. Scourged by God, they kick against the goad\* and grumble. By their own judgement they absolve themselves [from any guilt] and object to the sentence [levied upon them] by God. They hiss like serpents, oppressed and full of complaints. They judge themselves to be better than others who have not suffered such things and consider themselves undeserving of such scourging. Of people like these it is written: 'The heart of a fool is like the wheel of a cart'.\* It carries hay and rumbles and grumbles along, but its grumbling does not lighten the burden in the cart; it grumbles, but it still bears [the weight]. In the same way the fool is oppressed by the weight of affliction, and because of his impatience, he is himself his own burden — and [the burden is] truly one of hay, which is here today and tomorrow is cast into the oven.\* The fool speaks foolishness, and the mouth of fools bubbles out folly.\* What is more foolish than to extol oneself in adversity and to set one's mouth against heaven?\* To be weak and yet fail to acknowledge one's weakness and, through one's own anger, to arouse the anger of God? How much better are they who declare with blessed Job: 'As it has pleased the Lord so is it done: blessed be the name of the Lord'.\* Of such as these it is written: 'They will still increase in a fruitful old age. They will be well treated, so that they may proclaim that the Lord our God is righteous, and there is no iniquity in him.'\*

Ps 139:11[140:10]

Ps 11[12]:8

Ac 9:5

Si 33:5

Mt 6:30

Pr 15:2
Ps 72:9[73:8]

Jb 1:21

Ps 91:14–15[92:13–14]

## Of the Old Man, which is Earthly, Carnal, and Animal

The cross which the wicked bear, whether willing or unwilling, is on the left, a worthy cross for those who deserve it.³ On this cross the old man is crucified, for the Apostle, having spoken of the cross of Christ, goes on to add: 'Our old man is crucified with him'.* [Rm 6:6] He shows by this that the old man should be crucified together with Christ, that is to say, for the sake of Christ. Who is this old man but he who says, 'I have grown old among all my enemies'?* [Ps 6:8[7]] And who are the enemies among whom he has grown old but the members of God's own household?* [Eph 2:19] For the new man, however, the members of the household are his friends. They are fellow citizens of the saints and the household of God,*⁴ [Ibid.] and to them it is said, 'You are my friends if you do what I command you'.* [Jn 15:14]

The old man, however, is not like this. In his case, the members of his household are his enemies. The old man is an evil and unjust man—and he is myself, I who am now speaking!⁵ I, too, have grown old among all my enemies, and I am not speaking only of those enemies who are outside me, those among whom I dwelt when I dwelt with the inhabitants of Cedar.* [Ps 119:5[120:4]] I refer now more to those enemies who are within me, who inhabit the land of my heart and the land of my flesh. Canaanites and Jebusites and Perezites are dwelling there, and they have become my enemies. I myself, an evil and an unjust man, am so much my own enemy that I can as easily pray for myself as against myself and say, 'Deliver me, O Lord, from the evil man; rescue me from the unjust man'.* [Ps 139[140]:1] Deliver me, O Lord, from myself, for after you, O Lord, there is none that I should fear as much as myself. Who can lie in ambush for my soul as I can? Who is so opposed to my salvation as I am? Who is as skilled in [achieving] my destruction as myself? Who can coax and lure me to my ruin as I can? Who seeks my soul to take it away?* Who thinks to rob me of my reward?† Who is there, Lord, who tries as hard as I to sweep away that splendid inheritance which you have promised? Who is there more than I who hates my soul with so hostile a hatred?

Yet all this I do without cause? What evil have you done to me, O my soul? It is thanks to you that I live, thanks to you that I hear, that I see, that I am full of health and vigor; thanks to you that I perceive, that I understand, that I am wise—if indeed I am wise and not, in fact, foolish. Yet am I not ungrateful, am I not wicked and malicious in hating you and loving iniquity? Whoever loves iniquity hates his own soul.* O my soul, if I hate you who love me, is it not a great iniquity? And if I hate you, how can I not hate myself? Are you not my soul and my life? What else are you but my very soul and life? What right, then, have I not to love you, who are my life and my own unique [soul]?⁶

Woe to me if you should be lost for ever through my fault, and I [lost] for ever with you. If you should be lost, who is better fitted to take the blame than myself? If I should be lost (which God forbid!) whom should I blame, me or you? If both me and you, then woe to both me and you. But if it is through your fault that I am wicked and deserve to be lost, what reason could I have to love you since you are the cause of my ruin? If this should happen, it were better for me if I had not been born.* What counsel is left for me before I am lost which will

Ps 39:15[40:17]
†Ps 61:5[62:4]

Ps 10[11]:6

Mk 14:21

prevent me from being lost? For if it happens that one day I should be lost (and may it never occur!) what more could I do but to submit to such a loss? O Lord God, then is the time of your wrath,* then is the time when no counsel, no sagacity, no wisdom, no reasoning [will be of any use]. Someone who has once suffered such a loss remains lost.

I know what I will do before I am lost—or, more accurately, so that I may avoid being lost⁷—'I will cry to the most high God, to God who has done good to me'.* God is Most High, but I am in the depths of wickedness. Since he is Most High I need to give a strong cry, otherwise he may not hear me. To God, who freely sanctifies the wicked, I will tell my iniquities. I will confess that the Lord is good.* I will accuse myself and not spare myself, and I will loose my own eloquence against myself.*⁸ As a penitent goaded by sorrow I will speak in the bitterness of my soul and say to God, 'Do not condemn me!'* I myself will judge myself, and I will condemn myself. Do not you, O Lord, condemn me. Let me labor in this matter. You yourself once labored for our salvation; you considered labor and sorrow to deliver us into your hands.* Good Jesus, it is not in accord with your name to condemn him who condemns himself or to lose him who judges himself. The world calls you Saviour, not Destroyer. It is true that you will bring evil men to an evil end,* but [only] those who persevere in their wickedness. I have no wish to persevere in mine. 'Say to my soul: I am your salvation.'* O my soul, although you are accused of so much and guilty of so much and are therefore so terrified, can you not still smile at the hope of forgiveness in the most sweet name of

## Tractate XI

Jesus, who is most generous and exceeding bounteous?⁹ Why are you consumed with grief?* Why do you waste away in bitterness? Is there no one to give you counsel? 'Is there no balm in Gilead; is there no physician there?'* 'Why are you sad, my soul, and why do you disturb me? Put your hope in God, for I will still give praise to him, the salvation of my countenance and my God.'*

While I long to comfort myself in my soliloquy, my soul chooses to hang [on the cross] and my bones [choose] death,* for my soul is weary of life.† And no wonder! My life is evil, and I am an old man near to death,¹⁰ an evil man, an unjust man,* an earthly man, bearing the image of the earthly,* a carnal man sold to sin, an animal man, perceiving not the things that are of the spirit of God,* a man condemned to death and deserving the cross. But it is not just one cross [that I deserve]: there is one cross for earthly [man], another for carnal man, and another for animal [man]. But I, who am one man, am all of these, and all are in the one [man] who is me. Their thoughts are all against me [to lead me] into evil.* They will dwell [within me] and hide themselves; they will watch all my steps.*

How harsh and heavy, how miserable and wretched is our human condition! Our enemies are alive and are stronger than we,* and our enemies are we ourselves, earthly, carnal, and animal. There is neither peace nor security for us from ourselves until we are hung upon the cross and crucified with Christ. Then the body of sin will be destroyed in us, and we will serve sin no longer.* Then, when we are dead to sins, we may live to righteousness,* and being delivered out of the hand of our enemies, we

Mi 4:9

Jr 8:22

Ps 41:6, 12 [42:6, 14–15], Ps 42[43]:5–6

Jb 7:15
†Jb 10:1
Cf. Ps 139:2[140:1]:
1 Co 15:49

1 Co 2:14

Ps 55:6[56:5]
Ps 55:7[56:6]

Ps 37:20[38:19]

Rm 6:6
1 P 2:24

may serve him without fear, in holiness and righteousness before him, all the days of our life.\*

## Of Earthly Man

First of all, earthly man should be crucified in us, then carnal man, and finally animal man. We should then put on the man who was created according to God. Speaking of earthly man, the Apostle says, 'The first man was from the earth, earthly; the second man is from heaven, heavenly'.\* And again, 'Just as we have borne the image of the earthly, let us bear also the image of the heavenly'.\*

The earthly man is the old man, for he began [his life] in days long ago,[11] "the days of Adam's transgression. Those who bear his image have their minds set on earthly things.\* They think only of worldly things and of how they might be pleasing to the world. They are too much in love with earthly substance and earthly glory.

The psalmist shows us the nature of the image of earthly man when he says, 'Man is like vanity'.\* Someone who has turned from God, who loves vain things and does vain things, is himself also vain — or, more accurately, he becomes vanity itself. The nature of the deeds is the nature of the doer. What a person is outside himself, in the deeds he does, is also what he is within himself, in his heart, where he plans his deeds, for the doer expresses himself in what he does as if in a mirror.

Before sin, there was in man the image of truth,[12] the image, that is, of God, who is truth. After sin, the image of truth was disfigured in man, and there was portrayed in him the image of vanity. He became like vanity, and because he did not stand in the truth,\* his days pass away like a shadow.\* Man passes like an image.* Do you not see how earthly man has chased after greed? How he has neglected the image of God and has begun to love the image of money,* whose value lies only in the false and foolish opinion of men? A coin bears the image and superscription of a man, as though man makes it in the image and likeness of man and changes the glory of the incorruptible God into the likeness of corruptible man.* By his mistaken love of money, he serves the creature rather than the Creator,* and this is the service of idols.* What are these things of silver and gold stamped with the seal of the mint, but the effigies of kings and the works of the hands of men?*

It is these, these which are your gods, you greedy people, these whom you love with all your heart, all your soul, all your mind, these whom you treat with the highest honor, these in whom you trust, in whom you put all your hope for all your needs! Where your treasure is, there, too, is your heart!* But there will come a time when [God] will say to men like this: 'Where are their gods in whom they trusted, of whose victims they ate the fat and drank the wine of their libations? Let them arise and help you and protect you in your hour of need!'*

The way of life of earthly man is not in heaven,* but on earth. He does not look to heaven* but has determined to lower his eyes to the earth.* He licks the earth* and eats earth all the days of his life.* His belly cleaves to the earth;† he is stuck fast in the mire of the deep and has no foundation,* for he has not set his feet upon a rock.† He goes continually into the lower parts of the earth* until he is swallowed up by the earth, like Dathan and Abiron.* He disputes for the earth and fights for the earth, until a pit be dug for the

Ps 38[39]:7

Cf. Mk 12:16

Rm 1:23

Rm 1:25
Eph 5:5

Pss 113[115]:4,
134[135]:15

Mt 6:21

Dt 32:37–38
Ph 3:20
Dn 13:9
Ps 16[17]:11
Ps 71[72]:9
Gn 3:14
†Ps 43[44]:25
Ps 68:3[69:2]
†Ps 39:3[40:2]
Ps 62[63]:10
Nb 16:30

sinner* and he is buried in the earth, [once more] reduced to earth who was made from earth.*

Yet his whole life is [spent in] priding himself in his glory. He is envious of the happiness of others, since he is as full of cupidity as he is estranged from charity. He is not kind or patient, but ambitious and jealous. He acts falsely and seeks his own [interests], not those of Jesus Christ.* His heart is heavy; he loves vanity and seeks after lying;* his mouth abounds with evil, and his tongue frames deceits.* Of the earth he is, and of the earth he speaks. He is always in fear of want, and in taking precautions for the future, he is always conserving what he should augment and always augmenting what he should conserve! Each time a [new] need comes upon him, he [immediately] provides for it; his nostrils are always filled with the smell of profit and his right hand with gifts.* He refers to all the ways in which he can make more money as 'prudence'. He scoffs at poverty, and in his estimation, the very name of poverty is shameful. He puts all that he possesses in a safe place and continually promises himself the hope of a long life—until he is told, 'You fool, this night your soul will be required of you, and the things you have prepared, whose will they be?'* When he dies, therefore, he will take nothing away with him, nor shall his glory descend with him.* Such a person is a friend of the world and is made the enemy of God,* for it is he who cries out against Christ, saying, 'Take him away, take him away! Crucify him!'* Surely they were earthly men who said, 'If we let him alone, everyone will believe in him, and the Romans will come and destroy both our holy place and our nation'.*

## Tractate XI

The ill-will which the earthly man bears toward Christ has still not passed away, for he persecutes Christ in us to prevent Christ from living in us. If, then, anyone belongs to Christ, let him arm himself with vengeful zeal against those who persecute Christ. For the sake of Christ, let us cry out to each other against the enemy of Christ: 'Take him away, take him away! Crucify him!'* But what accusation do we bring against this man?* 'Behold the man that did not make God his helper! He trusted in the abundance of his riches and found his strength in his vanity.'* 'Take him away, take him away! Crucify him!' If you release this man, you are not God's friend.* Do to him what he has done! He crucified [Christ]; crucify him! He deserves the cross and is guilty of death!*

    Jn 19:15
    Jn 18:29

    Ps 51:9[52:8]

    Cf. Jn 19:12

    Mt 26:66

What is this man's cross, you ask. I hold it to be contempt for the world. Such a cross is made from two pieces of wood: [they symbolize] contempt for earthly substance and contempt for earthly glory. The earthly man certainly loves these two things, for he trusts in his own strength and glories in the abundance of his riches.* He trusts in the world, let it deliver him if it can!*

    Ps 48:7[49:6]
    Cf. Mt 27:43

Let those who despise the world stretch [the earthly man] out on the cross. Stretch him out completely, vertically and laterally! Since his height is his earthly glory, [a glory] in which he seeks to be raised [ever higher], let his height be stretched out by a contempt for earthly glory—that is, by voluntary abasement; and since his breadth is his earthly substance, which he seeks to extend to both left and right, let his breadth be stretched out by a contempt for earthly substance—that is, by voluntary poverty.

Let the earthly man hang on this cross; let him be stretched out upon it. When he has been stretched out, let him die; when he is dead, bury him; and do not ever let him rise again.* Let God destroy him for ever, let him remove him from his dwelling-place and his root from the land of the living.* Let his memory perish from the earth, since he did not remember to show mercy, but persecuted the poor man and the beggar.*

## OF CARNAL MAN[13]

There is another cross on which we should hang carnal man. For although it is the same man who is both earthly and carnal, it seems that we should distinguish between them on account of their [different] names and the different [sorts] of love [which apply to them].

When speaking of the law of sin which we have in our members, the Apostle says among other things, 'I am carnal, sold to sin'.* Someone sold to sin is not wholly free but is in a certain way a servant. He does not do the good which he wants to do, but the evil which he does not want to do. And if he is really intent on doing evil and does evil, he is then the servant of sin since he commits sin, for whoever commits sin is the servant of sin.* He is now completely sold to sin, and [in exchange] for the consent of his will, he receives the coin of unlawful delights.

The passions of sin work in our members to bear fruit for death,* and all of us, whether we are good or bad, share in feeling these passions. Not all of us, however, [feel them] to the same extent, nor do we all consent to them. But even if someone feels [them] and does not consent, he is still not wholly free from

sin, for he still does the evil which he does not want to do! By feeling the passion of concupiscence, he lusts[14] after evil while not wanting to lust after evil, and since lusting after evil is itself an evil, he therefore does the evil which he does not want [to do]! If someone lusts after evil and does not consent to it, he still commits evil in a certain way, [namely], to the extent that he lusts after evil; but because he does not consent to it, there is also a way in which he does *not* commit it, for having been tempted by concupiscence, he suffers unwillingly what he has no wish to suffer. The Apostle, therefore, who lusted but did not consent [to his lust] states both [points of view]: [he says] that he does the evil he does not want to do, and [he also says] that he does not do it – 'I do the evil that I do not want to do (that is, I lust, and I do not want to lust), but it is no longer I that do it, but sin which dwells within me.'* Rm 7:19–20
It is as if he said, 'I do not want to lust, and I do not consent to my lust, but I feel – against my will – the law of sin which is in my members. It moves within me so that I feel it, but it does not move me to the extent that I give it my consent.'

When someone who is just, therefore, is tempted by his concupiscence, he has some excuse, though not to the point that he is wholly free from fault. For if he is asked why he feels in his flesh the titillations of the flesh when he does not consent to them, he can reply: 'It is no longer I who do it, but sin which dwells within me'. It is not always in our power to feel or not to feel the passions of our members, but it is [certainly] in our power to consent [to them], for there is no [consent] without our will.

It sometimes happens that someone who feels [these passions] and does not consent [to them] is determined in his heart utterly to refuse them his consent. He has no desire to feel their temptation in any way at all. But what he feels comes from his weakness; the fact that he does not consent comes from his strength and virtue;[15] and his desire not to feel them at all arises from his eagerness for peace and security.

It also sometimes happens that a person intends to withhold his consent but still wants to feel such passions, because he expects and hopes for some profit from the temptation. The stronger the temptation he resists, the more glorious is his victory. There are some, therefore, who want to feel but do not want to consent, so that they might feel without consenting and resist when they are tempted. But it is dangerous to seek such temptation willingly, and [it is equally dangerous] not to drive out at once—so far as we can—[the temptations] which come upon us. It is safer not to be tempted than to fight with temptation, for the outcome of the battle is uncertain, and at the turning point of the conflict, the victory may go either way. For this reason, when the Lord teaches us to pray, he says, 'Pray that you do not enter into temptation'.\* But when the prophet says, 'Prove me, O Lord, and tempt me',\* he is referring to that temptation with which God tempts the just, for he tempts those he has chosen so as to find them worthy of himself.\*

A person who is tempted by the flesh, and who yields to this temptation, however, is someone who feels his passions and gives them his full consent. The more carnal he is, the more provision he makes for the flesh in gratifying its desires.\* He does not give his consent to the spirit against the flesh but allies himself with the flesh, whose desires are opposed to the spirit.* Such a person loves wine and good things,* ease and security and plenty. [He loves] to be clothed in purple and fine linen and to feast sumptuously every day.* Nor does he refuse his eyes whatever they desire. He allays all his desires impulsively and willingly, and whatever does not serve the delights of flesh he regards as vain. He reckons that the best thing for him is to enjoy good things in his lifetime,* and he gains nothing more than this by all the toil at which he toils under the sun.* The end that carnal man will come to is shown in the gospel parable of the rich man and the poor man, where it says, 'The rich man died and was buried in hell.'* And of Babylon it is written, 'As she exalted herself and lived in her delights, so give her a like measure of torment and sorrow!'* ⟶ Ga 5:17 / Pr 21:17 / Lk 16:19 / Lk 16:25 / Qo 1:3 / Lk 16:22 / Rv 18:7

It is better for us, then, to deliver such a man to death for the destruction of the flesh* than to be drawn with him into the pit of destruction.* Our flesh, therefore, should be mortified and crucified, so that the body of sin may be destroyed.* Such is in accord with the voice of the prophet speaking to the Lord:'Pierce my flesh with your fear'.* ⟶ 1 Co 5:5 / Ps 54[55]:24 / Rm 6:6 / Ps 118[119]:120

Because it is said to carnal man, 'You have hated discipline',*¹⁶ we can find no better cross on which to crucify carnal man than the austerity of regular discipline, for the discipline which he hates is a torment to him. Regular discipline is a cross, and the two pieces of wood from which it is built [symbolize] the laws of abstinence and continence. Abstinence tempers gluttony, and the law of continence restrains excess in all the senses of mind and ⟶ Ps 49[50]:17

body: and it is precisely these things which are [characteristic of] the carnal man.¹⁷

It is possible for us to restrain our excesses and to temper our gluttony so that we do not *consent* to the passions of sin which dwell in our members, but we cannot do so to the extent that we do not in any way *feel* the law [of sin] which is in our members. By the protracted practice of discipline and unremitting spiritual exercises, it is possible for righteous people to weaken and enfeeble concupiscence, which is innate and inborn, so that it does not prevail, but they cannot eradicate it completely—though this is not to put limits on the freedom of the spirit of God: his grace is bound by no law and abounds, or more than abounds, in whom he will and in the measure he will.

But just as there were certain peoples left in the midst of the children of Israel so that through them the Lord could instruct Israel, and just as it was impossible to cast the Jebusites out of Jerusalem,* so it is with concupiscence of the flesh. It always inhabits the land of our body or our heart so that we might be instructed by it and never lack enemies against whom we should fight. 'For the life of man upon earth is warfare.'* This concupiscence is our weakness; it continually exhibits us to ourselves lest we trust in ourselves. It shows us ourselves: what we are in ourselves and [what we are] from ourselves.

Someone who is tempted by his weakness and conquered by it is found to be weak beyond all measure, for he is shown to be weaker than the very weakness which conquers him. But in the case of someone who is tempted by weakness and is not conquered, part of him is weak, by which he feels his weaknesses, and part of him feels the strength

Jg 1:21

Jb 7:1

which is present in him, [the strength] by which he does not consent to his weakness, for strength is perfected in weakness.*18

If it is granted from above to one of the saints—as we devoutly believe in the case of the most blessed Virgin, especially after the Spirit came upon her— that in this mortal flesh he should feel nothing of evil concupiscence, then just as it is a rare and singular grace, so it is a rare and singular glory. If there be such a person, he no longer fights, but triumphs and reigns and has peace upon peace: peace from consenting, peace from feeling. He is no longer armed for battle, but unarmed in triumph. 'A man who is armed,' says the king of Israel, 'should not boast of himself as unarmed.'* But who will boast of having a pure heart? 'If we say that we have no sin, we deceive ourselves, and the truth is not in us.'*

But just as a person who is conquered by weakness deserves [to feel] ashamed, it also appears [at first glance] that someone who conquers weakness gains no glory to speak of. What is weakness, save what it says? What is it but weakness, infirmity, and feebleness? What glory, then, or what strength is there in conquering weakness? But if we who are weaker than weakness itself should conquer weakness, there is indeed great glory and great strength. This glory and strength, however, are not ours, but the strength of the Lord, the king of glory.* He is glorified in his elect and shows his wonderful mercies* in the weakness of his saints, and to him it is said, 'You are the glory of their strength'.* If we consider what we can do by ourselves, we who are not even adequate to resist weakness itself by our own powers, [we see that] we have no strength at all. But the

2 Co 12:9

1 K 20:11

1 Jn 1:8

Ps 23[24]:10
Pss 16[17]:7, 30:22[31:21]
Ps 88[89]:18

prophet says, 'My hope is in the Lord, I will not be weakened',* and again, 'The Lord is the strength of his people'.* If, then, our God is our virtue and strength, our strength is greater than we ourselves; or, to be more accurate, what can we not do in him who can do all things? What can we not do in that all-powerful strength?[19] 'I can do all things,' says Paul, 'in him who strengthens me.'* Thus, since we do not conquer weakness by our own strength, it does not [redound] to our own praise; since it is not our virtue, neither is it our glory. It is only right that the glory be ascribed to him by whose strength the victory was gained, and the Lord of strength is himself the king of glory,* the Lord glorious in triumph, the Lord mighty in battle.* This is why the prophet says, 'The Lord is my strength and my praise':* strength in the fight, praise in the victory. It is the Lord who fights for us and the Lord who conquers in us. When we feel our weakness within us but do not consent to it, the body of sin is destroyed so that we may serve sin no longer.

If by 'the body of sin' we rightly understand the consent [given] to sin, then the body of sin is truly destroyed when we do not consent to the temptation of concupiscence. Carnal man is like[20] a man of sin and a son of perdition:* he has a body of sin in which concupiscence plays the part of its soul and consent the part of the body. When he gives his full consent to concupiscence, it is like giving life to the body of sin, which then becomes the servant of sin.

It may perhaps seem to some of you that since concupiscence appertains to the flesh — [the flesh,] that is, whose concupiscent desires are contrary to the spirit — it should be likened more to the flesh; and that since consent [takes place] in the will and the will consents in the soul, consent [should be likened] more to the soul than to the flesh. In the spiritual man this is indeed the case: in him sensuality is ruled by reason, and it is subjected to it as an inferior to its superior. But in carnal man this is not so. By a reversal of the situation and a perversion of order, the will of the spirit, in giving its consent, is subjected to the concupiscence of the flesh, and that which consents is found to be inferior to that to which it gives its consent. Concupiscence moves the soul so as to make it feel what it did not feel before, and then, when it has been moved to feel this, it is further moved to consent to it.[21] In so doing it dishonors its dignity and abandons its positions by subjecting itself to its inferior. It is then, as it were, given life from the source which moved it, and it no longer acts as spirit but suffers as flesh. It is not unworthy, therefore, of being likened to the flesh. But by the law of discipline, consent is restrained, the body of sin destroyed, and the flesh chastised, and as a result, the mind is not subjected to the flesh according to the law of the flesh, but the flesh serves the mind according to the law of the mind. This is why the Apostle says, 'I chastise my body and bring it into subjection'.* 

1 Co 9:27

All that I have been saying refers to carnal man.

## Of Animal Man[22]

We can discover the nature of animal man from the words of the Apostle, for he says, 'The animal man does not perceive the things which pertain to the spirit of God; it is foolishness to him, and he cannot understand, because it is in spiritual things that he is discerned.[23] The spiritual man, however, judges all things and is himself judged by no one.'*

1 Co 2:14-15

Carnal man and earthly man are seen to differ in the characteristic qualities of their love: the former loves the works of the flesh; the latter loves the earth. But animal man is known by his judgement\* and his inclinations\*: his judgement is animal since he does not savor the things which pertain to the spirit of God, and his inclinations are animal since for him the things which pertain to the spirit of God have no savor.²⁴ Thus, to investigate the nature of animal man we should examine him in his relationship to spiritual things, for it is in spiritual things that he is discerned.²⁵ When animal man hears the words of God, he may not understand them because he is animal, or if he should understand them, he just refuses to listen, either through boredom, aversion, or contempt. Because he is animal, they are foolishness to him.²⁶ This is why the Apostle says, 'To them that perish, the word of the cross is foolishness'.\* For someone who does not believe in the cross, the word of the cross is indeed foolishness. He is animal in his judgement: he walks in the vanity of his own judgement, and his understanding is darkened.\* And for someone who believes in the cross of Christ but does not imitate the example of the Crucified, it is foolishness to take up the word of the cross for the sake of Christ. He is likewise animal, not in this case in his judgement, but in his inclinations.

Someone whose judgement is animal is ignorant and in error; he walks in darkness and does not know where he goes\*, and his foolish heart is darkened.\* He thinks that the wisdom of God, which is hidden in mystery,\* is foolishness, and the wisdom of this world, which is foolishness to God,\* he calls prudence. He judges one thing to be its opposite: he calls good evil and evil good; he regards darkness as light and light as darkness; he puts sweet for bitter and bitter for sweet.* Is 5:20

Someone of animal disposition is without feelings and does not sense within himself the disposition of divine love.²⁷ His heart is hard, intractable, and unfeeling. It is indifferent or stubborn or sluggish or stupefied and hates or disdains or despises or neglects the exercise of spiritual warfare. At the beginning of his watches he does not arise before the face of the Lord his God; he does not pour out his heart like water;* he feels in his heart neither the burning Lm 2:19 pricks [of conscience] nor the secret shouts of joy; he does not heave holy sighs nor flame with devout desires; he does not delight in the law of the Lord and is neither kindled by holy meditations nor caught up in contemplation; he does not sit solitary and silent so as to raise himself above himself;* Lm 3:28 he does not ask that he may receive nor seek that he may find nor knock that it be opened to him;* he is Mt 7:8 not busy with divine praises and does not speak in psalms and hymns and spiritual songs amid those who sing and make melody in their hearts to the Lord.* Like a sick man with a weak stomach and Eph 5:19 bitterness in his mouth, he disdains spiritual food, the food which does not perish but which endures for ever.* His soul finds every dish detestable, for Jn 6:27 he is close to the gates of death.* Ps 106[107]:118

Animal man is recognized by his soul rather than his body, for all who dwell in this mortal flesh have an animal body, not only those who are animal, but those who are spiritual as well. In its present condition, our body receives this [power of animal life] from the soul, and it is thereby endowed with sensation, just as is the case with the other bodies of animals. Weighed down by its bulk, [the body] is heavy and burdensome, subject to various passions and corruptions. It is bound fast to the necessity of dying, and to remain alive even for a little time, it requires nourishment, fomentations, and medicines. One day it makes progress, and the next it has grown weak; and even as it makes progress, it becomes weaker and more feeble. It is like an old garment which is continually patched: it grows older and older and more and more worn out.

The Apostle, however, says: 'If there is an animal body, there is also a spiritual body'.\* We should not believe that he said this with any doubt in mind. There was no uncertainty with the Apostle, nothing that anyone should call into question. No one disputes that we have an animal body, and no one, therefore, should dispute that we also have a spiritual body. Our actual experience and our common weakness inform us of the first; the conviction of faith and the example of the resurrection of Jesus Christ persuade us of the second. But it is the animal, not the spiritual, which comes first; the spiritual comes afterwards.\*

Our spiritual body will come into being when what is corruptible puts on incorruption,\* when that which is mortal is swallowed up by life,\* when our dwelling is perfected, when the temple of God — which we are — is consecrated and the front of the temple adorned with crowns of gold,\* when our flesh is made strong as bronze\* and endures as the hardest rock, when no injury nor violence of passion nor force of temptation can approach it or penetrate it.

The spiritual body will be glorious in its strength and [will be] light and nimble. It will no longer have need of food, as it had both before and after [the first] sin, and it will be freed from the service of corruption* and necessity. It will not be changed into the nature of spirit, but will be subjected to the spirit in complete freedom and without any contradiction.²⁸

In the meantime, however, both animal man and spiritual man are alike in having an animal body, and it is by the condition of their mind rather than their body that one is distinguished from the other. The spiritual man, in his heart, crucifies the animal man spiritually, and the cross [which he uses] is his zeal for God in the full knowledge of what he is doing.²⁹ Knowledge and zeal are the weapons of our warfare. They are not carnal but have the power of God to destroy strongholds. With them we are armed to destroy counsels and every height which raises itself against the knowledge of God, and to bring into captivity all our thoughts and make them obedient to Christ.*

In these words of the Apostle, note how a height is raised against the knowledge of God. What is this height but that of which it is said, 'Do not be highminded'?* This is the height of the animal man who walks in the vanity of his own judgement. But the height of the cross is the knowledge of God which brings into captivity all our thoughts and makes them obedient to Christ. The breadth of the animal man is his animal disposition, for in his unlawful [pleasures] he wanders about on the broad way which leads to perdition.* But the breadth of the cross is the disposition of devotion³⁰ in the breadth of charity.

There are some, however, who have a zeal for God, but a zeal not combined with knowledge.* And there are others who have the knowledge of God, but no zeal. But clearly, since a cross is constructed from two pieces of wood joined together,

Rm 8:21

2 Co 10:4-5

Rm 11:20

Mt 7:13

Rm 10:2

zeal should be united with knowledge and knowledge with zeal. There will then be no devotion without discernment nor discernment without devotion.[31] The clean animal is one that chews the cud and has a cloven hoof.[32]

Devotion without discernment generally [involves] tempting God with the temptation of impossible things, and because it does not know which things are profitable, it either presumes [to do] what is not expedient or neglects [to do] what is expedient. But in the case of discernment without devotion, although it makes no mistake in knowing what things are profitable, it is mistaken in what it chooses. It recognizes what is better and commends it, but it follows what is worse. But to choose what is worse is just as much an error as to be ignorant of what is better, and whoever approves by his choice what he reproves by his judgement condemns himself by his own sentence. If someone chooses one thing while judging another [to be better]—assuming he is not forced into it by necessity—then he shows himself to be doubly foolish.

If we want to examine the visible form of an object, the light inside our eyes is insufficient, and we must have the assistance of the light outside as well. The same is true of the reverse situation: if a visible object is to be seen, the light [outside] must be helped by the light [inside].[33] A closed eye sees nothing at midday, and an open eye sees nothing in the darkness of night.

There is a certain similarity here to discernment without devotion and devotion without discernment. Our desire and our hope is to be led to the contemplation of the form[34] of the invisible God. For this we need two eyes, and anyone who says,

## Tractate XI

'Enlighten my eyes so that I may never sleep in death',* beseeches God to enlighten them. The eye of discernment without the light of devotion, or the eye of devotion without the light of discernment, sees nothing: it is just like an eye which is closed in the light or open in darkness.

Ps 12:4[13:3]

Discernment, therefore, should be joined to devotion and devotion to discernment, so that there may abound in us charity with knowledge and knowledge with charity, in accordance with the counsel of the Apostle: 'May your charity abound more and more in knowledge and in all judgement, so that you may approve the better things and be sincere and blameless on the day of Christ.'* If someone has knowledge and does not have charity, then his knowledge makes a fool of him, for without charity neither greatness of knowledge nor contempt for the world nor the chastisement of discipline is of any account in God's eyes. Charity alone claims as its own the glory of the cross, and through [charity] we, too, should glory in the cross of our Lord Jesus Christ,* who, above all things, should be loved and blessed for ever and ever.
Amen.

Ph 1:9-10

Ga 6:14

## NOTES TO TRACTATE XI

1. This is a title of convenience, and does not appear in the manuscripts. It is customary nowadays to translate *vetus homo* in Rm 6:6 as something like 'old self' or 'former self', but Baldwin's exegesis demands a straightforward literal rendering. The subject-matter of the treatise would seem to indicate that it dates from the days of Baldwin's abbacy.

2. In Latin, patience and suffering are etymologically related (see Tr. IX/II, n. 15). *Patientia*, therefore, must sometimes be translated as patience, and sometimes as patient suffering.

3. The Latin word for left, *sinister*, can also mean unlucky, unfavorable, unfortunate, perverse. The English word 'sinister' is its direct descendant.

4. There is an omission in Thomas's text as a result of hom. After *domestici Dei* at the top of 39/62, add *Novus certe homo eosdem habet domesticos et amicos, qui sunt cives sanctorum et domestici Dei*.

5. There is a lengthy omission in PL 520A from 'and to them it is said' to 'I who am now speaking'.

6. *Unica mea* is a Hebraism for 'my soul'. See Ps 21:21[22:20] and Ps 34[35]:17.

7. *Imo ne peream* has been omitted in Thomas's text (39/68) by hom.

8. The whole of this sentence has been omitted in PL 521A.

9. *Benignissimus Jesus*. See also Tr. I, n. 16.

10. *Ego vetus homo sum, et morti vicinus*. Are we to take this comment literally as well as metaphorically? If so, it would imply that Baldwin was fairly advanced in age by the time he became abbot of Ford. Life-expectancy in the twelfth-century was rather longer than many people suppose, and the biblical span of three-score years and ten was by no means unusual. Edward Rosset, for example, using the life-tables provided by J. C. Russell in his *British Medieval Population* (Albuquerque [1948] 173–193), states that his computations 'would show a normal age of 68–71 years for England in the period of the late Middle Ages' (E. Rosset, *Aging Process of Population* [New York, 1964] 156–157). If, then, this comment of Baldwin's is indeed to be taken literally, it is quite possible that he was already in his sixties when he became abbot of Ford shortly before 1175, and this, in turn, would imply a birth-date of round about 1112–1115. It need hardly be added that all this is pure speculation.

11. *A diebus antiquis* has been omitted in PL 521D by hom.

12. *Imago veritatis* has been omitted in PL 522A by hom.

13. The basic ideas for Baldwin's lengthy discussion of carnal man may be found in Augustine, *De civitate Dei* XXII. 23; PL 41:787–788. Further accounts of the nature and importance of feeling and consenting (*sentire* and *consentire*) occur elsewhere in Baldwin's works. See Tr. IV, nn. 41, 44; Tr. VI, n. 30; Tr. IX/IV, n. 5.

14. The verb which I have translated as 'lusts' is *concupiscere*. In Latin, therefore, the relationship between lusting and concupiscence (*concupiscentia*) is immediately obvious.

15. *Virtus*. See Tr. IX/III, n. 10.

16. *Disciplina*. See Tr. I, nn. 31, 40; Tr. III, n. 20; Tr. IX/II, n. 7.

17. There follows here an editorial sub-heading: *Item unde supra* 'The same as the above', but since it is unnecessary, I have omitted it.

18. For another discussion of this idea, see Baldwin's account of the second reason for mourning in Tr. IX/III.
19. This sentence is omitted in Thomas's translation (39/95).
20. PL 527A reads *quia* instead of *quasi*: 'Because carnal man is a man of sin . . . .'.
21. There is a play on words here which is impossible to render into English: *. . .cum vero mota sentit, commoto consentit.*
22. For Baldwin's use of *animalis*. See Tr. I, n. 18.
23. The normal translation of this phrase from 1 Co 2:14–15 is '. . .it is foolishness to him and he cannot understand because it [God's spiritual domain] is discerned spiritually'. Baldwin, however, as is clear from his next paragraph, takes the subject of the passive form *examinatur* not as God's spiritual domain, but as animal man. It is by his attitude to the spiritual things of God that the latter is discerned. See n. 25 below.
24. There is a relationship between animal man's judgement (*sensus*) and inclinations or disposition (*affectus*) which is clearer in Latin than in English: 'He is animal in *sensus* who does not savor (*non sapit*) the things which are of the spirit of God; he is animal in *affectus* to whom the things which are of the spirit of God have no savor (*non sapiunt*)'. The verb *sapere* is the connecting link, and means both 'to savor' and 'to understand.'
25. An explanatory translation of Baldwin's Latin: *In spiritualibus enim animalis hominis examinatio fit; ibi examinatur quisquis animalis est.*
26. This sentence is omitted from Thomas's translation (39/101).
27. Baldwin plays on the terms *affectus* and *affectio* here: *Qui animalis est affectu, sine affectione est, divini amoris affectum in se non sentit.*
28. Cf. Augustine, *De civitate Dei* XXII. 21; PL 41:783–784.
29. *Crux autem est aemulatio Dei secundum scientiam*. This is based on Rm 10:2, and *aemulatio* (which is not always easy to translate: see Tr. IV, n. 30 and Tr. X/I, n. 2) here represents the Greek work *zēlos* 'zeal'.
30. *Affectus devotionis.*
31. Discernment (*discretio*), as we have noted before, is an important concept for Baldwin. See Tr. VI, nn. 9, 43, 45; Tr. VIII, n. 27.
32 The reader may be surprised by the sudden and unheralded appearance of this comment from Dt 14:6. Chewing the cud and having cloven hooves are presumably allegories of *devotio* and *discretio*, but this is not the first time that Baldwin has introduced an unexpected and unexplained allegory. See Tr. IX/I, n. 11.
33. To understand this passage we must also understand the medieval theory of vision, and Baldwin himself provides a full account in Tr. XIII (see especially Tr. XIII, n. 5).
34. *Species*. See Tr. IX/II, n. 27.

# TRACTATE XII
# AN EXHORTATION TO PRIESTS[1]

*Consider yourselves and the whole flock, in which the Holy Spirit has made you bishops, to govern the Church of God, which he has purchased with his own blood.*\*

      Ac 20:28

PRIESTS OF THE LORD and ministers of our God,\* it is to you that these words of the Apostle are addressed. You are told to consider yourselves and the whole flock: firstly, yourselves; and then the flock. Those who are involved with the business of the salvation of others should have a care for their own salvation. Those who are entrusted with watching over moral discipline ought to live their own lives correctly. Those who must first account for themselves should begin with themselves and not neglect themselves. Consider, he says, yourselves. Consider what you are according to the nature of your human weakness, what you are according to the demands of the mission imposed upon you, what you are according to the high and powerful office which you have received, and what you are according to the humble service which you should render. Consider what you are with others, what you are for others, what you are above others, and finally what you are below others.

      Is 81:6

What are you, along with others, but men like other [men], subject to suffering,\* conceived in sin,

      Jm 5:17

bound to the necessity of dying; and although you are freed by grace from sin, you are still within reach of temptations and still liable to be conquered by them. You too can still be tempted and conquered by temptations, for you yourselves are beset by weakness* so that you can have compassion² on the weaknesses of others.* This is the sort of priests you should be: men who know how to suffer with others since they themselves are subject to suffering. Because you are men, therefore, you are weak as men [are weak], in accordance with the nature of human weakness.

According to the demands which your mission lays upon you for the sake of others, you are angels of peace in whom God has placed the word of reconciliation.* Thus, you may say with the Apostle, 'We are ambassadors for Christ, and God makes his appeal through us. We beseech you for the sake of Christ, be reconciled to God.'* Malachi shows that you can be angels when he says, 'The lips of a priest guard knowledge, and men will seek the law from his mouth, for he is the angel³ of the Lord of hosts'* If you are angels, your life is in heaven,* for you are not of the flesh but of the spirit.* [You are] like ministering spirits sent to minister for the sake of them who receive the inheritance of salvation.* You are sent from God, who makes his angels spirits and his ministers a consuming fire.* As ministers of God, therefore, you should not only be called a flaming fire, but also—and rightly—a consuming fire; you should flame like the seraphim,⁴ like those close to God, consuming and enlightening the hearts of those in your charge⁵ so that they, too, may burn with the heat of your fiery eloquence and none of them find any place to hide from its heat.* To each

Heb 5:2, 4:15
Heb 4:15

2 Co 5:19

2 Co 5:20

Ml 2:7
Ph 3:20
Rm 8:9

Heb 1:14

Ps 103[104]:4

Ps 18:7[19:6]

of you is assigned the guardianship of a great number, and there is none among those in your charge who is without a guardian angel to protect him and guard him in all his ways.* Thus, in speaking of God, the prophet says to the just man, 'He has given his angels charge over you, to guard you in all your ways'.*

If, however, the priests of the Lord can be likened to angels because of the similarity of their office and can also be called angels, then just as they should always seek the fellowship of the good angels, so they should always avoid any similarity to wicked angels. Wicked priests are certainly not [grouped] with good angels, but are more appropriately compared to wicked angels, those who fell from heaven and did not stand in the truth,* who lost the honor of their angelic dignity. For if we can compare the heavenly way of life* of holy priests with heaven, is it not clear that those who have fallen from the elevated station of a life worthy of a priest to a base and unworthy [way of] life have fallen so far as to be like angels fallen from heaven? Even though they never achieved the highest pinnacle of virtue, they still lost the place which they could and should have occupied, but which they did not deserve. They have clearly fallen from where they might have been had they not been evil, [the place] where are still to be found those who are not as they are. It appears, therefore, that it is to such men as these, [men] who no longer deserve the name of angels, that the prophet's threat is addressed: 'You shall die like men and fall like one of the princes'.* One of the princes has fallen, and many were attached to him, like many[6] members to a single head.

Lest you too should fall, therefore, like one of the princes, consider that you are not only angels for

## Tractate XII

for sake of others, but that in accordance with the high and powerful office you have received, you are also gods above others. Thus, before threatening the wicked with the same destruction as the wicked angels, the prophet says of the good: 'I have said: You are gods; all of you are the sons of the Most High'.*

Ps 81[82]:6

Is your power from heaven or from men?* It is not from men, but from God, for who is able to forgive sins save God alone?* Yet the power to forgive sins has been given to you, for the God of gods, the Lord, has spoken* and said, 'Whatever you loose upon earth shall also be loosed in heaven'.* By this power of yours, God is always represented[7] by you on earth, and because you are the representatives of the one true God, you are called gods and you are gods. Thus, through your ministry, God is always present to those who seek him, not only by the presence of his majesty, but by your representing his authority and power.

Mt 21:23–25

Mt 9:6

Ps 49[50]:1
Mt 18:18

Consider how much honor you owe to him who has given you so honorable a name. In this name you should be both feared and honored: feared as judges, honored as fathers; feared for your power, honored for your holiness. But if one of you is lacking in holiness—which God forbid!—then it is he who should be afraid, for God is his judge. It is he who should be afraid, for God has stood in the congregation of gods and judges gods in its midst.* When he that is in heaven appoints kings*—those, that is, who should rule themselves and others—he judges the gods. He knows his own, and those who seek their own interests and not those of Jesus Christ* cannot hide from his eyes. But those who love the place of honor at feasts and the best seats in the

Ps 81[82]:1
Ps 67:15[68:14]

Ph 2:21

synagogues, salutations in the market place, and being called rabbi by men;* those who are hired servants; those who are thieves and robbers, who do not enter by the door;* those who are moneychangers and those who sell doves in the temple;* those who are dumb dogs and workers of evil;* those who are violent and quarrelsome;* and those who are not sober or chaste—all these types of gods should clearly be counted among the false gods. They are only imitations of priests, like the images of gods or idols of abominations in the temple.* If the worship of the one true God is unjustly given to an idol, it is idolatry, and in just the same way, if those who are not called by God (as Aaron was) take honor to themselves, they unjustly usurp the honor due to the gods—that is, to holy priests. The [following] text clearly refers to them: 'Whoever gives honor to a fool is like someone who casts a stone into the heap of mercury'.[8]*

Nevertheless, in every priest there is a holy ministry and the honorable sacrament of his priesthood,[9] and it is not for us to touch those anointed by the Lord,* nor to judge those whom God has appointed judges. There is One who seeks and judges:* it is God who judges gods!* Through them and in them, all faults, inasmuch as they have already been condemned by the judgement of God, are exposed to public reproach, but the indiscriminate open censure or public condemnation of specific individuals for their faults or of the faults of specific individuals is not permitted.

Priests of the Lord, you who show reverence for the power [you have received] as befits the ministers of Christ, consider, in all justice and holiness, how great is your dignity. Because you are angels of God,

## Tractate XII

you are more than men: [you are] like angel-reapers, who gather up out of his kingdom all causes of sin.\* And you are even more than angels, for just as [you bear] the name of gods, so too [you have] surpassing honor.

You have considered your dignity, how you are above others; consider now—I say it again—consider you humility, your function as servants, how you are below others. Do not think that I am insulting you: if you will listen, it was the prophet who first said what you are when he said to the Lord, 'The earth will be filled with the fruit of your works: it will bring forth grass for cattle and herbs for the service of men'.\* See what you are! Cattle and servants of men! From such a height you have sunk to such a depth, as it is written, 'They ascend to the heavens and descend to the depths.'\* And in another place it is written, 'The giants, and those that dwell with them, groan under the waters.'\* You [are] like giants whose stature is greater than that of others in accordance with your pre-eminent dignity; [but you are giants] groaning under the waters of the people, burdened with a multitude of cares and concerns. As the heavens are exalted above the earth,\* so are the gods exalted above cattle: in other words, [to that extent] you yourselves [are exalted] above yourselves.

You are gods and guides of souls, and among the other things you should consider, you should give special consideration to the difficulty of governing souls, of accommodating yourselves to the character of each, of conforming yourselves to all,[10] so that even though you are lords of all, you are no way different from servants. This is why he who is greatest among you becomes as the youngest\* and

Mt 13:39-41

Ps 103:14-15 [104:13-14]

Ps 106[107]:26

Jb 26:5

Is 55:9

Lk 22:26

is not ashamed to be called a servant of the servants of God.¹¹ The Apostle shows us the nature of this law of service when he says, 'Though I am free from all men, I made myself the servant of all. I became all things to all men so that I might save all.'*

There is also a text which shows us the reason for this service: 'The greater you are, the more you should humble yourself in all things'.* It is as if he said: 'The measure of your humility should be equal to the greatness of your dignity'. Humility in honor is itself the honor of honor and the dignity of dignity. No dignity deserves the name of dignity if it scorns humility, for just as humility engenders honor, so, too, it preserves it. Every advancement in honor, when it takes place in [due and proper] order, begins with humility and ends with a high position, and he who humbles himself will be exalted*—provided he does not humble himself in order to be exalted, but rather humbles himself so as not to be exalted. [Not to be exalted] in the world, I mean; in [the eyes of] God he is exalted. Someone who is truly humble does not strive for honor; when he receives honor, he does not snatch at it through ambition, but because of his humility he is himself snatched away to honor. Thus, he is not someone who plunders honor, but is like the plunder of honor itself. Humility without honor is sufficient in itself for honor, but honor without humility only brings upon itself confusion. Thus, just as humility justly precedes honor, it also justly preserves it. Those in [positions of] honor, therefore, should see that they show themselves humble in all things after the example of Christ. He was the master of humility. Since he took precedence, he became as a servant,* and since he was first, he became as the last,* abasing himself at the feet of his disciples.   Mt 19:30

By the example of his humility, Christ bears down upon you like a great and weighty mass, [driving you] to humility, so that you might be subject to those who are subject to you. Experience in yourselves, therefore, what Christ himself [experienced]. Although he was in the form of God, he emptied himself and took the form of a servant.*   Ph 2:5-7
You too are gods: empty yourselves and adopt the form of a servant, so that for the time being you become as men for the sake of men, weak for the sake of the weak, taking to yourselves every need and weakness, like him who says, 'Who is weak, and I am not weak? Who is made to fall, and I do not burn [with indignation]?'* You should labor   2 Co 11:29
more than all* because [you labor] for all. You are   1 Co 15:10
not only servants of men, therefore, but slaves of men, like oxen who tread [the grain],* like the   1Co 9:9, 1 Tm 5:18
beasts who serve the needs of men with their labor.

If you seek its gift, this earth, filled with the faithful subject to you,[12] produces hay and grass* for   Ps 103[104]:14
you at the proper times. These are your due, and you have them in your possession. [But] if you seek the fruit and not the gift, saying with the Apostle, 'I do not seek the gift, but I seek the fruit',* the fruit   Ph 4:17
of righteousness should abound in your land as in God's own field.* By reason of your ministry, hay   1 Co 3:9
and grass are owed to you, but what do you owe [in your turn]? First, all that you have; then yourselves, all that you can do , all that you are. In a word: your souls for the souls committed to you, and [you should give them] most gladly, like him who says, 'I will most gladly spend and be spent for your souls'.*   2 Co 12:15
You are debtors, therefore, not only to the one part

of the flock committed to you, but to the whole flock: to all and to each, to the wise and the foolish.\* You should render account for all.¹³

Consider, therefore, the whole flock in which the Holy Spirit has established you. This saying [of the Apostle] refers to those who do not take honor¹⁴ to themselves, but who are called by God, as Aaron was.\* They have not received the spirit of this world, but the Spirit which is from God.\*¹⁵ Those who are led by the spirit of this world are not established by the Holy Spirit and are not chosen by God as Aaron was chosen; instead, they have called their lands by their own names.\* And what are these [names]? Names of honor, perhaps, or names of dignity: archdeacon, bishop, archbishop, and the like; great names indeed. There are many who do not yet have these names, but who, in longing to possess what is not yet theirs, have called them to themselves, as it were, to make them theirs. These men, who are not themselves called to these [names], have called with loud voices: perhaps with obsequiousness, perhaps with gifts, perhaps with flattery, or with anything else that they are accustomed to use to make their voice heard. It is these who are led by the spirit of this world, the spirit of dizziness,\* the spirit of error.¹⁶ Since God has not called them, they have not been justified nor will they be glorified.\* They seek glory from men, not the glory which comes from God,\* and although they may find glory and favor in the eyes of men, in the eyes of God they are confounded, for God has despised them.\*

But you are not like this, [you] whom the Holy Spirit has made bishops to govern the Church of God. Since your name and the reason for your name reminds you of your office, you should never be

## Tractate XII

negligent in caring for those committed to you, but should govern the Church of God with all the care and concern that is necessary—more, indeed, than is necessary![17] The Holy Spirit has placed you here, and your function, in accordance with the two duties of a governor, is to direct and correct in righteousness and judgement. It is by these virtues that the throne of God is prepared or corrected, as it is written, 'Righteousness and judgement are the preparation of your throne',* and elsewhere, 'Righteousness and judgement are the correction[18] of his throne'.*

Ps 88:14[89:15]
Ps 96[97]:2

Your seat, or your throne, is the lay people subjected to you, and for the moment you preside[19] over them as deputies of Christ.[20] [Christ, however,] presides over you, and you are his throne. But he also presides over the people and sits upon them as on his throne, and although you too sit upon them as if they were your throne, it is more his [than yours].

Enthrone yourselves, therefore, as thrones in judgement, for righteousness and judgement are the preparation of his throne. Through your righteousness and your judgement you should prepare his throne[21] by directing [souls] to virtue, and to help you in this you have the grace of him to whom is said: 'You have prepared directions'.[22]* Through your righteousness and your judgement the throne of God should be prepared in those who have not yet offered themselves as seats for God to be enthroned: in those, that is, who have not yet begun to subject themselves to God in obedience. It should also be prepared in those who have begun, so that they go forwards instead of sliding backwards, and eventually bring to perfection that which they have begun so well. [Finally], it should be prepared in

Ps 98[99]:4

those who have fallen, so that with God's help they may be set on their feet, since God puts his hand under them.* [Ps 36(37):24]

The eyes of everyone are upon your righteousness and your judgement. On these [virtues] hang the salvation of those in your charge and the life of many. For your life is a mirror of holiness, an example of honesty, a seal of righteousness. There are many in the Church who look on you [as on a mirror] and see in their faces either the grace of beauty or the stain of disfigurement. They see in you what they ought to imitate and [the model] to which they long to be conformed. The life of those in your charge is symbolized by soft wax which can receive the express image of the seal of your holiness. 'Therefore love righteousness, you that are judges of the earth.'* [Ws 1:1] If you love Christ, love righteousness as well! God made him our wisdom and our righteousness,* [1 Co 1:30] when for our sake he made him to be sin who knew no sin, so that in him we might become the righteousness[23] of God.* [2 Co 5:21] Christ was made a victim for sin, and, as the good shepherd, laid down his life for his sheep,* [Jn 10:11] leaving you an example so that you might follow in his steps.* [1 P 2:21] To show the greatness of his charity with which he loved her,* [Eph 2:4] Christ purchased the Church with his own blood.* [Ac 20:28] Just as he poured out his blood for her, he also poured forth his charity.

This [Church] which he purchased so dearly and with so much love he has entrusted and committed to you. In you he has put his trust so that through you the heart of her spouse may trust in her.* [Pr 31:11] Therefore, just as you love Christ, and just as he can put his trust in you, so you must guard his bride in your faithfulness. You must protect her jealously, not for your sakes, but for his, so that you may present her as a chaste virgin to her bridegroom, Our Lord Jesus Christ,* who is above all things, God, forever blessed. Amen.*

2 Co 11:2

Rm 9:5

130                    *Spiritual Tractates*

## NOTES TO TRACTATE XII

1. Title as in PL 529–530. There can be no doubt that this is a sermon preached by Baldwin to a congregation of bishops and priests, and although it is possible that it could have been delivered while he was bishop of Worcester, it is more probable that it dates from his time as archbishop of Canterbury (1184–1190).
2. I.e. 'so that you can suffer with others'. For the etymological meaning of compassion, see Tr. I, n. 32.
3. Or 'messenger'. See Tr. VII, n. 3.
4. For the etymological meaning of *seraphim*, see Tr. II, n. 3 and Tr. III, n. 2.
5. Lit. 'of those subject to you'. Cf. Tr. II, n. 8.
6. Thomas (39/124) reads *multa*; PL 531D (incorrectly) has *una*.
7. The verb *repraesentare* (and its derivatives) must be understood in its literal sense, *viz.*, 'to re-present, to present again, to make present again'.
8. The M.T. of Pr 26:8 actually says 'Whoever gives honor to a fool is like a man who ties a stone in a sling'. The curious translation which we find in the Vulgate is perfectly explainable, but it would take us too far out of our way to demonstrate why.
9. See also Tr. II, n. 14.
10. The first part of this paragraph is based on RB 2:31–32.
11. A title of the popes which was first used by Gregory the Great. Its general use, however, dates only from the time of Gregory VII (1073–1085).
12. Lit. 'the earth of the lay-people subject to you'.
13. Cf. RB 2:34, 37, 38.
14. *Bonorem*, both in Thomas (39/136) and PL 534C, is a misprint for *honorem*.
15. This sentence is omitted in PL 534C.
16. *Spiritus erroris* is omitted in PL 534D.
17. This sentence is omitted in Thomas's translation (39/139).
18. The Latin *correctio* renders the Hebrew *māḵōn* 'foundation'. Baldwin, however, takes the word literally.
19. 'Preside' must be understood both in its normal sense and in its etymological sense. The word derives from *prae-sideo*, which means literally 'to sit in front of'. Hence Baldwin's association of presiding, sitting, and thrones / seats (*sedes*).
20. *Vicarii Christi*. 'Vicar of Christ' was a papal title from the eighth century, but it could also be used to refer to bishops in general. For details, see DLF s.v. *vicarius*.
21. Thomas (39/140) has *sedes illi*; PL 535A has *sedes Dei*.
22. *Tu parasti directiones*. Such is the Vulgate version of Ps 98:4. The M.T. actually says 'You have established equity', but the word for 'equity' (*mēšārîm*) has a plural form, despite its singular meaning. Hence 'directions' or 'straight lines' or 'correct ways'. Baldwin, of course, takes both the verb and the noun literally.
23. Thomas (39/142) has *justitia*; PL 536A (incorrectly) reads *gratia*.

# TRACTATE XIII
# ON THE LOVE OF GOD POURED FORTH IN OUR HEARTS[1]

*The love of God is poured forth in our hearts by the Holy Spirit who is given to us*\*     Rm 5:5

THE LOVE OF GOD with which he loved us before the foundation of the world and chose us in his beloved Son\* is itself the source and origin of all the good things which were bestowed upon us on the day of our creation, the day of our redemption, and the day of our justification and sanctification. But in addition to these, it is also [the source] of the things which will be bestowed upon us on the day of our glorification, when God will be glorified in us and we in him.\*     Eph 1:4

    Cf. 2 Th 1:10

God did not love us insignificantly or indifferently or meagerly, but fully and richly; not with a feigned or false [love], but purely and sincerely; not just in appearance, not just outwardly, as though it were only on the surface, but inwardly, from the bottom of his heart; not in word and tongue, but in deed and truth.\*     1 Jn 3:18

If you consider its character, this love is rich and opulent, for where did all the mercies which we have received from God come from if not from his continual kindness, his unmitigated liberality, his pure grace, his full and perfect benevolence? Whatever we may [gain] by our merits is by his grace, and beyond all our merits there is grace upon grace, for grace grows and grows.

If you want to know the extent of this love, its greatness is such that only God can measure it; as far as we are concerned, it is immense and immeasurable. If it were possible for us to comprehend its extent in some way with all the saints,* it is so great that we can comprehend it only with the greatest difficulty – although in reality [its comprehension] is wholly beyond our abilities. Its height and depth, its length and its breadth* are beyond anything we can describe or conceive.

Its height is the sublimity of glory which God has prepared for those who love him, [the glory], that is, which the eye has not seen, nor the ear heard, and which has not arisen in the heart of man.* Its depth is the emptying of himself by the only-begotten Son of God* and the descent of such majesty from the bosom of the Father to the shame of the cross, from the source of life to the end of life, from the highest point to the lowest, from heaven to hell, from one extremity to the other. Who is able to conceive these two extremes? Who can comprehend the height from which he came, or the vast distance between the summit from which he descended and the lowest depths to which he descended? The height of this love, therefore, is the ennobling of mankind; its depth is God's descent [into this world] – [a descent] which, as we have said, was from the highest point to the lowest, from the beginning to the end.²

Its length, however, has neither beginning nor end. Just as his love for us has no ending, neither does it have any beginning, for the mercy of the

Lord is from eternity to eternity upon them that fear him.* Its breadth is wide and far-reaching [and shows itself] in the way in which his benevolence and kindness are of universal benefit. [The benefit] of his benevolence is that he wants everyone to be saved and come to the knowledge of the truth;* that of his kindness is that he did not even spare his own Son, but delivered him up for us all.* It is his kindness, however, which we should value more highly because it extends not only *to* all things, but *through* all things, for in giving us his only Son has he not also given us all things with him?*

Ps 102[103]:17

1 Tm 2:4

Rm 8:32

Ibid.

Before the formation of the world, this love was enclosed in the purpose and intention of God, but it has [since] been revealed in its proper order: [it is] poured abroad, poured out, poured into [us], and poured forth.³ It was poured abroad in abundance when God created mankind in his image and likeness.* It was poured out in greater profusion and yet more abundantly when he redeemed mankind by the death of his only-begotten Son. It was poured into us when, by the grace of faith, he illuminated the heart of man so that he could understand the excellence of this love. And finally, it was poured forth when it filled up the breadth of our expanded heart with the intention of emulation, the desire for imitation, and an eagerness to return love for love. This pouring forth [of love] strengthens our hope so that we may have no fear of disappointment. 'Hope,' says the Apostle, 'does not disappoint us, because the love of God is poured forth in our hearts.'* The love poured forth in our hearts is certainly God's [love] for us,⁴ for it is this which the Apostle commends in this passage; but as a result of [God's love] being poured forth, there is also poured forth in our

Gn 1:27

Rm 5:5

hearts our [love] for God. And the way in which our [love] for him is poured forth through and in his [love] is similar to the way in which the light of our eyes, when they are illuminated by the sun, is poured forth in the light by which they are illuminated.[5]

Listen very carefully to this comparison so that your reason may be led from physical light to spiritual. [We must distinguish three forms of light]: light which illuminates — [the light] by which something sees or is seen; light which is illuminated, so that the specific form of an object can be seen; and light which is illuminated so that we ourselves can see.

Light which illuminates and enables something to see or be seen is the light of the sun which is poured out when morning first opens its eyes,[6] and it is this which we see first of all. When it is poured forth more extensively, we can see the different forms, the colors, shapes, and appearances of the objects presented to our eyes.

As for the light which is illuminated so that things can be seen, this refers to the forms of visible objects which cannot be seen here so long as they are in darkness. They are then like the darkness itself: unformed, indistinct, and confused. But when they are in the light, they are like a sort of light which is illuminated so that we can see them, for as the Apostle says: 'Anything that becomes visible is light'.\* The visible form of an object is seen in the light in such a way that the light may [also] be seen in the form,[7] and the greater the degree to which the illuminating light is brighter than the object it illuminates, the brighter is the light which is seen in the visible form.[8]

## Tractate XIII

The light which is illuminated so that we can see is the light of our eyes. They pour forth their own light in the light which is [first] poured forth, and whatever objects are illuminated by the light which is poured forth more abundantly then stand revealed to them.⁹

The spiritual light which illuminates our eyes is God's love for us. All the great favors which God has shown and accorded us draw into themselves, as it were, the light of love and reveal it to our eyes. In them we may see how much God loves and how much he ought to be loved. For when the greatness of his favors unfolds before our eyes, the immensity of the love of God, extending far and wide, is clearly revealed. When we contemplate it, the gaze of our mind pours itself out more widely, and when we have a worthy appreciation of God's favors and consider more deeply the love with which he loves us, it is communicated to our inmost senses and becomes sweet. It affects the heart with the wonderful sweetness of mutual love and expands it more and more so that it is able to receive God.¹⁰ In this interchange of love, love itself adjusts and conforms [the heart] according to its own height and depth, its own length and breadth.

The height of our love for God is when it hopes for the heights and desires the sublimities of glory, not in this world, but in God, [in him] who says, 'When I am lifted up from the earth, I will draw all things to myself',* and to whom the bridegroom says, 'Draw me after you'.* Its depth is when we strive for the truth for the sake of God and choose to be abased, [following] the example of him who said, 'I have chosen to be abased'.* We are shown

Jn 12:32
Sg 1:3

Ps 83[84]:11

by this that whoever chooses to abase himself has no wish to choose honor. Love is long when it perseveres to the end or, rather, when it has no end, for love never ceases.* It is wide when it is mindful of God's benevolence and kindness, when it continually delights in him, both in adversity and prosperity, when it rejoices in him and cries to him always in joy and exultation, in all places and with all gladness,[11] when it is not restrained by faint-heartedness or grumbling. The breadth of love is the expansion of the heart, which is also its delight in righteousness. This outpouring of love into our expanded hearts is effected by the love of God, [the love], that is, of the Father or the Son; it is effected through the Holy Spirit who is given to us, he who is himself the love of the Father and the Son and their mutual union.[12]

Leaving aside for the moment the rest of God's favors, [consider] the amount of love which is demanded from us since he gave us not only his only-begotten Son, so that in him we might find grace,* but also the Holy Spirit, who prepares our hearts so that the Father himself, with the Son and Holy Spirit, may come there and make his dwelling with us!* There are, of course, different sorts of graces,* but of all these love is the most excellent;* nor is it without good cause and reason that we say that its outpouring is effected by the Holy Spirit and that the Spirit himself is given [to us]. The gift of grace, in which the author of grace gives himself, is great and excellent, but in giving himself, he suffers no separation from the gift which is given by him. Whoever, therefore, receives love as a gift can justly glorify himself in God and say, 'The love of God is poured forth in my heart through the Holy Spirit who is given to me'.\* But if someone has the word of wisdom, or the word of knowledge, or diversity of languages, or the interpretation of tongues,\* or the grace of some ministry or activity—even though these are all gifts of the Holy Spirit—and does not have love, he does not have the Holy Spirit in him, and he confirms the truth of that which is written: 'The Holy Spirit of discipline will flee from the deceitful'.\*

Rm 5:5

1 Co 12:8-10

Ws 1:5

Love, however, both expands and contracts our heart in opposite ways. You can often feel how your stomach contracts and constricts itself when faced with food which it loathes and detests, for what is not accepted willingly gets down the narrow passage of the throat only with the greatest difficulty. No less can you feel it expanding and opening up when confronted with food it likes, and how easily it gulps down what it accepts with a real appetite.

In just the same way, when love is faced with unwelcome worldly desires, it contracts the heart, and when confronted with whatever is holy and beneficial it expands the will and freely opens itself to the things it desires. Cupidity,[13] however, expands itself for transitory things to the same extent that it contracts itself when faced with those which are heavenly, and the more the heart retreats from important things,[14] the more it is tied to trivialities. The things which are eternal are great and grand, but those which are soon confined by the strictures of time and quickly come to a close in a brief burst of sensual pleasure are truly small. Cupidity has its height in an ambitious striving for honor; it has its depth in feigned humility or in a striving for grandeur; it has its length in implacable obstinacy;[15] and it has its breadth in its insatiable capacity.

We, however, have renounced the world. We have received not the spirit of this world, but the spirit which comes from God,* so that the love of God which is poured forth in our hearts may remain there, as befits our religious [profession]. Let us, therefore, love God with all our heart, with all our soul, and with all our mind,* by [the power of] this same Spirit working within us, who is, above all things, God, forever blessed. Amen.*

*1 Co 2:12*

*Mt 22:37*

*Rm 9:5*

## Notes to Tractate XIII

1. This is a title of convenience, and does not appear in the manuscripts. As is clear from Baldwin's comments at the end of this sermon, it was certainly delivered to a monastic congregation. In translating Baldwin, I have normally distinguished between charity (*caritas*) and love (*amor* and *dilectio*) simply on the grounds that in medieval spiritual writings the terms are not straight-forward synonyms. To maintain the distinction in the present tractate, however, leads to an awkward style and detracts from the message Baldwin was trying to convey. For once, therefore, I have rendered *caritas*, *dilectio*, and *amor* by the same term: love.

2. I suspect that Baldwin's discussion here (and also his discussions of the Incarnation elsewhere) has been influenced by the ideas and terminology of Leo the Great, whose eight sermons on the Feast of the Nativity (*Sermons* XXI–XXVIII) are particularly important.

3. *Profusa et effusa, infusa et diffusa*.

4. The first part of this sentence has been omitted in PL 537B by hom.

5. The discussion which follows is by no means easy to understand, and some preliminary comments are essential if the modern reader is to appreciate it. For the medieval scientist, vision was normally regarded as an active, not a passive, phenomenon. I.e. it was not the result of the eye receiving passively the light-rays emitted by some illuminated object; instead, the eye itself was thought to emit rays, and it was these which established visual contact with the illuminated object. There were a few writers who disagreed with this (Witelo, for example, following al-Hazen, considered it quite impossible), but theirs was certainly a minority view.

Baldwin's opinion was that of the majority and his theory of vision is as follows: (1) a source of light (*lux illuminans* 'illuminating light') illuminates both the object to be seen and also our eyes; (2) as soon as the object to be illuminated receives light from the source, it begins to shine in its turn, and therefore becomes potentially visible, and the brighter the illuminating light, the greater is the potential visibility of the illuminated object. This is what Baldwin calls *lux illuminata ut videatur*, 'light illuminated so that it can be seen'. (3) So far the object is only potentially visible; in order for us actually to see it, our own eyes must be illuminated. They also must receive light from the source, and once they have received it, they emit it in the form of rays which fall on the illuminated object and establish contact with it. It is then that it becomes actually visible to us. Baldwin refers to this part of the process as *lux illuminata ut videat* 'light illuminated so that it can see', and parts (2) and (3) of the act of vision occur at the same time. Baldwin's own warning to his congregation—*audi attentius*, 'listen very carefully'—still remains valid!

6. Lit. 'in the eyelid of dawn': the phrase derives from Jb 41:9.

7. For *in spiritu* in PL 537D, read *in specie* with Thomas (39/160).

8. This is an explanatory paraphrase of Baldwin's Latin: . . . *et tanto clarius, quanto clarior est lux, quam species*.

9. This—more or less—is what Baldwin says. What he means is that when there is a source of light lighting up an object, our eyes (as we explained in n. 5) see that object by picking up light from the light-source and emitting this light as light rays. In this way, whatever objects are illuminated by the light-source (this is 'the light which is poured forth more abundantly', because it is considerably stronger than the

light emitted from our eyes) are rendered visible to us. It is to be hoped that Baldwin's monks were giving their abbot their full attention at this point.

10. Lit. 'to make it *capax Dei*'. This is one of Baldwin's rare descriptions of contemplative ecstasy, and Thomas (39/163, n. 1) compares it with William of St Thierry, *The Golden Epistle* II. 14; PL 184: 347AB (SCh 223: 342–344; CF 12:92). The similarities, however, are no more than one would expect from two spiritual writes belonging to the same tradition, and there is no evidence of any inter-dependence.

11. A play on words impossible to reproduce in English: *tam lata quam laeta*.

12. This is the Augustinian doctrine of the Holy Spirit, and was universally accepted by latin writers of the Middle Ages.

13. As Thomas points out (39/169, n. 1), the contrast between cupidity and charity is not uncommon among the Cistercian writers, and Thomas provides a number of examples.

14. For PL 539A *magis*, read *a magnis* with Thomas (39/168).

15. Thomas (39/168) has *obstinatio*; PL 540A (incorrectly) reads *continuatio*.

# TRACTATE XIV
# ON THE ORDER OF CHARITY[1]

*He brought me into the wine-cellar; he set charity in order within me. Sustain me with flowers, encompass me with apples, because I am afflicted with love.*\*  Sg 2:4–5

LOVE IS AN AFFLICTION, and the suffering of a soul that is sick. The authority of the poet [Ovid] – even though it seems unworthy and unsuitable – affirms the truth of this, when he says: 'Woe is me, for no herb can cure love'.[2]

But for religious minds, it should be enough that this is the voice of the bride. She states what she feels and says: 'I am afflicted with love'. Let us consider, therefore, whether all love is an affliction.

[Firstly], there is natural love, with which parents and children love each other. This also shows its power in irrational animals, for these, too, show affection for their young in various ways. The she-bear growls softly to her cubs, and the hen weakens herself for her chicks.[3] Could anything but love make Jacob lament and say, 'An evil wild animal has eaten my son, a beast has devoured Joseph'?\*  Gn 37:33
Could anything but love drive David to lamentation, saying, 'My son Absalom, Absalom my son: would to God that I might die for you, Absalom my son, my son Absalom'?\*  2 K 18:33

[Secondly], there is social love, and it is this which

joins [friends] with the bond of friendship. It was this [love] with which David and Jonathan loved each other, and it was the grief [of this love] which tormented David when he said, 'I grieve for you, my brother Jonathan; you were so beautiful, and your love was more to me than the love of women. As a mother loves her only son, so did I love you.'\*

[Thirdly], there is conjugal love. With this a bride and bridegroom chastely love each other, and for them the anguish they suffer in being apart is usually greater than the joy which they feel in being together.⁴

[Fourthly], there is incestuous love and other impure [forms of love]. This love has its own sufferings, distress, and grief. We see it in Amnon's love for Thamar, when Jonadab said to him, 'Why are you so haggard day after day, son of the king?'\* We see it too in Sichem, who loved Dinah, whose soul was fastened to hers.\*

[Fifthly], there is vain love, the love of this world. With this we love the things that cannot aid us in achieving the blessed life and can only hinder us from doing so. The prophet shows us that this [sort of] love is wrong when he says, 'O children of men, how long will you be dull of heart? Why do you love vanity?'\* This vain love, like impure love, is not only an affliction, but also a defect of the soul and its death.

[Finally], there is holy love, and with this God is loved truly, chastely, and purely. This, too, is an affliction, for when [the bride] says, 'I am afflicted with love', she is troubled and ill at ease. But if the love of God is charity and charity is virtue and strength,⁵\* the greatest strength of all, how can the love of God be an affliction? Or is it that the love of God or charity is [at the same time] both weakness and strength, affliction and health, disease and remedy?[26] It was [charity] that cured the sickness of [that woman] of whom it is written, 'Many sins are forgiven her, because she has loved much'.* In what way, then, is it not both health and a remedy? How can charity be other than health if it cures the wounds of an afflicted soul and covers a multitude of sins?* But if charity is health, how can it be an affliction? And if it is an affliction, how can it not be an incurable affliction, when it is written, 'Charity never ends'?* Or is it that love acts in one way when it wants to possess something and in a different way when it possesses what it wants? This is clearly the case.

*Lk 7:47*

*Jm 5:20*

*1 Co 13:18*

In the meantime, however, love is obviously an affliction. Someone who loves, burns and yearns and sighs; he does not have what he wants, and if he is kept from the coveted embraces of the bride, he is tormented by this very fact. But he who heals all your infirmities,* O bride, will also cure this affliction when he reveals himself to you. He is your bridegroom, and when you see him as he is,* eye to eye, face to face, then, in seeing him, you will be able to possess him and enjoy him,[7] united with him once and for all and never parted from his conversation, his appearance, his kiss, or his embrace. From that time forth your affliction—but never your love—will pass away. There will then be no occasion for you to say, 'I am afflicted with love', but rather 'I rejoice in love'. Joy will be yours, for the bridegroom shall rejoice over the bride, and your God shall rejoice over you.* This is the end of affliction, but it is not the end of love.

*Ps 102[103]:3*

*1 Jn 3:2*

*Is 62:5*

What, then, of [our condition in] the meantime? The bride is gravely ill and confined to her sick-bed:

may the Lord help her on her bed of sorrow!* But since there is no remedy for love at hand, what help, what counsel, what solace will we give her? [The remedy for love] is far away, beyond the ends of the earth, and cannot be found under heaven.

[The bride, therefore,] cries out [in her affliction] and feels the full force of her sufferings, and because she cannot hope for a remedy either at this time or in this place, she at least begs the members of her household to comfort and console her until she overcomes her infirmities. But first, as is the practice with anyone afflicted, she states the origin, cause, and progress [of her sickness], and only then asks for comfort. She does not yet hope for a cure, because she knows that this must be deferred for a while.

If someone were to say to her: 'Afflicted woman, where did you contract this sickness?', she would reply: 'He brought me into the wine-cellar'.[8] 'Who brought you?' 'I sat down in the shadow of him whom I desired; I ate his fruit, and it was sweet to my palate.* Then, when I had eaten, he brought me into the wine-cellar so that he could give me a drink from the cup of love which he brought from the wine-cellar and mixed for me, and when I tasted it, I wanted to drink [it all]. This is how I am afflicted with love.'

You, whose desire is to drink with the bridegroom the cup which brings health and salvation[9] (for here affliction itself is health), consider what the wine-cellar signifies, so that you may be brought into it. And if you will listen, the wine-cellar is none other than the cellar of the heart, where we find the wine of compunction*[10] and the wine of love. The cellar of the heart, I say, but [only] of those who are

## Tractate XIV

turned to their own hearts.* For those who roam about outside themselves and walk in [the way of] deceitful desires, those who have strayed far from their own hearts like madmen, those who are concerned with vanities and lying follies,* all these are outside the wine-cellar. It is they who are recalled to themselves by the Prophet when he says, 'Return, you transgressors, to your heart!'*

Ps 84:9[85:8]

Ps 39[40]:5

Is 46:8

All those who return to their hearts, however, are not necessarily brought into the wine-cellar immediately. First of all, the bride sits in the shadow [of the bridegroom], desiring him and praising the sweetness of his fruit, and only after that is she brought into the wine-cellar. And there are many who do begin by using this world* in the right way. They sit in his shadow and desire him. They praise the sweet fruit of righteousness and discuss with themselves the way of perfection, and when they are goaded by the grace of the divine mercy, they decide to give up everything for the sake of Christ and to cleave to him alone in complete purity of heart. Then, when they judge all things as contemptible for the sake of Christ and dissociate them from their heart, they enter the wine-cellar. But it is not as if the bride enters [the cellar] by her own [power]; instead, she is brought into it. No one, in fact, can enter the way of perfection properly or return to his heart unless the voice of [Christ] grows strong within him, for to him was said through the Prophet: 'You have said: Turn back, O sons of men!'* and again, 'He has turned back my soul'.* The bride, therefore, is brought into the wine-cellar when, through her contempt for the world, she wholly excludes from the whole of her heart the love of the

1 Co 7:31

Ps 89:2[90:3]
Ps 22:2[23:3]

world and yields up the whole cellar of her heart to the love of God, for if cupidity is not excluded, charity is not perfectly ordered.[11]

Thus, when she has been brought into [the wine-cellar] and has put all cupidity behind her, when the wine of compunction has made her forget the world in a sober inebriation of mind, and when she feels within herself nothing but charity, she says, 'He set charity in order within me'.* (Sg 2:4)

By charity, you must understand here [the love] of God and also [the love] of your neighbor. But [the love] of your neighbor really amounts to the love of God, since you should only love your neighbor with God, in God, or for the sake of God. Charity is the order of virtue, and virtue is the order of love[12] — but in a different way. Virtue is [called] the order of love because it is set in order by love, but charity is [called] the order of virtue because it sets [virtue] in order — but only after [charity] itself has been set in order to make the ordering [of virtue] possible.

Charity is set in order by evaluation, by zeal, and by choice.[13] [It is set in order] by evaluation when the mind judges it truly and values it as better, more worthy, and more precious than anything else. Ask the Apostle about the evaluation of charity, and he himself will tell you how worthily and splendidly we should value it: 'I will show you,' he says, 'a still more excellent way.'* (1 Co 12:31) And again he says, 'There now remain faith, hope, and charity, these three: but the greatest of these is charity'.* (1 Co 13:13) And again, 'To know the charity of Christ, which surpasses all knowledge'.* (Eph 3:19)

It is not enough, however, to feel this way about

charity and to prefer it to everything else by evaluation alone. We must also give it first place by our zealous intention [to possess] it. We will then desire it before and above all other things. Peter reminds us of this when he says, 'Above all, hold unfailing your mutual charity for one another',* and Paul, too, when he says, 'Be zealous for the better gifts',* and again, 'Above all these things have charity'.*

1 P 4:8
1 Co 12:31
Col 3:14

There are some, however, who show their approval of charity in their evaluation of it and their zeal for it, but who do not show their approval in choosing it or pursuing it. [Charity], therefore, must also be set in order by choice, for we will then seek it in such a way that we possess it and keep it. If we want to acquire charity, it is not enough just to combine whatever zeal we may have with [a proper] evaluation of it: we must also be eager to pursue it. There are some who aspire and sigh for [charity], but who do not establish themselves in it.[14] They long for it, but they do not seize it, and as a consequence, their longing is in vain. It is vain because they have made no resolution[15] [to pursue charity], and in their conduct, therefore, they show their disapproval of that which they approve by their judgement and desire but not by their resolution!

Evaluation [lies] in the judgement of the reason, zeal in the desire of the will, and choice in the resolution [which results] from discernment. But there is no discernment of choice in choosing what is inferior! The Apostle, therefore, says, 'Pursue charity',* for by pursuing it—by acting, that is, in accordance with your own resolve and God's own counsel[16]—charity is attained. This is the resolution [you should make]: to renounce all unlawful things

1 Co 14:1

for the love of Christ in order to gain charity, and to abstain as much as possible from lawful things in order to gain something which is more perfect. This is the resolution [you should make]: to rid yourself completely of cupidity in order to arrive at the acquisition of charity. This is the counsel given us by him who says, 'If someone were to give all the wealth of his house for love, he should despise it as nothing'.* If we despise the things that pass away, we acquire the love of eternal things. By our contempt for cupidity we gain the gold of charity. 'I have suffered the loss of all things', says the Apostle, 'and I have counted them as dung, in order to gain Christ.'¹⁷*

When you have set charity first in your heart by a just judgement of its value, by all the desire of your zeal, and by all your eagerness to pursue it, you have then established it in its own place, and it is therefore set in order. This is the place which is due to it, and when you have set it in order in this way, it sets everything else in order, so that everything may be done in order. For when the Apostle says, 'You should do everything in order',* and 'You should do everything in charity',* we can conclude that what is done in charity is done in order and what is not done in charity is out of order.

Charity orders the angels in their offices and ministries; it orders the lives and conduct of the just in their occupations and endeavors; it orders the host of the virtues in their stations so that the ordered troop of virtues—that is, the ordered battle-line of the army—cannot be broken or routed by the enemy.

In ordered charity is to be found the law which [was ordained] by angels through the Mediator,* for by the power of Christ shining forth in charity— [the charity] he entrusted to us—we have received after the spirit of fear the spirit of adoption as sons.* We do not serve him in fear, therefore, as we did under the Law, or from severity or compulsion, but in the joy of our heart, from a love which stems from the depths of our being.

Ga 4:5

It is charity which sets in order that covenant which is greater than sacrifices of good works, since the covenant promised by God is greater than all the good that we do. Through the love of God, we continually reflect on our eternal reward and judge it to be greater than all our merits [deserve.] 'The sufferings of this time are not worth comparing with the glory to come which will be revealed in us.'*

Rm 8:18

It is charity which ordered the mystery of our redemption; [charity] which, as it were, displaced God from his exalted place and placed him in the place of condescension, making him a little lower than the angels,* and setting him as a man among men. 'I was set in order from eternity',* says the Wisdom of God, and we cannot doubt that [he was set in order] as the equal of the Father, so that he through whom all things were made might rightfully be above all things. But 'he reaches from end to end'—from one end, which is the fount of life, to death, which is the end of life; 'mightily'—because by his death he destroyed death; 'disposing all things well'—setting them all in order in humility and charity, pacifying,* restoring, and reconciling them, so that they might all be subject to him.*18

Heb 2:9
Pr 8:23




Col 1:20
1 Co 15:28

When all things are under him from whom they took their being, then are they set in order. [Lucifer], however, refused to stand in his place. He wanted to be with God as his equal, not subject [to him] in humility. 'I will be like the Most High,'* he said, and abandoned his order. But 'It is by your ordinance,

Is 14:14

O Lord, that the day abides'\* — by *your* [ordinance], and not by one's own personal [ordinance]. [Lucifer], therefore, did not abide [in his place] because he presumed to confuse his order and gave no heed to the fact that all things serve you.\* This is why the angel of light became the prince of darkness; he who was like celestial day became the gloom of night.

Charity, however, subjects everything to God in obedience and disposes everything by its authority: sometimes it recommends what is more perfect; sometimes it commands what is necessary; sometimes it permits what is not unlawful; sometimes it chooses what is better; and sometimes it accepts what is necessary. For although it is true that freedom and charity are bound together, there are times when charity yields to necessity and disregards what is better so as to avoid something worse. Thus, it often happens that we have a zealous desire for the good which is better, more worthy, and more perfect, but are hindered [from attaining it] by the authority of a superior power, whether it be the violence of some difficulty or the feebleness of our own infirmity. As a result, we find that that which occupied first place in our zeal occupies a lower place when we come to choosing it or pursuing it. Thus, when charity arranges what has to be done, it sometimes uses the order of freedom and dignity, and sometimes the order of judicious selection[19] and necessity. When there is no opposition to it, either from the power of a greater authority or from some difficulty or from the trepidation which comes from timidity, [charity] freely chooses whatever is more worthy and more perfect and pursues it. But when freedom of choice — or rather the choice of what is better—is hindered in some way, by some topsy-turvy order (but [remember that we are talking about] order still), then charity accepts what necessity imposes or what weakness suggests. Thus, when charity makes use of its freedom, it agrees to what is better; when it yields to necessity or submits to weakness, it subjects itself to a lesser good.

As a result of this, when [charity] has a zealous desire for what is better but is urged by some power of reason[20] to a lesser [goal], it sometimes hesitates in its choice and does not know which to choose. But it does know which it prefers. Thus, when Paul had a greater desire to be with Christ, since that was something much the better, but also felt the necessity to remain in the flesh for the sake of his brethren, he was torn between two choices and said, 'I do not know which I will choose'.\*   Ph 1:22–23

In all the just, however, whether in those who freely choose better things or in those who accept lesser goods, charity itself is always ordered. It is always [ordered] by being valued above all else, by zeal, and by pursuing it or choosing it. No one can be called good—whether more good or less good is irrelevant—if he does not set charity before all other things, even if he puts first in his love what he puts second in his choice. When charity has been set in order and when it has ordered [everything else] in whatever way it has ordered it, then everything else is likewise set in order. [Charity] is itself the order of the things it regulates, and nothing which is done in charity can be out of order.

[Consider then] the bride, who now despises the world, who now has charity set in order, and who now has so great a love that she cannot bear its heat within her breast. Can you imagine the sufferings that vex her and the sorrows that torment her? How she is beset by sorrow and fear, cares and concerns, affliction and confusion?[21] How she is racked by hatred and weariness in the midst of her temptations? How burdensome is the delay and the waiting which keep her from her hope and her desire? Who can describe the distress and afflictions of the bride who suffers for love and for whom all that she suffers is too little? She herself refers to her affliction when she says: 'Do not consider my blackness, for the sun has altered my color.'\* *Sg 1:5*

But where we find an abundance of the sufferings of Christ, do we not also find an abundance of the consolation of Christ?\* Truly an abundance! The bride, therefore, sometimes finds consolation in her own goodness and sometimes in the examples given her by others who are good. For in the ranks of good people, she sees some who are just starting, who blossom, as it were, with the beginnings of virtue, and some who have reached the pinnacle of perfection by the maturity of their conduct. All these examples of those who love and those afflicted with love, whether beginners in virtue or those in whom it has come to fullness, whether in the initial stages or a well-trained maturity of patience, all of them, surely, are flowers and the fruit of honor and respect?\* The bride rejoices when she surpasses the beginners; she rejoices, too, when she equals those who are stronger. She rejoices when the former are beneath her, because she can then rest there gently as if she were borne up by flowers. And she rejoices when the latter are about her and around her, for being encompassed and enclosed, as it were, by apples, she veers neither right nor left, but presses

*2 Co 1:5*

*Si 24:23*

on inflexibly and strongly to greater and greater strength. This is why she says, 'Sustain me with flowers; encompass me with apples.' It is just as if she said to the members of her household: 'Comfort me, all my inmost senses and affections. Let me gently rest with flowers spread beneath me; let me be encompassed with apples all about me so that I may never turn to any other end. I am glad that I am sick like this, for those who suffer the same [pains] and those who are afflicted with the same sadness are with me for my solace.'

In addition to this, the bride also finds solace for her afflictions in her merits and the rewards of her merits. She takes note of the three things which the Lord promised her as a reward when he said: 'There is no one who has left this or that for my sake and for the gospel who will not receive a hundred-fold now in this time—although he will also be persecuted—and in the age to come eternal life.'[22]* After advancing for a long time in the gradual stages of virtue and exercising herself strenuously in the labors of spiritual discipline, then indeed she finds [she has received] a hundred-fold in peace and tranquility of heart, in serenity and security, in the delight of righteousness and the ineffable sweetness of spiritual joy.

Such are the apples, such are the fruits of righteousness, which grow from the flowers of incipient discipline. But these are not the only [fruits]: there are also the apples of tribulation and persecution which, as an example of patient suffering,*[23] God sometimes allots to those who want to suffer, or even die, for the name of Jesus.* Thus, when Job was suffering in patience, he said: 'I wish that he who has begun would destroy me; that he would let loose his hand and cut me off. This would be my

Mk 10:29-30

Tb 2:12

Ac 21:13

consolation: that he afflict me with sorrow and not spare me.'* And again: 'If he should scourge me, let him kill me at once and not laugh at the pains of the innocent.'* When he says this, does he not seem to be calling down scourgings upon himself and saying: 'Encompass me with evils'?²⁴ But unless he were sustained by the flowers of virtue, he would not have said this. He was simple and upright; he feared God and avoided evil.*

The bride, therefore, in her zeal for perfection, not only considers as God's favors the gifts of the virtues and the joys of inner peace, but also recognizes the gifts of God in her tribulations. She accepts his scourging joyfully as if it were a favor. 'It has been granted to you,' says the Apostle, 'that for the sake of Christ you should not only believe in him but also suffer for his sake.'* If, then, the bride wants to be encompassed by these apples [of misfortune],²⁵ as if they too were fruits of righteousness, how much more does she yearn for those inestimable fruits of righteousness which are reserved for the life to come? When she says, 'Encompass me with apples,' she can also be thinking of these [latter] fruits, and while she is here [on earth], it is in these that she finds comfort—at least in hope—from all her evil tribulation and all her sorrow, until she sees him whom she loves, her bridegroom Jesus Christ, who is above all things, God, forever blessed. Amen.*

## Notes to Tractate XIV

1. This is a title of convenience, and does not appear in the manuscripts. There can be no doubt that this brief sermon was delivered to a monastic congregation and dates from Baldwin's time as abbot of Ford.
2. Ovid, *Metamorphoses* I. 523. The actual text of Ovid reads *Ei mihi, quod nullis amor est sanabilis herbis*. Baldwin has *medicabilis* instead of *sanabilis*, which actually belongs to the very similar *Epistulae* 5.149: *Me miseram, quod amor non est medicabilis herbis*.
3. The same image appears in Tr. VIII, and derives, as Thomas notes (39/179 n. 3), from Augustine, *Tractatus in Iobannem* xv. 7; PL 35:1512–1513.
4. Natural, social, and conjugal love are also discussed at the beginning of Tr. VIII.
5. *Virtus*. See Tr. IX/III, n. 10.
6. The punctuation of this passage in PL 540B is obviously incorrect.
7. The intimate association of loving, possessing, and enjoying God derives from Augustine. Cf. *De moribus ecclesiae catholicae* I. III. 4; PL 32:1312.
8. Once again, the punctuation in PL 541A needs some correction.
9. *Poculum salutis. Salus* means both health and salvation. See Tr. IX/III, n. 4.
10. PL 541B omits *vinum compunctionis et*.
11. The last part of this sentence has been omitted in PL 541C by hom. The antithesis of cupidity and charity has been noted earlier (see Tr. XIII, n. 13) and occurs again later in this present treatise.
12. This is Augustine's definition in *De civitate Dei* xv. 22; PL 41:467: 'Thus it seems to me that a brief and true definition of virtue is "the order of love"'. Or, as we could also translate it, 'rightly ordered love'.
13. *Ordinatur autem caritas aestimatione, aemulatione, et electione*. On *aemulatio*, see Tr. IV, n. 30; Tr. X/I, n. 2; Tr. XI, n. 29.
14. Baldwin is playing on the root *spir-*: *Nonnulli enim ad eam aspirant et suspirant, qui in ea numquam respirant*. Cf. also Tr. III, n. 18.
15. *Consilium* means resolve, resolution, or decision, as well as counsel or advice. See also Tr. IV, n. 8; Tr. VII, n. 22.
16. The Latin simply reads *Dei consilio utendo*, but Baldwin implies both meanings of *consilium*. God's counsel should be our resolve.
17. Ph 3:8 with *arbitratus sum* instead of the Vulgate *arbitror*, and *lucrifacerem* instead of *lucrifaciam*. The latter variant may be due to the influence of Augustine. Cf. *De civitate Dei* XVII. IV. 6; PL 41:530; *Sermo* 169. IV. 6; PL 38:918.
18. This sentence is a running commentary on Ws 8:1: 'He reaches from end to end mightily, and disposes all things well'. It is used as the *Magnificat* antiphon of 17 December Vespers.
19. *Dispensatio* here means carrying out the most economical and judicious course in the circumstances. Cf. Tr. I, n. 6 for a rather different usage.
20. Thomas (39/202) has *rationis*; PL 544A (incorrectly) reads *actionis*.
21. This sentence has been omitted in PL 544C by hom.
22. The three things praised in these verses (Mk 10:29–30) are (1) a hundred-fold reward now; (2) persecution now; and (3) eternal life to come. Baldwin concentrates on the second of these.
23. *Ad exemplum patientiae*. For the meaning of *patientia*, see Tr. IX/II, n. 15; Tr. XI, n. 2.
24. In Latin, *malum* can mean both an apple and an evil, and Baldwin's play on words is impossible to reproduce in English. *Stipate me malis* can mean 'Encompass me with apples' or 'Encompass me with evils'.
25. Once again, *malum* is being used with both its meanings.

# TRACTATE XV
# ON THE CENOBITIC OR
# COMMON LIFE[1]

*The grace of our Lord Jesus Christ, and the charity of God, and the fellowship of the Holy Spirit be always with you all.** 2 Co 13:13

IT IS BY NO SLIGHT or mean or ordinary authority that the institution of the common life is supported and sustained. The primitive Church was built on the common life, and the infancy of the newborn Church began with the common life. It is from the Apostles themselves that the common life has received its form and expression, its title of honor, the privilege of its high position, the testimony of its authority, the protection which defends it, and the foundation of its hope.

It was the Apostles who were established by God as princes over all the earth;* princes of the people, gathered together with the God of Abraham; strong gods of the earth who are exceedingly exalted; friends of God, who are greatly honored and whose principality is greatly strengthened;* nobles of heaven, judges of the earth, to whom was made the promise that they should sit on twelve thrones and judge the twelve tribes of Israel;* members of the [celestial] senate,[2] who receive swords in their hands to execute vengeance upon the nations and chastisements upon the people, to bind their kings with fetters and

Ps 44:17[45:16]

Ps 46:10[47:9]

Ps 138[139]:17

Mt 19:28

their nobles with manacles of iron, to execute upon them the prescribed judgement.*     Ps 149:6–9

Such men as these, so powerful and so noble, were clothed in virtue from above, and by the inspiration of the Holy Spirit they undertook to observe the common life. They confirmed it by their example, sanctioned it by their conduct, and handed it down to us so that we might also keep it. Thus, through the common life, we who are set upon the earth can begin to be fashioned in the likeness of the angels of God, for in the eternal life to come, we shall be united with them as their like and their equal. The common life was instituted by celestial models; it was brought down from heaven and adopted by us from the heavenly way of life of the holy angels.

If the fact that the common life came down from the angels of God to the Apostles and from the Apostles to us is still not sufficient to recommend it to you, then there is a further factor which we can add, something beyond all praise: the common life flowed out from the Fount of Life itself. I am speaking now of that fount of which it is written, 'With you is the fount of life, and in your light we shall see light'.* The common life, then, is a sort of radiance     Ps 35:10[36:9] from the eternal light, a sort of emanation from the eternal life, a sort of effluence from the everlasting fountain, from which flow living waters, springing up into eternal life.*     Jn 4:14

### Of the Common Life of the Father, Son, and Holy Spirit

God is life. The holy and indivisible Trinity is one life. The Father is not one life, the Son another, and the Holy Spirit a third, but these three are one life. Just as they have one common essence and one common nature, so they have one common life. God is not alone or solitary, for God is three and one; nor is the life of God not common, for there is but one indivisible and undifferentiated life for all three persons.

It may perhaps seem to some, without giving offence to devout faith, that the essence or power or wisdom of God exists separately and discretely since each is incomparably supereminent and superexcellent, and that although each is indeed common, it is, as it were, *individually* common. Thus, it may perhaps be thought that each is a separate and discrete [power].[3]

But to prevent us from doubting what is certain as a result of the ambiguity of words, we are told that 'As the Father has life in himself, so he has granted the Son also to have life in himself',* and it is therefore established beyond any doubt that the life of God is not in this way a separate and discrete life which is not common to all. It was not fitting for God to be alone, nor was it consistent with his dignity to be lacking a partner [to share] in his glorious and blessed life.

According to the faith of the holy Fathers, it is a true profession of faith, a true assertion, a true declaration, that God is three and one, and not one alone; and in a certain way our own reason can offer support to this faith. God dwells in inaccessible light,* but since he has no wish to be totally unknown and, as a consequence of being unknown, also unloved, he therefore shines with a sort of light—albeit faint—in our hearts. To this extent he reveals himself to us more [clearly] and shows us his nature, and it is this which helps us to come to a better knowledge of his nature, which, according to the little knowledge given to us, we should love with all our heart, all our soul, and all our strength.* God, however, is charity,* and, as the Apostle says, his charity is poured forth in our hearts through the Holy Spirit who is given to us.* This charity is in us by grace and reveals to us in a certain way the nature of that incomprehensible charity which is God himself, whose nature is charity or generosity; and by a sort of inward feeling of charity itself, it indicates to our innermost being that the nature of charity is to love and to wish to be loved.

    Just as it is impossible for fire not to burn, so it is impossible for charity not to love. Love, after all, is a fire, and to love, therefore, is to burn. Fire does not contain itself within itself, but always seems to be trying to reach out for whatever it is burning. It has no wish to live only in itself, and it therefore shares its heat with the things it has touched and burned. In just the same way, love, by a certain instinctive movement,[4] longs to pour itself forth and transfer the good it possesses to someone it loves with all its love; [it longs] to have it in common, to take the other as a companion and to share its possession with him. In the view of charity, everything good shines with a more beautiful [light] when—so far as is proper—it is held in common with another. With regard to those goods which can satisfy both the lover and the one he loves with all his love, charity loves to share them and prefers to have them in common with the beloved rather than possessing on its own that which can satisfy both. And with regard to the goods which cannot satisfy both, charity itself often prefers to go without, so that a friend,

Lk 10:27
1 Jn 4:8

Rm 5:5

whom it knows to be in need of its generosity,⁵ should not be lacking. In displaying this liberality, charity always acts so as to arouse the love of the one it loves, so that it is not alone in its love.

As we have said earlier, [charity] always loves to be loved. A love of sharing is not enough for the lover: there must also be a sharing of love.⁶ And since it wants to share its goods, [it wants] much more [to share] love itself. Love does not know what it is to be ungenerous, and it hates to be solitary. By bestowing things so freely and profusely, it strives, as if through the love of sharing, to bring about a sharing of love. If love wanted to keep its goods for itself alone and did not want to have them in common, where would be its generosity? Or if it stood alone in loving another and not being loved [in return], where would be the comfort of love? It is written, 'Woe to one that is alone'.* A love which is solitary is its own torment, and in a certain way it hates itself, for since it wants to be mutual, it is wholly averse to being solitary. And just as it cannot be deprived of its generosity and its nature, so it cannot but love to share both its good and its very self.

With regard to the desire of charity, therefore, the charity which is in us [is characterized] by two factors which are inseparably connected: the love of sharing and the sharing of love. And if one or the other is absent, then charity is not yet blessed, for charity seeks its joy and blessedness⁷ only in the sharing of the good [it possesses] and the sharing of its own self. If we have a common good but not a common love, then charity lacks something which it wishes to have. And if there is a common love but not a common good, then charity lacks something

## Tractate XV

which it has no wish to be without. Both of these should be present[8] in that charity which is ours, which is in us, and which is among us; and [although] this charity has not yet brought us to the fullness of joy and blessedness, such blessedness will be ours in the future in the communion of the supreme good and in the communion of mutual love. The former can satisfy all, and in the latter there will be nothing which is not common to us all.

See, my soul,[9] and consider how the experience of that very charity which is so familiar to you shows you as much of the nature of God as God himself reveals to you through the grace of faith. If you were not so darkened by sin, my soul, you could know God with complete intimacy in your own nature, as in his image. But now you are nearly blind, and neither in yourself nor through yourself can you discern either God or yourself! You should be my eye for seeing God, but if my eye is blind, how am I not blind myself?[10] To the best of my ability, I recognize that I am totally blind in this way, and [the words of the Psalmist] are truly my own words: 'My strength has left me, and the light of my eyes itself is not with me'.\*

Since I began by speaking to you, my soul, I will continue to do so: I believe that your desire is to see God and to go to God, but because you are blind, you are in need of a guide. If you follow the guidance of faith, you will not go astray, but in the light of faith itself you will be able to see God even now!

But does this mean that it is only in faith that God is seen? Is he not [seen] in charity? Indeed he is seen in charity—and even more in charity [than in faith]! For charity is a commandment which is full of light, enlightening the eyes.\* There is nothing

*mens mea*

Ps 37:11[38:10]

Ps 18:9[19:8]

in us more similar to the charity which is God than the charity we have in us from God. Through [charity] the image of God is reformed in us; through [charity] God is seen and sensed in us much more completely than he is known by faith alone. If, then, we see clearly the invisible things of God by means of the things which were made within us,* if we are permitted to judge the nature of God from his grace, if it is given us to recognize the giver of the gift from the gift itself, then there can be no doubt that the love of sharing and the sharing of love correspond to the nature of God.

<sub>Rm 1:20</sub>

He whose nature is charity and generosity naturally loves and wants to be loved, and the extent to which he loves is the extent to which he wants to be loved. The sharing of love should not be less than the love of sharing, and he cannot bear it if he whom he wants to love him as much as he deserves to be loved should lack the full sharing of his joy and blessedness.

So great is the charity of the Father that the life he has in himself he also gave to the Son to have in himself,* so that the Son, who is the equal of the Father and who shares in common the glory of the Father in all the fullness of eternal honor and indivisible power, might be one life with the Father.

<sub>Jn 5:26</sub>

Without a partner—and therefore without sharing—charity is not happy or blessed. But blessed charity is blessed life, and the blessed life is blessedness, and blessedness is the supreme good; and the supreme good, by its very nature, is common [to all]. Everything good is worthy of praise simply because it is good, but if it is both good and common it has a double glory: [the glory] of goodness and [the glory] of sharing. The supreme goodness of good is the sharing of itself, and it therefore follows that the Supreme Good cannot be deprived of the praise [due to] its sharing itself. If such a quality of praise and praise of such a quality were lacking, then it would not be the Supreme Good. Since the Supreme Good is the full and perfect good, such good deserves all praise and should be lacking for none. By its nature, therefore, it is common, and it can be shared through grace, for it is the source and origin of all good things.

Such is the eternal life, the blessed life, the common life, infinite and incomprehensible charity, common to God the Father and his only-begotten Son. For as the Father has life in himself, so he has granted the Son also to have life in himself.\* In himself the Son has the life which the Father also has, because he is one life with the Father. But the Son does not have the life which he has in himself from himself; because it is life, he has it from the Father. For everything which we say the Son is or has substantially,[11] he is in common with the Father and has in common with the Father, that is, he has it from the Father. These are the things he has from the Father: that he is the living God, that he is blessed, omnipotent, and wise, that he is life itself, and blessedness and virtue, and wisdom. From the Father, too, he has [his being] as the Son, but he did not *begin* to have what he received from the Father: by being begotten he received what the Father bestowed upon him by the very act of begetting him.[12] He is coeternal with the Father, consubstantial and coequal, and like him in all things: God from God, light from light,[13] the brightness of his glory, the expression of his substance,\* and the image of the invisible God.\*

*Ibid.*

Heb 1:3
Col 1:15

The Father, who granted the Son to have life in himself as he has life in himself, loves the Son as himself; and the Son [loves] the Father as himself; and their [mutual] love is the Holy Spirit, who is the bond and the communion of both. Their love is so indivisible that whoever loves the Father also loves the Son, and whoever is not loved by the Son is not loved by the Father. Their love is one, and their honor indivisible; there is one power and one single operation.[14] Their communion is such that the Son can say to the Father, 'All that is mine is yours, and all that is yours is mine'.* And John the Baptist says, 'The Father loves the Son and has given all things into his hands'.* And the Lord himself says again, 'The Father loves the Son and shows him all that he himself does'.*

Jn 17:10

Jn 3:35

Jn 5:20

### Of the Sharing of the Angels

The common life of the angels is a sort of copy[15] of that common life which is in God, of God,[16] and is God. It is united in perfect peace by the Holy Spirit, who is its love, its bond, and its communion. 'By the word of the Lord the heavens were established, and all their virtue by the spirit of his mouth.'* The heavens are the angels in whom God dwells as their common life and common blessedness,[17] and in his love they live in concord and happiness. Each of them loves all the others, and all of them love each; they all want the same things and all are averse to the same things; what pleases one is displeasing to none, and what one wants, they all want. There is one purpose and one will for all; all feel the same thing, and all sense the same thing.

Ps 32[33]:6

There is no one here puffed up with pride, no one consumed with envy, no outbursts of anger, no quarrels or discord, no murmurs of impatience,[18] and no one is defamed by treacherous tongues. Here all is at peace, all is calm, all is tranquil. There is nothing disordered, nothing undisciplined, nothing contrary to order or obedience, nothing secretly put away with the intention of keeping it for oneself. Everything is open and aboveboard, everything is plain, and things which are proper to each individual are common to all through the sharing of love and the love of sharing. They are all [assembled] in one temple and raise their shouts of joy to God in common; all at the same time read and meditate and contemplate in the book of life; and they all refresh themselves communally at one and the same table. They take their rest together in the place of eternal[19] repose, and there is no one who does anything on his own which can disturb or damage their common peace, obedience, or order. Such is the fellowship — the happiest and most joyous [of fellowships] — of the citizens of the realms above who live the common life, and we who are still upon earth should follow their way of life by [living] the common life after their example. Thus, we might deserve to be joined with them in intimate companionship, a companionship which will be the more intimate the more it is granted us from above to imitate their life, through the grace of our Lord Jesus Christ, the charity of God, and the fellowship of the Holy Spirit. Amen.\*     2 Co 13:13

### Of the Sharing of Nature, to which is added the Sharing of Sin

Sharing is the basis of the common life, but there is a certain sharing of nature, a certain sharing of grace, and a certain sharing of glory.

The whole human species is united by sharing a single nature. It has descended from a single parent, accompanied by the transmission of sin, and is now disseminated far and wide in all the vast numbers of human beings. Joined to this sharing of [a common] nature there is also a certain sharing of sin and wrath, for nature is corrupted at its root, and its propagation is accompanied by [three things]: this corruption, original sin, and the wrath which this sin originally aroused.[20] By nature, we are children of wrath, for we are all of us born wicked and miserable. The blemish of sin has so infected human nature that it cannot be cleansed by lye, or soap,* or anything else we use to wash and clean ourselves, but only by the blood of our Lord Jesus Christ, into whose death we are baptized. 'For all of us who have been baptized have been baptized into his death.'* But the wrath of God's indignation has come forth from his hidden righteousness like an arrow from its quiver. It has pierced deep into human nature; it has reached its inmost parts and is so firmly fixed that the only force that can pull it out is the inconceivable strength of the hand of the omnipotent God. This is the arrow of which it is said through the prophet: 'He has shot into my loins the daughters of his quiver'.* In his zeal for [justice and] righteousness, God became [filled] with indignation against sin and poured forth his wrath. This is the wrath which is upon us from our birth, and this is why we are children of wrath by nature.* Such is the daughter of the quiver which is taken from God's hidden righteousness as if from a quiver. There [in heaven] it came into being; here [on earth] it is born in us, innate in us, the daughter of the quiver, born when we were born, like a twin sister to our nature. This is [the arrow] which the prophet says was shot into our loins, and he is right [to say] the loins: for it is here we find the seat of concupiscence, and it is from here that the affliction of our nature is generated.

By our sharing of this corrupted nature, a single nature in which we are all participants, we are subjects of sin and held in bondage to the debt of death, and there is imposed upon us a threefold necessity: [the necessity] of charity, humility, and pious devotion. 'You shall love your neighbor as yourself,'* says the Lord. If human curiosity inquires into the reason for the divine commandments—although the fact that God has so commanded should be enough to restrain any curious inquiry, since all his commandments are faithful, made in truth and equity*— but if someone is still anxious [to know] why God wished this commandment to be kept so meticulously, then faith does not lack a reply. The conviction of faith knows that God loves him who is consubstantial with him, him who shares in his nature, and following this example it can say in reply to mankind, 'Do likewise':* love him who shares your nature and who, in the future, will also share the glory promised to you. Love your nature, love that which you are by birth, for if you do not love in others the nature which is in you, you will not love yourself either.

Thus, we are drawn by the very example of God himself to love [our neighbor] who shares our nature. We are urged [to it] by the authority of him who gave the commandment, and we are constrained by our sharing of [the same] nature. Because of the awareness of our common infirmity, each should humble himself before the other, and each should

Lv 19:18, Mt 22:39

Ps 110[111]:8

Lk 10:37

feel pity for the other, and there will then be no proud self-glorification to divide those whose common condition of infirmity renders them equal. Whoever presumes to despise in another the nature he has in common does not yet know how to love himself, and whoever does not recognize [in another] the rights he has [from being created] in the image of God does injury to his own condition. Whoever refuses to honor in his neighbor the nature which he shares with him violates the rights of human fellowship, and whoever fails to extend the sentiment of mercy to his brother when he is in need debars himself from the chance of mercy.

### Of the Sharing of Grace

Up to now I have been speaking of the sharing of nature,[21] but there is also a certain sharing of grace in the case of all who profess themselves to be Christian, all those—whether good or evil—who, in general, are embraced by a single confession of faith and participation in the sacraments. This is a field in which there grow both tares and wheat.\* This is a region where we have grain mixed with chaff.\* This is a net in which there are good fish which should be sorted into vessels and bad ones which should be thrown away.\* This is the ark of Noah, and there are animals here both clean and unclean, the crow as well as the dove. There are some who have faith, but who do not have a worthy respect[22] for the works of faith; and there are some who participate in the sacraments of the Church whose conduct annuls for them the virtue of the sacraments. There is thus a division among those who confess the faith and communicate in the sacraments, and one group is divided from the other as the good from the bad.

Among them we can count schismatics, who refuse the yoke of canonical obedience, and false brethren, who pretend rather than practise the humility of their Christian profession.

The just, however, participate in the sacraments of the Church in faith and in the obedience proper to faith, and all of them [enjoy] a special and singular communion which a stranger does not share. Nor does a person who finds himself in this communion share it with strangers, and he can therefore say with the prophet. 'I will not enter into communion with their elect.'*     Ps 140[141]:4

This communion of the just is the unity of the Church, and it keeps the unity of the spirit in the bond of peace* in all the members of Christ. This     Eph 4:3 is the seamless garment of Christ which was not divided and of which Christ says, 'They parted my garments among them, and for my clothing they cast lots'.* As we have said, those who profess the     Ps 21:19[22:18], same faith and participate in the [same] sacraments     Jn 19:24 are divided one from the other as the garments of Christ are parted. One [group] receives the sacraments of the Church worthily, the other unworthily; the faith of the latter is dead,* since it is without     Jm 2:26 works, but the just man lives by faith.*     Heb 10:38

The lot was cast on the garment which was not divided. If someone unites himself with the fellowship of the Church in the charity of Christ and in obedience, he belongs to that lot of which it is written, 'The Lord will not leave the rod of sinners upon the lot of the just'.* Through the unity of peace     Ps 124[125]:3 [which reigns] in the Church and through the communion of obedience and charity, the just, wherever they might be found, whether living communally or alone, are like the members of one body and admit of no division. The birds—the turtledove, that is, and the pigeon—were not divided when Abraham, by God's command, took a cow, a she-goat, and a ram, cut them in two, and laid each half over against the other.* [Gn 15:9-10]

The Apostle alludes to this communion of the just when he says, 'One Lord, one faith, one baptism',* [Eph 4:5] and Christ himself clearly shows us that we owe obedience to one Lord when he tells us that 'No-one can serve two masters'.* [Mt 6:24] But obedience is the inseparable companion of charity, as [Christ] again testifies, when he says, 'If anyone loves me, he will keep my word',* [Jn 14:23] and 'Whoever does not love me does not keep my words'.* [Ibid.] Thus, obedience to one Lord, [together with] one faith and one baptism, make one communion of the just. Whoever remains in this communion until the end will find his lot among the elect and will not perish from among the people of God. There are many in this communion, however, whose lives are marked by indulgence and negligence, although not to the extent that they are past recovery.²³ It is they who build on the foundation (which is Christ) not with gold, silver, and precious stones, but with wood, hay, and stubble. It is true that they will be saved because of the merit of the foundation [on which they built], but [they will be saved only] through fire.* [1 Co 3:12-15]

There is no doubt that this communion of grace which we are now discussing is essential for instituting what is normally referred to as 'the common life', but on its own it is wholly inadequate for the common life of a religious community.

### Of the Sharing of Grace which makes the Common Life

There is still another sort of communion: that of

those who live in a [monastic] community. It is said of them: 'The multitude of believers had but one heart and one soul; no one said that any of the things he possessed was his own, but they had everything in common'.* What makes the common life, therefore, is one heart, one soul, and having everything in common. Such a life is an earthly copy—so far as human weakness allows—of the life of the angels.

Ac 4:32

Since they have but one heart and one soul and all things in common, there is concord and unanimity[24] throughout, and they always put the general profit and the common good before their own individual convenience. They so far renounce themselves and what is theirs that none of them, if indeed he is [truly] one of them, whether in [making] decisions or in [giving] advice, presumes to make a stubborn defence of his own opinion, nor to strive hard after his own will and the desires of his own heart, nor to have the least thing which could be called his own. Instead, as servants of God, they humble themselves for the sake of God under the hand of one of their fellow-servants,[25] and in him all power is vested. His judgement alone determines the decisions, regulates the will, and governs the needs of all. He alone can want something or refuse it, for the others have renounced their own power and freedom [of will]. Thus, they are not permitted to want what they want, nor to be able [to do] what they are able [to do], nor to feel what they feel, nor to be what they are, nor to live by their own spirit, but by the Spirit of God. It is he who leads them to be sons of God,* and it is he who is their love, their bond, and their communion. The greater their love, the stronger is their bond and the more perfect is their communion: and conversely, the greater their communion, the stronger is their bond and the more perfect is their love.

Rm 8:14

I am speaking now of that love with which we should love God before all things and above all things, the love which informs every life which [can be called] a good life—whether it be lived alone or in a community—and which makes it good. If it has not been made good by the charity of God, then it cannot be called a good life; indeed, it should not even be [referred to] as life, but rather the image of death. People who love themselves and serve their own desires are dead while they are still alive. They are like a widow who spends her time enjoying herself, and of whom the Apostle writes, 'The widow who spends her time enjoying herself is dead while she is still alive'.\* But whoever is truly alive gives his consent to the will of God, since life is in his will;\* and whoever truly loves God consents to his will, for it is by giving our consent to his will that God wants us to love him. In just the same way, we want others to love us by giving their consent and agreement to our will, and the more they consent, the more we think they love us. Thus, since love loves having things in common, and consent is necessary [for having things in common], it is clear that love always loves consent. If someone gives his consent, he feels something in common with another.²⁶

Now because it is possible for a person to have both a good will and a wicked will, it is also possible for a man to be loved both well and wickedly. But it is better to be hated well than to be loved wickedly, just as it is better to have hated someone well than to love him wickedly. To love well and to hate well are both good, and we owe both to our neighbor. This is why we are commanded to love our enemies and hate our friends!\* Yes, indeed! This is really what we have been told to do! And it was absolutely right that we should be told to do it! Otherwise our will would be much too hasty in hating our enemies and liking our friends. Our feelings, [both of love and hatred], would exceed all measure. They would burst all bounds and spread themselves far and wide. Our love for our friends, therefore, should be tempered with hatred, and we will not then praise the sinner in the desires of his soul,* even if he is our friend. No one loves his neighbor well unless he hates him well.²⁷     Ps 9B[10]:3

The case of the love of God, however, is entirely another matter. Just as we should love him with all our heart, all our soul, and all our mind,* so we should love all of him. He is wholly lovable, wholly desirable, and in him can be found nothing worthy of hatred, nothing unworthy of love.     Mt 22:37

O God of goodness and liberality; O God, so lovable and desirable, so worthy of our love; O God who is love; O God who is charity; O God of so sweet a nature, how great is the iniquity of those that hate you without a cause,* for you have not deserved [their hatred]. Why have the wicked provoked your name?* What benefit is there, what profit, what advantage, for those who provoke your name? Those who love your name find great peace,* but those who hate you hate life itself, and salvation, and generosity, and mercy. In a word, it is charity they hate, since you, O God, are charity! Whoever hates charity is hated by charity and is far, far from salvation.* How foolish it is to hate charity! For the hatred [of charity] is the hatred of wisdom, since you, O God, are the Supreme Wisdom, and to know you is perfect understanding.* It is through love that we know you, for love itself is knowledge,²⁸ and if someone does not love you then he does not

Ps 68:5[69:4]

Ps 9B:13[10:14]

Ps 118[119]:165

Ps 21:2[22:1]

Ws 6:16

yet know who you are in the way that he should. However much he prides himself on the glory of his brilliant eloquence, however much he extols himself for his knowledge of marvels and wonders, however much he displays his abundance of desirable things, if he does not love you, then he is foolish and stupid. If he does not love you, he is a beggar and a pauper, for the riches of salvation are wisdom and knowledge.* But the wisdom with which someone who loves you savors you²⁹ is more precious than all riches, and of all the things that we desire, there is none that can compare with it.

Is 33:6

'Keep me, O Lord, as the apple of an eye.'* Keep me from the grave sin which I fear so much. [Keep me] from hating your love lest I sin against the Holy Spirit, who is your love and your bond, [who is] unity, peace, and concord. Otherwise, in sinning the sin which is forgiven neither here nor in the world to come,* I shall be far from the unity of your Spirit and the unity of your peace. Keep me, O Lord, among my brothers and my neighbors, so that I may speak peace of you.* Keep me among those who keep the unity of the spirit in the bond of peace.*

Ps 16[17]:8

Mt 12:32

Ps 121:8[122:7]

Eph 4:3

Beloved brothers, we must take the greatest care in practising what pertains to the profession of the common life. [We must] keep the unity of the spirit in the bond of peace,* through the grace of our Lord Jesus Christ, the charity of God, and the fellowship of the Holy Spirit. From the charity of God comes unity of spirit; from the grace of our Lord Jesus Christ [comes] the bond of peace; from the fellowship of the Holy Spirit [comes] that communion which is essential to those who love communally, if indeed they are to live communally. The

Ibid.

## Tractate XV

charity of God brings about unity of spirit, for he who cleaves to God is made one spirit [with him].* The charity of God—the [charity], that is, with which we should love God—is necessary in one way for those that live on their own and in another way for those who live communally, but the charity which corresponds to the common life is more akin[30] to the charity which is God. God loves righteousness,* and the greater the righteousness, the more he loves it. But he also hates iniquity, and the greater the iniquity, the greater is his hatred.

It is the things of this world—[the things] in which and for which we normally find the self-glorification of human pride, the malice of jealousy, the quarrels of cupidity, and the delights of sensual pleasures— it is these temporal things, I say, which, for the sake of our love and desire for eternal things, God wants us to despise rather than love. Nevertheless, in accordance with the demands of our human needs and provided we scorn all extravagance and excess, he permits us to use them in moderation. But he certainly hates those who spend their time in useless vanities.*

If, then, the charity of God which is in us can be so much in accord with the charity with which God loves us that it loves that which he himself loves, if it always pursues the better things in its zeal for perfection and is always careful to avoid even the lighter sins, if it regards as contemptible what God also wants regarded as contemptible, then this charity of God brings about in us unity of spirit, and as the only-begotten Son of God lives with God the Father in the unity of the Holy Spirit (for there is but one Spirit of the Father and the Son), so we too, as adopted sons, live under God the Father in the unity

1 Co 6:17

Cf. Ps 44[45]:8
Heb 1:9

Ps 30[31]:7

of the Holy Spirit, and it is in this [Spirit] that we cry, 'Abba, Father'.* We do not, of course, say this in the same way as the only-begotten Son. He is at the right hand of the Father and equal to him in all things, whereas we are inferior and far and away unequal. In his case, we should not say that he cries out [to God], but rather that he calls him by name,³¹ as it is written: 'He will call to me: You are my father.'* Our cry, therefore, certainly comes from far away, but yet, in a certain way, there is a similarity.³² The unity which is brought about in us by the charity of God is preserved in the bond of peace through the grace of our Lord Jesus Christ. He who makes two to be one* is himself our peace. At his birth the angels sang together, 'Glory to God in the highest, and on earth peace to men of good will,'* and when he was about to ascend into heaven, he said to his disciples, 'Peace I leave with you, my peace I give to you.'*

What exactly is this peace which we have been given by Christ, the peace which preserves unity of spirit in its bond? It is the mutual charity with which we love each other, and it remains intact provided we all say the same thing and there are no divisions among us. Blessed Peter brings this to our attention when he says, 'Before all things, hold unfailing your mutual charity'.* What is mutual charity but that which is both mine and yours, so that I may speak of it with someone I love? If I should love you without your loving me, or if you should love me without my loving you, then charity is not yet mutual, since it is not both mine and yours. Mutual charity is common and does not lack the sharing of love. As it is mutual, so it should also be unfailing, otherwise there will be no bond of peace nor tie of love.

Unfailing [charity] has truth as its foundation. It is not broken apart by distrust, but is always nourished and cherished by mutual service and mutual patience. It is guarded carefully and diligently so that it does not fail and is not clouded by any hypocrisy. This is the charity of those who truly love themselves in Christ, not in word and tongue but in deed and truth.* This is the charity which Christ impresses, infixes, inscribes so deeply on our hearts by his word and his example when he says, 'This is my commandment, that you love one another, as I have loved you'.* In this charity, unity of spirit is preserved as in the bond of peace. This, therefore, is the law of the common life: unity of spirit in the charity of God, the bond of peace in the mutual and unfailing charity of all the brethren, the sharing of all the goods which should be shared, and the total rejection of any idea of personal ownership in the way of life of holy religion. [Our hope is] that this may be found in us and remain in us, as in those who have but one heart, one soul, and all things in common, [and therefore we pray that] the grace of our Lord Jesus Christ, the charity of God, and the fellowship of the Holy Spirit be with us all always. Amen.*

1 Jn 3:18

Jn 15:12

2 Co 13:13

### Of Mutual Charity among Those Who Live the Common Life

With regard to the concord of mutual charity, let us ask advice from our own nature, the nature of our own body, [and we will find that] it instructs us as to how peace should be preserved. We who are

Rm 12:5 — many are yet one body and members one of another.* And there is one spirit which animates the whole of our body through its members, joints, and structure. It brings about that mutual peace by which unity of spirit is preserved and achieves it by the mutual service and mutual patience of all the members.

If you think about it, you will see how all the individual parts, each with its own characteristics, serve the common welfare. The eye does not see simply for itself but directs our feet in their steps and our hands in their work. The mouth does not eat nor the stomach digest only for itself, but both work for a common end. What is consumed by the mouth and digested by the stomach nourishes the whole body, meeting all its needs and aiding its growth. If part of the body is wounded in some way, does it not seem as if the tongue suffers with it? It speaks as if it suffered itself and cries out against the one who wounds it, 'Why do you wound me?' And is it not true that the heart is careful to decide and dispose things for the common welfare, as much for the other [members] as for itself? [Consider, too,] our hands, which are born to service and are devoted to it. Does our everyday experience not teach us how they humble themselves in the service of our feet? And what if one hand wounds the other, as sometimes happens? Does the one which is hurt rouse itself with zeal for revenge and, once it has been struck, strike the other in turn? Or is it not the case that the one that gave the hurt, as if aware of its guilt and goaded by sorrow and remorse, hastens to make amends and to apply to its wounded sister the best possible remedy and cure? Is this humble service not a plea for forgiveness, an appeal for pardon? Does its earnest devotion and assiduous kindness not excuse it from any suspicion of malice? And here is something else which can enlighten us: if our eye sees a sword being brandished round our head and threatening to strike it, then immediately, without being asked, in the heat of love or anger, our hand puts itself in the way and blocks the sword, or even attacks it. Its fear for the head [annuls] its fear for itself, and it therefore rushes to put itself in danger. To spare the head it does not spare itself.

Beloved brothers in Christ, where do these examples lead us but to mutual patience, mutual humility, mutual charity? Has God not written within us a law of love which should teach us about ourselves? If only he who gave the law would also give us his blessing! If only he would feed us in the innocence of our heart and lead us by the skill of our hands[33] into the way of peace!\* Then we would preserve the unity of the spirit in the bond of peace and maintain the love of God by loving our neighbor. If we love God with one heart and one soul[34] in accordance with the purity of our profession, there is no doubt that the charity of God will be poured out in our hearts by the Holy Spirit and that the one Spirit of God will animate all of us as if we were one body. None of us then will live for himself, but for God, and all of us together will live in unity of spirit through the one spirit that dwells in us.

It is by the charity of God that this unity of spirit is found in us, and it is preserved in us by the love of our neighbor. In this way we may all remain together in the love of God, and by remaining in this love remain also in God and God in us.\* The love of God is made known, strengthened, and fortified in the love of our neighbor.

God can certainly find contentment within himself.

Ps 77:72[78:73]

Cf. 1 Jn 4:13

He is sufficient to himself in every good thing and has no need of our goods. If someone does not love him, he cannot be harmed, and if someone does love him, he cannot aid or help him. Thus, when we do everything well, we should say, 'We are unprofitable servants',* for whatever good we do profits us rather than him.

Nevertheless, God should not be loved with word and tongue,* as they loved him of whom it is written, 'They loved him with their mouth, and they lied to him with their tongue'.* God, I say, should be loved so that the love of him shines forth in deed and in truth.*[35] Since God has no need of any benefits himself, he has put in his place, as it were, our brothers and neighbors who need these things, so that they might receive from us those outstanding benefits which are due to him. No one, therefore, should flatter himself that he loves God, no one should deceive himself by thinking that he loves God, if he does not love his neighbor, [for if he does not love his neighbor] he does not love God. If anyone lacks the means of experiencing this, of proving it for himself, [let him consider the following]:[36] if he does not love his neighbor whom he sees, who is present with him as one who stands in the place of God, to whom shall he pay the debt of charity? How can he love God whom he does not see,* who does not reveal his presence to him, and who is not in need? How else can he offer benefits to God, except by offering them to someone in whom God does have a need, who in himself needs nothing? It is God who, in his members, asks and receives; [it is God] who is loved or despised. The love of our neighbor, therefore, is the tie of love and the bond of peace by which we maintain and preserve in

ourselves the charity of God and the unity of spirit.
Anyone who does not love his brother separates
himself from unity of spirit. He does not love God,
and lives not by the spirit of God but by his own
spirit; he now lives for himself and not for God.

### A Further [Discussion] of the Sharing of Grace

Sharing things in common is characteristic of the
love of one's neighbor, and where love is complete,
sharing is complete. There cannot be a sharing more
complete[37] than the sharing of everything, as it is
written: 'They had everything in common'.* But we     Ac 4:32
might be worried by [the text] which follows: 'Distribution was made to each one according to his
need'.* How [can we reconcile] having things in     Ac 4:35
common with distribution [to individuals]? How
[can we reconcile] having things in common with
individual ownership?[38] If distribution was made to
each one according to his need, then to each one
was granted the use and possession of whatever his
need required. If each one had different needs, each
with its own satisfaction, if [each one had] his own
sickness and his own cure for it, if each one [had] his
own wretchedness and his own solace to counter it,
how could they have had all things in common
when a number of things pertained to each one
individually?

The question is made even more difficult by the
Apostle saying, 'To each is given the manifestation
of the Spirit for the benefit [of all]',* and 'Each has     1 Co 12:7
his own special gift from God, one of one kind, and
one of another'.* And again, 'There are different     1 Co 7:7
sorts of gifts, different sorts of service, and different
sorts of working'.* How, then, can all things be held     1 Co 12:4-6

in common when such different sorts of gifts and graces are given to different individuals? What can we say about this? Who is capable of giving an answer? 'It is a labor in my sight.'\*

Ps 72[73]:16

Let us, then, see whether the knot of love, which should not itself be untied, can untie this knotty problem. Indeed it can! For by its judgement, charity knows how to convert individual ownership into common ownership, and it does so not by doing away with individual ownership, but by making individual ownership serve a common end. In this way, [whatever is individual] is not separated from what is common and therefore does not detract from the common good. But since charity loves to share things in common, a distribution of personal ownership which does detract from the common good is contrary to charity. [Charity], however, also loves individual ownership when it promotes the common good and does not hinder having things in common. Indeed, although it is possible to have individual ownership[38] without the common good, it is impossible to share things in common unless there is also individual ownership. How can anything be held in common if those who have it in common are not distinguished from each other by what they possess individually?

In the supreme and indivisible Trinity there is one unity,[40] one eternity, one power, one wisdom, one life, one essence, common to all three persons. But one person is distinguished from another by what they possess individually, even though there is one common blessedness. Thus, the fact that the Father alone is [the Father] does not detract from the common good. The Father, after all, is not Father to himself but to the Son, whom he begot from his

## Tractate XV

own substance and to whom, in begetting him, he granted to have life in himself. And if I may turn from this and speak instead about something with which we are more familiar, [something which accords more] with our normal experience: the individual characteristics by which a man is a father do not hinder his sharing in human nature. On the contrary, this nature is passed down from one to another by [the process] of generation, and the fact that one particular individual is responsible for this generation does not impair the sharing of a common nature.

Now the power of grace is not less than that of created nature, and charity, which is poured forth in the hearts of the saints and poured out by being shared,[41] is a very high grace. It is through the Holy Spirit that charity is poured forth, and he loves this outpouring since he himself is that which is poured out. 'I will pour out my spirit,'* says the Lord. Whoever, therefore, has [received] from God an individual gift should have it in such a way that he has it not only for himself but also for God and his neighbor: for God, so that he seeks the glory of God in God's gift and not his own glory, and for his neighbor so that he always considers the common benefit and not his own. 'Charity seeks, not its own inteests, but those of Jesus Christ.'* [Charity] loves to have things in common, not to possess them individually without sharing them. In fact, it loves to share them so much that it is sometimes unwilling to reclaim goods which rightfully belong to it and which someone else has taken. Charity is generous and shuns disputes; it does not seek its own interests and has no wish to enter into legal controversy, when charity itself would be in danger. It prefers to be

Ac 2:17, Jl 2:28

1 Co 13:5, Ph 2:21

cheated rather than to perish; [it prefers] to suffer the damages than to be awarded the costs. Why would it be eager to reclaim what it does not have when it is so quick to give away what it does have? Individual gifts are led by [charity] to [serve] the common good, and a gift which one person has received as his own personal possession becomes of benefit to another because its usefulness is shared with him.

This is why blessed Peter says, 'As each has received a gift, employ it for one another. If anyone speaks, [let him speak] as if it were the words of God. If anyone renders service, [let him do it] by the strength which God supplies, so that in all things God may be honored.'* Paul also says, 'To each is given the manifestation of the spirit for the benefit [of all].'* What is this manifestation of the spirit which is given for the benefit [of all] if not the gift of grace which should be manifested for the benefit of our neighbors and (so far as is proper) made available to all? A wise man should not be [wise] for his own sake but should say, 'That which I have learned without guile, I have shared without envy'.* Someone who has should share with those who have not, as we are taught by him who says, 'Give, and it shall be given to you'.*

Avarice, which has no desire to share things in common, keeps what it has for itself and is as opposed to sharing things as it is inimical to charity. If one of the pagan poets* praises a pagan who had neither the true faith nor the true God nor the true hope of a true resurrection or of true blessedness by saying of him that 'He believes that he is born not for himself but for the whole world',[42] how much more should Christians — and especially those men bound by vows who profess the common life—hold fast to the idea of having all things in common and prefer it to all else. Thus, whoever is good to himself should also be good to others and not troublesome. Whoever has the utterance of wisdom or knowledge, whoever has the gift of work or of service,* whoever has any other gift, whether greater or lesser, should possess it as having been given it by God for the sake of others. He should always be afraid that a gift he has received may turn against him if he does not strive to use it for the benefit of others, for we receive the gift of God in vain if we do not use it to seek the glory of God and the benefit of our neighbor. But if the personal gift which someone [has received] from God is turned to the common good, it is then that this gift is changed into the glory of God, and when the gift given to each one individually is possessed in common through the sharing of love, then the fellowship of the Holy Spirit is truly with us.

1 Co 12:5f

### A Further [Discussion] on the Sharing of Grace and the Sharing of Glory

The Holy Spirit is communion [and sharing], and he loves so much to share things that he wants to give himself. He is generosity itself, and it is not enough for him to give the things he has: he must also give himself. But [he gives himself] only to those whom he himself has made worthy to receive so great a gift, for he is the gift and was, from eternity, the supreme good and the supreme gift.

Whoever has received a gift from God and shares its use and benefit with his neighbor truly possesses what he has received, and to him that has will more be given, and he will have abundance; but from him who has not, even what he seems to have will be taken away.*⁴³ The gift which God has entrusted to us and which we have received is, as it were, given into our keeping and put in our name as a loan. [Such a gift] binds the one who has received it both to God and to his neighbor: to God, in that he should return glory to him; and to his neighbor, in that he should share with him his gift. Whoever shares his gift shows mercy to his neighbor; whoever returns glory pays [his debt] to God.⁴⁴

These are the marks of a just man: he shows mercy, and he pays [his debts]. If a man did not pay his debt, if he did not honor a contract, if he went against the whole system of lending and borrowing, then he would be unjust. This is why it is written: 'The sinner shall borrow and not pay back'.* He borrows when he receives; he does not pay back when he refuses to repay; and in this he is a sinner since he borrows and does not pay back. He does not pay back because he neither shares with his neighbor nor glorifies God. God demands [repayment] both for the gift which he has bestowed and for that which he may not yet have given. He requires interest. He reaps where he did not sow and gathers what he did not scatter.* He reaps among the wicked and gathers among the good. At the end [of time], he will send his angel-reapers to the wicked,* to those whom he condemns for not returning a profit,⁴⁵ and the angels will gather up the tares and bind them in bundles to be burned.* But he will gather the good into his granary like wheat* and repay them for what he himself gave them. [He will give them back] the profit which they returned and which he received.

'He gathers that which he did not scatter.' The text refers only to God. He alone gathers for himself what he did not scatter. It does not refer to those to whom he gave his gifts,[46] those who received them and shared them with their neighbors. They certainly scattered. They went forth and bore fruit like those of whom it is written: 'They went forth and wept, sowing their seeds'.\*     Ps 125:6[126:7]

Now it seems as if the reference to God's hardness [in the parable we are discussing[47]] must refer not to the good but to the wicked, but whether the two phrases refer to the good or the wicked, then without offending either the piety of faith[48] or the lovingkindness of God, we must somehow show that God is indeed hard. 'I reap where I did not sow,' he says, 'I gather what I did not scatter', and by these two statements he certainly shows his hardness either to one group or to both. Is it not true, then, that God is a hard Lord?\* Who dares to say it? On the other     Cf. Mt 25:24
hand, who dares to contradict the Spirit of God? Does not the prophet speak in the Spirit and say: 'With the holy you will be holy, and with the perverse you will be perverse'?\* And when the prophet     Ps 17:26–27[18:26]
said, 'How good is God to Israel,' he added, 'to them that are of a right heart',\* indicating [thereby]     Ps 72[73]:1
the ones to whom he is good. [Thus, we see that] the Lord appears hard to those who are hard of heart, those whom he has himself hardened by a just—but secret—judgement.

It may seeem [to you] that I am now destroying all that I built up earlier. I began by talking about the generosity and charity of God and have now rescinded this by demonstrating the hardness of his wrath against the wicked! But it sometimes happens that when two contrasting [ideas] are brought together, the truth shines out all the better. Now it is written that 'The Spirit of wisdom is generous, but will not acquit the evil speaker from his lips'.* These first words, 'The Spirit of wisdom is generous', [might imply] that God does not mean to punish sins severely; and therefore to prevent us from taking the generosity of God as an excuse for carefree sinning, the following is added:[49] 'He will not acquit the evil speaker from his lips'. He is generous to those who, by striving to be generous themselves, love the good of having things in common.[50] He is generous to someone who possesses for another the good he has himself. He is generous to someone who loves in another the good which the latter possesses and which he does not have himself.

The different [spiritual] gifts are made common in two ways: [firstly] when the gifts given to individuals individually are possessed in common by the sharing of love, and [secondly], when they are loved in common by the love of sharing. In a way, a gift is [always] common to the one who has it and the one who does not. If he who has it shares it with another, he has it for the sake of the other; and he who does not have it actually does have it in the other because he loves him! And by the fellowship of the Holy Spirit, the individual needs and weaknesses of each person are also made common to all, for just as charity is patient, it is also compassionate,[51] and someone who suffers with another who suffers makes the other's need his own. Thus, there is one need common to both, for the need of the former [consists] in the pain of suffering and that of the latter in feeling his pain with him.

If the needs of the just are common [to all], then it follows that their consolations are also common. If, by the disposition of charity,⁵² a person knows how to weep with those who weep, he also knows how to rejoice with those that rejoice.\* What an abundance of love and affection, what depths of charity are shown by the Apostle when he says, 'Who is weak, and I am not weak? Who is made to fall, and I do not burn [with indignation]?'\* He teaches us that we should do as he does by saying, 'Bear one another's burdens',\* and when he says, 'Each one shall bear his own burden,'\* he does not contradict himself. This is rightly understood to refer to the burden of sin, for sin alone is not admitted to the communion of charity.

Whatever good we do is for the common benefit, although its good may not be shared equally by those [united] in love. We hope to aid each other in the sight of God by our mutual prayers and mutual merits and by the merits and prayers of the saints whom we love; and we wish [in turn] to be loved by them so that we may be quite certain of obtaining forgiveness of sins and the glory which we deserve in the sight of God. We love them most of all, most ardently and zealously, if we recall their merits and consider their faith, charity, devotion, and patience, and are thereby stirred to rival [their achievements] and inflamed to imitate their virtues.

If someone were to be judged on his own merits, — as if the merits of others, which are shared in common through charity, were not there to give him support, — how could he bear the weight of the divine judgement? Many and great are our iniquities, and the prophet says, 'If you, O Lord, keep

Cf. Rm 12:15

2 Co 11:29

Ga 6:2
Ga 6:5

count of our iniquities, Lord, who shall stand it?'* [All] our good works are insufficient, and all our righteousness is like the rag of a menstruous woman.* And as it is written, 'The sufferings of this time are not worth comparing with the glory to come which shall be revealed in us'.*

Shall we then despair? In no way! Far from it! For God is charity!* O God who is charity, I suffer violence, answer for me! What shall I say, or what will he answer for me?* But if—or rather because—I am old enough to speak for myself,* I will declare with my mouth what I believe in my heart. I believe, O, Lord, in the Holy Spirit, the holy catholic Church, the communion of saints.* Here is my hope, here is my trust, here is my confidence, here is my security—however small it may be—which I have in the confession of my faith, in the generosity of the Holy Spirit, in the unity of the catholic Church, in the communion of the saints. If it be granted me from above to love you and to love my neighbor, then even though my own merits are poor and meager, I have a hope which is above and beyond all my merits: I am sure that through the communion of charity the merits of the saints will profit me and that the communion of the saints can make good my own imperfection and insufficiency. The prophet comforts me when he says, 'I have seen an end of all perfection, but your commandment is exceeding broad'.*

O charity, so broad and so extensive, how great is the house of God, how vast is the place of his possession!* We need not be distressed in our heart; we need not be confined by the boundaries and limits of our insignificant righteousness. Charity extends our hope to the communion of the saints, and we can therefore share with them their merits and their rewards. But the sharing of their rewards is [reserved] for the time to come, for it is the sharing of the glory which shall be revealed in us.

There are thus three sorts of sharing, [three forms of communion, three ways in which we have things in common]: the sharing of nature, which is associated with the sharing of sin and the sharing of wrath; then the sharing of grace; and thirdly, the sharing of glory. By the sharing of grace, the sharing of nature begins to be restored and the sharing of sin is removed, but by the sharing of glory, the sharing of nature will be fully and perfectly restored and the sharing of wrath wholly removed. It is then that God shall wipe away all the tears from the eyes of his saints.* It is then that all the saints will be as one heart and one soul, and they will have all things in common when God will be all in all.*

[Our hope is] that we, too, may come in common to this communion and come together as one [and therefore we pray that] the grace of our Lord Jesus Christ and the charity of God and the fellowship of the Holy Spirit may be with us all always. Amen.*

Rv 21:4

1 Co 15:28

2 Co 13:13

## NOTES TO TRACTATE XV

1. Title as in PL 545-546. I think there can be little doubt that this tractate originally comprised three separate sermons, each ending with the same doxology (2 Co 13:13). The first ends at PL 550C, the second at 556B, and the third at 562D. The three have then been placed together—probably with some minor editing—to form a single lengthy treatise on the common life. But since the development is logical and each successive part depends on the preceding part, the treatise is best left as it is and not divided up as in the case of Tractates IX and X. It need hardly be added that this little set of sermons was unquestionably delivered to a monastic congregation, and there can be no doubt that Abbot Baldwin knew what he was talking about. The tractate is an extremely important discussion of the monastic life, and a significant part of the heritage of twelfth-century cistercian spirituality. For further discussion, see C. Hallet, 'La communion des personnes d'après une oeuvre de Baudouin de Ford' in RAM 42 (1966) 405-422; idem, 'Notes sur le vocabulaire du *De Vita Coenobitica* de Baudouin de Ford' in *Analecta Cisterciensia* 22 (1966) 272-278; and D. N. Bell, 'Heaven on Earth: Celestial and (Cenobitic Unity in the Thought of Baldwin of Ford' in E. R. Elder, ed., *Heaven on Earth*, Studies in Medieval Cistercian History, IX, CS 68 (Kalamazoo, 1983) 1-21.

2. *Patres conscripti* 'elected fathers': this is a standard term in classical Latin for members of the Senate.

3. The word which I have translated by 'separate and discrete' is *singularis*, and Baldwin seems to be referring here to the contemporary controversy over appropriation, i.e. if the Trinity is truly one God and has 'one operation' (see n. 14 below), and if whatever can be said of one person of the Trinity can also be said of either of the other two, is there anything which can be attributed *specialiter* to the Father, or to the Son, or to the Holy Spirit? In 1140, Abelard had been condemned for 'tritheism' in attributing power to the Father, wisdom to the Son, and benignity or goodness to the Holy Spirit (see D. E. Luscombe, *The School of Peter Abelard* [Cambridge, 1970] chapter IV), and there was considerable debate at the time as to where, when, and how such terms as *specialiter*, *principaliter*, and *proprie* could be used. Baldwin does not enter into the debate, and merely stresses that as far as the Trinitarian life (*vita*) is concerned, it is indisputably common to all three persons. For a useful bibliography on the appropriation problem, see J. Châtillon (Ed.), *Achard de Saint-Victor, Sermons inédits* (Paris, 1970) 136, n. 14.

4. *Quodam sensibili conatu.*

5. This part of the sentence could also be translated as 'charity itself often prefers to go without, since its generosity makes known to it that its friend is in need'. But I think this is less likely.

6. Baldwin is contrasting *amor communionis* and *communio amoris*, and there is a lengthy discussion of this idea and this terminology in the two articles by Charles Hallet cited in n. 1 above. To translate *communio* simply by 'communion' can lead to very peculiar English and obscure sense, and I have therefore rendered it by sharing, sharing in common, having in common, and communion, depending on the context.

7. *Beatitudo* sometimes means joy, sometimes blessedness, and frequently both joy and blessedness.

## Notes to Tractate XV

8. *Habent*, in Thomas's text (40/25) is a typographical error for *habeant*.
9. *Mens mea*. Cf. IX/I, n. 18; X/II, n. 2.
10. The first part of this sentence has been omitted in PL 548C by hom.
11. *Secundum substantiam*. *Substantia* is used here in its specific Trinitarian sense. It follows, therefore, that since the Trinity is three persons but only one substance, what the Son is or has 'substantially', he is or has in common with the other members of the Trinity.
12. In other words, Baldwin is no Arian. The Son has no beginning in time, and we cannot say 'There was when he was not'.
13. *Deus de Deo, lumen de lumine* – phrases from the Nicene Creed.
14. *Individua operatio*. I.e. when the Trinity acts, it acts as a unity. What the Father initiates proceeds through the Son and comes to completion in the Holy Spirit. This is standard Augustinian (or Cappadocian) orthodoxy. Cf. Augustine, *De Trinitate* II. v. 9; PL 42:850–51, and a number of other places.
15. *Repraesentatio*: a re-presentation. For the significance of this word, see Tr. XII, n. 7.
16. *Et Dei est* has been omitted in PL 550A.
17. Most of the first part of this sentence has been omitted in PL 550A.
18. This same sentence appears in Tr. IV, n. 26, in a section which closely parallels this present discussion.
19. For *externae* in PL 550B, read *aeternae* with Thomas (40/35).
20. Lit. 'by original sin and original wrath'.
21. For the sake of style, I have taken the liberty of transposing this sentence from the end of the last section to the beginning of this one. We might also note in passing that this three-fold division of *communio* into nature, grace, and glory is not Baldwin's own invention. We may compare Bernard of Clairvaux, Gra III. 7; PL 182:1005C; (SBO 3:171; CF 19:62): 'There are said to be three liberties: the first, of nature; the second, of grace; the third, of life or glory'.
22. Thomas (40/41) has *digna reverentia*; PL 551D reads *congruentia*.
23. *Sed non perdite*.
24. This is clearer in Latin than in English: one heart (*cor unum*) and one soul (*anima una*) naturally imply *concordia* and *unanimitas*.
25. I.e. their abbot. Cf. RB 5:15 and 5:12.
26. *Qui consentit, cum altero communiter sentit*. Once again, we find Baldwin playing on the relationship of *sentire* and *consentire*. See also Tr. IV, nn. 41, 44; Tr. VI, n. 30; Tr. IX/IV, n. 5.
27. We may compare Aelred's discussion in his Spec Car III. XXVI. 60–64; PL 195:598D–600D (CCCM 1:133–136).
28. Baldwin is quoting the famous *dictum* of Gregory the Great, *Homiliae in Evangelia* 27.4; PL 76:1207A, which was so important for William of St Thierry. For a useful discussion of its significance for the spiritual writers of Baldwin's day, see R. Javelet, 'Intelligence et amour chez les auteurs spirituels du XIIe siècle' in RAM 147 (1961) 273–290; 148 (1961) 429–450.
29. *Sapientia* (wisdom) is derived from the verb *sapere* 'to taste, savor, sense, understand'. The relationship between wisdom, love, and 'tasting' ( = experiential knowledge) is a very important key to the understanding and appreciation of twelfth-century spirituality.

30. Thomas (40/55) has *similior*; PL 555A reads *similis*.
31. *Ipse enim magis invocare dicitur, quam clamare.*
32. In the interests of clarity, I have rearranged the order of these last four sentences.
33. Baldwin is quoting a phrase from Ps 77:72[78:73]: *in intellectibus manuum nostrarum*. The construction is peculiar both in Latin and English, and Thomas (40/66) uses an explanatory paraphrase to convey the sense: 'If only he would lead us in the way of peace by assuring the wisdom of our works'.
34. *Unanimiter et concorditer*. See n. 24 above.
35. This sentence has been omitted in PL 557C.
36. The PL text and the majority of the manuscripts read: *Si non habet omnis homo unde experimentum capiat sui, unde seipsum probet: si non diligit proximum quam videt*, etc. MS Troyes 876, however, contains the interlinear explanatory gloss: *diligat proximum ut diligat Deum*, and Thomas (40/67) inserts this in the text after *seipsum probat*. Nevertheless, it does not appear to be what Baldwin actually said, and I have therefore omitted it in this present translation.
37. For PL 558A *plena*, read *plenior* with Thomas (40/69).
38. *Proprietas*. The word means not only physical possessions, but any individual characteristics, e.g. possessions, looks, illnesses, comfort, etc.
39. PL 558C omits *proprietas*.
40. Thomas (40/73) has *una unitas*; PL 558D reads *unica unitas*.
41. PL 559A omits 'and poured out by being shared'.
42. Lucan, *Pharsalia* 2.383.
43. The background to this and the next four paragraphs is part of the Parable of the Talents in Mt 25:24-30. This must be kept in mind if we are to follow Baldwin's somewhat laborious exegesis.
44. Both PL 560B and Thomas (40/79) have *Qui communicat gratiam, misereretur proximo. Qui reddit, gloriam tribuit Deo.* In this present version, however, I have translated the last sentence as if the punctuation were *Qui reddit gloriam, tribuit Deo*, firstly because the two sentences are then rhetorically balanced, and secondly because it fits the context better.
45. Baldwin is referring to the wicked servant of Mt 25:26-27.
46. *Congregat quae non sparsit, ipse scilicet per se sine illis, quibus dedit.*
47. Baldwin is now referring to Mt 25: 24: 'Master, I knew you to be a hard man'.
48. PL 560D omits *pietate fidei*.
49. For PL 561A *sive adjungitur*, read *hic adjungitur* with Thomas (40/85).
50. Thomas (40/85) reads *studio communionis bonum*; PL 561A has *studio bonum collationis*.
51. In Latin, the words patient (*patiens*) and compassionate (*compatiens*) both imply suffering. See Tr. I, n. 32; Tr. XII, n. 2; Tr. IX/II, n. 15; Tr. XI, n. 2; Tr. XIV, n. 23.
52. *Per affectum caritatis.*

# TRACTATE XVI
# IN PRAISE OF THE PERFECT MONK[1]

*[The Nazarites were] whiter than snow, purer than milk, ruddier than old ivory, more beautiful than the sapphire.* \*   Lm 4:7

THIS PASSAGE from the prophet describes the beauty of the Nazarites. It lavishes upon it wonderful praises and extols it—indeed, more than extols it—with wonderful titles and commendations. It praises the whiteness of the Nazarites, it praises their purity, and it praises their ruddy color; and since these three things are characteristics of beauty and add to the grace of beauty, [the text] finally praises beauty itself by name. When all these are praised, however, they are not [praised] without reference to anything else, but certain comparisons are drawn,[2] so that by being compared with other things which are themselves worthy of praise, they might shine forth more and more [brightly]. Nor are they compared with things whose quality is equal to their own, but with things whose dignity and honor stand out as preeminent. The glory of praise is increased when that which is [already] eminent is made preeminent and that which is [already] superior is made yet more so; and the glory of praise reaches perfection when something which in itself is obviously worthy of praise, being founded on its own virtue and its own proper merits, distinguishes itself by the very praise [which it bestows] on other things which are worthy of more praise.

The beauty which is praised in the Nazarites is that not of their bodies but of their conduct, the glory not of the flesh but of the mind, of virtue, of integrity. In the eyes of the flesh the glory of the flesh has no little attraction, but it is actually vain and deceitful, as it is written, 'Attractiveness is deceitful, and beauty is vain'.* What is vain beauty if not a beautiful vanity? And what is deceitful attractiveness if not attractive deceit? It is attractive but deceitful; it is deceitful but attractive. Those who see it are gloriously pleased, but when they look at it they are deceived, and when they gaze at it, it deludes their eyes like a sort of conjuring-trick. If they would use the keen sight of their inner eye to penetrate the depths of the human body, [they would find that] the beauty of the flesh is nothing but a veil over depravity, nothing but an outward display [which covers] a hidden ignominy and confusion. Under the glory of the flesh shameful secrets lie concealed, [secrets] which are disgusting to name and which people shudder even to think about. Man indeed is rottenness and the son of man a worm.* If this is so—or rather because this is so—what is the beauty of the sons of man but the beauty of the worm? And what is a beautiful person but a beautiful rottenness? And finally what is proud man but the noble offspring of the most vile corruption, someone who, with blessed Job, can say to rottenness, 'You are my father', and to worms, 'You are my mother and my sister'.*

Bodily beauty, therefore, may have glory in the eyes of men, but not in the eyes of God. It lacks the virtue of merit and has no hope of reward. God is the inner judge and sees into the heart,* and he loves the beauty which is interior. When the prophet addresses the king's daughter, he says, 'The king shall greatly desire your beauty',* and so as not to hide the fact that it is an inner beauty, he adds, 'All the glory of the king's daughter is within, in golden borders'.*

The beauty of the Nazarites is inward, not outward, and they are therefore named after the flower of holiness, not the flower of the field, which is the flower of the flesh. 'For all flesh is grass, and all its glory as the flower of the field.'* It is written, 'The just shall flourish like the palm tree',* and again, 'Those who are planted in the house of the Lord shall flourish in the courts of the house of our God'.* And another scripture says, 'Flourish as the lily, and put forth leaves in grace'.* Where does the lily flourish? Christ is conceived in Nazareth, a flower in the flower of virginity and holiness. As the Father says of Christ, 'Upon him shall my holiness flourish'.* And Christ [says] of himself, 'I am the flower of the field and the lily of the valleys'.* In the book of Wisdom we read, 'Flourish as the lily'.* Christ says, Be holy, because I am holy'.* All the Nazarites breathe forth the odor of this lily and emit its scent. Those who were Nazarites in the days of the Law, consecrated to the Lord, were prefigurements of Christ, and by their abstinence and their conduct they also represented those who would imitate Christ in the future. They abstained from wine and intoxicating drinks and everything which could result in inebriation. But the sons of Jonadab also abstained from wine, for Jonadab instructed his sons not to drink wine, and they obeyed the voice of their father. Because of this, the Lord says, 'Jonadab

Pr 24:12

Ps 44:12[45:11]

Ps 44:14[45:13]

Is 40:6
Ps 91:13[92:11]

Ps 91:14[92:12]

Si 39:19

Ps 131[132]:18

Sg 2:1
Si 39:19
Lv 11:44

shall never lack a descendant to stand in my sight'.*

Jr 35:19

If, then, according to the voice of the Lord, Jonadab never lacks a descendant to stand in his sight, there must be sons of Jonadab, imitators of Christ, who now, in our own days, stand in the sight of the Lord. For it is Christ who is the true Jonadab, one who is always ready and willing to obey in all things, which is what the name Jonadab means.³ Someone who says to God, 'I will willingly sacrifice to you'* is always ready. The Nazarite, too, is ready, and this verse of the psalm [alludes] to him: 'My flesh has flourished again, and with my will I will give praise to him.'* The phrase 'with my will' refers to the Holy Spirit, for where the Spirit is, there is liberty;* but [the phrase] which precedes this, 'my flesh has flourished again', refers not to the present glory of our feeble flesh, which is the flower of the field, but to the hope of a glorious resurrection and the flower of the sanctified flesh, which is put to death with its vices and its lusts.*

Ps 53:8[54:6]

Ps 27:7[28:8]
2 Co 3:17

Ga 5:24

OF THE WHITENESS OF THE NAZARITES

The abstinence of the Nazarites and the sons of Jonadab was a sacrament,⁴ an example, and a sign. For them it was a sacrament [which led] to their sanctification; for us it is an example to imitate, a sign for our instruction. In it we find the model of a threefold spiritual abstinence, for there are three things which, by an inebriated forgetfulness or a forgetful inebriation, alienate the human mind from the love of God: the love of the soul, the love of the flesh, and the love of the world. In other words, the love of one's self-will,⁵ the love of carnal pleasure, and the love of worldly vanity. The love of the world is vain, the love of pleasure is sweet, the love of self-will is tenacious.

The more the soul loves itself tenaciously and obstinately and [thereby] cleaves to itself in a certain way, the greater its difficulty in being able to detach or separate itself from itself. It is scarcely possible to find anything which a soul loves more than its own self-will and its own opinion, and therefore when it is dragged away from its own will, it is as though it were severed from itself, and it bleeds as if it had been wounded. The love of self-will is a wine which intoxicates the mind and throws all its senses into confusion: [it confuses our] hearing, for example, so that it fails to hear what it should obey; [it confuses] the eyes of discernment, so that they fail to see the truth; and it robs the other senses of their proper functions and mingles in the midst of them the spirit of giddiness.* This is not the wine which we are told to give to those who are sad.* Those who are sad and those who weep for the sins of self-will are intoxicated with the wine of compunction.* They are given to drink of the wine which cheers the human heart* with the promise and hope of forgiveness. 'For blessed are those who mourn, for they shall be comforted.'* It is said of such as these, 'Give wine to those that are sad, and strong drink to those that are grieved in their soul'.* But contrary to this is another saying, 'Do not give wine to kings, Lamuel, not to kings; for there is no secret where drunkenness rules. Otherwise they may drink and forget the judgements of God.'*

The wine of self-will is strained and pressed out in the wine-press of disobedience. [It is made] from a sour grape which our fathers have eaten and which

Is 19:14
Pr 31:6

Ps 59:5[60:3]

Ps 103[104]:15

Mt 5:5

Pr 31:6

Pr 31:4-5.

has set the children's teeth on edge.\* Adam, the father of disobedience, mixed this wine of self-will and passed on the draught of death to his children[6] as if to say, 'Drink of this, all of you'.\* And all the sinners of the earth are still drinking from it!\* Christ, on the contrary, came not to do his own will but that of his Father\* and passed on the cup of obedience even to death, saying to us, 'Drink of this, all of you'.\* [Drink] of this, he says, which I serve, not that which Adam served.

When the Lord was hanging on the cross and thirsting for their salvation, the unbelieving and disobedient Jews offered him wine, [wine] which was of the same nature as their wicked conduct, but when he had tasted, he would not drink.\* He did not approve of it but abstained from wine like a Nazarite. This was [wine which came] from grapes of gall, from the vines of Sodom and the land around Gomorrah.\*

This wine of self-will and disobedience is forbidden to the Nazarites and the sons of Jonadab, and they must not drink of it. It is good for us not to drink this wine. Those who know this distrust the whole of their own will; they do not put their trust in themselves but entrust themselves to the rule of another's judgement;[7] they are always fearful of willing something from themselves, as if it were a product of their own [self-will]. Therefore, they bind themselves with the bonds of obedience and confine themselves by the laws of regular discipline. They change their will into obligation and reduce their freedom to servitude.\* But all this [they do] for Christ, so that in Christ their servitude may be freedom and their obligation freely given. The more

## Tractate XVI

they are bound to obey Christ because of their contract with him, the more freedom they have in him. Such is the first and most important [type of] abstinence of the Nazarites.

With regard to the strong drink of carnal pleasure, it too is pressed out in the wine-press of disobedience, as if from the fruit of the forbidden tree. For the woman saw that it was beautiful to look at and pleasant to eat.* It was there that the voluptuous pleasure of gluttony was born, and concupiscence of the flesh, and concupiscence of the eyes.* The Nazarites abstain from such strong drink; they make no provision to gratify the desires of the flesh,* and through their abstinence and continence and discipline, they always carry in their body the death of Jesus.* They abstain, too, from everything which can cause drunkenness, for they flee from the manifold shortcomings of the secular life. They do not put their faith in things which will perish, but look at the earth from far away* and trample all the glory of the world beneath their feet.

In the perfection of this threefold abstinence is to be found the whiteness of the Nazarites, and this whiteness is whiter than snow. [The whiteness of] snow is the whiteness of those that abstain, but just as [we distinguish] perfection from imperfection, so we must distinguish one sort of abstinence from another and one sort of whiteness from another. This is why it is written, 'When he that is in heaven distinguishes between kings, they shall become as white as the snow of Selmon'.* Those who use the world* legitimately are white as snow, but those who do not use the world at all are whiter. The whiteness of the former [comes] from their abstaining

Gn 3:6

1 Jn 2:16

Rm 13:14

2 Co 4:10

Is 33:17

Ps 67:15[68:14]
1 Co 7:31

from things which are unlawful; the whiteness of the latter [consists] in their refraining even from things which are lawful. The former are troubled and anxious about many things,* because although there is nothing that they love more than God, they love many things other than God, and not for the sake of God. Their love, therefore, is divided,* for the more we concern ourselves with the love of perishable things, the more we detract from the perfection of divine love. That which is scattered about is always less than that which is collected together. When [a body of] water is split up into a number of streams, there can be only a little [water] in each one, and the same is true of love. This is why a certain [poet]* says of love—even though [he is speaking] of vain love—'When the spirit is cut in two and runs in different ways, the powers of love detract from one another.'[8]

Let us, therefore, collect together all our love lest it be scattered among many. Let us recall all the affections and intentions of our love from all that host of things [to which we have attached them], so that the whole force of our love may rush to One alone and into One alone: to that One, namely, who is worthy of all love and to whom all love is due, to him who is so worthy of love that all love is scarcely sufficient. For it would be no small affront to take away a part from him to whom all is due. This is the whiteness which is whiter than snow. This, perhaps, is the whiteness desired by him who says, 'You will wash me, and I will be whiter than snow'.*

### OF THE PURITY OF THE NAZARITES

By being called whiter than snow, the Nazarites are honored with a praiseworthy title, but in order that praise should be heaped on praise, there is added, 'purer than milk'. Oil, milk, tallow, and fat are all pure, and this [purity symbolizes] mercy, of which the Lord says, 'I desire mercy and not sacrifice'.* Those who have the purity and sweetness of milk are those who, in mercy, relieve the needs of the indigent, so that they might have milk to drink and be filled from the breasts of their consolation.*

Ho 6:6

Is 66:11

There are certain needs, however, which are bodily, and others which are spiritual. The body requires many kinds of support for its needs and requires many remedies for its infirmities. The soul, too, requires those things which are necessary for its spiritual consolation and its true health [and salvation].

Generally speaking, those of the just who are themselves infirm in the flesh are stirred with a greater devotion and affection for the bodily needs of their neighbors [than for their spiritual needs]. They are more concerned with striving to feed the hungry than with leading those who are in error back to the way of truth. I think that the infirmities which they themselves have to endure make them weaker and more tender-hearted, so that for the sake of Christ they love to have compassion on the poor* as if they had been taught by their own personal example.

Cf. Jb 30:25

But those who love the souls of their neighbors more perfectly than their bodies sustain them in their suffering for Christ. They are zealous for God and are stirred with a greater affection for spiritual needs. They are weak with those who are weak and burn [with indignation] for those that suffer a fall.* In the midst of their secret tears and secret conversations with God, they pray and lament for their enemies, and suffer and mourn for the sins of others;

2 Co 11:29

and from the depths of their charity and the very heart of their piety, sighing and weeping, they commend to the God whom they serve in his spirit* their neighbors who are ignorant and who have gone astray. With regard to bodily needs, however, they often seem hard and unfeeling, and it may be that, because they themselves suffer poverty willingly, they have less compassion for it when it appears in others. They do not hold poverty to be a misery, but rather a way to salvation, and they think it safer to be moderately in want than to have too great a profusion. They judge the rich who perish in their abundance to be more wretched than the poor who, for a while, live in a condition of healthy want which leads to their salvation.[9]

True mercy, however, has compassion on both kinds of needs, but it has more [compassion] on that which is more [important] and less on that which is less [important]. It is indeed a great mercy to suffer with one's neighbor when he is in want, but it is a much greater [mercy] to take such care of him that he does not perish. To feel pain for the evils which people suffer is to be affected by great mercy.

Christ in himself showed us an example of both kinds of mercy. When he saw that the multitude was near to fainting [with hunger], he said, 'I feel pity for the multitude',* and when he multiplied the bread, he symbolized by an action which was of benefit to the body the mystery of a spiritual grace. But when he saw the city of Jerusalem, he wept over it, saying, 'If only you had known',* and to explain why he wept, or why the city made him weep, he added, 'even now, today, the things that make for peace!'* Such a lamentation should be pronounced on every rich man who abuses temporal peace to his own ruin: '[If only you had known] even now the things which make for peace!'¹⁰ When the Lord was being led to his passion, he turned to the women who were present there and wept, saying, 'Do not weep over me, but [weep] for yourselves and for your children.'*    Lk 23:28

Zeal for souls, therefore, is superior to a sympathetic feeling¹¹ for the sufferings of the body. The latter is the purity of milk; the former that of oil, which surpasses all other liquids. The latter is like the external fat of a sacrifice; the former is the internal tallow. The latter is characteristic of the rich who, in mercy, distribute [their goods to the poor]; the former is more suited to the Nazarites, for it is there that we find the very marrow of sincere love for one's neighbor.¹² What better reason is there for loving our neighbor with whom we share the same nature than that we both might participate in a common glory? The Nazarites, therefore, who give first place to their zeal for souls while in no way despising the needs of the body, shine forth with a double brightness: being whiter than milk, they always possess the brightness of grace and [the brightness] of glory in the eyes of God, who says, 'Blessed are the merciful, for they shall obtain mercy'.*   Mt 5:57
Those who have professed the common life and who, in the future, will have everything in common, meanwhile share what they have in such a way that each of them wants to have nothing more than that which can benefit the others. Anything which is not brought into the grace of communion they consider as superfluous, and they take no pleasure in owning anything themselves, just as they are forbidden to take anything [which belongs to] another.

## Of the Ruddy Color of the Nazarites

In describing the face of the Nazarites, one color is painted on another: to whiteness and brightness there is added ruddiness. Thus, the grace of whiteness brings to their face its bright color, and the grace of ruddiness gives it its cheerful expression. A red face normally indicates either heat or shame. The Nazarites are reddened with the heat of burning devotion and ashamed as a consequence of their reverence for integrity. In their fervent zeal for the law of God, they do not only burn with their eagerness for virtue, but they also have an ardent love for the beauty of integrity. Their senses are so refined that they blush at everything unseemly. They abominate everything dishonorable and are ashamed at whatever is unbecoming. Their senses are chaste and modest. They are ashamed to see anything dishonorable; they are ashamed to hear anything unseemly – not only about themselves but also about others; they are ashamed to say anything unseemly, and in company with him who says, 'I made a covenant with my eyes that I would not even think about a woman',* they are ashamed to think it. They are also ashamed if they have done anything unseemly, as the Apostle says in reference to certain people, 'What return did you get from the things of which you are now ashamed?'*[13]

To say simply that the Nazarites are ruddy is insufficient praise: they must stand out as being [ruddy as] old ivory. Ivory, we are told, is the bone of an elephant. The elephant is an animal whose bones are so huge and tough and strong that it can support on its back war-machines and towers. Such is the strength of the saints who possess the outstanding glory of stability, firmness, and beauty as ivory among their bones. If the flesh is so weak that it can symbolize the weakness of the saints, why can we not use the bones to indicate their strength? The following passage certainly refers to them: 'The Lord guards all their bones'.*     Ps 33[34]:20

Old ivory is the strength of the just, whether of the just under the Law in the days of old or of those who are now their imitators. Among the ancients there was great gravity of conduct, a great maturity, a great firmness and steadiness of mind, an unshakable strength of the unconquerable soul in the harsh and undeserved things it had to endure for the sake of its Law. No adversity, no human perversity, no injuries, no insults, no terror, no shame could separate them from their reverence for holy religion. This is why one of the saints speaks for all of them[14] and says, 'All day long my shame is before me and the confusion of my face has covered me, from the voice of him that reproaches and abuses me, from the face of my enemy and my persecutor. All these things have come upon us, yet we have not forgotten you. We have not acted wickedly in your covenant, and our heart has not turned back.'*   Ps 43:17–20[44:16–19]

All this, however, was under the Law, and [the Law] led no one to perfection* since the perfection   Heb 7:19
of the gospel was still absent. It had not yet been said that 'If you wish to be perfect, go and sell all that you have and give it to the poor'.* It was this   Mt 19:21
which was still being said: 'An eye for an eye, a tooth for a tooth, a blow for a blow'.* And not yet   Ex 21:24
this: 'If someone strikes you on one cheek, offer him the other also'.* The world did not yet know   Lk 6:29
the secret and consummate counsels of perfection

brought down from heaven by Christ and proclaimed in Christ, counsels which not all could take: [counsels] of consecrated virginity in the service of God, of voluntary poverty embraced for the sake of Christ, of the love of humility,[15] of scorn for [earthly] dignity, of the refusal to seek revenge, of the forgiveness of every injury, of not entering into arguments to get our property back [if someone has taken it], of hating our father and mother and all our friends, and even [hating] our own life, of loving our enemies, of laying down our life for our friends, even though they be our enemies, of enduring all injuries, insults, abuse, invective, and whatever harsh and undeserved things [we suffer] for the honor and love of Christ, and not only enduring them, but [enduring them] cheerfully in the joy of the Holy Spirit, as it is written, 'They went forth from the presence of the council, rejoicing that they were accounted worthy to suffer insults for the name of Jesus'.\* It is these and such as these which are the counsels of christian perfection, and although in the old days they were communicated to certain of the just by divine inspiration, they were not promulgated through the Law. They were reserved for Christ, who gave perfection to the Law, but who did not destroy the Law.\*

O good Jesus, may I, with all due respect, ask you why have you done this to us?\* We were hoping that when you came into the world you would lighten our burdens\* and mitigate your anger†, and by being made a human being would become humane unusually humane in fact! But now you add to our burdens and weigh us down with a heavier load! Were the hands of Moses not heavy enough?[16] Did you come to beat us with scorpions and make our

## Tractate XVI

yoke still heavier?* Are we not allowed to love our friends? Are we not allowed to hate our enemies? O Creator of new laws, who can [bear to] hear your words?* Are you looking for a chance to ruin us? Is not your name Jesus?¹⁷ Are you not our God, the God of our salvation?* Will you then destroy us? God forbid!

Why do you command me not to hate my enemies, but to love them instead? How can I do this? Look, if I am provoked by the slightest insult, I catch fire inside and flare up! My heart burns for revenge, and my tongue falls headlong into abuse. For the moment I am ignorant of God and do not know your laws, and you say, 'Whoever is angry with his brother shall be in danger of judgement'.* If I say to my brother, 'Raca!' or 'You fool!,' you frighten me even more, for I am in danger of the council or of hellfire!* Surely 'you have commanded your commandments to be kept most diligently!'*

To be quite honest, I can forget the benefits, but I cannot [forget] the injuries. I am by nature such a child of wrath* that it is impossible for me not to be angry! But you,¹⁸ Jesus, are you angry,* you who forbid me to be angry or to be the slightest bit annoyed with my enemy, or even to grumble in my heart? Where can I find the power¹⁹ to make my heart so stable that I will never be annoyed at all, or that I may be, as it were,²⁰ insensible to all injuries? Where can we find the power to do what you want us to do and suffer what you want us to suffer unless you who gave us the laws also give us your blessing? Where can we find the power unless you come to us first with blessings of sweetness,* unless we remain in the charity of your sweetness?

In this [charity] all that is bitter becomes sweet

1 K 12:14

Jn 6:61

Ps 67:21[68:20]

Mt 5:22

Ibid.
Ps 118[119]:4

Eph 2:3
Cf. Is 64:5

Ps 20:4[21:3]

and all that is hard is softened. Here alone your yoke is sweet and your burden light.* What is difficult for someone who loves?²¹ The more strictly something is imposed upon us, the easier it becomes by the devotion of charity. Charity is patient, charity is strong, labor does not tire it, nor does any burden weigh it down. It bears all things, it endures all things,* and although it is conscious of a holy modesty, it is also, in a reverent way, shameless. It blushes at all unseemly things, but not at the words of Christ, not at the reproach of Christ,* not at the example of Christ. Christ, who added to the law its perfection, taught us what we should do, and all that he taught²² he fulfilled in himself, and he gave us himself as an example.*

All that Christ did himself and all that he taught us to do may appear contemptible to the world, but in itself it cannot be lacking the grace of true honor. To the world, the poverty and humility of Christ are vile, but to the poor in Christ it is the world which is vile; and since the world despises those that despise it, they despise each other with a mutual contempt! The fact that the world despises them is truly [a result of] its arrogant pride; the fact that they are despised is [a result of] their noble humility. The true humility of Christ seems to have in itself a type of noble pride, for it disdains to submit itself to the yoke of sin, and by its own strength it dares to trample upon the neck of swollen pride* and all the arrogance of vanity.

Anyone whose zeal for Christ has reached perfection²³ is mindful of the fact that he was created in the image and likeness of God,* and mindful too of the price with which he was redeemed by the Son of God.* Thus, on account of this awe-inspiring,

## Tractate XVI

dignity, he takes a noble pride in opposing that [worldly] pride which is unworthy of any dignity, and judges it unworthy of his nobility to love the vanity of worldly honor, and not to love the promises of God which surpass all our desires.

This is why it is written of the Church, 'I will put you in a proud position for ever'.* And it is said of the ministers of God, 'You will eat up the strength of the nations, and you will pride yourselves in their glory'.* What is the strength of the nations, what is their glory, but that which they love? 'They trust in their own strength and glory in the multitude of their riches.'* But the glory of those whose minds are set on earthly things lies in their confusion.* It is written that 'All who owned lands sold them and laid the price at the feet of the apostles'.* At their feet indeed, as if to trample underfoot what was unworthy to be touched with the hands. Peter said, 'Silver and gold have I none',* a saying worthy of the primacy of the prince of the apostles, the prince of the Church. What was silver or gold to Peter? Was it not Peter who said, 'See, we have left everything and followed you. What, then, shall we have?'* He was not promised gold or silver as the reward he sought, for he despised these since he found his pride in the glory of the nations. Paul, too, despised them when he said, 'We have food and clothes, with these we are content'.* He who worked day and night and never ate anyone's bread without paying* did not blush at the poverty of Christ; nor did he blush at Christ's humility but said, 'We have become, and are now, like the refuse of the world, the offscouring of all things',* and again, 'We have become a spectacle to the world, to angels, and to men'.*

Is 60:15

Is 61:6

Ps 48:7[49:6]
Ph 3:19
Ac 4:35

Ac 3:6

Mt 19:27

1 Tm 6:8
2 Th 3:8

1 Co 4:13

1 Co 4:9

The Nazarites, therefore, with their ruddy color, are the perfect disciples of Christ. Their double confusion and ruddiness* renders them more ruddy than old ivory, just as they are so much more perfect than the just of old times. Their strength, too, is greater, in proportion to their greater zeal for christian discipline.[24]

Is 61:7

### OF THE INTENTION[25] OF THE NAZARITES

Praise is further added to praise and honor heaped on honor. [The Nazarites], we are told, are more beautiful than sapphire. The perfection of beauty is [here] shown to us by a beautifully ordered sequence. The first stage of perfection is to keep ourselves unstained from all the corruption of this present life,* so far as human frailty permits it. The second stage is never to neglect in any way the care of our neighbor, so far as opportunities for help or advice present themselves. The third stage is to endure steadfastly, by the heat of holy devotion and the blush of holy shame, everything harsh and undeserved, so far as human weakness allows it.[26] The fourth stage is to keep the eye of intention always directed to God whenever we do good or endure evil, and to restore all to the glory of God, so far as human ability can manage it. The first virtue is perfect innocence with regard to oneself; the second is the plenitude of mercy with regard to one's neighbor; the third is unconquerable patience with regard to one's enemies; the fourth is the pure and simple awareness of a sincere intention with regard to God.

Jm 1:27

The first virtue is achieved either by a devout hatred of oneself or by being harsh in one's mercy to oneself. The second [is achieved] by charity which is kind, charity for one's neighbor. The third by charity which is patient, charity for one's enemy. The fourth by charity which is outstanding, our charity for God. This last gives the others their form and makes them [truly] virtues; it establishes and completes them so that they will not be worthless. For whatever good a person does or whatever evil he endures is reckoned to be totally worthless—neither genuine nor worthy of praise—unless the eye of intention is directed to God, so that it may be pleasing in his sight, in the light of the living.* [It is totally worthless] unless it considers the honor of God to such an extent that it does not seek its own glory.

Ps 55[56]:13

The purity of intention in the heart of the Nazarites is like the beauty of the eyes in an attractive face. There is nothing which adds more to the loveliness and glory of such a face than the beauty of the eyes. Attractive eyes in an attractive face are the beauty of beauty, the loveliness of its loveliness, and [in a similar way], the principal beauty of a good action is the purity of the intention.[27] It is this which is the beauty of the sapphire. A sapphire is the color of heaven and imitates the appearance of a pure and cloudless sky. But although it imitates the purity of heaven, it is not entirely its equal; it is surpassed by that which is superior to it, for the purity of heaven itself is more beautiful than that of a sapphire.

Thus, when a devout and upright intention is joined with the hope and desire for celestial things, it possesses among some the purity of the sapphire which imitates the appearance of heaven, but among others it displays a greater beauty since it is patterned on the purity of the purest heaven of all. For there are some whose love for God is utterly pure, who love God in preference to all other things, and whose love for him is not mixed with any other love. But there are others who also love God in preference to all else, but whose love for him is mixed with a love for other things as well.[28] In the case of the former, the love [of God] occupies the only place; in the case of the latter, it occupies the highest place. A love which holds the highest place does not exclude other loves, but a love which holds the only place admits no other love into its fellowship. That which refuses to admit any admixture from an inferior stock is itself more pure in its own lineage. In the case of those who love God before other things but also in company with other things, God holds the first place in their love, and they very often direct on him the eye of pure intention in what they suffer and what they do. They hope confidently that the promises of God will be fulfilled in themselves, and they desire them before all else and above all else. Nevertheless, because they also love a number of things vainly,[29] [things] in which they do not love God since they do not love them in the right way, [that is], for the sake of God, they often turn the eye of their intention away from its concern with supernal retribution and direct it in a quite different direction, to those things, in fact, which they love vainly. 'For where there is love, there, too, is the eye.'[30]

Thus, they hope and desire and pray that their desires for the things they love will be fulfilled for their pleasure, and because the whole of their heart is not lifted upwards, it falls back little by little to [a concern with] lesser things. But in the case of those who love God alone and the things which are of God with a pure [love], the purer the sincerity of their intention, the more beautiful than the sapphire they are. They meditate always on heavenly things and say to the Lord with the prophet, 'The meditation of my heart is always in your sight'.* Whoever has no desire for the eyes of intention to be turned to vain things says, 'Turn away my eyes so that they may not see vanity'.* To show forth the purity of his desire he says, 'My heart has said to you: My face has sought you; your face, O Lord, I will seek.'* And to declare the purity of his hope he says, 'The Lord will reward me according to my righteousness and according to the purity of my hands in the sight of his eyes.'*

Ps 18:15[19:14]

Ps 118[119]:37

Ps 26:8[27:9]

Ps 17[18]:25

The Nazarites are established in such purity of intention, desire, and hope that it is as though they always see God, and God, who always rejoices in his works, always sees them in the glory of his beauty as the works of his hands.* They regard each other, therefore, with a mutual regard and take delight in their mutual vision. For the prophet says, 'The eyes of the Lord are upon the just',* and the just man says, 'My eyes are ever on the Lord'.* See how it is that even now, in this present life, there is a certain way in which the Nazarites see God eye to eye. See how even now they anticipate the joy of the future vision. See how even now they gain a first foretaste of the sweetness of their future satiety, a satiety which will be more complete when there appears
the glory of God,* who is blessed
above all things for ever
and ever.
Amen.*

Ps 103[104]:31

Ps 33:16[34:15]
Ps 24:15[25:14]

Ps 16:15[17:16]

Rm 9:5

216    *Spiritual Tractates*

## NOTES TO TRACTATE XVI

1. Title as in PL 561–562. There can be no doubt that this treatise dates from Baldwin's days as abbot of Ford.
2. *Non simpliciter, sed ex comparatione.*
3. For the etymological meaning of Jonadab, see, for example, Jerome, *De nominibus hebraicis* (PL 23:817–818) or Augustine, *Enarratio in Ps* 70. 1.2 (PL 36:875–876).
4. See Tr. III, n. 10; Tr. VIII, n. 8; Tr. X/I, nn. 7, 8.
5. On *propria voluntas*, see Tr. v, n. 38.
6. For PL 565A *solus*, read *filiis* with Thomas (40/109).
7. As Thomas indicates (40/112, n. 1), this is possibly an echo of RB 5:12.
8. Ovid, *Remedia Amoris* 443.
9. The Latin simply says *quam pauperes ad tempus salubriter egentes*, but Baldwin is playing on the two meanings of *salus*: health and salvation. Cf. Tr. IX/III, nn. 4, 19; Tr. XIV, n. 9.
10. The whole of this sentence has been omitted in PL 567B by hom.
11. *Pius affectus.* What Baldwin means here by this loaded term is a sympathetic and compassionate fellow-feeling of our neighbors' suffering, feeling arising from a good inner disposition, and which it is our devout duty to bestow.
12. There is a further exegesis of fat, tallow, and marrow in Tr. VI.
13. A similar discussion of whiteness, ruddiness, shame, modesty, etc. may be found in Tr. VII.
14. *Unus caeteros sanctos in se transfigurans* . . .
15. Again, as Thomas suggests (40/128, n. 1), this is very probably an echo of RB 7:49, which defines the sixth degree of humility.
16. This is based on Ex 17:12, and the hands of Moses symbolise the Old Law and the commandments.
17. I.e., 'He who saves his people from their sins' (see Mt 1:21).
18. For PL 569C *at tu*, read *an tu* with Thomas (40/131, n. 1).
19. *Unde hoc mihi* . . .
20. PL 569C omits *quasi*.
21. See Tr. VI, n. 7.
22. *Decuit*, in Thomas's text (40/133), is an error for *docuit*.
23. Lit. 'The perfect *aemulator* of Christ'. For the significance of *aemulator / aemulatio*, see Tr. IV, n. 30; Tr. X/I, n. 2; Tr. XI, n. 29; and Tr. XIV, n. 13.
24. Lit. 'the more they are made true emulators (*aemulatores*) of Christian discipline'. See n. 23 above.
25. By the *intentio* of the Nazarites, Baldwin means the one-pointed directing of their minds and wills to God and the things which pertain to God. Thomas (40/138) renders the term as 'élan vers Dieu'. It is a rich word and comprises within itself devotion, application, direction, intention, attention, and disposition. See further DLF s.v. *intentio*.
26. These first three stages correspond to the first three comparisons drawn in the verse at the head of this discourse, and summarise what Baldwin has said up to this point. Stage I corresponds to 'whiter than snow' and summarises 'Of the Whiteness

of the Nazarites'; Stage II corresponds to 'purer than milk' and summarises 'Of the Purity of the Nazarites'; Stage III corresponds to 'more ruddy than old ivory' and summarises 'Of the Ruddy Color of the Nazarites'. The fourth stage, which corresponds to 'More beautiful than the sapphire', summarises in advance the material which Baldwin is now about to present in this final section of his discourse.

27. Thomas (40 / 141) has *intentionis*; PL 571B reads *voluntatis*.
28. This is a wordy rendering of some very concise Latin: *non quasi cum ceteris, sed prae ceteris. Alii vero prae ceteris, sed cum ceteris.*
29. Reading *vane* with Thomas (40/143) for PL 572A *vana*.
30. See Tr. VIII, n. 15.

## INDEX OF PRINCIPAL LATIN WORDS

(References are to Tractates [roman numerals] and Notes [arabic])

*Aemulatio* IV-30, X/1-2, XI-29, XIV-13, XVI-23, 24
*Affectio* III-9, 30, 32, VI-14, XI-27
*Affectus* III-9, VI-13, 16, 31, 33, IX/II-8, 13, IX/III-17 IX/IV-5, 6, X/1-15, XI-24, 27, 30, XV-52, XVI-11
*Amor communionis* XV-6
*Angelus* VII-3, XII-3
*Animalis* I-18, XI-22
*Apex mentis* VIII-26, X/II-4
*Appetitus* VI-28
*Aquilo* IX/1-11
*Auster* IX/1-11
*Beatitudo* XV-7
*Beneficia* III-8
*Benignissimus Jesus* I-16, XI-9
*Capax Dei* XIII-10
*Coimagino* X/1-3, 10
*Communio* XV-6
*Communio amoris* XV-6
*Compassio* I-32, XII-2, XV-51
*Comprehendo* IV-34
*Concordia* III-12, 13, 14, XV-24, 34
*Concupiscere* XI-14
*Consentio* IV-41, 44, VI-30, IX/IV-5, XI-13, XV-26
*Consilium* IV-8, VII-22, XIV-15, 16
*Contritio* VI-22
*Conversio* V-6, 13, IX/II-6, IX/IV-4
*Correctio* XII-18
*Credo* I-27, IX/I-12
*Disciplina* I-31, 40, III-20, IX/II-7, XI-16
*Discretio* VI-9, 43, 45, VIII-27, XI-31
*Dispensatio* I-6, IX/II-24, XIV-19
*Durus* X/1-18
*Excessus* VI-21, VIII-18, IX/III-5
*Exercitatio* III-29
*Fides* I-5, 25
*Fingere* VIII-17, 24
*Individua operatio* XV-14
*Infans* IX/II-18
*Intentio* III-30, 32, XVI-25
*Israel* V-23, 25

*Jerusalem* IX/II-33
*Laboro* V-5, 12
*Lactens* IX/II-18
*Libertas* VII-21
*Lux illuminans / illuminata* XIII-5
*Malum* XIV-24, 25
*Mansuetudo* IX/II-3
*Mens* VI-19, 29, 37, VIII-26, IX/1-18, X/II-2, 4, XV-9
*Modicum* IX/III-5
*Modus* III-15
*Necessitas* VII-21
*Obedio* IV-40
*Oculus simplex* VIII-12
*Operor* V-5, 12
*Patientia* IX/II-15, XI-2, XIV-23, XV-51
*Patres conscripti* XV-2
*Perfectus* II-20
*Petrus* IV-13
*Pietas* I-15, IX/III-3
*Pius* IX/1-14
*Plectrum* IV-22
*Praesideo* XII-19
*Principale mentis* VIII-26, X/II-4
*Principaliter* XV-3
*Proprie* XV-3
*Proprietas* XV-38
*Prudens* V-19
*Pudicitia* VII-11
*Pudor* VII-11
*Ratio fidei* VI-5
*Rector* II-7, 10
*Regio dissimilitudinis* IX/II-12
*Repraesento* XII-7, XV-15
*Sacramentum* III-10, VIII-8, X/1-7, 8, XVI-4
*Salubriter* IX/III-4, 19, XIV-9, XVI-9
*Salus* VII-2, XIV-9, XVI-9
*Salutatio* VII-2
*Sapientia* XV-29
*Sapio* XI-24, XV-29
*Scintilla rationis* VI-35, X/II-4
*Sentio* IV-41, 44, VI-30, IX/IV-5, XI-13, XV-26

## Index of Principal Latin Words

*Seraphim* II–3, III–2, XII–4
*Sermo* VI–1
*Similitudines rerum* VIII–2
*Singularis* XV–3
*Sinister* XI–3
*Specialiter* XV–3
*Species* IX/II–27, XI–34
*Substantia* XV–11
*Supergloriosa* VII–16
*Supergratiosa* VII–16
*Superscriptio* I–17
*Superspeciosa* VII–16
*Sustineo* V–24, IX/II–26

*Terra* IX/II–5
*Unanimitas* XV–24, 34
*Unica mea* XI–6
*Utor* IX/1–22
*Verbum* VI–1
*Verecundia* VII–11
*Vertex mentis* VIII–26, X/II–4
*Vetus homo* XI–1, 10
*Vicarius Christi* XII–20
*Virtus* IX/III–10, XI–15, XIV–5
*Visio pacis* IX/II–33
*Voluntas propria* V–38, XVI–5

## INDEX OF PROPER NAMES

(References are to Tractates and Notes)

Abelard xv-3
Achard of St Victor xv-3
Adam of Perseigne viii-15
Aelred of Rievaulx xv-27
Al-Hazen xiii-5
Ambrose of Milan v-25, vi-42, viii-9
Anselm of Canterbury vii-16
Arius xv-12
Augustine i-34, iii-10, iv-29, 31, v-25, 29, vi-4, 7, 18, 35, 40, vii-9, 14, viii-2, ix/ii-16, ix/iii-6, x/i-20, xi-13, 28, xiii-12, xiv-3, 7, 12, 17, xv-14, xvi-3
Becket, Thomas ii-12, 15, 16
Bernard of Clairvaux i-10, iii-6, 15, 16, iv-32, vi-7, vii-1, 21, viii-3, 9, xv-21
Bethune-Baker, J. F. iii-10
Bradfield, N. viii-25
Brito, R. ii-12
Burnaby, J. v-5, ix/iii-16
Châtillon, J. xv-3
Cicero vi-7
Corson, R. viii-25
Gilson, E. iii-6, v-38, vii-21, ix/ii-12, ix/iii-5
Gregory the Great ix/ii-4, x/i-16, xii-11, xv-28
Gregory VII xii-11
Guébin, P. i-1, ix/i-1, x/i-1
Hallet, C. xv-1, 6

Henry II ii-13, 16
Hilary of Poitiers x/i-3, 10
Hunt, R. W. ii-20
Isidore of Seville ii-3
Javelet R., viii-26, ix/ii-12, xv-28
Jerome i-9, 12, ii-18, vi-42, viii-5, ix/iii-9, xvi-3
Leo the Great xiii-2
Lucan xv-42
Luscombe, D. E. xv-3
Moorman, J. R. H. i-39
Munrow, D. iv-22
Ovid xiv-2, xvi-8
Pantin, W. A. ii-20
Pelikan, J. vii-1
Philo v-25
*Regula S. Benedicti* vi-42, 43, xii-10, xv-25, xvi-15
Richard of St Victor viii-15
Rosset, E. xi-10
Russell, J. C. xi-10
Smalley, B. ii-12
Thierry of Chartres viii-15
Tissier, B. ix/i-1
Tracy, W. ii-12
Uthred of Boldon ii-20
Virgil viii-10-ix/ii-30, 32
William of St Thierry iii-4, viii-3, ix/i-9, 23, ix/ii-11, xiii-10, xv-28
Witelo xiii-5

*Spiritual Tractates*

## SYSTEMATIC INDEX

Abbot 2: 171
Abstinence (see also Renunciation)
   2: 197ff.
   abstinence from both lawful and
      unlawful things 2: 201f.
   threefold spiritual abstinence 2: 198ff.
Angels 1: 108
   angels greeting women 1: 191
   the angel's salutation to Mary
      Tr. VII *passim*
   the just and the seraphim 1: 69, 79
   guardian angels 2: 120
Animals
   not made in the image of God 2: 57
   cannot be saved or condemned 2: 57
Ass
   its symbolism 2: 40f.
Atonement 1: 56ff., 2: 39f.
Avarice 2: 184

Beauty
   defined 1: 194, 2: 213
   of the Nazarites 2: 196ff.
   of the Virgin 1: 194ff.
   inward and outward beauty
      1: 194f., 2: 197
   the illusory nature of bodily beauty
      2: 197
Becket, Thomas
   his martyrdom 1: 71f.
   and priestly corruption 1: 71f.
Bishops 2: 126
   the duties of a bishop 2: 127
   as deputies of Christ 2: 127
Blessings
   of creation, restoration, and conso-
      lation 1: 82ff.
   of the Virgin 1: 202ff.

Charity (see also Love) Tr. III *passim*,
   Tr. XIV *passim*, 2: 114f.
   the nature of charity 2: 183f., 210f.
   as the love of God 2: 142
   as the love of God and one's neigh-
      bor 2: 146

   as the order of virtue 2: 146
   as the root of all good 1: 143
   as both health and affliction 2: 143
   as the blessed life 2: 162
   and cupidity 2: 20f., 100, 146, 148
   and the love of sharing 2: 159ff.
   and necessity 2: 150
   and obedience 1: 92f., 2: 150, 170
   and patience 1: 105
   and pride 2: 20
   God as charity 2: 161ff., 173, 190f.
   God is seen in charity 2: 161f.
   charity in us reveals the charity
      which is God 2: 159
   how God displays his charity
      towards us 1: 215ff.
   our charity should be in harmony
      with God's charity 2: 175
   the ordering of charity Tr. XIV
      *passim*
   how charity is set in order 2: 146
   what charity itself orders 2: 148f.
   finds it impossible not to love 2: 159
   loves having things in common
      2: 159
   loves to be loved 2: 160
   requires a partner 2: 162
   binds two souls together 1: 163
   produces unity of spirit 2: 174f.
   converts individual ownership into
      common ownership 2: 182
   is our link with the merits of the
      saints 2: 190f.
   must be put before all other things
      2: 151
   mutual charity 2: 176ff.
Chastity 1: 197ff., 2: 206f.
   holy chastity 1: 198
   of body and mind 1: 207
   of the Virgin 1: 198
Christ
   as the power of God and the wis-
      dom of God 1: 49, 107, 130
   as our wisdom and our righteous-
      ness 2: 128

Christ (continued):
  as Savior, not Destroyer 2: 96
  as the unique high priest 2: 74f.
  as the model of humility 1: 55, 195ff., 2: 125
  as the model of mercy 2: 204
  as the model of obedience 1: 107, 125
  his being is from the Father 1: 55f.
  he is consubstantial and coeternal with the Father 2: 163
  he assumed nature and communicated grace 1: 216
  he was made sin who knew no sin 2: 40, 129
  he was born of the seed of David without seed 1: 209
  he alone is free 1: 210
  Christ's love for us 2: 39
  he is present in the Father, in the incarnation, and in the eucharist 1: 44
  the different ways in which he is present to us 1: 46f.
  Christ seated on an ass and on us 2: 40ff.
  Christ is made our righteousness 2: 68
  Christ is our head 2: 39
  our inheritance is in Christ 2: 40
  the consolation of Christ 2: 152
Church and State: their relationship 1: 70, 73, 156
Community and the Common Life Tr. xv *passim*.
  the Holy Spirit as the key to the common life 2: 157ff., 185
  sharing as the basis of the common life 2: 165ff.
  common life in the Trinity 2: 157ff.
  common life among the angels 2: 164ff.
  received its form from the apostles 2: 156
  what makes the common life 2: 171
  the law of the common life defined 2: 177
  the ideal community 1: 112, 2: 164f., 171, 205
  mutual love in community 1: 113
  dwelling together in unity 1: 113
  both good and wicked together 1: 140
  peace in the community 2: 36f.
  causes of disruption 2: 36f.
  the earthly community as a symbol of a heavenly community 1: 142
  the communion of the just is the unity of the church 2: 169
  communion of grace 2: 170
  how individual spiritual gifts are made common 2: 188f.
Compassion (see also Mercy, Suffering) 1: 57, 138
  compassionate suffering with one who is loved 1: 163
Concupiscence 1: 175ff., 206f., 2: 27, 108f., 167
  its nature 1: 176
  two sorts of concupiscence 1: 177ff., 2: 69f.
  may be enfeebled but not eliminated 2: 106
  the triumph of evil concupiscence 1: 180
  concupiscence and death 1: 176f.
Conscience
  how conscience may be divided in two 2: 52
Consent
  the interaction of craving, consent, action, and pleasure 1: 173ff., 2: 58f., 69ff., 102ff., 108f.
  desire and consent 1: 53, 2: 58
  love loves consent 2: 172
Contemplation 1: 124, 166, 219, 2: 111
  the rapture of contemplation described 1: 221, 2: 135
  of God's love 2: 135
Contrition 1: 169

Conversion to God 1: 139
Corruption (see also Misery, Mourning)
    the corruption of society at present Tr. 11 *passim.*
    our total human corruption 2: 52f.
Covenant, made with us by Christ 1: 115
Craving (see also Consent)
    craving for wickedness is not within our control 1: 175ff.
Cross and Crucifixion 1: 133, 217, Tr. xi *passim.*
    the symbolism of the three crosses 2: 91ff.
    cross of the earthly man: voluntary abasement and voluntary poverty 2: 101
    cross of the carnal man: regular discipline (abstinence and continence) 2: 105f.
    cross of the animal man: knowledge and zeal 2: 113
    what the cross of Christ demands of us 1: 60f., 109, 2: 92, 94
    as Christ died for us, we should die for Christ 1: 63
    cross of Christ stands opposed to sensual pleasure 1: 60
Cupidity 1: 95, 145, 147
    as the root of all evil 1: 143
    and charity 2: 20f., 100, 146, 148
    how cupidity expands and contracts itself 2: 137
    the height and depth of cupidity 2: 137
    vain cupidity 2: 20

David, as type of Christ, 1: 115
Death
    and concupiscence 1: 177
    and disobedience 1: 91, 103, 114
    and love Tr. x/1 *passim*
    is a sign both of hatred and love 2: 76f.
    is a sign both of anger and mercy 2: 77
    is universal 2: 77
    man's possibility of not dying 2: 75f.
    the double strength of death 2: 78
Desire
    the interrelationship of desire, resolution, and action 1: 177ff.
    and consent 1: 53, 2: 58
    and love 2: 20
    holy desire and holy resolve 1: 178f.
    desire for good 2: 59
    desire for righteousness 2: 70f.
Discernment 1: 184ff.
    as the mother of the virtues 1: 184
    as the union of upright thought and devout intention 1: 185
    discernment and devotion 2: 114f.
    discernment without devotion, and devotion without discernment 2: 114f.
    the comb of discernment 1: 225
Discipline 1: 111, 2: 153
    is abstinence and continence 2: 105f.
    and penitence 1: 58f.
    the necessity of christian discipline 1: 57, 2: 105f.
    the holy spirit of discipline 1: 225
    its effects on concupiscence 1: 176
Disobedience
    and death 1: 91, 103, 114
    the sin of disobedience 1: 207, 2: 85
Disquiet
    the three forms of disquiet 1: 145ff.
Docility (see also Meekness)
    with regard to oneself 2: 30ff.
    with regard to God 2: 39ff.
    with regard to one's neighbor 2: 35ff.
    docility, patience, and obedience 2: 35ff., 41
    as the companion of peace 2: 37

Eucharist Tr. 1 *passim*
    Christ is wholly present in the eucharist 1: 44
    Christ is united to us in the eucharist 1: 48

the conversion of bread and wine
  in the eucharist 1: 43
the effects of the eucharist 1: 56, 63
leads to eternal life and true salvation 1 :48
contains the power for our restoration and the price of our redemption 1: 63
imitation of the eucharist 1: 56
Eve 1: 52f.

Faith 1: 44, 135
is put to proof in the eucharist
  1: 44ff., 63
is based on divine authority 1: 50f.,
  2: 13
is founded on Christ 1: 51
is shaken by the conflict of divine
  and human wisdom 2: 48
is the knowledge of salvation 1: 51
fights with human reason 1: 49
restrains human reason 1: 49
and hearing 1: 153
and obedience 2: 36
and understanding 1: 153f.
the certainty of faith 1: 51f., 2: 167
the humility of faith 1: 49, 2: 13f.
the reason for faith (*ratio fidei*) 1: 154
the touch of faith 1: 118ff.
Christ dwells in the heart by faith
  1: 153
Faithful
how the faith, hope, and love of
  the faithful are tested 1: 44, 63
Fall, the story of the 1: 52
Fat, the symbolism of three types of
  fat 1: 171ff., 2: 203f.
Fear
the fear of God, 1: 125, 161, 2: 17f.
holy fear and holy love 1: 217ff.
holy fear and holy obedience 1: 225f.
and hope 2: 15f., 18ff.
Flesh
where the desires of the flesh lead
  1: 59ff.

desires of the flesh are contrary to
  those of the spirit 1: 117
the threefold condition of the flesh
  2: 28ff.
the works of the flesh 2: 30ff.
flesh, reason, and will 2: 30f.
Flood
how the Flood prefigures judgment
  1: 68f.

God
as Supreme Truth, Wisdom, and
  Power 1: 51, 2: 173
as Supreme Peace and Supreme
  Rest 1: 130
as Supreme Beauty and Supreme
  Sweetness 2: 42
as the Supreme Good 2: 162f.
as Charity 2: 161ff., 173, 190f.
as the Breath of Life 1: 124
as a kind-hearted creditor 1: 81
as a just judge 1: 89f.
should be loved in his blessings
  1: 81ff.
should be loved in his promises
  1: 85ff.
should be loved in his judgments
  1: 87ff.
should be loved in his commandments 1: 91ff.
requires our whole heart 1: 83, 146
rests in Christ 1: 134
God's unchangeability 1: 130f.
Grace
fullness of grace: what it signifies
  1: 193ff.
triple grace: of beauty, favor, and
  honor 1: 193ff.
different sorts of graces 2: 136
the communion of grace 2: 170ff.
the sharing of grace 2: 168ff., 170ff.,
  181ff., 185ff.
prevenient grace 1: 98
Hair
its symbolism 1: 224ff.

## Systematic Index

medieval hair-styles 1: 225
of the Nazarites and of Sampson
  1: 225
Harp
  its symbolism 1: 109ff.
  how it is played 1: 110
Hatred
  devout hatred 2: 212
  hating well and loving well 2: 172f.
Heart 1: 79ff.
  the significance of the word 1: 84
  as the wine-cellar 2: 145
  loving God with one's whole heart
    1: 79ff.
  God demands our whole heart 1: 83
  returning to the heart 2: 145
  purity of heart 2: 145
  the heart expanded and contracted
    by love 2: 137
Honey
  honey and milk: their symbolism
    2: 42f.
Hope
  hope and fear 2: 15f., 18ff.
  hope in God 2: 17, 19
  hope in the good things we do 2: 19
  founded on humility 2: 61
  vain hope 2: 15ff.
Humility
  five kinds of humility 1: 202ff.
  the nature of true humility 2: 124
  Christ as the model of humility
    1: 195ff., 2: 21, 125, 210f.
  Mary as the model of humility
    1: 196ff.
  of judgment and will 1: 55
  of reason and will 1: 54f.
  and dignity 2: 124f.
  and poverty 2: 12, 21f.
  as the foundation of hope 2: 61
  mutual humility 2: 179

Ignorance
  devout ignorance 1: 54
Image of God 1: 82, 2: 133, 210
  we are made in God's image in
    judgment of reason and freedom
    of will 1: 54, 2: 57
  since we are made in God's image
    we can be saved or condemned
    2: 57
  the image of God is deformed by
    the image of money 2: 99
  the image of God is deformed by
    proud reason 1: 55
  our formation and reformation in
    God's image and likeness 2: 75
  the image of God is reformed by
    the humility of reason 1: 55
  the image of God is reformed by
    charity 2: 162
  the image of love 2: 74, 161
  the image of the earthly and of the
    heavenly 2: 79
  the image of Truth 2: 98
  Christ as the image of God 2: 163
Imitation 2: 133
  of Christ is as hard as hell 2: 80f.,
    82f.
  of Christ's resurrection 1: 104
  of Jacob 1: 142
  of the Bridegroom 1: 122
  of the eucharist 1: 56
Impatience
  may be a virtue 1: 85f.
  patient impatience 1: 86
Incarnation (see also Christ) 1: 47, 200f.
  as an example of humility 1: 195ff.,
    2: 125
  as an example of obedience 1: 106ff.
Intention
  the importance of intention 1: 184ff.
  the intention of the Nazarites
    2: 212ff.
  devout intention and vain intention
    1: 184ff.

Jerusalem
  as the vision of peace
    2: 44

Judgment 1: 103
   past and future judgment 1: 68ff.
   by water and by fire 1: 69f.
   signs preceding the day of judgment
     1: 70
   God's judgments 1: 87ff.
   the need to judge ourselves on
     earth 1: 89, 104

Knowledge
   knowledge of God on earth as
     compared with heaven 1: 79, 82
   love itself is knowledge 2: 173

Labor 1: 130ff.
   what it means for God to 'labor'
     1: 131ff.
   labor of endurance and labor of
     suffering 1: 132
   labor and lamentation 2: 51f.
Laity
   look to the clergy in vain 1: 71
Love (see also Charity) Tr. III *passim*,
   Tr. XIII *passim*.
   three forms of love: natural, social,
     and chaste 1: 214ff.
   four forms of love 1: 81ff.
   six forms of love: natural, social,
     conjugal, incestuous, vain, and
     holy 2: 141f.
   the first degree of love 1: 84
   and the Holy Spirit 2: 136f.
   the nature of God's love for us
     2: 131ff.
   God's love poured abroad, out,
     into us, and forth 2: 133ff.
   the extent of God's love 2: 132
   the length and breadth of our love
     for God 2: 135f.
   love of God should have no
     measure 1: 85
   a pure love for God and a mixed
     love for God 2: 214
   loving God with the whole heart
     1: 79ff.
   love of God and love of obedience
     1: 91ff.
   on earth God is loved only in part
     1: 79ff.
   love of God must replace love of
     the world 1: 79, 162, 2: 145f.
   love of God and of one's neighbor
     1: 144f., 147, 2: 146, 179ff.
   love of neighbor preserves unity of
     spirit 2: 179
   Christ's love for us 1: 47
   Christ's love is our example 2: 79
   our love for Christ and Christ's
     love for us 2: 78f.
   how we should love Christ 2: 79ff.
   loving ourselves for the sake of
     Christ 2: 81
   love is an affliction 2: 141ff.
   love is a fire 1: 69, 2: 159
   love itself is knowledge 2: 173
   love and death Tr. x / i *passim*.
   love is strong as death 2: 77
   the glue of love 1: 115
   the wounds of love 1: 216ff.
   the remedy for love 2: 144
   begins with hatred and contempt
     1: 83f.
   conforms our hearts to its own
     length and breadth 2: 135
   expands and contracts our hearts
     2: 137
   demands love in return 1: 46f.,
     141, 2: 79f.
   loves consent 2: 172
   loving well and loving wickedly 2: 172
   loving well and hating well 2: 172f.
   mutual love in community 1: 113,
     141, 144f.
   love of sharing and sharing of love
     2: 159ff.
   love, divided and unified 2: 202
   holy love and holy fear 1: 217ff.
   vain love for vain things 2: 214
   solitary love is its own torment
     2: 160

## Systematic Index

love of unnecessary things leads to misery 2: 88
where love is, there too is the eye 1: 220f., 2: 214
Lucifer 2: 149f.

Man Tr. XI *passim*.
   earthly man 2: 98ff.
   carnal man 2: 102ff.
   animal man 2: 109ff.
Martyrs
   two sorts of martyr 1: 160f., 2: 10f.
   are true imitators of Christ 2: 80
   martyrdom as the renunciation of self-will 1: 161f.
Mary the Virgin Tr. VII *passim*
   as Mistress of the World and Queen of Heaven 1: 200
   as agent and collaborator in the work of salvation 1: 201
   as Mother of Mercy 2: 18
   how God rested in her 1: 139
   her compassionate suffering with Christ 1: 164ff.
   her glorious sort of martyrdom 1: 164
   her beauty, humility, glory, etc. Tr. VII *passim*.
   her humility is our model 1: 196ff.
   her uniqueness 1: 199
   her exemption from the general curse 1: 208
   she felt nothing of evil concupiscence 2: 107
Mary and Martha 1: 219f., 2 86f.
Mary Magdalen
   how she "touched" Jesus 1: 118ff.
   how she is our consolation 1: 119f.
Meditation 1: 93, 166
   meditation and action 1: 93f.
Meekness (see also Docility)
   meekness, gentleness, and docility Tr. IX/ii *passim*.
Mercy (see also Compassion)
   God's mercy and the fear of God 2: 18
   God's mercy and God's hardness 2: 186f.
   the nature of true mercy 2: 204
   Mary as Mother of Mercy 2: 18
Milk
   milk and honey: their symbolism 2: 42f.
Mind (see also Reason, Spirit, Will)
   its nature and function 1: 91
   must be obedient to God 1: 91
   may be divided *to* God, but not *from* God 1: 167
   the mind unified (Mary) and divided (Martha) 1: 219
   controls craving, consenting, and pleasure 1: 181
Misery (see also Corruption, Mourning)
   our miserable condition in this world 2: 50f., Tr. X/ii *passim*.
   the source of our misery 2: 50
   misery and need 2: 87
Modesty 1: 197ff.
   holy modesty 1: 198
Mortification (see also Discipline)
   and abasement 1: 57
   the necessity for mortification 1: 57
Mourning (see also Tears)
   five reasons for mourning Tr. IX/iii *passim*, 2: 57 (summarized)
   two sorts of mourning 2: 49
   devout mourning 2: 49
   labor and lamentation 2: 51f.
   good tears and useless tears 2: 60
   the water of sorrow and the wine of joy 2: 63

Nazarites Tr. XVI *passim*.

Obedience, Tr. IV *passim*, 1: 123f., 126, 2: 30ff.
   four types of obedience 1: 95ff.
   and the abolition of self-will 2: 199f.
   and charity 1: 92f., 2: 150, 170
   and faith 2: 36

and life 1: 91
and love 1: 91ff.
and patience 2: 41f.
and perseverance 1: 104ff.
and rest 1: 139
the necessity of obedience 1: 53
love of obedience stems from love of God's commandments 1: 94
leads to resurrection and eternal life 1: 102
unites the soul to God 1: 118
the obedience of Christ 1: 105ff.
obedience, discipline, and reason 1: 111
double obedience 1: 126
the yoke of obedience 1: 225, 2: 31
holy obedience and holy fear 1: 226
Opinion
  false opinion 2: 13f.
  vain opinion 2: 15

Patience 1: 90, 2: 153
  and obedience 2: 41f.
  and perseverance 1: 105ff.
  as the virtue of charity 1: 105
  mutual patience 2: 179
Peace
  preserved through gentleness and docility 2: 36f.
  and mutual charity 2: 176f.
Penitence 1: 58f., 84, 111, 126, 2: 27, 60, 68, 96
  the necessity of penitence 1: 168
  the medicine of penitence 2: 53
Perfection
  the four stages of perfection 2: 212f.
Perseverance Tr. IV *passim*.
  in glory 1: 104ff.
  in humility 1: 196
  in love 1: 144f., 2: 136
  in obedience 1: 104ff.
Pleasure (see also Consent)
  an analysis of its origins and its dangers Tr. VI *passim*.
  the mind's role in seeking pleasure 1: 182

as the source of sin 1: 170f.
and the desire for sin 1: 180
pleasure, craving, and consent 2: 58f.
Possessions (see also Riches)
  the dangers of possessions 2: 87ff.
  how they should be used 2: 23
  desire and possessions 2: 20
  shared possessions 2: 159
  individual and common ownership of possessions 2: 181ff.
Poverty Tr. IX/i *passim*.
  the poor in spirit 2: 7ff.
  loving poverty, enduring poverty, and neither loving nor enduring it 2: 8
  holy poverty 2: 21f.
  voluntary poverty 2: 8, 101f., 208
  poverty and humility 2: 12, 21f.
  poverty and purification 2: 8
  the poverty of Christ 2: 21
Prayer 1: 222
  pure prayer 1: 122
Pride 1: 173
  as the beginning of sin 2: 16
  corrupts reason 1: 52ff.
  deserves a curse 1: 202
  and vain opinion 2: 15f.
  the pride of charity 2: 20
  noble pride 2: 210
Priests Tr. II *passim*, Tr. XII *passim*.
  as angels of peace 2: 119f.
  as gods 2: 121f., 123f.
  as guides of souls 2: 123
  as ministers of God 2: 119
  as representatives of God 2: 121
  as servants 2: 123ff.
  as thrones of God 1: 74, 2: 127
  how priests should consider themselves 2: 118ff.
  what priestly conduct should be 1: 61ff., Tr. XII *passim*.
  should live an ordered life 1: 72ff.
  must guard the Church, the Bride of Christ 2: 128f.
  their lives should be imitated by the laity 2: 128

they are justly persecuted by the
  laity 1: 71
sinful priests 1: 70ff., 2: 120, 122
imitation priests 2: 122
holiness of the priestly ministry
  1: 71, 2: 122
priests and the distribution of the
  eucharist 1: 62
Promised land, its symbolism 2: 35ff.
Promises
  God's promises 1: 85, 122, 184, 2: 7,
    26, 59, 214
Propriety
  two types of propriety 1: 197f.
Psaltery, its symbolism 1: 113ff.

Reason (see also Mind, Spirit, Will)
  2: 147
  its powers 1: 49f.
  its relationship to faith 1: 49ff.
  its place in the Fall 1: 53
  and pride 1: 52ff.
  proud reason and proud will 1: 53
  cannot comprehend the wisdom of
    God 1: 55
  the humbling of reason 1: 54f.
  the spark of reason 1: 179
  reason, will, and the flesh 2: 30ff.
Renunciation (see also Abstinence)
  2: 138, 147f.
  three degrees of renunciation 1: 172f.
  renouncing the world for the sake
    of Christ 2: 145
  the renunciation of the Nazarites
    2: 197f.
  in the common life 2: 171
Resurrection 1: 63, Tr. IV *passim*.
  twofold resurrection 1: 102ff.
  of life and of judgment 1: 103ff.
  the resurrection of Christ is our
    model 1: 104
  imitation of the resurrection 1: 104
  the nature of the resurrection body
    2: 112f.
Rest Tr. v *passim*.
  something which all crave 1: 137

impossibility of perfect rest here
  1: 142
rest and boredom 1: 138
Riches (see also Possessions)
  danger of riches Tr. IX/i *passim*,
    esp. 22f., 2: 100, 204
  the rich still desire more 2: 87
Righteousness Tr. IX/iv *passim*.
  the stages in the acquisition of
    righteousness 1: 171ff.
  six stages in the development of
    righteousness 2: 71
  two types of righteousness whose
    reward is not postponed 2: 9f.
  its nature 1: 172f.
  how it is formed 1: 184
  in what it lies 2: 59
  its recompense 2: 7, 26
  the fruits of righteousness 2: 154
  the shoot of righteousness 1: 210f.
  is food and drink 2: 72
  is the acquisition of immortality
    2: 72, 75
  desire for righteousness and love of
    righteousness 2: 69
  consenting to righteousness 2: 70
  love of righteousness 2: 68ff.
  righteousness and peace 2: 34f.
  of Christ, the saints, and us 1: 210
  of the martyrs 2: 10

Sacraments 1: 82, 2: 168f., 198
  sacrament of Christ's resurrection
    2: 78
  sacrament of redemption 2: 77
Sacrifice
  how the O.T. sacrifices prefigure
    the eucharist 1: 45, 48
  of ourselves 1: 122
Saints
  how the strength and weakness of
    the saints helps us 2: 54
  how God strengthens and humbles
    them 2: 55
  the communion of the saints 2: 190
  the merit of the saints 2: 189f.

the strength of the saints 2: 206f.
Salutations
  the angel's salutation to Mary
    Tr. VII *passim*.
  two types of salutation 1: 192
Satiety
  two types of satiety 2: 71
  true satiety and false satiety 2: 67
Schismatics 2: 169
Seal, its meaning and symbolism
    Tr. x/i *passim*.
Security
  good and evil security 2: 17f.
  true security and the fear of God
    2: 17ff.
Self-Will 1: 98, 117, 2: 199ff.
  the love of self-will, of carnal
    pleasure, and of worldly vanity
    2: 198ff.
  the misery of self-will 1: 148
  the wine of self-will 2: 199
  the martyrdom of self-will 1: 161f.
  self-will endures to the end 1: 148
Senses
  the bodily senses 1: 117
  the five spiritual senses 1: 118ff.
Sharing Tr. xv *passim.*
  of nature 2: 165ff., 205
  of sin 2: 165ff.
  of grace 2: 168ff., 170ff., 181ff., 185ff.
  of glory 2: 185ff.
  three sorts of sharing summarized
    2: 191
  complete sharing 2: 181
  sharing things and individual
    ownership 2: 181
  how spiritual gifts are shared 2: 188f.
  sharing of love and love of sharing
    2: 159ff.
Simplicity 1: 141, 144, 219
Sin (see also Pleasure)
  the reasons for sinning 2: 58f.
  the habit of sin 2: 58, 69
  how sin leads to sin 1: 167f.
  sin and pleasure 1: 170f.
  the body of sin 1: 169
  is an affront to God 2: 76
  is as hateful as death 2: 75f.
  original sin 2: 166f.
Sorrow: see Mourning
Soul (see also Mind, Reason, Spirit,
    Will)
  defined 1: 162f.
  what it is and what it does 1: 86,
    116f.
  what the word signifies 1: 86f., 158f.
  soul and spirit distinguished 1: 158f.
  stands midway between God and
    the flesh 1: 114
  cleaves either to God or the flesh
    1: 116
  provides motion and sensation 1: 159
Spirit (see also Mind, Reason, Soul,
    Will)
  distinguished from soul 1: 158f.
  two types of spirit 2: 10f.
  its divisions and unitings 1: 166f.
  of man, of this world, and of God
    2: 11, 126
  how the human spirit becomes
    puffed up 2: 12f.
  how the human spirit is conformed
    to the spirit of God 2: 14
  lack of spirit and abundance of
    spirit 2: 11, 14
  renunciation of spirit 2: 14
  timidity of spirit 2: 16
Suffering (see also Compassion)
  all the just must suffer for Christ
    2: 10
  suffering in tribulation and rejoicing
    in tribulation 2: 55

Tears (see also Mourning)
  good weeping and useless weeping
    2: 60
  holy tears drawn from humility and
    charity 2: 61
Temptations 2: 104
  our life on earth is temptation
    2: 53f.
Transubstantiation 1: 43

## Systematic Index

Trinity (see also God, Christ) 2: 157ff., 182f.
   and appropriation 2: 158
   the common life of the Trinity 2: 157f.
   one single operation of the undivided Trinity 2: 164
Truth
   Christ as Truth 1: 48

Understanding
   two ways in which it should be understood 1: 153f.
   essential to the beginning of faith 1: 154
   and hearing 1: 153f.
Union 1: 121
   of the soul and God 1: 116
   proceeds by love of obedience 1: 118
Unlikeness
   the region of unlikeness 2: 32

Virginity Tr. VII *passim*.
   always dear to the angels 1: 192
   always pleasing to God 1: 205
   the perfection of virginity defined 1: 198
   holiness of virginity above the Law 1: 204
   virginity, integrity, and incorruption 1: 207
   barren virginity and fertile virginity 1: 204
Virtues 1: 158
   faith, hope, and charity 1: 135f.
   the flowers of virtue 2: 154
Vision, how it operates 2: 134
Vision of God 1: 144, 2: 42, 143
   God is seen in charity 2: 161f.

Will (see also Mind, Reason, Spirit) 2: 147
   three meanings of 'the will of God' 1: 99
   our will and God's will 1: 96ff.
   what it means to will with the whole will 1: 96ff.
   proud will and proud reason 1: 53
   the humbling of the will 1: 54
   the misery of an evil will 1: 148
   will, reason, and the flesh 2: 30ff.
Wine
   its symbolism 2: 55f., 144, 199ff.
   is necessary for our frequent weaknesses 2: 56
   the wine of compunction and of love 2: 144, 146
   the wine of self-will 2: 199f.
   the wine offered to Christ on the cross 2: 200
   wine mixed with tears 2: 56
   the wine of joy and the water of sorrow 2: 63
   the wine-press of disobedience 2: 201
Wisdom 2: 174
   human and divine wisdom 1: 157, 2: 47ff.
   the limits of human wisdom 1: 50, 157
Women
   responsible for the Fall 1: 208
   bound by a curse 1: 208
   saved by the Virgin 1: 208
Word of God
   three ways in which the word is revealed 1: 152ff.
   its effectiveness 1: 155
Wounds
   the wounds of love: their nature, variety, and importance Tr. VIII *passim*.
Zeal 2: 203, 206
   zeal and knowledge united 2: 113ff.
   zeal, evaluation, and choice 2: 146f.
   zeal for souls superior to sympathy for the body 2: 205
   zeal for Christ 2: 210
   zeal for christian discipline 2: 212

www.ingramcontent.com/pod-product-compliance
Lightning Source LLC
Chambersburg PA
CBHW032022290426
44110CB00012B/633